Second Wind of the
Aerial Leviathans

Second Wind of the Aerial Leviathans

John Andrew Reed

"Now that *their* DC-7 just exploded on the ramp, that makes mine that much more valuable." *—from the author's 1992 phone conversation with the owner/operator of a cargo airline at Miami International Airport, regarding a competitor's preventable fueling mishap (no fatalities).*

First Edition, 2022

ISBN: 979-8-218-05208-9

DEDICATION

The true stories that comprise this book are dedicated to the thousands of air transport crews who, while flying grossly obsolete equipment during the tumultuous *Second Wind* era, ushered countless passengers and tons of cargo over millions of miles in "reasonable safety," and who dealt with hundreds if not thousands of serious emergencies with total professionalism, and who despite their quick reactions and by-the-book heroics sometimes could not conquer fate's worst outcome.

This is a true account. However, the names of some corporate entities and individuals have been disguised to protect the guilty (and me from them) as well as to maintain professional ethics regarding certain former business relationships.

CONTENTS

AUTHOR'S NOTES AND ACKNOWLEDGMENTS

This book covers a lost era of propeller-driven airline history through a chronological series of interlinking short stories. This history does not encompass the "golden era" of the 1930s into the 1960s but it picks up with a confusing period that began in the 1960s and lasted into the turn of the millennium. Except for our several necessary "field trips" to provide readers with summary context, each chapter or short story portrays one or both of two perspectives.

The *first-person* perspective consists of my eyewitness accounts starting in 1969. These accounts take on an aesthetic, even an ethereal tone at times—*feelings* for a dying breed of aircraft if you will—as you might expect from a teenage kid who hasn't figured things out yet. As life's lessons are learned over time, he realizes that an old, nostalgic airplane is not meant as a piece of art or eye candy, but as a practical tool in a typically brutal and unforgiving environment.

The other perspective is a very important *third-person* view, the *pragmatic*. This is chronologically integrated into my first-person eyewitness accounts, but there are no aesthetics here. This second perspective emphasizes the harsh realities of real life, where ugliness often rears its head. This reality perspective is viewed through the lenses of serial airline entrepreneurs Joseph E. and Mark G. Morris (Joe's son), through their trials and tribulations of running their company, Mark Aero, Inc.—an aviation services company that Joe founded in 1958 at St. Louis Lambert Field. This includes Mark Aero's *five* offspring airlines that one or both of these entrepreneurs founded and ran—primarily Mark as time went on. This book's recurring theme is the dysfunctional worldwide re-employment of an old, obsolete piston airliner technology—decades past its intended usefulness.

I call this re-employment era the *Second Wind of the Aerial Leviathans* or the *Second Wind*. The Mark Aero lineage was a key participant in the *Second Wind* among hundreds of others, mostly *fly-by-nighter* corner cutters who did not follow procedures or maintain their cheap equipment. But compared to all the others, the Mark Aero lineage was one of the most—if not *the* most—*unique* and *impactful* of these legacy aircraft operators. Due to the extreme challenges and intense frustration it endured due to decades-long collusion among the major airlines and the federal government, the Mark Aero lineage had a key role in tearing down and then reshaping the entire airline industry into what it is today. More specifically, Mark Aero and its offshoot airlines had a direct, far-reaching impact on the overnight air courier industry through what is now the third largest in the world, DHL, as well as the *entirety* of today's deregulated passenger airline industry and more relaxed international flight rules.

I would first like to thank my wife Karen for her unending patience during my endless hours working on this project. Had I not met her on December 5, 1980, by providence or twist of fate, the chain of events leading to this book would not have happened. With that, I need to mention that this book could also not have been written without the daily assistance and enthusiastic cooperation of major contributor Mark G. Morris, who is where that chain of events led. Mark spent hours with me through emails, phone and Zoom calls, and five-hour scotch-and-bourbon dinners during his regular travels to St. Louis, straightening out what I thought were "facts" and adding meaningful stories that gave incredible depth to everything. He also provided numerous newspaper and magazine articles written about him and his enterprises—by local and national outlets—as well as photographs featured here. Most important is our great friendship that developed.

I also owe thanks to Jerry Riebold, a former Mark Aero pilot and instructor who became Mark's trusted chief pilot for his first big airline, and later for their client Peabody Holding (initially known as Peabody Coal, now Peabody Energy), the world's largest coal energy producer. I met Jerry years ago through Karen who worked in the executive suite at Peabody, where one of her jobs was flight department scheduling. Jerry and fellow Peabody pilot Dick Horowitz are two of the nicest guys on the planet and accepted me as a "peer pilot" even though I was just a lowly private pilot who only flew "Wichita Reynolds Wrap," which is code for "light airplanes." Both retired, Jerry also kindly provided many photographs that are presented in this book. Jerry was the key link in the chain of events as he introduced me to Mark Morris. Also, my thanks go to Jerry Riebold's wife, Patti, for sharing her recollections. She was Mark Morris's highly valued can-do administrator/coordinator for his airlines and other business ventures for many years.

Special thanks go to Alan J. Bacon, West Point graduate, Army Ranger, and UH-60 Blackhawk pilot who retired as Lieutenant Colonel, only to spend the rest of his working decades as the consummate proposal and technical writer for Boeing Defense, Space & Security in St. Louis. He was invaluable in the editing this manuscript and book cover design.

I would also like to thank Jack L. King, Jr. and Jim King. They are the son, and stepson, respectively, of engineering test pilot Jack L. King (the step brothers coincidentally have the same last name "King"). Their father was one of the test pilots and manual writers on the Martin 202 and 404 airliners in the late 1940s and early 1950s, and the author of the excellent book *Wings of Man: The Legend of Captain Dick Merrill*. Often referred to as the *Martinliner*, the Martin 404 was a 44-passenger twin-engine big-piston/propeller short-haul airliner that was a fixture with TWA and Eastern Air Lines during the 1950s, and later flown second-hand with many others, including the airline fleets of Mark Aero.

Also, in years past I had worked with the late Harry Gann, historical curator at the former McDonnell-Douglas manufacturing facility in Long Beach, California, and noted vintage aviation author, who provided photographs and permissions for my aviation magazine articles and videos I was producing back then. Mr. Gann provided me with hard-to-get detailed information on the big, four-engine Douglas DC-6 airliner that was also a big part of the Mark Aero fleet, even more so than the Martinliner. Gann later wrote *the book* on both the DC-6 and its further development, the DC-7, which is included in the bibliography. Finally, I would like to also thank Steve Kreitmeyer, another retired Peabody pilot who was an integral part of the *chain of coincidences* leading to this book.

John Andrew Reed
St. Louis, Missouri
December 1, 2022

PHOTO SOURCES

John A. Reed
Mark G. Morris
Jerry Riebold
Douglas E. Teel
Jeffry K. Reed
The late John J. Reed
The late Walter "Willie" Davis
Wikimedia Commons: Creative Commons
Wikimedia Commons: GNU Free Documentation License
Public Domain
Unknown

The vast majority of photographic images are the author's own; therefore, no attribution or credit is placed with these photos. A few photographers/sources on included photographs are unknown and could not possibly be tracked down online or otherwise, which is always unfortunate but sometimes a fact of life. We believe our use of these few photos, which are usually cropped portions of larger subjects, is both transformational and educational, providing a linking component within our total work. All images are presented with descriptive captions strictly to enhance our broader story or convey our unique experiences or understandings related to such images that the original photographer would not possibly know in most cases.

Most Creative Commons (CC BY) or GNU Free Documentation License (GFDL) images presented in this book are color photographs that were necessarily converted to black and white due to printing requirements. As required, we attribute the author/owner and license type of each. Some of these photographs were cropped for emphasis or formatting purposes. We do not believe these minor alterations detract from any photographer's desired original impression in any material way, and we do not restrict the use of these photographs beyond what is specified with each license. Simply use your search engine to link to any license associated with a "CC BY" or "GFDL" image.

Also, note that some of my early photographs do not meet today's photo quality standards as they were taken many decades ago with off-the-shelf retail chemical film, with some of them *screen-captured* from my father's 8mm or Super8 home movies. And finally, some of those old images had to be enlarged to illustrate the desired point, deteriorating their sharpness.

INTRODUCTION

Leviathan: 1.a. A sea monster defeated by Yahweh in various scriptural accounts. 2. Something large or formidable.

Anachronism: 2. A person or thing that is chronologically out of place, especially: one of a former age that is incongruous with the present.
—Excerpts from Merriam-Webster

This is a tale of two journeys as told through a series of interlocking, chronological short stories. The journeys complement each other and give us an in-depth perspective on the *Second Wind* of a dying class of fire-breathing *Aerial Leviathans*. In the end, both journeys wind up in the same place. Both are wrapped within the context of a now obscure period in commercial aviation history, as shaped by a confusing transitional paradigm that existed at the time. Our main journey is one of left-brained hard *reality*, taking us on the highway to hell and back—multiple times. It is the history of fixed base operator (FBO) Mark Aero, Inc. headquartered at what was then called Lambert Field (now Lambert-St. Louis International Airport), its offspring airlines, the entrepreneurs that ran them, and the aircraft they flew. Mark Aero and its lineage were *major* operators at Lambert from the late 1950s into the early 1980s and are hardly mentioned in any context these days.

Why? One possible reason was that Mark Aero's old, greasy, oil-spitting, flame-throwing piston/propeller-powered *Aerial Leviathans* that dominated its ramps reeked of extreme obsolescence. These images lingered well into the adolescence of a new era—that of jet propulsion. The lasting preponderance of old iron on their apron was an *anachronism*, at Lambert and at most major (and many small) airports at the time. Some might say the presence of this grossly outdated, sometimes junky hardware was a nuisance—as it was no vision of progress by any outward appearance—only a backward look. Mark Aero, as a dealer and operator of these hand-me-down aerial clunkers, could only be considered as a slice of, or portal to, a much larger, more universal reality that existed at the time. And unlike the hundreds of other reality slices comprising the *Second Wind of the Aerial Leviathans*, the Mark Aero slice was unique in that it out of its frustrations it formed a catalyst for worldwide jet-age change that impacts us all today.

The other journey is mine which started 50 years ago when I was a teenager. This resulted from my personal discovery and growing awareness of Mark Aero and its related entities, thrusting me into a proactive lifelong legacy aviation quest that unfolds in this book and continues to this day, feeding the interests of a growing audience. This journey started as a right-brained odyssey of aesthetics and sentiment that started as simple eye candy—in this case, the beauty of a forgotten machine. The actual purgatory behind this eye candy was at first not visible to me but became seriously evident as time went on.

My journey began with a single epiphany in August 1969 emanating from behind the widened eyes of this teenager, peering through an airport chain-link fence. Sitting there was a thing of engineering beauty, previously taken for granted, but familiar again. This sparked a realization that what's behind that fence represents the sunset on a familiar discarded generation of overly-complex heavy piston flying transport machines, or so he then thought. These flying vestiges were only known as "obsolete prop jobs" or just "those old passenger planes" to the general populace. Not its fault per se, and why should it care? But to me, these machines had just risen from the dead—as they truly had.

A short decade earlier, these piston monsters were cutting edge in the peak of their *First Wind*, carrying millions of passengers and tons of freight to destinations all over the world. In the two decades after World War II, they were the technical capacity that expanded the size of the airline industry by a factor of 50, but being an airline passenger was still mostly for the elite. Looking at them passing overhead, they growled in a labored slow motion—they did not *rocket* over you like the familiar jet. The populace enthusiastically embraced heavy piston aviation on any Sunday afternoon, with most wishing they could afford to fly in one. Families crowded outdoor airport observation decks to watch and soak in all the sweet 115/145 avgas exhaust and the fiery ramp activity that they possibly could—yes, the engines made smoke and *fire* when they started. Then poof! The enthusiasm vanished in the blink of an eye and the crowded decks disappeared forever as though they never existed. A more exciting thing called the "Jet Age" was emerging.

Postcard reflecting a typical Sunday afternoon at St. Louis Lambert Field on the public observation deck over the TWA concourse to the left, circa 1960. If this were New York or Chicago, the deck would be packed elbow to elbow. The big planes in the foreground are TWA's triple-tailed Lockheed L-749A Constellations, representing one of the most iconic propeller-driven airliners of that era, which—when considering the 707 jetliner tail barely visible in the background—is near coming to a close. (Collection of David L. Troupis)

Characteristic of today's obscure steampunk retro-future cult, the first thing today's interested person might notice is that these giant piston-powered artifacts with giant propellers have too many moving parts—pistons, valves, pushrods, crankshafts, superchargers, gearboxes, and auxiliary drives, prop governors, times 4, 8, 12, 36, 72, 56, 112, 144 or 224, *all* bent on self-destruction. Not so in today's sterile, glass cockpit jet environment. Now, it's just two or three neatly spinning coaxial turbine shafts affording safety and reliability, which is unheard of in the entire technical history of mankind. Also, there are no more "stick-and-rudder" pilots in the airplane front office—whereas during the piston days aircraft were almost entirely controlled manually by the lost art of eye coordination, muscle, and overall *feel*. With today's jetliners, we have highly trained and skilled, safety-conscious *computer monitors*—using GPS—as the plane is on pre-programmed autopilot for almost the entire flight, from just after takeoff to just before touchdown. While this does not detract from their high skill levels, currencies, proficiencies, and extreme responsibility, it has been shown that *some* of today's jetliner drivers seem a bit rusty on old-fashioned stick-and-rudder skills when losing autopilot or GPS functions in emergencies.

Stick-and-rudder aside, the piston *Aerial Leviathan* of yesterday can be considered a *death trap* as measured by today's safety standards. Engine failures, loopholed regulations, primitive navigation and weather procedures, failure-prone mechanical instruments, bad management (and pilot) practices, and the bad accidents that accompanied all this were accepted as "normal" risks. It is said that airline pilot trainees in the late 1940s were told they had a 20% chance of being killed on the job sometime in their careers, which did not seem to faze them. The logic was that the 20% was for the other pilot. Still, back then, airline travel was statistically *totally safe*. Safer than a drive to the 7-Eleven. Today airline crews—and *you*—are safer flying with most airlines than just sitting around the house in front of the TV with a bag of Cheetos you just got at 7-Eleven.

The big piston transport aircraft were propelled by very large propellers, perhaps second in diameter only to a large ship's screws. Each plane had two or four massive air-cooled powerplants driving the propellers that developed from 1,200 to 3,500 horsepower apiece with 14, 18, and even 28 cylinders, radially wrapped around a massive crankcase, like kernels of corn around a cob (that particular 28-cylinder engine was nicknamed the "Corncob" to be described later). Many required *water-alcohol* injection right into the atomized fuel mixture at maximum takeoff power to cool the engines in avoidance of blowing them up during maximum takeoff heat and stress. Under normal circumstances, they spit out exhaust fire, smoke, and oil like they were going out of style, darkening airport aprons and making them slippery for ground support personnel.

In recent decades this machinery has been coined as "propliner" equipment by a small cult of vintage aviation enthusiasts, but actual pilots and crews of these aircraft seem to favor the term *heavy-recips*, short for *heavy-reciprocating piston engine aircraft*, or "*heavy piston*" aircraft. We may use any of these terms interchangeably. However, we should point out that the term *propliner* is a broader term that typically includes first-generation 1950s commercial turbo*prop* airliners such as four-engine Lockheed L-188 Electra and the earlier Bristol Series 100-300 Britannia from the UK, so we will use that term most often. A turboprop powerplant is little more than a jet engine that drives a propeller for most of its thrust, rather than using exhaust.

The Electra turboprop, as flown by the major airlines, was part of the final generation of the major propliners that comprised a big part of the *Second Wind* and was in service simultaneously with them in the latter part of the *First Wind*. Turboprops were an efficient stopgap transition between piston power and pure jets, but to this day smaller turboprop applications thrive with regional airlines. Since the dawn of the jet age, the general populous never liked turboprops and still doesn't—because they have old-fashioned *propellers*. Also, because of its superior propulsion and other technologies, Electra's ultimate phaseout from front-line service occurred about a decade later than the heavy-recip propliners. The Electra might have seen wider use had the traveling public not had a preference for faster, more exciting pure jets, and had it not had a rash of terrible fatal crashes early on (mainly in-flight wing separations) that destroyed its reputation. Lockheed, therefore, was forced to cut production short, but all existing Electras were structurally strengthened around the wings and engine nacelles and flew successfully for years with major airlines until 1977 (with Eastern Airlines) when they were relegated to secondary operators.

With the advent of the commercial jet age, hundreds of newly formed second-hand and mom-and-pop airline wannabes were looking for a quick buck with cheap surplus heavy piston airliner castoffs that flooded the market. This was the beginning of an uneasy renaissance of sorts not seen since the flood of surplus heavy-piston C-47s after World War II.

In this *Second Wind* resurgence, most propliners were converted from passenger carriers to freighters, but a few of them retained glamorous passenger roles such as transporting (and regularly killing) A-list celebrities, rock stars, and top executives the world over. At the same time, many of the cheap, low-time freighters were forced into near-prostitution, flying drugs, illegal arms, and other contraband for the worst and most violent organized elements mankind has to offer. Illegal drugs were the real stigma that was associated with the *propliner glut* of the *Second Wind*. And then there was the hauling of everything in-between—the realm of college sports teams, conventioneers, high-school bands, courier and general cargoes, and more specialized cargoes such as livestock, automotive just-in-time inventory, cargoes under military and CIA logistics contracts (LogAir) and many other legitimate, *kinda legitimate* and *not-so- legitimate* operations.

A book published by Alvin Moscow in the early 1960s coined the heavy-recip transport aircraft as a *Tiger on a Leash*—the title of the book. Slight inattention while operating a big, complex propliner could result in it the tiger's master (read *aircrew*) being badly maimed or killed, along with tens or hundreds of innocent passengers and people on the ground. If these old and overly complex machines were not maintained and flown by the book, an incremental buildup of mechanical discrepancies could snowball into a disaster when least expected, eating crews and innocents alive. This happened with disturbing regularity.

For the most part, when propliners were their frontline equipment, the major airlines and regulatory authorities of the *First Wind* looked at safety as seriously as today, even though now it would not seem so. The baseline safety standards of the past were comparatively *primitive* and could not possibly reflect the serious lessons to be learned in future decades.

By contrast, for many of the hundreds of inexperienced hand-me-down operators that arose out of the *Second Wind*, the temptation was complacency and *not* respect the *Tiger*. To save money, maintenance was deferred, crew qualifications were relaxed, and checklists and load limits were ignored. This led to inexcusable disasters. Propliners became little more than flying coffins on a lottery wheel, and the federal regulators discovered that their rules then in place were badly loopholed, therefore *unwittingly encouraging* this bad behavior. Every fly-by-night operator and crew knew this, and crews concerned about corner-cutting often heard from their bosses, *if you can't take this flight, we'll find someone else who can.* These chastised crews were forced to rationalize as they reconsidered, *"It hasn't happened to me yet, so I suppose it won't happen this time."* In many unfortunate instances, the unthinkable *did* happen *this time*.

Mark Aero, Incorporated. at St. Louis's Lambert Field was one of these secondhand propliner operators, but not one of the sloppy ones just described. It was founded, owned, and operated by a flamboyant aviation pioneer Joseph E. Morris who in 1958 started it all by managing and operating Monsanto CEO Edgar M. Queeny's fleet of converted World War II Consolidated PBY Catalina amphibious *Flying RVs* that flew all over the world. Later assisted by his calm yet short-fused multi-tasking son Mark G. Morris, Mark Aero morphed into one of many *Second Wind* propliner-centric fixed base operators (FBOs) that were common at many US airports from the 1960s into the early 1980s. To the Morrises and all others who built their earlier careers around large obsolete piston aircraft, the rationale was that a perfectly good, inexpensive low-time airplane was a *terrible thing to waste*, obsolete or not.

Still, "rogue," "renegade," "loose cannon," and "nuisance" could be typical descriptions that *might* have been associated with Mark Aero. Its thick-skinned father/son team had a habit of unwittingly stepping on the toes of the major airlines and their Civil Aeronautics Board (CAB) partners when they tried to form and run their own common carrier interstate airlines. On the contrary, the other Lambert FBOs stuck to the traditional FBO knitting (training, ground services, outfitting, refurbishing, and sales) and were not a threat. But the Morrises seemed to be in constant battle with the government regulators who protected the turf of the majors—back then it was nearly impossible for anyone to start an interstate airline in that hostile oligopolistic environment. Joe and Mark were more than once threatened, even roughed up by thugs who were hired by the big airlines on an "as needed" basis. All the public ever heard from these airlines was the cheerful "Up, Up and Away" jingle on the radio, while behind the curtain their spooks were doing their dirty work.

As well, the propliners that were a fixture on Mark Aero's premises were a kind of ball-and-chain eyesore on the image of civic progress. At times, junky-looking, clapped-out old planes, some of them engineless, faded hulks, half-hulks, and pieces and parts, littered the premises, infuriating bureaucrats. Some of that was used to keep the good ones flying. Large airports were always looking for the first opportunity to shut such operators down and clean things up. However, the City of St. Louis and the Lambert airport authority seemed a bit more lenient.

Mark Aero was not managed by bottom-feeder types that characterized many of its peers. The Morrises got along well with, and entered business relationships with, the other big FBOs at Lambert, and drank after work with top aerospace executives, celebrities and entertainers, high-profile U.S. congressmen, and even moon-walking astronauts, almost seeming to mimic Howard Hughes' flashy style—and yes, the Morrises knew Howard well. As a matter of necessity, they were well plugged into St. Louis high society and had those very necessary aviation industry contacts all over North America. Mark Aero served as the outsourced flight operations for several of America's largest corporations before they took their flight departments in-house, and continued to provide ground support for several of these new internal flight departments.

The company operated out of the obscure northwest corner of Lambert Field, butting right up against the west side of the McDonnell Douglas facilities, which at the time produced most of the nation's modern jet fighter aircraft, as well as the Mercury, and Gemini manned spacecraft that propelled the U.S. into the space race with the Soviet Union. Mark Aero leased 52 acres of ramp space there and utilized the airport's oldest two hangars, plus a couple of other smaller ones to the south. The two main hangars were the historic Navy hangars that were the very first structures at Lambert, built in the 1920s. They were a stone's throw from where Charles A. Lindbergh, chief pilot for Robertson Aircraft Corporation, departed with the mail to Chicago every evening in a flimsy, wood, wire, and cloth World War I deHavilland DH.4. One of these moonlit flights to Chicago inspired his far-fetched desire to make a record-breaking solo transatlantic flight. Today, the world has a deeply faded awareness of the outcome of that insane idea.

Later, Mark Aero became the last tenant of Lambert's original 100,000 square-foot passenger "Old Terminal" on its ramp that was completed in 1933, and in the early 1970s, it poured its money into considerable leasehold improvements. Under Mark Aero, it was known as Lambert's "International Terminal" becoming the sole U.S. Customs and international passenger terminal there, despite the airport's main terminal that dominated the south side, designed by famed architect Minoru Yamasaki years before he designed the World Trade Center. The historic Old Terminal was itself a work of art-deco, featuring the roof gazebo where aviation's *very first* air traffic controller, Archie League, worked for many years with his giant spotlight. The Old Terminal was built adjacent to the site where Robertson Aircraft previously operated, which later became a key component of American Airlines. The Old Terminal was unceremoniously demolished in 1979 with the vague excuse of "future expansion," leaving only the original old Navy hangars standing for the time being. That future expansion did happen two decades later, but bad timing proved the $370 million runway expansion unnecessary.

Mark Aero did everything. For almost twenty years it was the most diversified operation at Lambert and Spirit of St. Louis Airport in St. Louis County, and *the* tie-down spot for most light aircraft based at Lambert. They operated a Part 141 flight school and in 1970 they trained select St. Louis County policemen to fly their newly-formed Bell 47 helicopter surveillance and search team. The police initially leased the two 47s (and later 3 more) from Mark Aero which featured high-powered searchlights. One article on the new operation appearing in the St. Louis Globe-Democrat in March 1971 stated, *"If, some night, your neighborhood is suddenly bathed in floodlight, remember—it's only the eye in the sky."* Sure enough, two weeks later on a chilly night our extensively wooded backyard acreage was lit up like daylight under a powerful swinging beam of a hovering Bell 47. In the dark of night, I could see every familiar detail of our wooded property like it was daytime—right where I played while growing up. Suspects? Hiding in my backyard? I never found out whom they were chasing or if they were apprehended.

Mark Aero, Inc. founder, sole shareholder, and president Joe Morris meets with his secretary, Rose Joly, circa the late 1960s. (Mark G. Morris)

Mark Aero initially had Part 135 and Part 135.2 Certificates to conduct air taxi and charter operations using light aircraft. Starting in 1967 they initially operated a single *large* aircraft as a non-commercial leisure "travel club" under the then-new FAR Part 123 that became effective in 1968 (and rescinded in the early 1980s). Part 123 provided tighter rules governing large transport-category *club* aircraft previously operated under the badly loopholed Part 91 rules governing non-commercial operations. Travel clubs were a major phenomenon by the late 1960s and early 1970s that found a use for old propliners, which could serve as an entrée into at least the contract (non-common carrier) or intrastate airline business. After considerable effort and expense, Mark Aero was eventually awarded their Part 121 Commercial Operator certificate allowing them to operate large transport category aircraft on a contract basis rather than just as a club.

On the tarmac, Mark Aero provided airline ramp and all ground handling services at the International Terminal, including baggage handling, use of terminal facility counters and baggage conveyor, passenger manifesting and check-in, aircraft cleaning as requested, airstart and ground power, heating and air conditioning, airstairs, catering and ground transportation. It provided line check assistance and fueling for private, common carrier, and military customers.

Mark Aero was an FAA Certified Repair Station. Its hangars housed its main offices, engine and avionics shops, an airframe overhaul shop, an upholstery and woodworking shop, an aircraft paint shop, ramp vehicle service bays, and storage and aircraft work areas. These facilities provided 24-hour line service, licensed FAA mechanics, switchboard, and telex. The engine and accessory overhaul shop consisted of employees qualified to overhaul heavy reciprocating engines up to and including the Pratt & Whitney R-2800 C-Series engine used on both the Martin 404 and Douglas DC-6 that it operated, as well as the ubiquitous Convair twins that in the propliner heyday competed with the 404.

Mark Aero V.P. Maintenance William "Red" Hindman (in front of prop blade) makes the rounds as mechanic Jim Hardcastle works on an R-2800-CB17 hanging on a customer's DC-6 during the 1960s. (Mark G. Morris)

In a nutshell, the several Mark Aero divisions and related subsidiaries were owners, flight instructors, refurbishers, overhaulers, painters, cannibalizers, scrappers, brokers, lessees, and lessors typically involving big obsolete aircraft and their engines and systems. Their flight training school was a big deal in all of this, providing everything from primary through the most advanced airline transport training. They put good pilots on an unusually fast track. A new private pilot in a little Cessna 150 trainer could have his Airline Transport Pilot rating (ATP) and several type ratings in less than 18 months. Training went hand-in-hand with its corporate flight department first utilizing a few Beechcraft 18s, Lockheed Lodestars, and Douglas DC-3s, and then later advanced turbine equipment such as the Mitsubishi MU-2 *hotrod* twin-engine turboprop, and also the de Havilland DH-125 corporate jet. If all that wasn't enough, Mark Aero started, owned, and operated *airlines*. So, we can see that Mark Aero morphed into the collective broad experiences of the multi-talented personnel that ran it.

Mark Aero's three *primary* operational groups included:

- **Mark Aero:** Ground support, engine and avionics overhaul, pilot training, and a lessor of seasoned pilots and other crew to Mark Aero Supplemental Carriers, outside supplemental carriers, or private owner/operators, as well as administrative support for Mark Aero and its affiliates. Satellite operations were in Greenville, Illinois, and later Spirit of St. Louis Airport, both of which were shut down by 1971.

- **Mark Aero Supplemental Carriers:** Started, operated, grew, and wound down various affiliated air taxi, contract, and charter airlines.

- **Alpha Aviation:** An aircraft broker/lessor operation that transitioned mostly large aircraft through various stages of storage, refurbishment, cannibalization, and scrapping. Many aircraft ultimately operated by Mark Aero were registered to Alpha Aviation at one time or another, when either coming, going, or both.

Fifty or more business enterprises, private aviators, and public institutions relied on the services of Mark Aero, including universities such as the University of Missouri and Illinois University, corporations such as the McDonnell-Douglas, Peabody Coal, Banquet Foods, Emerson Electric, Ralston Purina, Kellwood, Chromalloy, Angelica, and government agencies such as the Missouri State Highway Department, and the Missouri Conservation Commission.

There were at least two other general aviation FBOs at Lambert that had existed before or emerged somewhat simultaneously with Mark Aero in the late 1950s. These were the longstanding Remmert-Werner located down the line to the southwest quadrant, who specialized in modifying and operating surplus twin-propliners including DC-3s and then larger Convairliners for executive use. They also had pilot training and charter operations which were soon deemphasized in favor of the DC-3 work. Joe Morris hatched Mark Aero with the support of Edgar Queeny, his then-employer, who happened to be one of the founders and original stockholders of Remmert-Werner. As mentioned, Mark Aero would become the servicer and operator of Queeny's PBY aircraft fleet, but also became one of the first dealers for the Aero Commander line of small piston general aviation aircraft (hence the term *Aero* in the name *Mark Aero*). Remmert-Werner went on to be the exclusive dealer for the Sabreliner corporate jet, and later became the Sabreliner Division of Rockwell International, moving to new facilities at the northwest corner of Lambert.

Young Aviation was the other major FBO that was founded about the same time as Mark Aero. Located at the southeast airport quadrant, Young and its successor, Midcoast Aviation would eventually dominate the FBO scene (ground, fueling, and turnaround services) at Lambert starting in the mid-1970s after Mark Aero was formally shut down. These ground operations were

Joe Morris (second from left) with a few of his key employees inspects a Continental "flat-six" engine block used on many light aircraft. (Mark G. Morris)

Floyd Napier, head of the Mark Aero engine shop, next to a freshly overhauled R-2800 C-Series aircraft engine, in the 1960s. These engines powered aircraft such as the Douglas DC-6, Martin 404, and Convair 240/340/440. At 2,500 horsepower, it was a little beyond your stock automobile automotive V8. (Mark G. Morris)

rolled into a new subsidiary, Airport Terminal Services (ATS) in the early 1980s, which would expand to other airports nationwide. Midcoast would also become an outfitter of the Canadair Challenger and Dassault Falcon corporate jets. Unlike Mark Aero, these other two Lambert FBOs were more tuned into the emerging jet age but did not seek to own and operate airlines. They also did not place their *long-term* bets on old technology just because it was plentiful or they might have known it well.

Mark Aero took a different path. Instead of outfitting and marketing the emerging corporate jets, *they just wanted a platform to start and run airlines* by the most expedient means possible. They invested considerable monetary and intellectual capital toward that end, but *not* for budget-busting jet-age equipment. The company and its spinoff successors started and ran several airlines using the old and slow heavy-recips. However, due to a rapidly changing economic and regulatory environment, each airline had an unimpressive lifespan ranging from zero to just seven or eight years. Yes, a few corporate turboprops, jets, and even a large Boeing 720 did find their way into Mark Aero's fleets, but the low-hanging fruit of the propliner dominated their visible spectrum for years.

As mentioned, Mark Aero got started in the big transport airline business in 1967 by forming and servicing their travel club affiliate with a single Douglas DC-6, and years later adding a DC-7, another DC-6, and even a Boeing 720 Intercontinental jet. In mid-1972 Mark Aero acquired its own DC-6 and then took over three Martin 404 twins with the shutdown of one of its good customers, a restricted charter airline called *Interstate Airmotive*. Mark Aero made several attempts to form *scheduled* airlines to employ these Martinliners and DC-6s, but could never get out of the starting blocks. The major airlines, with the help of their regulatory CAB "partners," did everything they could to keep Mark Aero in its place, and there was an energy crisis and a resultant economic recession that did not help. This bad alignment of the planets put Mark Aero into voluntary dissolution in 1975. That did not deter the Morrises.

In what seemed to be a seamless transformation, 27-year-old Mark resurrected things out of the smoldering ashes just like the Phoenix. This risen Phoenix, unveiled later in this book, manifested itself in what would become the largest *Second Wind* Douglas DC-6 airline in the world. Owned and run by Mark himself, he had just become one of the youngest if not the youngest founder of an airline at that time. This specialty airline utilized a fleet of 25 four-engine Douglas DC-6 airliners and the three former Interstate/Mark Aero Martin 404 twins on passenger and cargo missions for offshore oil services companies. They quickly expanded into dedicated freight service for auto manufacturers and freight forwarders all over North America. The former Mark Aero facilities in St. Louis became one of its largest hubs. All this was happening at a time when all other airlines of this size were flying jets and turboprops.

The big DC-6 airline would be sold to a large air transportation company only two years after its founding, but both Mark and Joe continued to manage it. One highly unusual feature was that it was profitable every year of its existence. It survived for another three years under the new ownership before being abruptly shut down and liquidated as a "non-strategic" asset during the economic storm of 1981, despite its continued profitability. Despite the deplorable safety records of many of their peers, neither Mark Aero nor its big airline successor had a fatal accident, but they did have a few close calls as all operators do. Also, the big DC-6 airline would *not* be Mark's last airline, but from there it would be jetliners only.

Over the next two decades, former Mark Aero's northwest corner of Lambert would become a wasteland for a few decaying propliners. Broken, rusty support equipment was scattered randomly everywhere, with tall weeds popping out the seams of the dried oil-stained ramp. One could witness several large propliners being scrapped on site, probably contracted out by ATS or the airport authority.

Amid this decay, transient propliner freighter operators—all former competitors of Mark Morris's DC-6 airline—saw *increasing* operations here, mainly with DC-6s, C-46s, Convairs, and Electras. They were operated by the remaining "hot shot" just-in-time auto parts haulers out Willow Run Airport near Detroit (where Mark's airline had its largest hub) and the growing overnight courier operators that were still serviced and turned here (under ATS). The historic Navy hangars' final role was to house at least one or two satellite dispatching offices for these cargo operators, and overnight package haulers, well into the 1980s. Even into the 1990s very few old propliners *still* cycled in and out, but not for long.

One might ask, why chronicle an obscure airline-oriented operation that never seemed to reach a critical mass—and is now long dead, gone, and forgotten? Well then, why did writers chronicle all the well-known legacy majors such as Pan Am, Eastern, Braniff, TWA, Continental, National, and Northwest? They are long gone too. Many just died, but most just lost their

This is a *normal* heavy-recip startup scene. In this case, a Curtiss-Wright R-3350 radial engine mounted on a Lockheed L-1049H Super Constellation gets a fiery start out of the exhaust dumps, not to mention the thick churning smoke behind it that is not visible. In the 1950s, everyday passengers were accustomed to this kind of scene at the beginning of almost any flight, as well as on takeoff when the flames often got even worse. (Walter Davis)

identities in mergers. What about *all* the local service airlines that existed in 1955 that were chosen and blessed by the Eisenhower administration—Allegheny, Bonanza, Central, Frontier, Lake Central, Mohawk, North Central, Ozark, Piedmont, Southern, Pacific Air, Trans-Texas, and West Coast? There were books written about them too. But *none* of these airlines exist today. As the late rock singer Jim Morrison of the Doors was known to have said, *"No one gets out of here alive."* Yes, all these airlines are long dead, but *as we shall see*, unlike their fly-by-night bottom-feeding peers, Mark Aero and its successors left legacies that *changed the world* in a surprisingly big way, just like many of these legendary, longer-lasting, but now defunct, airline pioneers did. Just *how* you say? Read on.

Mark Aero and its offshoot airlines started it all for me as a 14-year-old teenager staring in from outside the airport chain link fence. As will become apparent, this directly impacted many of this kid's lifetime decisions, thrusting him headlong into the *Second Wind of the Aerial Leviathans*. While by 1982 Joe and Mark Morris gladly exited the heavy-recip world, I was finally able to get "inside the fence" and continue to seek it out, experience it, and even broadcast it to a worldwide propliner cult that was emerging. This odyssey of mine lasted for two more decades until the *Second Wind* reached its inevitable, permanent calm.

Captain Mark G. Morris during his "jet years" circa 2005. (Mark G. Morris)

CHAPTER 1

St. Louis National Air Races 1969

It's a big weekend in August. *The* legendary rock festival is in progress at Woodstock, New York, only three weeks after Neil Armstrong takes humanity's very first steps on the Moon. Privately-owned Spirit of St. Louis Airport is hosting the National Air Races, a major event held on a 3-mile course over the cornfields of its western perimeter, under the sanction of the now long-defunct Professional Race Pilots Association (PRPA). Spirit is a fairly new reliever airport to what was then called Lambert Field and is located in the fertile Missouri River basin in Chesterfield in far west St. Louis County, so the young airport is probably looking for publicity. Crop farms are all over and the sleepy Lobmaster Sky Ranch airport is only a half-mile to the north are its only neighbors. Lobmaster is home for an inactive, faded yellow World War II North American SNJ trainer (Navy designation for the North American AT-6 Texan military trainer) always visible from Highway 40 looking north, and a handful of banner-towing Piper Cubs and a few old Cessnas. Many of these planes don't even have radios. Years earlier it was proposed to expand Lobmaster as Lambert's reliever airport, but the surrounding farmland owners would hot have it. This vast and rich farming area in Chesterfield Valley is known by St. Louis natives as "Gumbo Flats," or just "Gumbo."

But to grow the new Spirit of St. Louis reliever airport authorities want light manufacturing, warehousing, and offices surrounding it, not farmland. And the uncontrolled Lobmaster had become an air traffic hazard for the new higher-density, tower-controlled Spirit operations just to the north, and they were so close that Spirit tower even had to control Lobmaster takeoffs and landings with colored light guns. By chance, and perhaps to the relief of Spirit airport operations, Lobmaster had been finally closed down in late 1968 with the re-routing of Highway 40 right through the south end of its runway. The industrial development did materialize over the next five decades, and even a cataclysmic flood that submerged the whole valley in 1993 did not stop the airport or industry expansion. After the reinforcement of the levy, a *massive* THF retail development sprung up in the valley just east of Spirit and industry greatly expanded from there.

Starting in the late 1960s my dad had been close friends with Paul Haglin who conceived, built, and then opened Spirit Airport in 1964. Haglin did this because he, as a private pilot of light aircraft, was tired of the sometimes dangerous congestion at Lambert where general aviation seemed always second fiddle to airline operations. Back then, the Mark Aero Lambert facility was the place for droves of light planes based there and was most likely the largest tiedown facility on premises. This may likely have been Haglin's Lambert base.

Now, in 1969 Haglin is still Spirt Airport's owner (a decade later he would sell to St. Louis County), which has about a 5,000' runway able to handle medium- and some larger-size airliners and transports of the day. Dad gets free airshow tickets from Haglin for the three-day event, so he hauls his dad (Gramps), my younger brother Jeff and 14-year-old me to the races. This is nostalgic for both Gramps and dad—it's the very first air race at St. Louis since the last one they attended at Lambert Field in 1937, thirty-two years prior when dad was only 10 years old.

Scale replica of the 1939 Keith Rider R-4 racer, named "Schoenfeldt Firecracker." I built this for my dad for his 65th birthday because it was his favorite winner in the 1937 National Air Races in St. Louis which he attended. Its wheel brakes were so sensitive that when pilot Gus Gotch applied them on landing rollout after winning the 50-mile event he nosed over, busting the prop to pieces. In 1939, famed pilot Tony LeVier raced this plane in the National Air Races in Cleveland, clocking a record speed of 300 m.p.h. He didn't win because he passed and then miscounted the former leader's number of laps, permitting this competitor to retake the lead and win. The R-4 was powered by an inverted inline six-cylinder air-cooled Menasco engine that developed 500 hp or more.

Back in 1937 aviation was learning the meaning of *speed*, and the general public was *all- in* for air racing during aviation's adolescence, just like it is now with major league sports. Dad and Gramps saw one of the Menasco-powered Folkerts racers slap into a flock of birds at around 250 miles per hour during one of the race heats, resulting in a spectacular crash landing. Or so they told me. Some sources suggest the crash was caused by an improperly secured propeller, not birds. At least pilot Roger Don Rae walked away from his badly damaged Folkerts.

Air racing is now back in St. Louis 32 years later and that excites me. As a growing teenager, I have a slowly evolving interest in airplanes and other things mechanical like cars and fast boats. A month before this airshow I had gotten back from three weeks at a boys' horseback riding camp called Ute Trail near Gunnison Colorado (are "boy's camps" still allowed?). Us campers learned how to be cowboys and herd cattle. How did that prepare us for real life in the city? I'm not sure. I guess that just taught us "discipline" as we experienced some of the realities of the wild west culture that we always saw on those old black-and-white tube TVs growing up (excluding the shootouts, train robberies, women, saloon fights, etc.).

To get to Ute Trail, Jeff and I get our first airline ride ever on a Frontier Boeing 727-100 to Denver. We, along with all the other campers are shuttled to Gunnison by a huge Frontier Airlines Convair 580 twin-engine turboprop, which impresses me to the gills. To top that off, at Gunnison a completely white and unmarked DC-3 taxis right by us just after we deplane, swinging around for an immediate full-power takeoff just a stone's throw away. Wow!

This summer I'm getting pretty good at building plastic airplane models, and I'm flying a bright yellow Cox .049 piston-powered control-line plane. It is a very basic design I had just built out of balsa, paint, and dope, called the "American Boy" by the kit manufacturer. The Cox engine develops a whopping 1/16 horsepower at something like 20,000 rpm. A *control-line* model plane is where you fly it in circles around you, connected by two elevator control lines. Due to centrifugal force, there are no other control inputs required such as ailerons or rudder. Your body is spinning in circles from its stationary point, with the elevator lines attached to your handheld control harness. Control line planes are noisier than hell, often irritating neighbors. You get very dizzy at first, but that goes away with experience. But now, back to the races.

In my backyard in August 1969 with my bright yellow "American Boy" flying control-line model I named "Bad Penny." Even with only one control axis (pitch), it was a handful to fly and flew quite fast, making me very dizzy at first. (John J. Reed home movie frame)

Upon parking our car at a cleared-out weed field, we climb into what looked like a dark blue prison shuttle bus (there was a brand-new medium-security prison near the airport at the time) for transfer to the spectator drop-off point. At this time in my life, I don't know the names of any general aviation manufacturers other than Cessna, Beechcraft, and Piper, as my dad is with Goldman Sachs and all three manufacturers are his very good clients. He always buys me their airplane postcards and brochures (that show all the cool instrument panel layouts) when he gets back from his Wichita and Lock Haven business trips.

We reach the tarmac and on the way to the spectator field, we pass a field of tied-down light aircraft and homebuilts, with manufacturer names I never heard of. We later walk around this line of aircraft, and I am awestruck by a new, maroon-colored two-place (side-by-side) aircraft called the "American Yankee," designed by the well-known homebuilt designer Jim Bede. It's a sleek and fast-looking low-wing machine, though with a fixed-pitch prop and fixed landing gear, with no rivets and the cleanest, shiniest skin covering I ever saw. The cockpit instrumentation grabs me, and this is not a brochure picture—the panel, in "full 3D reality mode" looks like that of a jet fighter. I couldn't possibly believe that decade later I would be racking up flying hours in two of its direct descendants, the four-place Grumman/Gulfstream American models.

We find a spot at the mowed, chigger-infested spectator area. A well-known St. Louis Aviation fixture, Pappy Downs, is the airshow announcer. He is good at it. In 1967 he became the very first Ozark pilot to retire, flying Douglas DC-3s exclusively his entire career there. He is now an FAA Regional Examiner and flight instructor. During my flight training a decade later I would meet Pappy and talk with him extensively, but he was never one of my instructors. That was probably my loss.

The main racing class at the Spirit National Air Races was called the "Formula One" class, formed way back in the 1930s. One of the older designs in this class at that time was called the "Shoestring," a pretty neat-looking plane, but the more common later design was the "Ole Tiger" which had more modern-looking angular and squared-off features. All were very small mid-wing designs that were hardly bigger than the pilot that was strapped into them. Under Professional Race Pilot's Association (PRPA) rules, all Formula Ones had to be powered by the 4-cylinder Continental O-200 flat-four engine. This was the same engine that powered the ubiquitous little Cessna 150 that I trained in years later. However, the Formula teams were allowed to beef up the engines beyond the normal 100 horsepower rating for competition purposes, and it seems they ran at much higher RPM than the stock engine. While this was one of the fastest competition classes at this event, average speeds of up to 200 miles per hour were a full 50 miles per hour slower than the averages at the 1937 racers.

Just as in 1937, today in 1969 dad and Gramps once again witness a race plane auger in, this time with us boys looking on, slamming into the cornfield right in front of us with a loud reverberating thud and a cloud of dust. Its green tail section then rises out of the cornstalk line,

An "Ole Tiger" Formula One racer at Spirit of St. Louis Airport, August 1969. (John J. Reed home movie frame)

A couple of AT-6s get ready to round a pylon at the August 1969 National Air Races at the west perimeter of Spirit of St. Louis Airport. Several of these AT-6 pilots were killed 2 years later in a multiple midair pile-up at a Cape May, New Jersey race. (John J. Reed home movie frame)

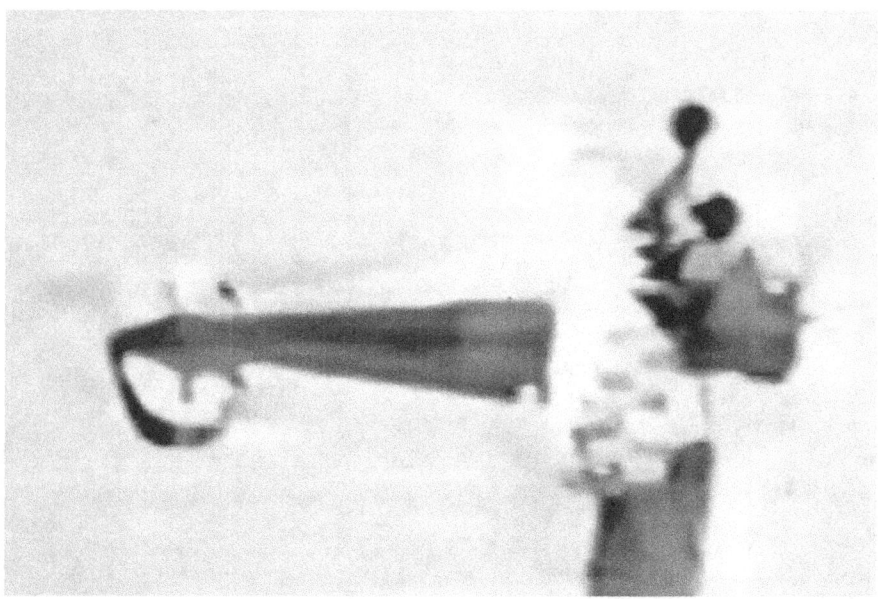

Bevo Howard performing in his Bücker Jungmeister biplane at the National Air Races, Spirit of St. Louis Airport, August 1969. In those days, cutting-edge aerobatics was tame compared to what you see today. Within 24 months of when this frame was taken, Bevo perished while practicing maneuvers in this plane. (John J. Reed home movie frame)

seemingly in slow motion, then rapidly flips over before being swallowed once again by the cornfield and rising dust cloud. The crowd gasps in horrified unison—this time, however, it's engine failure and not birds or a departing propeller. Thankfully, as in 1937, this 1969 Formula One crash pilot walks away uninjured, but this is still not a very pleasant continuation of generational tradition. I don't remember who this latest lucky pilot was.

There is a similar biplane racing class that is slower but also fun to watch, but this is the first time I see a North American AT-6 World War II advanced trainer in action. It's the Army version of the yellow Navy SNJ that sat deteriorating at Lobmaster Sky Ranch. The AT-6 racing class is a big part of this event and impresses me the most, even as the heat, humidity, and insects become unbearable. They pass with a sharp, slapping propeller buzz which to me is very annoying, but as the gaggle of planes recedes the sound changes to something more pleasant—you only hear the thundering 9 pistons of the 600 horsepower in unison from each of the Pratt & Whitney R-1340 engines. These machines are the epitome of piston *POWER.* That is until I shortly prove myself wrong.

There are also aerobatic acts at this airshow. Bevo Howard is there with his vintage Bücker Jungmeister biplane. Other biplane and monoplane aerobatic acts also perform, including Howie Keefe, Mary Gaffney, Bob Herendeen, Charlie Hillard, Harold Krier, and Duane Cole, among others. It is too bad that some of these performers, including Bevo, would be dead from practice or airshow accidents within a few short months or years. Most of the others eventually succumbed to their flying professions as well.

Between aerobatic acts, I see a big, twin-piston engine, twin-tail tail-dragging machine

A C-119G Flying Boxcar similar to the Marine jump ship used by the Navy parachute team at the 1969 National Air Races at Spirit of St. Louis Airport. I think this is the loudest heavy-reciprocating aircraft ever with its two 3,700 hp Turbo-Compound engines, with its cavernous airframe acting as a giant amplifier, almost like a bullhorn bell. I was spellbound by this machine. I took this photo at the Wright Patterson Air Force Museum in 1987.

thunder down the runway on takeoff. It seems a bit larger and louder than the similarly-configured Beech 18s I was somewhat familiar with. Dad tells me that the big thing is a "Lockheed Lodestar," an old 1940s transport plane. However, it was not part of the airshow and I wonder who would be flying an old thing like that in this day and age.

The U.S. Naval Precision Parachuting Team is also performing. The jump plane is an extremely large twin-engine Fairchild C-119 twin-boom "Flying Boxcar" assault transport flown by the Marines. Today, giant piston planes of this size no longer exist so they are no longer parachute team platforms. As I would find out in due course, this aircraft was powered by two Curtiss-Wright R-3350 18-cylinder Turbo-Compound engines developing 3,700 horsepower each (compared to the AT-6's *measly* 600 horsepower). On low climb out after takeoff, the C-119 seemed to just hang on its propellers, hardly moving, howling like a thousand reverberating organ pipe demons, killing my eardrums. Now, *this* is the epitome of *power*, not the AT-6.

After the conclusion of the final day's show, we climb back into the prison bus, hot, sticky, dusty, and tired. We head east past the general aviation display area where I had seen the American Yankee. Then we pass by some large hangars along a chain-link fence, where the bus hits "stop and go" traffic. We idle along the fence, right next to an old *four-engine propeller airliner* that I immediately recognize, right there in my face, seemingly out of place with the wimpy light planes tied down nearby. It's some sort of old "DC plane" in all-natural metal color—sparsely painted including the script letters "Pegasus Club" smartly painted above the passenger windows. This name, which of course denotes the winged horse in Greek mythology, fascinates me.

The spark that ignited it all for me. A *very rare* image of the four-engine Pegasus Club "DC plane" I gawked at in August 1969 from a prison shuttle bus at the National Air Races at Spirit of St. Louis Airport—the only known image of this plane in its early Pegasus Club paint job. Here, this plane's fuzzy image was inadvertently caught in the remote background of a wide-angle promotional photograph from the late 1960s. This Pegasus DC-6 N90710 was all-natural metal with the "Pegasus Club" script lettering and color trim in navy blue. Entering service with American Airlines in 1947, it had been only recently retired by them in 1966 from its long stint as one of their Flagships. American's "lightning" fuselage livery remains intact here—the main difference being that American's trademark bright orange colors were simply painted over in navy blue. As I found out several years later, this aircraft *had* to be registered N90710 as that was the only DC-6 operated by Pegasus at that time.

Long black and brown exhaust stains emanate along each of the four big piston radial engine nacelles with big paddle-blade propellers, sort of similar in size to those of that big C-119. My memory flashes back to seeing these kinds of passenger planes on the apron at Lambert and regularly flying over my house only 5 or 10 years ago but not anymore. These were mainly blue-nacelled Delta airliners heading south on their way to Memphis or New Orleans. I remember the Delta engines "singing" in a deep harmony while they struggled *slowly* overhead, rather than the more typical growling of a twin-engine DC-3, or the organ pipe demons I just heard on the C-119.

A thought hits me as I think of all the four-engine Delta planes of a decade ago—*Man! This machine is awesome! I just don't see these giant four-engine propeller planes anymore.* I subconsciously put this realization on my mental backburner, without knowing that this one impression is permanent and life-changing. It would be a while before I would learn who this giant flying horse *Pegasus* was. As it turns out that big Lockheed Lodestar dad and I saw taking off earlier during the airshow intermission had something to do with it.

CHAPTER 2

Aviation Pioneer

Joseph E. Morris was born in 1917 and raised on a Minnesota dairy farm by his aunt and uncle. His father was a World War I combat pilot before barnstorming through the 1920s. During prohibition, Joe's dad smuggled alcohol with his planes as a lucrative side business. This aerial circus performer and part-time smuggler was a typical adventurer who was never home— he was not a family man. Nor was Joe's mother for that matter, who apparently didn't want to be a "family woman" and they both left Joe when he was very young.

While he grew up working very hard on the dairy farm, Joe could not imagine this line of work as his destiny. One thing he liked about the farm and got good at was maintaining, modifying, and rebuilding the farm machinery. Stimulating, yes, but it was just plain old farm equipment.

When the rebellious Joe was 14 years old he acquired a junked-out, completely inoperable Harley-Davidson motorcycle. He is said to have fixed it up and gotten it running well, allowing him to one day hightail out of Dodge without even informing his aunt and uncle, never to return (like parents like son?). At some point thereafter he wound up at Bryce Canyon Utah at a flying school, owned by none other than Edgar Bergen, the world-famous ventriloquist. There, Joe earned his private pilot's license, probably as a bartered benefit for doing odd jobs at the school. He took his Harley down to Santa Anita, California, and worked at the race track there to advance his flight training and attend aeronautical engineering classes at UCLA. This was the start of an impressive 24,000-hour flying career that most pilots never achieve.

Joe was taken by an attractive and personable assistant at the Bergen flying school. They married and in 1933 they went to Alaska so he could get a flying job. Joe became a bush pilot and learned the ins and outs of some of the most dangerous flying in the world—dodging "cumulo-granite" in bad, low-visibility weather. In those days, the life expectancy of a bush pilot was not that great.

After gaining bush flying experience, Joe and a partner formed a flying service with a couple of single-engine Beech Staggerwing biplanes. Details are scarce, but apparently, this operation was absorbed by Alaska Star Airlines which flew Lockheed Model 18 Lodestars, with Joe becoming a captain there, just as World War II was heating up. One day, this airline would evolve into today's major airline known as Alaska Airlines—but Joe Morris had moved on by then.

It's one of those World War II "flat feet" stories all over again. Joe had them, so he could not be a military combat pilot in the war. If he could not serve directly, he would serve indirectly, like so many other flat-footers. As it turned out, this indirect participant would have a much greater impact on the war and beyond than if he were just a combat pilot.

He started as a production test pilot for Boeing, which was turning out hundreds of B-17 Flying Fortress heavy bombers for the war effort. Joe went on to San Diego to become an experimental test pilot for Consolidated Vultee (which later became Convair), the designer and manufacturer of two legendary aircraft that helped win the war—the four-engine B-24 Liberator heavy bomber, and the twin-engine PBY Catalina amphibian which was a multi-role maritime transport, rescue, and attack aircraft. The Liberator looked like a clean, modern bomber, while the PBY looked like a throwback to the late 1920s, with a big high wing that resembled a giant rectangular slab mounted atop a "sail" structure on the fuselage, further supported by old-fashioned wing struts. Its two engines were mounted uncharacteristically close together at the wing leading edge, just above and behind the flight deck. Both the B-24 and the PBY were powered by versions of the 1,200-hp 14-cylinder Pratt & Whitney R-1830 Twin Wasp engine that was developed in the early 1930s.

Joe Morris (right) on his Harley in the early 1930s with one of his good buddies who worked with him as a "form runner" at the Santa Anita, California horse race track. This provided him with funds for further flight training and aeronautical engineering courses at UCLA. (Mark G. Morris)

Joe spent much of his work at Consolidated developing and improving the PBY amphibious aircraft, one that he fell in love with. He did not yet know that his work with this machine would save hundreds of lives if not thousands, during World War II and the decades beyond even to this day. But now, the South Pacific theatre of the war covered a vast, desolate, and unforgiving geographical area, comprising 30% of the earth's surface, and almost all of it was *blue ocean* territory. It represented by far the largest and most thinly-spread war theatre ever. Downed pilots and survivors of wartime ship and submarine disasters found themselves in a situation that was a thousand times worse than being a mere needle in a haystack.

Why did this Pacific theatre exist? In its quest for petroleum, refining, and other mineral resources and primary manufacturing, the Japanese military overtook and occupied most South Pacific island groups both large and small, stretching into larger land masses such as the Philippines, New Guinea, Borneo, Indonesia, Burma, and even Malaysia in the Indian Ocean, with its sights on Australia. It was the job of the U.S. and its allies to locate, extract and kill this enemy one by one, island by island, but U.S. combat and transport aircraft ranges were stretched to the max in this vastness. If a ditched aircraft didn't do so because of fuel starvation, it had to be

Lockheed Model 18 Lodestar similar to that flown by Joe Morris at Alaska Star Airlines. I first saw one of these taking off during an intermission at the 1969 National Air Races at Spirit of St. Louis Airport. It was probably being operated by Mark AeroFirst flown in 1939 the Lodestar was active in commercial and private aviation for decades. It's powered by two 9-cylinder Curtiss-Wright R-1820s of 1,200 hp maximum takeoff power. There were several programs to modify this plane, including installation of 2,500 hp R-2800 CB-17 engines.

Consolidated PBY-5A. (Wikimedia Commons, Alan Wilson CC BY-SA 2.0)

because of that all-too-common mechanical failure—not to mention being shot down by the enemy. These three factors resulted in many situations where parched and sunburnt life-rafted survivors had to be rescued amid extremely rough, shark-infested seas, in the middle of "absolute nowhere." Aviation had never seen a Search and Rescue (SAR) environment of this vast magnitude, and of course, never will—it cannot get any worse.

Consolidated was trying to figure out how to best land its PBY in an open ocean rough sea rescue attempt. *Intuitive wisdom* suggested approaching and touching down on one of the large wave crests from a perpendicular angle. Unfortunately, experience and later live tests showed that after touching the first big wave and bouncing over the trough, the now-stalled aircraft would plow nose-down into the next wave to be swallowed whole by the next surge, killing everyone on impact. So much for human intuition.

Joe realized that there just *had* to be a better heavy sea technique. His counter-intuitive theory was for the aircraft to land approximately, but not quite parallel to the waves, right on top of a crest. If done with the correct technique, the seaplane's hull would stay glued to the surface after the initial touchdown, rather than develop into the "bounce, stall, and auger-in" condition. The aircraft track would remain straight and secured to the water as the crest becomes a trough and the trough becomes a crest again. Comprehensive tests proved that this technique worked, and so it was adopted worldwide as the standard rough sea landing procedure for seaplanes and ditching landplanes.

This did certainly did not hinder Joe from being promoted to chief experimental test pilot at Consolidated. Because he was considered one of the world's top seaplane hydrodynamics experts, the eccentric billionaire Howard Hughes took notice and hired him as one of his contract pilots/engineers for the behemoth eight-engine H-4 Hercules "Spruce Goose" seaplane. It is commonly known that while Hughes had an incredible number of major business interests in the oil, movie, and gambling businesses, he was best known as the controlling shareholder of Trans World Airlines (TWA) from 1939 until 1961.

Near the end of the war in 1945, Joe finally spent ten months as an in-theatre Air Transport Command (ATC) pilot over the western South Pacific. In the more dangerous flight sectors, his flights were escorted by Army Lockheed P-38 fighters that sometimes had to chase off Japanese fighters that were setting up for an attack. He survived all that and made it back home.

Over the next nine years, life got back to normal, whatever that means for people like him. Joe plunged right back into the airline business, where he would build the expertise and skill set needed to run airlines. Airline operations and flying planes would fuel his passions for the rest of his life.

Pacific Northern Airlines was founded by Arthur G. Woodley and purportedly began Alaska's first scheduled airline service in 1932. A federal mail contract for most of south-central Alaska was its ticket to its early establishment and survival. Airline historian Robert Serling, in his 1978 book on Western Airlines, described Woodley as *". . . a man of iron will, unimpeachable integrity, awesome profanity, a streak of sentimentality in the approximate depth of Carlsbad Caverns, the liquor capacity of a 747 wing tank and a hair-trigger temper."* This may have been a good way to describe Joe, who seemed to share some of these characteristics.

Joe wound up as Woodley's chief pilot and Operations Manager for the airline and was responsible for operation policies, flight safety, training, scheduling, engineering, and maintenance, forming a well-rounded basis for what was to come later in life. He prepared the airline to become a scheduled carrier in the lower 48 states, mainly in the northwest. Beginning in 1951, Joe oversaw this expansion, using mostly DC-3 equipment, and soon four-engine Lockheed

Joe Morris (center), during a jovial break with his buddies from water evacuation practice, sometime during World War II. (Mark G. Morris)

Howard Hughes' 320-foot wingspan H-4 Hercules "Spruce Goose." Only one was built, and it flew briefly, only skimming a few feet above the water, just once in 1947. It had *eight* 28-cylinder Pratt & Whitney Wasp Major piston engines developing 3,000 hp each. It was made out of plywood due to aluminum shortages during World War II. Joe Morris was a contract pilot/consultant for Hughes on this project. (Wikimedia Commons)

Constellations. This thrusted Pacific Northern into the big leagues, in fierce direct competition with both Alaska Airlines and Western Airlines. This experience would mold Joe into an incessant, seasoned fighter against competitive and regulatory constraints as the number-two man at theairline. Joe helped grow the airline to a critical mass whereby it was eventually merged with Western Airlines in 1967—thirteen years after he departed his nine-year career with the airline. Twenty years later in 1987, Delta Airlines would acquire Western.

So, in 1954 Joe took a respite from airline work to join the Monsanto Company in St. Louis, Missouri as a corporate pilot flying converted executive DC-3s. Despite some of the written records, son Mark Morris maintains that his dad only worked indirectly for Monsanto because his actual boss was its chairman, Edgar Monsanto Queeny. But at that point, Queeny and Monsanto could be roughly considered one and the same, and at least Joe would shed the administrative baggage and do what he loved most—flying. Little did he know that despite his first love of piloting aircraft, his combative *administrative* nature did not disappear from his psyche. While that aspect of him went dormant for a while, in just a few years he would have to unleash his combat soldiers again to a much greater extent than he had ever dreamed possible.

CHAPTER 3

Fiery Recips

The budding airline industry saw a uniquely glamorous evolution during the first half of the 20th century. It involved household aviation names like Lindbergh, Earhart, Hughes, Trippe, and Rickenbacker among a wide spectrum of other rich and famous people, including a broad range of celebrities and movie stars. During these times, the airlines made no money on passengers, and could only make money flying the mail with federal subsidies. They seemed to always be in legal trouble with the anti-trust crowd, which is another story. The main transition era or *Pivot* (as I call it) for this industry was during the 25 years from around 1935 to 1960, during which the glamour part and their Ford Trimotors faded away, and the airlines could finally make money flying passengers. This *Pivot* era was the age of the big propliner, an overstretched piston technology transition that served as a stopgap between the wood, fabric, and the corrugated aluminum prop-driven era of the celebrities, to the efficient turbofan-powered mass-transit "flying whisk tubes" of today.

During the *Pivot*, commercial air passenger transportation evolved from a dangerous novelty for the elite few, to a relatively safe transportation mode for the masses. The traveling public dumped trains and ships and jumped onto planes, and air travel increased by a factor of 50 between 1945 and 1960. Days became hours, oceans were drained down to rivers, and the world shrunk during this big propliner era, starting with the ocean-spanning Martin China Clippers and Boeing 314 seaplanes flown by Pan American, both large aluminum transports with four big engines. When this *Pivot* emerged after World War II, it was all on the back of that war's archaic, mechanically complex piston and propeller stretched to almost impossible technological limits in the postwar period—like squeezing water out of a rock. Jet propulsion, which held the promise of true efficiency at something like 6 to 10 times that of a big radial piston engine and its propeller, had the "unfair advantage" to seal the deal, but jet efficiency was nowhere near ready for commercial markets during most of the *Pivot* age. Only taxpayer-funded military interests could afford to tinker with the initial unreliability of the emerging gas turbines.

A discussion of the *Pivot* can *only* start with a conversation on the ubiquitous twin-engine Douglas DC-3. This airplane, now 85 years after its introduction, still has a small presence in commercial passenger and freight service, mainly in remote areas such as northern Canada and Africa. In its heyday during World War II and a few years thereafter, it had the overwhelmingly largest presence of any commercial airliner. The DC-3 evolved from the more experimental DC-1 and -2, and was more capable and practical than either of them. Its twin 1,200 horsepower, 14-cylinder Pratt & Whitney, R-1830 Twin Wasp engines ("R" = Radial and "1830" = approximate cubic inches displacement) or in the earliest cases 1,200 hp 9-cylinder Wright R-1820s, allowed it to carry 21 passengers over short- and medium-ranges, starting in 1936 with American Airlines. It became a "sort-of-long-range" plane only when it hopscotched across the country with required refueling stops.

Before these Douglas transports, the primitive airliners could carry a mere handful of passengers over a very short range, at first in partnership with passenger rail lines. This was little more than a daredevil publicity act for the elite, and otherwise very dangerous—many of these celebrity patrons paid the ultimate price. Notre Dame head football coach Knute Rockne was one of them.

The iconic Douglas DC-3. This aircraft revolutionized air transport during World War II. In military service, it was known as the C-47. The DC-3 *finally* allowed the airlines to carry passengers at a profit without mail subsidies from the federal government.

The DC-3 was the first aircraft that could make a profit for the airlines without mail contracts or subsidies. It truly ignited the prewar *Pivot* airline era with its service introduction by American Airlines in late 1936. It became the standard transport for the airlines and represented the start of the transition of this industry from a novelty to practicality. But many times more of them went into World War II service as the military C-47 with U.S. and allied forces, becoming best known as the front-line hero of D-Day as a paratrooper and paradrop platform.

Around 10,600 DC-3/C-47s were produced in the U.S. by 1946, with only 607 these being commercial DC-3s. After the war, thousands of C-47s were converted to commercial DC-3 standards and put into civilian service as commercial airliners and freighters. It also became one of the earliest corporate aircraft and quite a few earned revenues into the next millennium, especially as freighters. This is despite the unstoppable onslaught of much more advanced propliners, and, more importantly, within the permanence of the jetliner age. The DC-3 was truly the taproot of what the airline industry has become today.

From this taproot, piston/propeller airliner evolution forked into two different, but logical directions—four-engine medium- to long-range aircraft, and twin-engine short to medium-range

40

aircraft. Each fork evolved so fast that production runs for each new type ranged from less than 100 to just over a thousand each, none of which ever came close to total DC-3/C-47 or Curtis C-46 production (discussed later). While cruise speeds seemed to stabilize within the 250 to 300 miles per hour range, useful load and passenger capacity and comfort increased during this evolution, especially with the advent of cabin pressurization allowing for higher, more efficient cruise altitudes.

Most all the public attention went to the expansion of long-range, four-engine airliners, starting with the 50-passenger Douglas DC-4. This aircraft was conceived by the airlines and Douglas in the mid-1930s and a cumbersome three-tailed prototype flew later that decade. Once it was determined that this prototype was too large for the market, it was scaled back to a simpler design with a more conventional single tail. All but the earliest DC-4 versions were powered by four Pratt & Whitney R-2000 engines that would ultimately reach 1,450 hp apiece. That engine was simply a scaled-up carbon copy of the 1,200 hp R-1830 that powered the DC-3, the PBY, and the B-24 Liberator.

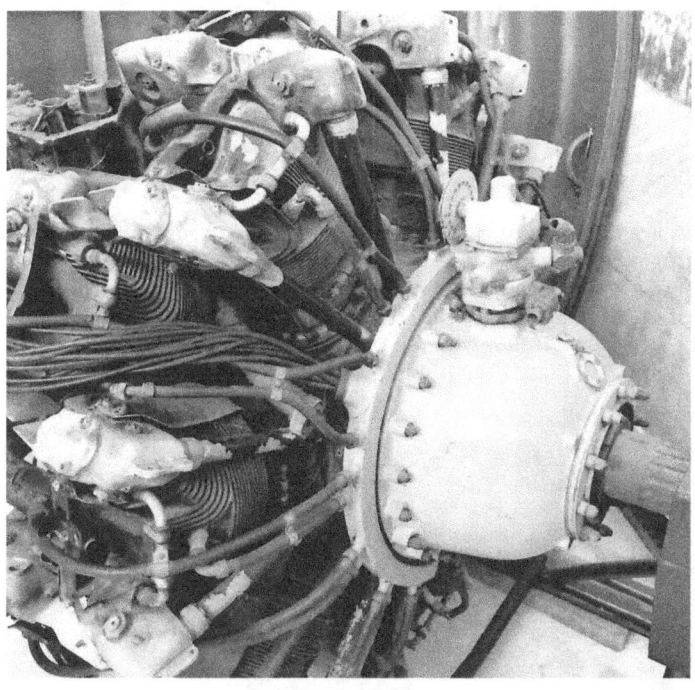

The 14-cylinder, air-cooled Pratt & Whitney R-1830 of 1,200 horsepower powered most DC-3s as well the four-engine Consolidated B-24 heavy bomber and twin-engine Consolidated PBY amphibian transport. This engine carried the airlines from the late 1930s through World War II. After the war, an uprated version developed 1,350 hp and was retrofitted to many DC-3s. A slightly scaled-up version of the R-1830 was the R-2000 which developed 1,450 horsepower in the four-engine Douglas C-54/DC-4. That engine appeared almost identical to the R-1830. C-54s saw reliable service for transoceanic crossings later in the war, and, despite their rapid obsolescence, flew passengers through the 1950s into the 1960s.

The redesigned DC-4 first flew in 1942 and was the first U.S. transport to use tricycle gear rather than a tailwheel. However, just like the DC-3/C-47, the DC-4 production was commandeered by the U.S. Army Air Force for wartime troop carrying and cargo service as the C-54. While it did not see the C-47's front line, "D-Day like" combat, it made thousands of wartime trans-Atlantic and trans-Pacific crossings with an impeccable safety record. A few civilian DC-4s were manufactured for the airlines after the war, but most postwar DC-4s destined for airline service were converted C-54s in mostly high-density, 80-passenger layouts. There were so many surplus C-54s that Douglas and Lockheed at first had trouble marketing their more advanced propliner offerings such as the DC-6 and Constellation, but this would soon change.

The Douglas DC-4 (commercial designation). Its production was commandeered by the U.S. Army during World War II where it became the C-54 military transport, making thousands of oceanic crossings during the war with few mishaps. After the war, it became the stopgap passenger flagship for the commercial airlines until its successors, the Douglas DC-6s and the Lockheed L-749 Constellations became established. The DC-4 represented the earliest of the practical-sized *trunk* airliners seen today. It flew with the U.S. military branches until the early 1970s, long after the commercial airlines got rid of them. (San Diego Air and Space Museum)

The Pratt & Whitney R-2000 Twin Wasp of 1,450 hp powered the DC-4/C-54. Like the later R-2800 and the earlier R-1830 from which it was developed, the R-2000 had a *very reliable* reputation. (Wikimedia Commons, Kogo GFDL 1.2)

CHAPTER 4

Awakening

I grew up in an affluent St. Louis suburb during the 1960s. My dad was an investment banker so we never worried about where our next meal would come from, so I didn't have to work as a child to put food on the table as you hear in most "growing up" stories. My brothers and I did have alternating chores, though, like emptying the trash, feeding the dog, and cutting the grass for a weekly allowance of a couple of bucks. At night our family watched TV shows like *Dick VanDyke*, *Hogan's Heroes, Get Smart, The Man from UNCLE,* and *The FBI*. All are great shows but most are no longer "politically correct." I love still being alive today, but I miss that era.

We also grew up with a summer house on the Niangua Arm of the Lake of the Ozarks in central Missouri. Why mention that? Because it will become apparent that this lake getaway played a role in my unquenchable thirst for aviation knowledge and the *Second Wind*. My father owned a succession of 18-foot-plus, hopped-up high-performance boats which galvanized my interest in things that *go*, by land, sea, or air. This was long before the *much larger* and more expensive Formula and Cigarette offshore racing boats began appearing on this lake and others like it around the country. Ours were from an era where they were smaller and closer to fresh-water quarter-mile racing drag boats or top-fuel hydroplanes rather than offshore racers. Long before I attended the National Air Races in 1969, our boats got me interested in horsepower, which is one important thing you need for a large aircraft.

Mom was slightly annoyed by these very noisy and uncomfortably fast boats, but she could not control dad's impulses or his "capital outflows." Dad was always challenging other boats on the lake to a drag race and he usually won. Our largest two machines, a Donzi Corsica and then a Sanger, were powered, respectively, by a highly-modified Ford 427 V-8 built up by Holman-Moody in North Carolina, and an Oldsmobile 451 V-8 which, according to dad, was "bored out to 480 cubic inches" by what is now Paul Pfaff Engines in California. Dad's Sanger was built up in California by blown-fueler hydroplane quarter-mile record holder Larry Schwabenland that he set with his hydroplane called "Climax," which was basically "all-engine" and "no-boat." The Donzi's Ford V-8 developed around 400 horsepower full-bore and the Sanger's Oldsmobile developed around 750 horsepower with its Holley 4-barrel high-rise carburetors. Speeds of almost 100 miles per hour were achievable in the Sanger (all you could hear during a speed run was the screaming carburetor jets), but we didn't do that very often due to concerns of *getting killed*. At that speed a sudden let-up on the foot throttle would do it.

Water skiing behind these boats was an insane experience, so we usually did that behind our smaller Sidewinder boat with a 115-horsepower Mercury outboard which put the fun back into that activity. We also had a fleet of dirt and street motorcycles we used for "family" trips around the lake countryside and through the woods. This started in 1967 when I asked my dad for a mini-bike for Christmas, that had a boxy 3-hp Briggs & Stratton lawn mower engine. Well, I didn't get "my" mini-bike that Christmas, but "we" did—I had to share. This single purchase grew into our fleet of motorcycles in a few short years, multiplying into at least two other such fleets outside our family—even spawning a Suzuki motorcycle dealer in St. Louis.

By a motorcycle "family" I mean dad, me, and my two brothers, along with any male cousins and friends—the women were not interested in riding along. Despite this, mom partook in all other lake activities. We and our extended family, friends, and dad's business associates had many great summers down there, and all accumulated fond lifetime memories. Despite all this silver spoon stuff, back in St. Louis, on more than a few occasions I *did* trudge two miles to school through the snow in zero-degree temperatures.

Back home we had a large wooded area behind our house in the St. Louis municipality of Frontenac, covering a few square miles, along the Two Mile Creek that ran through the north edge of our wooded property. About a quarter mile downstream to the east this creek ran through some of the Busch, Orthwein (Anheuser-Busch), and Griesedieck (Falstaff Brewing) family properties and polo fields in Huntleigh. Year-round we boys and our gang of friends spent considerable time in these woods, smoking dry weed stalks (real weeds, not "Weed" so to speak) and later "domestically lifted" cigarettes from our homes. We hunted birds, squirrels, and rabbits with pellet guns, caught crawdads, oversize minnows, and tadpoles, and played hockey on the frozen creek pools. We also build underground tunnel networks with rooms we called *forts*. We didn't bore tunnels into the ground, we only dug surface trenches and covered them with plywood sheets, further covered with dirt and brush to camouflage our networks. We would steal some of our plywood from nearby residential construction sites, but getting the rest of it was a different story.

Boys from other adjoining neighborhoods did the same thing along their stretch of the creek, and we often fought "turf wars" with different groups of them. Our weapons were mud balls, spears whittled out of bush taproots and their de-branched stalks, and sometimes BB guns. It was fun to spy on the other kids' encampments and come up with ambush strategies from the seclusion of the brush. Our spoils of war would be some plywood pillaged from enemy forts which helped make up for construction site inventory shortfalls. Yes, our plywood was pillaged too when we were attacked—all this before mom would ring the dinner bell.

It's a high-overcast, chilly November afternoon in 1969 at one of our wooded encampments. The awesome thunder of a four-engine propeller airliner approaches from the south. Through the leafless tree branches, I watch its familiar silhouette roaring overhead as it descends to Lambert Field only 12 miles to our north. In retrospect, it's probably intercepting the final approach course to runway 06. This single event resurfaces my memory of the Pegasus Club "DC-plane" ramp sighting three months earlier at Spirit Airport. *You know you don't see many of those old four-engine propeller airliners anymore* again pops into my mind. This is the inflection point that juggles my subconscious and launches a lifetime of curiosity into motion. I later realize (by recalling the sound) that this overflight was that of a DC-6.

In the fall of 1970, I'm a sophomore at Kirkwood High School. By this time I had spent almost a year taking special note of every twin- and four-engine heavy-recip flying over my house, starting with that November 1969 DC-6 sighting from the woods. One of my good schoolmates at this time is a guy named Pat Lane who lives not too far from my house. I don't quite remember, but he may have been one of the Two Mile Creek tribesmen (he lived close enough), but by now all of us kids were rapidly phasing out of that activity.

It turns out Pat's dad is a corporate pilot for St. Louis-based Ralston Purina, flying a Beechcraft Super 18. While Ralston has turbine equipment in their fleet at this time including a Falcon 20 jet and a Gulfstream I turboprop, Mr. Lane is one of the few who can still fly the -18 with its tricky ground-handling characteristics, but it will soon be retired. I always like to talk to Pat about his dad's neat job, as compared to my dad's "boring desk job." Ralston set up Spirit of

Depiction of a four-engine DC-6 silhouette passing overhead as I saw from deep within the woods on a gloomy, overcast late afternoon in November 1969. (Jerry Riebold)

St. Louis Airport's very first corporate flight operation in 1965 and Mr. Lane and the Super 18 are based there. Ralston Purina also happens to be one of my dad's major clients as he is managing the St. Louis office of Goldman Sachs. Pat and I, after consulting with our respective dads, find out that Mr. Lane regularly flies my dad with the Ralston executives in that very same Super 18. Pat also tells me that he sometimes flies with his dad on weekend maintenance test flights.

 The red-trimmed plane has trademark *checkerboards* painted on each wing tip. It is a very crisp and attractive scheme, and I would soon recognize it flying over my house on occasion. To this day I retain the obscure habit of *always* looking up at the sound of aircraft overhead, no matter where I am. One clear Saturday afternoon I gaze at the checkerboarded Ralston 18, *circling my house* at a low altitude, several times. Or so it seems—it's circling *Pat's* house instead, about a half mile to the west. That Monday I tell Pat I had seen the Ralston -18 circling overhead. Pat proudly tells me he was in the right seat on that flight and steering the circling plane. The father and son were doing some "safe-altitude buzzing" of their neighborhood on a minor maintenance check flight—a normal habit of pilots.

 At school, Pat and I talk about airplanes a lot, and about activities at Ralston's flight department at Spirit. I ask him if he had ever seen a "Pegasus Club" DC-6 parked there. *"Oh yes, me and dad have been through that airplane, it's always parked on the Ralston apron."* He tells me that Pegasus is a "travel club" that coordinates vacations for its members. I'm surprised and satisfied to so effortlessly get this piece of information that had eluded me for months. This once again fans the flames of getting the facts on these old airplanes. In an instant, I become a heavy-recip Sherlock Holmes.

I ask Pat what it was like inside the DC-6. He says half-jokingly, *"Well, it's musty and dark—kind of depressing. It's a little cleaner on the inside compared to most of those old, beat-up prop jobs these days. But it still has a few ripped and rumpled seats, faded and cracking upholstery, an all-around grayish interior, and a musty moldy oily smell throughout."* He smiles, *"As you always see with these worn-out crocks, some of the parts and switches on the flight deck are held together with scotch tape."*

Whether or not his description was exaggerated (it probably was), it was in stark contrast to the bright and cheery modern jetliner interiors that now defined air travel. I surmise that Pegasus Club personnel probably give cabin tours of the DC-6 for prospective members, so I'm not so sure that the interior was as bad as Pat said. Pat would eventually become a Secret Service agent and would serve on President Reagan's detail. The last time I talked to him at our 25th high school class reunion he was a professor of criminology at a major university.

Unmarked Beechcraft Super 18S, the identical model to that flown by the Ralston Purina until 1970 (in Ralston livery). My friend's dad was the Ralston pilot that flew it and my dad often rode in it on Ralston business trips. It is powered by two 9-cylinder Pratt & Whitney R-985 Wasp Junior radial engines developing around 450 hp each. (Wikimedia Commons, Adrian Pingstone)

CHAPTER 5

The Propliner Overdevelops

The Douglas DC-6s, then its DC-7 arrived on the four-engine scene in the earlier post-World War II years, quickly supplanting the DC-4s starting in the late 1940s. Compared to the DC-4, the DC-6 used the larger Pratt & Whitney R-2800 and the DC-7 employed the Curtiss-Wright R-3350 Turbo-Compound. The competing triple-tailed Lockheed Constellation, Super Constellation, and Starliner Constellations strictly evolved with R-3350 power. As with the R-1830 and R-2000 (see Chapter 3) all these heavy-recip engines utilized internal mechanical supercharging. All these higher-performing aircraft were pressurized, representing a considerable improvement in comfort, and were among the first to provide passenger and freight capacities that more closely represent most modern jetliners. With these new *long-range* piston airliners, engine technology had to be stretched beyond its original wartime limitations (that is, "overdeveloped") to serve as a stopgap measure to allow jet technology to catch up. Reliability and therefore safety suffered as a result.

Lockheed Aircraft was a fierce competitor for Douglas with its long-running Constellation series. Collaborating with TWA's controlling shareholder (and hands-on manager) Howard Hughes, Lockheed designed and built, and the U.S. Army Air Force tested, the huge Lockheed C-69 Constellation, a fast and powerful pressurized transport that could carry 14,000 pounds of cargo or 63 lightly equipped troops. It first flew in 1943 when the U.S. was in the thick of World War II. Its nearest competitor, the unpressurized C-54/DC-4 was then in full production for the Army and could not come close to the Constellation in terms of capacity, speed, and passenger comfort.

As originally envisioned before the war, the C-69 was first designed as the 049 commercial airliner and finally began service with Pan American and TWA after the war. The Constellation series would rapidly evolve into the L-749 and then the stretched L-1049 series Super Constellation, culminating in the L-1649 Starliner Constellation (see the Starliner photo in Chapter 12). The 049 was powered by four unreliable 2,200 hp R-3350 Duplex Cyclones, the same engine variant used in the World War II Boeing B-29 Superfortress. The ultimate Starliner Constellation of 1957 was powered by the final commercial R-3350 development, the 3,400 hp Turbo-Compound which was *temperamental* and still dangerous if not operated by the book. This represented a 55% increase in power out of the core engine of the same displacement over 12 years.

All branches of the U.S. military and many foreign militaries flew the C-121 variants of the L-749 Constellation and L-1049 Super Constellation, in both transport and electronic reconnaissance and combat control capacities. The first widely-used postwar AWACS aircraft were Super Constellations flown by both the U.S. Air Force and U.S. Navy. These EC- and RC-121s featured large, protruding dorsal and ventral radome installations.

Boeing, though a minor player in commercial aviation at that time (unlike today), competed in the long-range propliner market with its less-than-successful 377 Stratocruiser, which evolved from its famous World War II B-29 Superfortress heavy bomber. The Stratocruiser was powered by four Pratt & Whitney 28-cylinder turbocharged R-4360 engines of 3,500 horsepower each.

Lockheed 049 Constellation N90816, represents the earliest of the Constellation airliner series. This photo was taken in Ft. Lauderdale, Florida in March 1981 in the same blue trim it had in the early 1960s. In 1979 this plane made the very last 049 flight ever when it arrived here. It was gradually scrapped on site and was all "beer cans" by 1986. In August 1963 my family was in Jackson Hole, Wyoming when I was an 8-year-old. At that airport, dad took a home movie of this very plane in this exact blue trim when it was flying for supplemental carrier Edde Airlines. We caught it boarding smoke jumpers who were returning to their Salt Lake City base, taxiing out, and taking off to the south. (Permission of Mark Willis, Dublin Ireland)

Engine-exhaust turbocharging (not to be confused with the always present internal supercharger) allowed higher, more comfortable cruising altitudes than its competitors up to nearly 30,000 feet, which was above most turbulent weather on long-range transoceanic flights. The big engines, turbochargers, and propellers exhibited terrible reliability in high-intensity airline service, and the Stratocruiser's safety record was nothing short of sickening—almost a flashback to the wood-and-fabric days of the early 1930s. During the 1950s one-third of the 57 Stratocruisers produced were destroyed in crashes—mostly fatal—usually caused by mechanical failures.

During the growth of the long-range four-engine propliner, maximum all-coach passenger capacities stabilized at around 90-100, and realistic cruise speeds settled around 250 miles per hour or below (they always advertised higher). The longest-range development, the Lockheed L-1649A Starliner Constellation, could fly 6,280 miles with under 90 passengers. That was not exceeded until the ever-expanding development of the twin widebody turbofan jetliners of the 1990s that carried several hundred passengers. By comparison, the 21-passenger DC-3's range was only 1,500 miles.

On the other hand, technology did not need to be overdeveloped for the short- and medium-range markets. Most of these designs were reliable aircraft powered by World War II-proven proven R-1830s or R-2800s. In the immediate postwar period the public and the regulators realized that the big population centers like New York, Chicago, Denver, and Los Angeles were well served, but "main street" places like Cape Girardeau, Missouri, Jackson Mississippi, or Knoxville, Tennessee were not.

As a result, a gaggle of local service airlines developed, receiving federal mail subsidies so that smaller communities could be served, otherwise, these routes would be operated at a loss and

An early 2,200 hp 18-cylinder R-3350 Duplex Cyclone two-row radial that powered the military Lockheed C-69 and commercial 049 Constellations. The cast cylinder heads were so closely packed that the engine overheated and caught fire a lot, but many other problems contributed to that such as the forward-dumping front row exhaust ring (not shown).

Closeup of the unusual R-3350 Duplex Cyclone engine installation on an ex-TWA 049 Constellation. Note the forward ring exhaust dump stack which contributed to the engine's propensity to overheat and fail.

Boeing 377 Stratocruiser of British Overseas Airways Corporation (BOAC). This aircraft was the most complex propliner ever and it flew long-range overseas routes with several airlines including Pan American, United, Northwest Orient, and American Overseas (AOA). Its complexity, caused mainly by its 3,500 hp 28-cylinder Pratt & Whitney R-4360 and its unreliable propellers and turbochargers gave it the worst safety record ever in terms of the percentage of airframes lost. (San Diego Air & Space Museum Archives)

soon dropped like a rock. As time went on, even the majors got a piece of the more profitable local service markets with the introduction of new short-haul Martinliners and Convairliners. But the ubiquitous DC-3 (mostly converted surplus C-47s) would dominate local service operations for the first postwar decade and a half.

The Martin 202 and 404 were the less successful of the new short- and medium-haul airliners due to a rough start for the 202. Once introduced to airline service in late 1947, the 202 developed a "slight problem" with fatal inflight wing separations, and it never recovered from the resultant bad publicity. Accordingly, the 202's production was cut off at only 31 units. However, twelve structurally strengthened 202As were produced for TWA as an interim measure while the airline waited for the introduction of the improved 404—but they liked their 202As so much that they didn't retire them when their 404s went into service. In late 1951 the more comfortable, pressurized Martin 404 entered airline service. It was stretched to accommodate an additional row of seats, increasing passenger capacity from 40 to 44. Both the 202 and the 404 could cruise at about 280 miles per hour but in reality, probably less. Both the 202 and 404 were ultimately considered reliable and good performers, and they were well-liked by most passengers, pilots, and crews.

The Martin and Convair short-haulers were both powered by the air-cooled R-2800 C-Series engines developing either 2,400 or 2,500 maximum horsepower with water-alcohol injection. This engine was considered one of the most, if not *the* most reliable heavy-reciprocating aircraft engines ever produced. Both aircraft types had similar performance, but the more successful Convair 240/340/440 series were developed into *slightly* more capable aircraft in terms of passenger capacity, comfort, and aircraft range.

The Convair models were manufactured from 1947 into 1958, including a sizeable fleet of military C-131s and T-29 trainer variants as derived from all three commercial variants. Their main differences from the Martinliners included a flatter wing dihedral and a special engine exhaust "augmentation" system that was claimed to provide a token "exhaust jet thrust" for slightly increased cruising speeds, which was negligible.

The 28-cylinder air-cooled Pratt & Whitney R-4360 developed up to 3,500 horsepower in the commercial Boeing 377 Stratocruiser airliner. In military applications such as the six-engine Consolidated B-36 Peacemaker heavy bomber (ten engines when four auxiliary J-47 jet engines were added later) and the four-engine Douglas C-124 Globemaster II, it was rated at 3,800 horsepower for takeoff. Each of these engines on a four-engine Stratocruiser developed 1½ times the power of an entire Douglas DC-3. How this engine ran for even one minute without destroying itself—much less for 15 hours on repeated transoceanic flights—is a minor miracle.

The 240 was of slightly smaller dimensions with a wingspan of 91 feet 9 inches, with the stretched 340 and 440 having identical dimensions with an extended wingspan of 105 feet 4 inches. The 240's capacity was 40 passengers while the 340 and 440 could carry 50. From the mid-1960s onward, many 340 and 440s were retrofitted with Rolls Royce Dart or Allison 501/T-56 turboprops, giving them a second life with major airlines and then secondary operators. Eventual turboprop retrofit was the intention of Convair, so they built all of them with beefier wings, unlike the Martinliners which were not intended to be so retrofitted. Also unlike the

The Douglas DC-7B, which was the second-generation descendent of the DC-4. This aircraft, with its R-3350 Turbo-Compounds, developed more than 120% of the power of the DC-4 and 30% more power than the R-2800 used in the DC-6B.

Martinliners many Convairs, both piston, and turboprop were converted to dedicated freighters for secondary operators. Lighter cargoes that could fit through the narrow passenger doors were carried by some Martinliners with seats removed (mostly in South America), but cabin floors were never properly reinforced for heavy cargo as with the Convairs.

Just over a thousand Convairliners were produced in total, compared to only 133 Martinliners. Both remained popular with second-tier local service airlines after the majors started moving into new short-haul jets such as the DC-9, and less than a handful of piston and turboprop Convairs were still flying freight, mainly in the Caribbean, as late as 2020. The last revenue Martin flight is said to have taken place in Venezuela in the year 2000, and the last Martin to fly *ever* was a museum restoration that made its final flight in February 2008. The United States Air Force retired their last handful of C-131s during the 1980s.

Finally, we should mention a medium-range dedicated freight hauler, the WWII twin-engine Curtiss C-46 transport, which looked somewhat similar to the DC-3/C-47 but could carry a payload of 11,630 pounds, or 75% more than the DC-3, cruising at about the same speed. Just over 3,160 C-46s were built. They became famous during World War II for flying the "Hump" over the Himalayas between India and China in support of Claire Chennault's Flying Tigers mercenary fighter group. Powered by the early R-2800 B-Series engine of 2,000 horsepower apiece, dwindling numbers of these aircraft flew for many decades after the war with militaries and commercial airlines, from the majors down to small commercial operators. Less than a handful of C-46s remain in service flying freight in Alaska and the Northwest Territories of Canada more than 75 years after rolling off the assembly line during World War II.

We should probably discuss *time before overhaul* or TBO for big piston engines versus turboprops and jets. TBO is a manufacturer's certification as to when an engine needs an *off the wing total overhaul* in terms of accumulated engine operation hours as shown on a gauge called the "Hobbs" meter. A completely overhauled engine is deemed to be *zero-timed* (zero hours on the Hobbs meter—like resetting a stopwatch to zero). For big radials, as design and metallurgy improved and as experience was gained, average TBO peaked at something like 2,000 or 2,500 operating hours by around 1960. This compares to the 1940s when TBO was lucky to reach 500 hours— but usually less.

The Curtiss-Wright 18-cylinder air-cooled R-3350 Turbo-Compound engine had a 20% higher displacement than the R-2800 (using larger cylinders), this and the R-4360 were the largest and most complex, overdeveloped piston engines used in aviation. Accordingly, they suffered notable diminishing returns on reliability. The most powerful commercial versions of the R-3350 Turbo-Compounds used in the four-engine DC-7 and Super Constellation developed 3,400 horsepower on takeoff, but military versions used in the Navy's Lockheed P2V Neptune and Martin P5M Marlin seaplane patrol aircraft developed up to 3,700 takeoff horsepower. This engine used a two-speed geared supercharger and three exhaust-driven power recovery turbines (PRT) that were fluid coupled directly to the crankshaft (two PRT exhaust shrouds are visible here). The PRTs delivered the last increment of power—20% of the total—at altitude.

Convair 240 short-range airliner of the 1950s and slightly beyond, powered by the R-2800 C-Series engine normally developing 2,400 hp each on takeoff. Minor variants of this engine powered the competing Martin 202 twins and the Douglas four-engine DC-6 series. Like the Martin 202, this Convair carried approximately 40 passengers. (Wikimedia Commons, RuthAS CC BY 3.0)

The very reliable Pratt & Whitney 18-cylinder air-cooled R-2800 C-Series engine powered the Martin 202/404, the Convair 240/340/440/C-131/T-29, and the DC-6/C-118. This is a CA-3 variant off of a Martin 404 with a single-speed supercharger that powered over half of them (all for Eastern Airlines). As mentioned, internal cylinder dimensions and displacement were identical to those on the R-4360, though they were of different designs. The CB-16 with a 2-speed supercharger powered the remainder of 404s (all for TWA). TWA needed the 2-speed superchargers because they operated 404s at higher altitudes over the Rockies. Eastern routes were mostly in the east (obviously) where lower altitudes could be maintained. This engine was rated at 2,400 horsepower on takeoff, but the CB-17 used in the Convairs and most DC-6s could develop 2,500 horsepower with water/alcohol injection. On top of the nose case (housing the propeller reduction gearing) are the magneto and two distributors serving 36 sparkplugs (2 per cylinder in aviation applications). Mark Aero was a major maintenance and repair station for this engine, which powered most of its heavy-recip transports over the years.

The simplicity and reliability of turbines changed all that, with earlier off-the-wing TBOs increasing to around 6,000 hours and then to 10,000 hours and beyond. With today's predominant turbofans such as the CFM-56 found on Boeing 737s, there is *no recommended* off-wing TBO at all—just a rotating inspection and replacement schedule for different engine components while it remains on the wing, based on the number of operating cycles. An *operating cycle* consists of one takeoff, flight, and landing cycle. Eventually, every engine needs an off-the-wing overhaul at some point, based on the results of normal rotating inspections and not a recommended engine hour interval. It is rumored that one CFM-56 lasted for some 14,000 cycles before removal from the wing. That is an equivalent TBO of 40,000 hours. This makes the cumbersome heavy-recip engines look like they were designed and built by Neanderthals, which they were not. They were designed and built by smart and talented people, just like those who build today's turbofan engines.

A civilian Curtiss C-46 in postwar freight service, in this case under a U.S. Navy contract. A proven transport for the U.S. in World War II, it was widely used in commercial freight service after the war, and several remain in freight service today in Northern Canada and Alaska. (Wikimedia Commons, Bill Larkins CC BY-SA 2.0)

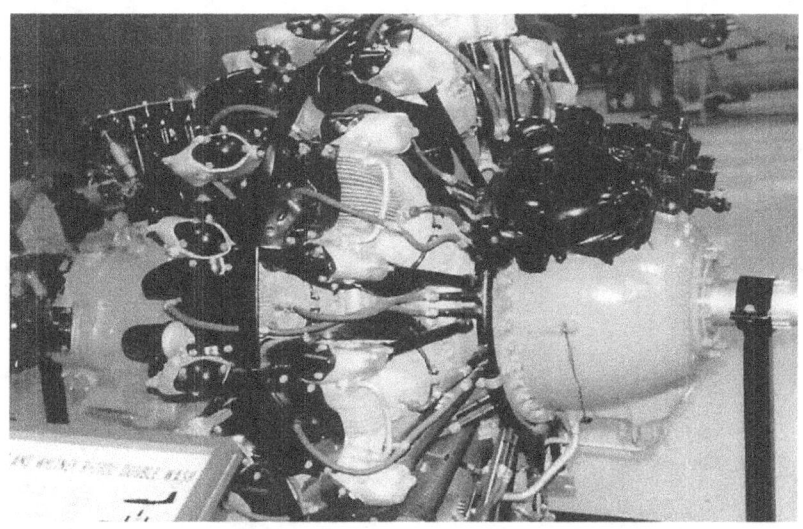

The earlier-design 2,000 hp Pratt & Whitney R-2800 B-Series was used in most C-46s and many World War II fighters such as the Vought F4U Corsair, Grumman Hellcat, and the Republic P-47 Thunderbolt, as well as the twin-engine Martin B-26 medium bomber. This lower-powered earlier version of the R-2800 had a bell-shaped single-piece nose case (for propeller reduction gearing) and cast cylinder heads (versus stronger forged heads and two-piece nose case on the later C-Series engine). Compare this photo to the C-Series (CB3) photo above in this chapter.

Of the *Aerial Leviathans* described above, the DC-6, Martinliners, C-46, Convairliners, and the DC-3 were by far the most reliable and economical of all, with their well-behaved R-1830 and R-2800 engines. It's no surprise that these were the ones that were most in demand during the *Second Wind*. The problematic R-3350 Turbo-Compounded Constellations and DC-7s found their way there too—in much fewer numbers but with deadlier results.

Production of the last piston-powered propliner transports ceased in 1958 with the advent of jets and turboprops. While certainly not the case today, the *Pivot* airline era that ended around that time was dominated by the U.S. designed and built equipment that had an unassailable competitive advantage worldwide

CHAPTER 6

Queeny

At the end of World War II William F. Remmert and D. Robert (Bob) Werner formed Remmert-Werner Air Service operating from the southwest hangars of Lambert Field. It started as a diversified general aviation services company, but it soon moved into a new core business for which it was known. This business was the conversion of overabundant surplus World War II military C-47s into luxurious DC-3 executive chariots. Monsanto Company, also headquartered in St. Louis, initiated and bought the first such conversion aircraft at the urging of its aviation-minded CEO, Edgar Monsanto Queeny, who, as mentioned, was a Remmert-Werner founder and stockholder. Remmert-Werner expanded its C-47 conversion business to a point where it was almost out of control, and, as a result, deemphasized or otherwise shut down its flight training, ground services, and charter operations.

The DC-3 rework business expanded rapidly, and Remmert-Warner soon became the largest non-airline commercial operation at Lambert (as a reminder, McDonnell-Douglas was a military contractor). The company expanded its conversion activity to other airplane types such as Convairliners but became known for its DC-3 work, installing luxurious *lounge-type* interiors with panoramic passenger windows, more powerful 1,350 horsepower R-1830s, modern radio equipment, and, later, weather radar. In 1951 the company opened a subsidiary operation south of St. Louis in Perryville, Missouri, and thereafter opened locations all over the U.S.

In the early 1960s, Remmert-Werner became the exclusive developer, outfitter, and distributor for the North American Sabreliner corporate jet, a new derivative of the military T-39 trainer. This would be one of the first executive jets to be introduced to the corporate aircraft market. While the initial passenger capacity was limited to seven, the corporate community turned its head away from the high-capacity DC-3s—plush, roomy interiors and all. Remmert-Werner was forced to follow suit by mapping its conversion activities over to the Sabreliner.

In 1968, Remmert-Werner was acquired by North American Rockwell, which was the surviving iteration from the earlier merger of North American and Rockwell Standard. Sabreliner production was moved to Perryville, Missouri just south of St. Louis. The Remmert-Werner name survived for now, and in the following year, its Lambert headquarters was moved to new hangar and office facilities at the northeast corner of Lambert, where its FBO ground services were expanded. In 1974 Remmert-Werner lost its identity to become the Sabreliner Division of Rockwell International, but from then on had a tumultuous existence resulting in financial distress and the ultimate shutdown of production in 1981. A New York investment banking firm acquired the Sabreliner assets strictly to service the diminishing Sabreliner fleet.

Monsant Company was a chemical manufacturer founded in 1901 by John Francis Queeny. Its kickoff product was the popular sweetener *saccharin*. Monsanto grew into a leading publicly-traded chemical and later agribusiness technology company, and in 1928 son Edgar Monsanto Queeny) took the helm (*Monsanto* was his mother's maiden name, which is also the Indian tribe from which she descended. In the 1950s Monsanto was one of the nine companies that manufactured the infamous herbicide *Agent Orange* as mandated by the U.S. Government— before anybody knew of its harmful impact on humans. Decades later, after John Francis' death, Monsanto would become an even more familiar household name starting in the 1970s with its weed killer *Roundup*. Monsanto has more recently been acquired by Bayer Corporation.

We previously mentioned that upon retiring from Pacific Northern Airlines in 1954, Joe Morris was hired by Queeny as Monsanto's chief pilot, flying their Remmert-Werner DC-3 conversion. We should mention that during this timeframe Joe Morris and Bob Werner became close friends and they would eventually spend many hours flying together at Mark Aero, both before and after Remmert-Werner was sold to North American Aviation. But beforehand, Joe had a reputation as a very good, safety-conscious pilot. It is rumored that a few Monsanto executives, including Queeny, would fly only if Joe were the pilot-in-command, infuriating Monsanto's chief pilot. Despite that, it didn't take long for Queeny to pull Joe off the Monsanto flight line to become his personal pilot. Joe was known as *the top* Consolidated PBY and seaplane operations expert and Queeny was a conservationist and adventurer who started using his personal PBY for his exploits. This was a perfect formula for what came next.

Edgar M. Queeny

In the postwar period, the Consolidated PBY Catalina became a popular aircraft for civilian adventurers, probably the most famous owner being Jacques Cousteau (whose son was eventually killed in it). Queeny was a naturalist, conservation proponent, *and* aviation enthusiast, making him the perfect match for the PBY amphibian, many of which were being converted to *aerial RVs* for the rich and famous. In short order, Queeny accumulated a small St. Louis-based fleet of these aircraft.

It was clear that Queeny's growing PBY fleet needed regular maintenance. St. Louis possessed little, if any, PBY expertise, even though there were rivers and lakes all around that might attract at least some recreational PBYs—were it not for the bridges, submerged logs, surprise sandbars, invisible power transmission lines, and other obstructions in the most unexpected places. In the late 1950s, Joe took some of his savings and formed a company to perform Queeny's PBY servicing. In 1959, this new company was legally formalized as Mark Aero, Incorporated., based at the northwest corner of Lambert Field, which included the two old Navy hangars (and two smaller ones on the southwest side of the airport) that were among the first structures at Lambert built during the 1920s. Joe and his other trusted pilots flew Queeny around the world in his PBYs, but mostly in Africa where they were capable of setting down on the ubiquitous supply of lakes and rivers. With Joe's help, Queeny produced several nature documentaries that were aired on network TV. In short order, Mark Aero's service offerings would multiply beyond PBY operations DC-3s, larger propliners, and traditional FBO services.

In the November 1959 issue of *Popular Mechanics Magazine*, there was a short blurb entitled *Super Catalina*. It states, "*Powered by two Wright R-2600 engines of 1,600 hp each instead of the Pratt & Whitney R-1830s of 1,200 hp of the standard Catalina. Modification was performed by Timmins Aviation of Montreal, Canada. The plane shown here belongs to Edgar Monsanto Queeny, Chairman of Monsanto Chemical. Cruising speed is 187 mph, range 2,500 miles.*" This modified aircraft was designated as the *PBY-5AY Super Catalina*.

Timmins may have done the work, but Queeny funded the modifications and then obtained ownership of the associated Supplemental Type Certificate (STC) valued at around $2.0 million.

A PBY-5AY conversion owned by Queeny (with early cowl panels). This was the conversion as performed by Timmins that was featured in *Popular Mechanics,* and dubbed by Queeny as "The Pelican." With the replacement of the stock R-1830s with larger R-2600s, horsepower per engine increased from 1,200 hp to 1,600 hp. Compare this engine cowling to the *tighter* cowling on the definitive PBY conversion in the photo below. The trim is green. (Mark G. Morris)

A definitive modified PBY with the 30% more powerful 1,600 hp Curtiss-Wright R-2600 engines . Edgar Queeny and then Joe Morris owned the STC for this significant modification. Compare these fat engine nacelles to those in the PBY photos in Chapter 2. (Wikimedia Commons, SkagitRiverQueen CC BY-SA 3.0)

A 2-row 14-cylinder Curtiss-Wright R-2600 radial engine similar to that used on Joe Morris's PBY conversions.

In subsequent years Queeny sold around 26 of the STC engineering drawings, and Joe coordinated and supervised most of the major conversion work which was performed by several engineering firms, but mostly by Stewart-Davis in California, with Remmert-Werner in St. Louis doing much of the finishing and interior work on a lot of the conversions. Other major changes incorporated in the PBY-5AY included a wider wing chord and slightly greater span that allowed for more fuel for the thirstier engines and greater range, as well as the squaring off of the tailfin. Joe became owner of the STC at the time of Queeny's death in 1968, as Queeny had previously bequeathed it to him in his will.

The R-2600's most well-known standard application was the twin-engine North American B-25 Mitchell medium bomber of World War II. Most of the engines used on the PBY STC were salvaged from retired B-25s. The R-2600 was not adopted as a commercial airliner engine in postwar aircraft, though in limited numbers it did power Pan American's *prewar* and *wartime* four-engine Boeing 314 Clipper seaplane. One thing I have noticed in watching R-2600s operate in restored B-25s is that they are unapologetically *noisy* compared to other large radial engines.

One of these PBY-5AYs was featured in the 1989 Stephen Spielberg movie *Always*, a fictional story about aerial firebomber operations in the western U.S. The last of the R-2600 PBYs to fly took on a serious leak near an Alabama-Florida border beach on the Gulf of Mexico during another movie shoot in 2015. It slowly worked its way onto the beach, but could not be salvaged and had to be scrapped on site. There were no casualties, but it was an anticlimactic end to a great aircraft.

Around 1964, after Mark Aero expanded into areas beyond PBYs, Joe Morris became plagued with a persistent, serious problem. The St. Louis mafia wanted to acquire Mark Aero, probably to obtain assets and operations that would allow them to consolidate and control the movement of contraband in and out of St. Louis. The St. Louis mob was particularly powerful at this time. The harassment continued to fester, which escalated into real threats on Joe and his family if he didn't give in and sell. Joe resorted to calling his old friend Howard Hughes to help, who at the time was highly influential with the mobsters that had converged on Las Vegas from all over the U.S. Mark Morris, a teenager at the time, said he saw several limousines pull up to their Ferguson home. Several men in dark suites escorted Howard himself out of one of the limos. He was sporting a tie but was otherwise dressed in a crumpled sport coat and khakis. Mark immediately recognized Hughes and had no idea as to why he was coming to their front door.

A meeting of Joe and his high-profile guests in the living room ensued without pleasantries, and Mark, who had several awkward eye contacts with Hughes, said the conversations were strangely subdued almost to a whisper, and *short*. Then Hughes and his handlers escorted Joe into Hughes' limo and the caravan drove off. My *speculation* is—and Mark Morris has verified this as plausible—that this was all for a meeting with Morris Shenker, the St. Louis-based defense attorney for the Teamsters (and personal lawyer for Jimmy Hoffa) who had *very close* ties to Hughes' operations in Las Vegas at the time (this was a few years after Hughes gave up control of TWA). When the caravan returned to drop Joe off, Mark asked him what was going on. "*Howard is going to take care of my problem*" was the short answer. Mark suddenly realized what this was about. Joe never heard a peep out of the St. Louis mob again and not surprisingly, Morris Shenker became a regular charter customer of Mark Aero in the years ahead.

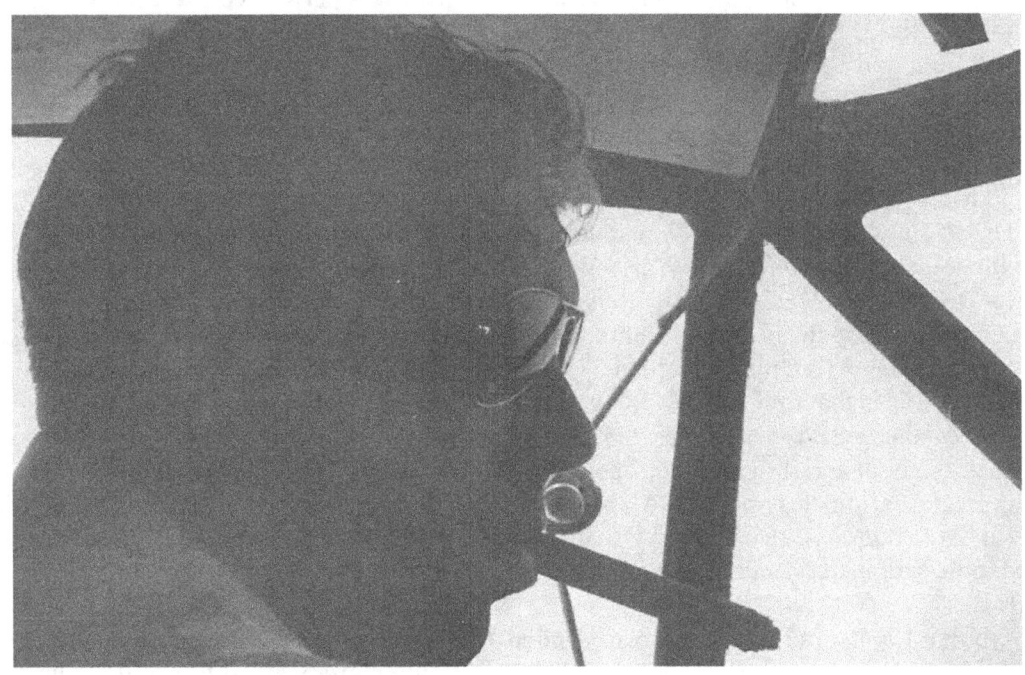

Joe Morris at home in the left seat of a Consolidated PBY Catalina in the early days of Mark Aero, Inc. (Mark G. Morris)

CHAPTER 7

Beginning to Figure it Out

On a hot, hazy July afternoon in 1970, I am drawn out to the front yard by the *distant singing* of slowly climbing R-2800 engines arcing around me to the west. The fairly low DC-6 suddenly banks sharply toward me, now heading easterly right at me. It screams directly overhead, propellers churning madly, before receding toward the eastern horizon. It is *here* I begin to develop an unnatural affection for this big, howling aerial machine. I personify it. It is *truly alive*.

The owner of a Volkswagen dealership called Mid America Motors lives across the street from us. He gives dad a deal on a brand-new beige VW Squareback station wagon, a boxy little vehicle that proves not to be the car for impressing the chicks when I get my driver's license next year. On one Saturday afternoon, I ride along with dad in the Squareback as we head north up Lindbergh Boulevard on the way to Mid America Motors for scheduled service on our new car.

At around mile 12, Lindbergh skims the western perimeter of what is now called Lambert-St. Louis International Airport. We head around a bend and up a short rise in the road, and off to the right, I see an old hanger with the prominent words "Mark Aero" painted above the cavernous hangar door. Parked right in front of the open door, facing outward, is a monster of a silverish twin-engine propeller airliner with a fierce wing dihedral, standing smartly on its tricycle gear, and dwarfing the several light aircraft tied down nearby. Its two oil and exhaust-stained engine installations with their big dorsal air scoops and large three-bladed "paddle" propellers look like they mean *business*. At the two engine cowl openings, I glimpse the complex front details of large radial engines. This is not the DC-3 twin that I know fairly well, but something much larger. It is not sitting at an angle on its tailwheel like a -3. It is sitting level on a smart set of tricycle gear.

This heavy twin seems vaguely familiar to me, as though I had lived it in another life. It is unmarked with a typical white topped fuselage and imposing vertical tailfin, and a greenish "cheat line" painted along the passenger window line. The tailfin has three green "swallows" in the form of two intersecting swooshes each. Now I know why this plane looks familiar, for those swallows mean it was a former Ozark Airlines plane, of which I had occasionally seen operating out of Lambert a few years ago, not thinking much of it. I ask dad if he knows what kind of plane it is, telling him I think I've seen one of these before. *"I flew on those all the time. I'm pretty sure that's a Martin, either a 202 or a 404."* As we pass by the Mark Aero hangar again on our way back, I ask dad slow the car down so I can get a long look. I am dying to see it start up, run up and taxi out, but that sure *ain't happnen'* now. As it turned out, this *was* a Martin 404.

Around this time, my dad attends a McDonnell Douglas dinner banquet honoring the 50th anniversary of Douglas Aircraft. This major Santa Monica and Long Beach-based aircraft manufacturer was acquired by McDonnell Douglas in 1967. Douglas Aircraft founder and aviation legend Donald W. Douglas, Sr. is the guest of honor at this banquet, and my dad is fortunate enough to sit at his table and share conversation with him. Dad brings home a commemorative booklet that covers the details of every aircraft that Douglas designed and built, including photographs, from the cloth-and-wire Cloudster of 1921 through the monocoque DC-3 of 1936, and on through the giant DC-10 tri-jet on the design table at the time of the 1967 merger. The Douglas DC-4, DC-6, and DC-7 look very similar with their four engines and straightforward airframe design. While to the average person they all look the same, the pressurized DC-7 represented a major technological improvement unpressurized DC-4. The pressurized DC-6 fell in the middle of that. It is from this booklet that I finally discern the subtle differences in profile between these three Douglas aircraft that look almost identical to the average person.

And just where do I get more information on them? Since I'm only 15 years old I must ride my bicycle to our county library to dig it up. I check out old, wrinkly, plastic-wrapped books and magazines on airliners, airports, operations, and even major airline crashes during the *First Wind* or *Pivot* era, and am soaking in tons of information on the planes, their engines, their technical evolution, and their operations, mainly from dated annual issues of *Janes All the World's Aircraft*, which gets very technical on both airframes and engines and therefore much to my liking. I photocopy pictures and articles at a nickel per page and organize and build scrapbooks with these copies. I confirm that the DC-3 is not the only large *twin-engine* airliner from that era that I recognize, but I confirm there are even bigger, more advanced, and more powerful piston twins designed and built by Martin (like I just recently saw at Mark Aero) and Convair, that I vaguely recalled when I was much younger. It feels strange to immerse myself into a fading technology when nobody else is—I'm using my valuable time to look *backwards* into a forgotten hospice of jettisoned machinery while the rest of the world looks toward the future. I further personify these machines—they become my friends. Weird? Yes, but so be it.

The helmsmen of these *Aerial Leviathans* become nothing less than godlike to me. Their giant machines, generating thousands of throbbing horsepower and spitting huge tongues of fire, fuel a passion in me that just grows *worse*. As described earlier, the title of a book by Alvin Moscow described it best. These heavy-recip crews were masters at throttling a complicated 100,000-pound *Tiger on a Leash* for hours on end, at a couple of hundred miles per hour through the skies. Each flight was multiple times riskier than flying in a modern jetliner. In any given second there were countless opportunities for inattention, misstep, mechanical self-destruction, or plain bad luck, any one of which could snowball into a full-blown disaster. Yes, the *Tiger* could turn on any of its masters, attentive or not, when least expected.

But in its heyday, this was accepted by the traveling public as the safest transportation mode in the history of mankind. Looking back on this long-gone generation and its clumsy excuse for technology, we should realize *nobody knew any better*. Just like we don't know any better now as to what the future holds, some people arrogantly joke about just how *naive* everyone was during the times of the steam engine, the 8-Track player, the Atari, or the landline.

I soon learn more about the long-range four-engine, triple-tailed Lockheed Constellations, and Super Constellations, and suddenly tie this with recollections of my dad stepping down from these serpentine TWA planes at Lambert Field just in from New York as a 5-year-old. In the summer of 1970 when I am 15 years old, I am convinced I will never see a Constellation again. But on an August afternoon at our lake house, one of these Super Constellations roars *very low,* perhaps only 500 feet above ground level (AGL) over us heading due west as we sit on our balcony, apparently just having departed the lake area's brand-new Lee C. Fine Airport with its long 6,500-foot runway. It just so happens that the governors from all 50 states are holding their 1970 annual Governors' Conference at the nearby Tan-Tar-A Resort, hosted by our Missouri Governor, Warren E. Hearnes who was then head of the Governors' Association. The new lake airport was built strictly in anticipation of this event. This conference hits close to home as on the same day of the Super Constellation flyover, David Cargo, then governor of New Mexico anchors his rented cabin cruiser yacht in our cove, perhaps only 100 yards from our house. How do I know? He strikes up conversations with our neighbors on their docks.

I am convinced this thundering Super Constellation must be tied to this big meeting, so I naturally assume some bigshot governor is riding in it. Years later after my heavy-recip body of knowledge had grown exponentially, I hypothesized this overflight had most likely been commanded by a pilot named Frank Lange, who ultimately racked up more Constellation and Super Constellation hours than any other pilot in the universe. In August 1970 Lang was the chief pilot for Governor Ronald Reagan of California. Was Lange flying low and level to give the governor a view of the lake? The plane probably took off on Runway 21 at Fine Airport to make a shallow right turn to a heading near 270 degrees just south of our house, west toward California. That course would give him a view of all arms of the 129-mile-long lake. Maybe that's a long shot, but the circumstances seem to fit nearly perfectly like a well-broken-in pair of cowboy boots.

Four decades after the actual event—and just for fun—I re-create the Lockheed Super Constellation low flyover of our lake house, using the Microsoft FSX flight simulator—cranking in the weather conditions of that August 1970 day near the end of the Governor's Conference at Tan-Tar-A Resort (now a Jimmy Buffett Margaritaville resort). Our lake house was located on the far side of the closest peninsula--visible between the #3 and #4 engines—on the Niangua Branch of the lake. Confluence with the winding Osage River arm is seen in the upper right with Tan-Tar-A located at the center of the horizon. The likely *hypothetical passenger* looking out the cabin window to the northeast is California Governor and future President Ronald Reagan.

Referring back to my initial research period, I come to discover that weird-looking Boeing 377 Stratocruiser that was flown by Pan Am, United, and others during the 1950s. It looks more like a blimp with wings rather than an airplane. It's powered by those big 28-cylinder R-4360 Wasp Major engines we discussed previously. I was never able to see one as they were transoceanic aircraft that had no reason to operate near St. Louis and, they were slightly before my time. Because of its complexity, unreliability, and prohibitive operating expenses that came with it, it had a minimal role in the *Second Wind*. However, during my high school and college years into the mid-1970s I would witness the military KC-97 Stratotanker variants of the

A Boeing KC-97 Stratotanker that was similar to those flown by the Missouri Air Guard's 180th Air Refueling Squadron. Note the auxiliary jet pylons/engines mounted outboard the reciprocating engines. These auxiliary jets were needed to keep up with the jet fighters they refueled in the air. This reasonably *successful* U.S. Air Force tanker was based on the comparatively *unsuccessful* commercial Boeing 377 Stratocruiser airliner. These planes just *roared*, they did not have a distinctive *singing* or *growling* sound like other heavy-recips. (USAF)

Stratocruiser over St. Louis and operating into Lambert, and even an aerial refueling flyby display at a 1973 airshow at Spirit of St. Louis Airport. All of these Stratotankers were from the 180th Missouri Air Guard at Rosecrans Municipal in St. Joseph, Missouri. Decades later, a handful of surplus KC-97s did make it into second-hand commercial freighter service out of Miami International Airport in the late 1980s and early 1990s. As we describe later, it is one of these that was packed with horses that crashed on takeoff in Mexico City with messy results. *Lotsa* dead horses and people on the ground. The crew of three somehow walked away.

Passing west on I-70 by Lambert on several occasions that summer of 1970, I notice a lone but purposeful-looking Douglas DC-7 with its big stationary 4-bladed props parked just west of the Young Aviation hangar with the big "Gulf" sign, facing east. It is the first -7 I see since my propliner interest started. It has no identifying markings and had the ubiquitous white-top fuselage and bare metal underside, separated by an aqua blue strip along the window line. The -7 has bigger, more aerodynamic, and tight-looking engine cowling and nacelles than its predecessors, with large air scoops, with the 4-bladed propellers as the giveaway—this is the cream of the Douglas pistonliner crop. It has a long HF wire antenna stretching from a mast near the roof of the flight deck to the top of the vertical stabilizer of the tail assembly. On another day it is gone, never to be seen again.

During this phase of my life, it is typical for me to grab my binoculars for a couple of hours on warm evenings. I sit on our patio on the north side of our house with my library books, facing Lambert that's 20 miles north of me, looking for overflying propliners. I can normally catch at least one such overflight per hour, while perhaps 10 to 15 jetliners pass overhead in the meantime. If I had been doing this same thing ten years earlier, these counts would have been reversed. I keep a meticulously written log of all heavy-recip overflight sightings to plot their dwindling numbers.

Over time at the approximate rate of only one sighting per hour, I begin discerning sound different sound signatures between the various heavy-recip aircraft. The DC-4 sounds like an amplified version of the grumbly DC-3, the DC-6 *sings* overhead, and the DC-7 sounds like a gaggle of low-pitched muffled organ pipes. The Martin and Convair twins sound just like the DC-6. The KC-97 just *roars* with no discernable note. I recorded the aircraft sounds overhead with my cassette tape recorder—there was no such thing as a consumer video camera.

I also notice military Convair piston twins flying over my house, mostly east and west and almost always at the same medium altitude. At first, I think they are commercial airliners flying revenue service way past their prime, but they are not. Upon closer examination with my binoculars all have "USAF" painted on their left-wing undersides and big red crosses painted on

Departing Medivac C-131 Samaritan, Military Air Transport Service. I started noticing quite a few of these over my house in the early 1970s a few years after Military Air Transport Service (MATS) became Military Airlift Command (MAC) in 1966. (USAF-Scott AFB)

their tails. It turns out the Air Force calls these C-131 Convairs "Samaritans." They are from the 375th Aeromedical Airlift Squadron of the Military Airlift Command headquartered at Scott Air Force Base, only 30 miles to the *east* of my house.

All these east-west overflights are likely tracking the Maryland Heights VOR, which is about 15 miles due *west* of my house near Spirit of St. Louis Airport. The 90-degree radial goes almost right over my house and the Convairs are going either inbound or outbound to/from Scott. I think this VOR was also the final approach fix for the final approach course for the VOR approach to runway 6 at Lambert. This VOR was located adjacent to the former Lobmaster Sky

The remains of the old Maryland Heights VOR, ½ mile directly north of Spirit of St. Louis Airport and looking north from Highway 40 (I-64) in January 2020. It was decommissioned in the mid-1970s. The C-131 Samaritans flying west/east over my house in the early 1970s were likely tracking a radial from this VOR to/from Scott Air Force Base. The VOR "cone" normally protruding from the middle of the round roof is long gone. This VOR was adjacent to the long-closed Lobmaster Sky Ranch airport, and I-64 cuts right through the south end of its former runway. The sleepy Lobmaster Sky Ranch, home to a derelict SNJ and a few Piper Cubs and Cessnas, was closed in October 1968 due to rerouted highway incursion. After this VOR was decommissioned circa 1978 it became a concession stand for a sports complex, which is now also gone as a new complex was built west of here.

Ranch Airport and decommissioned in the late 1970s. It was replaced with a new one further to the northwest at Foristell, Missouri.

Then I discover more patterns. On Friday and Sunday evenings I notice repetitive north-south routing into and out of Lambert. These are mainly U.S. Navy C-118s (military DC-6) and C-121s (military Super Constellations) out of Naval Air Station Millington near Memphis,

Tennessee, as well as a few C-54s (military DC-4). I research this and find these planes are flying weekend Navy reservists back and forth from weekend duty at Millington in a north-south pattern over my house. Sometimes it's a twin-engine Navy Lockheed P2V Neptune patrol bomber pretending to be a transport that ferries them back and forth. The Neptunes sound just like the DC-7 because they, like the C-119, are powered by R-3350 Turbo-Compounds with 4-bladed propellers.

Many years later I found out one of my industrial sales customers was a former Navy reservist plane captain on these Millington to St. Louis Neptunes. He told me the reservists were haphazardly packed inside these Neptunes like sardines. Neptunes are patrol bombers, not passenger planes by any stretch. I'm sure that during the normal work week, these weekend reservists were all suits and ties, blending with my office-bound dad in the downtown financial district.

On various occasions, I ride my bike to the local hobby shop looking for plastic models of any of these propliners I've been seeing. I cannot find a *single* model of *any* of them. Only jet airliners and fighters, and World War II propeller combat planes—nothing in between—as though the 25-year-long *Pivot* airline era never existed. This is because nobody has good reason to even *think* about wallowing in this hospice of out-of-favor technology as I do.

CHAPTER 8

Martin 404

Founded in 1912 by its namesake, the Glenn L. Martin Company was first widely known for its then huge four-engine transpacific seaplane airliner called the M-130 China Clipper. Only three were built, all for Pan American Airways in the mid-1930s. It carried up to 36 passengers and was powered by four early-version Pratt & Whitney R-1830s developing 950 hp each.

However, Martin was *never* a big builder of airliners. It was best known for two twin-engine combat aircraft that were heavily utilized in World War II. These were the B-26 Marauder medium bomber used by the U.S. Army Air Force, and the PBM Mariner anti-shipping and patrol bomber used by the U.S. Navy. While experienced pilots praised the B-26 as an excellent flying aircraft, it was promptly retired after the war due to persistent training casualties thanks to its high wing loading, unreliable engines (early on), and high rotation and landing speeds. On the other hand, Martin's docile PBM Mariner continued service for more than a decade after the war and evolved into the larger and more powerful P5M Marlin seaplane used by the Navy into the Vietnam war, to be retired as late as 1967. Other noteworthy Martin postwar aircraft included the P4M Mercator landplane patrol bomber, the massive single-engine AU-1 Mauler dive bomber and ground attack aircraft, and the behemoth four-engine JRM Mars seaplane used for Navy cargo and passenger flights, mostly between Oakland, California, and Honolulu, Hawaii. Certainly, the pilots of all these wartime and postwar Martin seaplanes were trained in rough water landing

Martin B-26 Marauder medium bomber (left) and the very last Martin PBM Mariner seaplane in existence, a rare PBM-5B amphibious version. The B-26 has some characteristics later adopted for the Martin's 202/404 series of short-haul airliners, but all Marauders were powered by the earlier, less reliable B-Series R-2800s (1,800-2,000 hp), similar to those found on the Curtiss C-46 transport. This PBM-5B was the last Mariner to be flown *ever*—on the ferry flight from California to Pima Air Museum, Tucson, Arizona in 1972, and I shot this photo in 1987 before the museum restored it in its Navy colors. This is a later version that was powered by the more refined and more reliable 2,100 hp R-2800 C-Series engines similar to the Martin 202 and 404 airliners. The earlier PBM-3 variants were powered by later versions of that noisy Curtiss-Wright R-2600 up to 1,900 hp each. (B-26 photo USAF)

techniques formulated years earlier by Joe Morris. All these aircraft evolved using the various heavy piston radial engines we summarized earlier. Martin ceased building aircraft for good when its last P5 Marlin seaplane came off the assembly line in 1960, almost a full decade after its very last Martin 404 airliner came off the line. That was when the company decided to exit the commercial airliner business.

Both the Martin 202/404 and the Convair 240/340/440 were powered by similar advanced versions of the air-cooled 18-cylinder CA or CB Series (both C-Series) Pratt & Whitney R-2800 radial engine, developing 2,400 horsepower, and later 2,500 horsepower on takeoff in the Convair 340 and 440. The Martin's had more conventional engine installations (both the engine and the support structures around the engine). The Convairliners sported unconventional but aerodynamically cleaner installations, running engine cooling air and exhaust through augmenter tubes exiting at the wing trailing edge, eliminating a lot of the drag-producing features of a standard installation.

Martin decided not to compete with Lockheed, Douglas, or Boeing in the *long-range* commercial aviation market, causing the Martin 202/404 to appear somewhat as an afterthought considering its competence as a builder of behemoth long-range military aircraft. That aside, they felt that their commercial opportunity lay with the short-haul markets. Design work for the 40-passenger unpressurized Martin 202 commenced late in World War II in response to airline

The *oversize* Martin JRM Mars flying boat served as a Navy shuttlecraft between Oakland, California, and Honolulu, Hawaii from late World War II until 1956. Seven were built, and all but one were powered by 2,500 hp R-3350 Cyclone-18s (without PRTs). This one, named "Caroline Mars" was initially powered by 3,000 hp R-4360's which were later swapped out with the R-3350s. Two of these survived until 2016 as firebombers for several western Canadian concerns, the last one being Coulson Group. (U.S. Navy)

Martin P4M-1Q Mercator maritime patrol bomber. It was powered by two Pratt & Whitney R-4360 Wasp Major radials and two auxiliary Allison J33-A-10A turbojet engines mounted in the lower rear engine nacelles under the wings. Built contemporaneously with the Martin 404, most P4Ms were re-configured into electronic countermeasures "ferrets" that surveilled international waters just off the communist Chinese and Russian coasts. Several P4Ms were shot down by communist fighters, with a significant loss of crews. (U.S. Navy)

interest in a "DC-3 replacement" on short intercity routes. This predecessor of the 404 appeared almost identical to the definitive 404, though the fuselage was slightly shorter. First flown in featured innovative built-in ventral airstairs which later proved popular with both passengers and airlines alike and featured a major vertical stabilizer redesign. Unlike the production versions, the prototype had a small straight tailfin, with no tail spine along the fuselage top and minimal wing dihedral. All this caused stability problems. The outer wing panel dihedral was increased substantially, requiring altered wing fasteners at the nacelle juncture.

A by then very rare Martin 202 sits at Fort Lauderdale, Florida in 1973. It is in the light blue and gold trim of its Colombian operator Aeroproveedora. (Wikimedia Commons, RuthAS CC BY 3.0)

Former TWA Martin 404 restored in Pacific Air Lines colors, taken in early January 2008 less than two months before it made the very last flight ever of a 404. During the late 1970s and early 1980s as a converted corporate aircraft for Tiffany Industries, N636X was based at Lambert-St. Louis International Airport sporting a somewhat gaudy brownish paint job (as described later in Chapter 38). I spotted this very Martin flying over my house several times between 1977 and 1982. (Wikimedia Commons, Tomas Del Coro CC BY-SA 2.0)

In spring 2020 I had several phone conversations with both the stepson and the son of the late Jack L. King, Sr. (Jim and Jack L., Jr., respectively—both coincidentally with the last name "King"). The senior King was the assistant test pilot at Martin on the flight test certifications programs for both the 202 and 404 in the late 1940s and early 1950s. During the design phase of the 202, there were three vertical tail sizes under consideration, each now with a long dorsal spine extending forward over the fuselage to add further stability. The plan was to mount test each of the designs on the prototype. But Martin founder and president Glenn Martin overrode this process, telling engineers to only go only with the largest tail because it "looked better." This was done, and the test crews allegedly referred to the new tail as "The Presidential Tail." In this day and age, aircraft design decisions like this—based *solely* on *looks*—just don't happen.

According to the book *The Martinliners* by Gary L. Killian, Jack King, Sr. purportedly said the 202—which was unpressurized—flew like a rocket compared to the DC-3. Another favorable feature was that it had a very wide center of gravity range, from 12.4% to 37% of the mean aerodynamic chord (center of wing lift), allowing passengers to sit almost anywhere despite the load factor. King, Sr. also wrote the crew familiarization manuals for both the 202 and 404 and took part in much of the design work refinements, including the engine nacelles and cowling.

There was one concern among future Martin pilots about the innovative autofeather feature that was installed. In a twin-engine aircraft, the ability to promptly secure and feather the propeller of a failed engine on takeoff is always a life and death proposition. There was an element of unease about taking manual feathering control away from the pilot, along with the possibility of a rogue feathering signal that would secure a prop when there is no engine emergency.

However, autofeather took care of the problem more quickly than the manual procedure, allowing the pilot to tend to other issues during the emergency, mainly *flying the plane* while

Former Systems International Martin 404 N145S sits in front of the old terminal at Kansas City Downtown Airport on December 11, 1990. It started its life in the early 1950s with Eastern Airlines. It is now a static display in a "semi-TWA" paint job at the Airline History Museum in Kansas City.

adjusting the power of the good engine, and trimming the rudder and ailerons. If the signal were triggered by a drop in manifold pressure as in earlier autofeather systems, a harmless backfire (causing a momentary drop in manifold pressure) could trigger an unnecessary false signal. However, the Martin system was triggered by the torquemeter, which is the true measure of power being developed by an engine and is minimally affected by a temporary backfire. Chief Martin test pilot Pat Tibbs demonstrated the system before a group of pilots when he cut the left engine at V1 (liftoff decision speed) on takeoff, the worst one to cut. The autofeather system immediately kicked into action, and the plane easily maintained a safe climb rate on the right engine only, clearing the high-tension wire obstacles at the end of the runway by a wide margin. Pilot trust in the system was rarely a problem after that.

There was an economic slump in 1946-1947, and the several 202 launch airlines canceled all of their 202 orders, except for Northwest, which halved their order from 50 to 25 units. Ultimately, there were only 31 Martin 202s built to cover an order of 25 for Northwest and 6 others for South American airlines. Before all the Northwest planes could be delivered, disaster struck in August 1948 when a Northwest flight lost a wing over Winona, Minnesota due to a random structural failure, killing 37 people. This was shortly followed by two other fatal crashes of Northwest Martins which were not structurally related but still caused Martin crews and the public to feel the "jinx factor" and shun the aircraft. A defective outer wing fastener, associated with the change in the dihedral during flight testing two years earlier, was found to be at fault in the Winona crash. These fasteners were redesigned and beefed up along with the wing spars, and 202 crews and the public slowly came back, but not before Northwest got rid of all their 202s in 1951.

The probable reasons it was not as successful as the follow-on 404 were a bad economy and its rough start with Northwest, and that its passenger cabin was unpressurized. Post-Northwest secondary airlines that flew 202s included Pioneer Airlines, California Central, Transocean,

Maybe the cleanest Martin 404 powerplant package you will see today. This restored 404 belongs to the Mid Atlantic Air Museum which flew it to airshows in the early 1990s but is now on static display.

Pacific, Allegheny, Southwest (not today's Southwest), Modern Air Transport, Baja, and several non-U.S. airline and charter operations.

The 202A was an interim solution for TWA that was *almost* like the 404 except for the lack of 4 extra seats and cabin pressurization, so they grabbed it. They kept most of the 202As in interim service throughout the 404 delivery cycle, 202As flew alongside the 404s until both were retired in by 1961. Secondary 202A operators included names such as Allegheny, Pacific Air Lines, Lone Star, and Southeast, and private charter companies used them to transport 1960s rock bands including Herman's Hermits and The Animals. Most were scrapped after Allegheny retired its 202A fleet in 1966, with the remaining small handful going to miscellaneous South American operators. The final *revenue* 202 flight is thought to have occurred in 1977 with an obscure Colombian operator. Only one unairworthy Martin 202 exists today (a 202A) at the Aviation Hall of Fame Museum of New Jersey at Teterboro, and is purportedly under restoration for static display.

The *pressurized* Martin 404 follow-on had a fuselage stretch of 39 inches for a row of extra seats, increasing passenger capacity from 40 to 44, and maximum gross takeoff weight to 44,900 pounds, from the 39,000 pounds of the 202. The overall appearance of the 404 was similar to the 202 except for the windscreen and fuselage length. Pilot visibility was improved with larger, raised window panes. TWA wanted the 404 to replace its ancient Boeing B-17-based Model 307, but the 404s were not ready. However, Martin had twelve unsold 202s available and could convert them to new but unstretched 202A standards, with further beefed-up airframe structure and higher altitude CB-16 engines (to be used on TWA's 404s), allowing a higher gross weight of 43,000 pounds.

The maiden flight of the Martin 404 occurred in October 1950. Of only 103 built, 61 went to Eastern Air Lines and 40 to TWA. The other two went to the U.S. Coast Guard as RM-1s. The Eastern planes had weather radar in a pointy nose and CB3 engines with single-speed superchargers that were altitude limited as Eastern flew in the eastern half of the U.S. which did not have extremely high mountainous areas. They also had their rotating beacon on the top of the vertical stabilizer. The TWA ships did not have weather radar and had slightly blunted noses as a result. They had CB16 engines with two-speed superchargers that allowed for higher cruise altitudes over the Rocky Mountain environment of the western U.S. The rotating beacon was located atop the fuselage rather than atop the vertical stabilizer.

Captain and first officer flight deck stations on the Martin 404.

TWA unloaded all its 202As and 404s by 1961, while Eastern did the same the following year. Many 404s went to aircraft brokers such as California Airmotive, where they found their way to local service airlines such as Piedmont, Southern, and later Ozark Airlines. Southern did not retire their 404s until 1977. Scheduled and charter airlines such as Marco Island Airways, Systems International, and Provincetown Boston flew them well into the 1980s. From then on, only a few miscellaneous charter operators remained, including meat haulers, mostly in South America. These were all-cargo flights whereby just the seats were removed—no widened cabin doors or reinforced floors as would be found with a true freighter conversion.

And, of course, musicians and rock bands such as Ray Charles and The Doobie Brothers utilized 404s on concert tours. Recently I was contacted by one of the Doobie Brothers' former pilots who told me they always used two Martin 404s when on tour—one for the band and one for the road crew. He distinctly remembers flying them into Columbia, Missouri in 1976 when I saw them in concert as a student at the University of Missouri.

The last revenue Martin 404 flight was a passenger operation out of Venezuela known as Rentavion, which occurred during the year 2000. The last 404 flight ever was in February 2008, a flying restoration by aviation entrepreneur Jeff Whitesell, which was N636X, a flying restoration that was painted in Pacific Airlines colors—that I knew well. That plane spent several years as a corporate aircraft conversion based at Lambert in the late 1970s and early 1980s. N636X is one of less than a handful of intact Martin 404 airframes surviving in 2021. While they may look operational, none remain airworthy today.

The last production airplane built by the Glenn L. Martin Company was the P5M Marlin maritime and anti-submarine warfare (ASW) seaplane as operated by the U.S. Navy as their last seaplane. The last one came off the assembly line in 1960, and the Navy retired it in 1967. This one made the last Marlin flight in 1968 from San Diego NAS North Island to Patuxent River, Maryland for museum preservation. (U.S. Navy)

CHAPTER 9

Spreading it Thin

As the 1960s wore on, Mark Aero evolved. Edgar Monsanto Queeny was getting up there in age with the health issues that come with that. He passed away in 1968 at the fairly young age of 70. Beforehand, the Mark Aero PBY operations began to taper off. Joe Morris focused on his flight school, which would become the largest at Lambert. Mark Aero trained pilots at all levels, from primary to the most advanced training—private pilot, instrument, commercial, multi, CFI, large aircraft type rating, and airline transport pilot (ATP) rating.

Their aircraft fleet and instructor pool grew to meet all these training requirements, from single-engine Cessnas to Piper Twin Comanches and Cessna 310s to Beechcraft Barons and 18s to vintage Lockheed 10 and 14 Electras and that Lockheed 18 Lodestar, and finally the big DC-3s. A few smaller turbine-powered aircraft would find their way into the fleet. Many of the fleet planes were owned by other investors or operators where Mark Aero provided the crews and maintenance.

There was an airframe and powerplant (A&P) school, and the company became a certified airframe and piston engine repair and overhaul shop for several manufacturers, up to the 2,500 horsepower Pratt & Whitney R-2800. Refurbishing services, including sheet metal and paint shops, were added. While Lambert was always an operational base, in the early to mid-1960s there were significant satellite operations in nearby Greenville, Illinois including an interior outfitting and upholstery shop, paint shop, maintenance shop, and pilot training facility there, where corporate DC-3s, piston Convairs, and deHavilland corporate jets were typically serviced.

In 1966 after a fire burned down the Greenville facilities, many operations were moved over to Spirit of St. Louis Airport in Chesterfield due to a deal from Paul Haglin they *couldn't refuse*. Recall that this is where the "Pegasus Club" DC-6 was based when it first caught my eye. However, Mark Aero left Spirit when it expanded its Lambert facilities starting in 1971. Mark Aero rounded out its full-service FBO status Lambert, involving flight training, renting, servicing, fueling, loading, unloading, and passenger boarding and deplaning—working with both local and transient operators. While early on the Lambert ramp became almost overwhelmed with tied-down light general aviation aircraft, this began to thin out a bit with the opening of Spirit of St. Louis Airport and Downtown St. Louis Parks Airport. Mark Aero's aircraft brokerage and lessor operation, under its Alpha Aviation subsidiary, was kind of a placeholder where it could decide to *keep*, *lease*, *refurbish*, *sell*, or *scrap* any aircraft that came its way.

A corporate flight operation had been formed, first using the smaller piston twins, then DC-3s, and later with smaller turbine-powered twin-engine corporate aircraft. Mark Aero obtained its FAR Part 135 Air Taxi certificate which allowed operations of *smaller* aircraft up to the Lockheed Lodestar. This enabled these planes to be used on daily or nightly contract mail runs to places like Chicago and Kansas City, as well as charter passenger runs. The Chicago mail route they flew was Charles Lindbergh's own, who departed each evening in his World War I DH.4s just down the line near Mark Aero's two smaller hangars on the south. Joe certainly had a lot of previous aviation experience and seemed to be on the road to using it all. He was possibly spreading Mark Aero a bit thin, like a thin slice of butter on a giant pile of pancakes. For most of us it's hard to focus that way, but maybe not for the Morris family.

Mark Morris, was born in 1948 in Anchorage, Alaska while Joe was with Pacific Northern. For someone who wanted to be a pilot like his dad, Mark was fortunate to be born right into the thick of it. After a few years of odd jobs and "supervised underage flight time" at Mark Aero, Mark got his private pilot's training and license at Greenville in 1964 when he was 17 years old. He paid for it by painting aircraft and performing odd jobs there. It seems like many people who get their private pilot's license at that magical age evolve into successful, high-time military and/or commercial pilots, with thousands of career hours in the widest variety of aircraft types, small and large, piston and turbine, slow and fast. Mark Morris was no exception.

Mark "blew through" the earning of his relevant airman certificates from Private to Commercial Pilot as well as his Aircraft & Powerplant mechanic (A&P) certification. When he reached the required age of 23, he earned his Airline Transport Pilot (ATP) certificate in one of Mark Aero's new de Havilland DH-125 corporate jets. The same was true regarding his relevant ratings: Single-Engine Land, Multi-Engine and Instrument Rating, and then multiple type ratings in numerous aircraft—as required to command any aircraft with a maximum takeoff weight (MTOW) of over 12,500 pounds.

To do all this in his early years he was able to build both left- and right-seat piloting time quickly in all these advanced, complex piston aircraft such as Cessna and Piper twins, Beechcraft Super 18s, vintage Lockheed Electra Twins, the heavier Lockheed Lodestar (after getting the type rating), and then into his type ratings for really big piston iron such as the Douglas DC-3 and much later the Martin 404 twins and the giant Douglas DC-6 and DC-7. During all this he worked on building time in the turbines and jets—the Mitsubishi MU-2 twin turboprop, the de Havilland DH-125 (later the Hawker HS-125 when Hawker acquired the design), and even a right-seat checkout in the massive four-engine Boeing 720 jetliner. Joe urged mark to get his Certificated Flight Instructor (CFI) certifications, but Mark refused, fearing he would be stuck flying little single-engine Cessna 150 trainers yelling at green students all his life. However, Mark did do extensive introductory and advanced fixed-wing ground-school instruction for all types of groups during his tenure at Mark Aero, including future helicopter pilots for the St. Louis County Police.

In the latter half of the 1960s, Mark's first job was production test pilot for Piper Aircraft, but not for long. He soon found himself back at Mark Aero working for his dad, as well as being a leased-out pilot to an outfit called Skyways. There he flew mail, canceled checks, and small package freight all over the Midwest, as well as Army personnel and cargo out of Ft. Leonard Wood. In due course, after an *eventful* stint flying Pilatus Porters for the CIA's Air America in Southeast Asia from 1969 to 1970 (that is a completely different story where we cannot elaborate but will touch on later), Mark would eventually become the chief pilot for the corporate division at Mark Aero, flying Fortune 1000 executives all over the map.

However, in 1967, two larger transport aircraft appeared that would become fixtures on the Mark Aero aprons. These were ex-Eastern/ex-Ozark Martin 404 registered N471M and ex-American Airlines DC-6 registered N90710. The 404 had the white top but was unmarked, but for the green center stripe and the 3 green swallows on its tail. The DC-6 was still in the original bare-metal finish of American Airlines, but soon received that blue trim job and the name "Pegasus Club" in blue letters over the passenger windows. The 404 was registered to "Interstate Airmotive" and the DC-6 was registered first to "Mark Aero" and then to "Pegasus Club," respectively. This was just a start.

CHAPTER 10

Douglas DC-6

Douglas Aircraft Co was founded by Donald Wills Douglas, Sr. in 1921. Douglas took a different track from Martin, especially when it came to commercial aviation after 1935. Both manufacturers were heavy into military aviation, but while Martin dabbled sporadically in commercial aviation, Douglas became the worldwide commercial aviation juggernaut (with Lockheed a close second) from the mid-1930s starting with its game-changing DC-3. It continued its leadership in commercial aviation through the early 1950s and into the 1960s with its DC-4, DC-6, and DC-7 advanced piston airliners. Starting in 1959 it entered the jet age with its DC-8 and DC-9 jetliners (the DC-9 which entered service in 1965) until Boeing finally eclipsed it with its 707, 720, and 727 (the 727 entered service in 1964). This forced Douglas to merge with McDonnell Aircraft in 1967, where under the McDonnell Douglas umbrella jetliner production was further leveraged to include stretched versions of its DC-8, DC-9, the DC-10 widebody, the MD-80 through -95 as developed from the DC-9, and the MD-11 as developed from the DC-10. This all abruptly ended in 1997 when the again struggling McDonnell Douglas was acquired by Boeing. For a short time, Boeing continued with, and then dropped the MD-95, briefly marketing this final McDonnell Douglas commercial aircraft as the Boeing 717.

As World War II was concluding, it was clear that Douglas Aircraft needed an answer to the Lockheed Constellation, and it was only logical that the DC-4 would serve as the baseline design for this new aircraft, designated DC-6. The most important change was to replace the 1,450 horsepower Pratt & Whitney R-2000 engines of the DC-4 with the advanced 2,100 takeoff horsepower Pratt & Whitney R-2800C. The fuselage would see a 6-foot 11-inch stretch to allow for 10 more passengers in 52 – 86 passenger configurations. The vertical stabilizer was redesigned with a somewhat squared-off profile, and the round cabin windows were replaced with larger square ones that passengers favored. A new stronger and lighter aluminum alloy was used for the main wing spars and other key structural components. Like the C-69/049 Constellation, the DC-6 cabin was pressurized for higher altitude operation between 10,000 and 20,000 feet. This afforded better engine efficiency, rough weather avoidance, and otherwise optimal passenger comfort.

The sole DC-6 prototype was built under U.S. Army Air Force direction and designated XC-112, and first flew in February 1946. With the war's end, the Army Air Force stepped away and all aircraft were produced to commercial specifications. However, the new U.S. Air Force and just a few years later the Navy would buy stretched versions of the DC-6 to military specifications as the C-118 and R6D, respectively, until a decade later the Navy was forced by Secretary of Defense Robert McNamara to standardize with the "C-118" designation.

The maximum gross weight of the original DC-6 variant was 97,200 pounds. Both American Airlines and United Airlines took delivery of the first commercial DC-6s in November 1946 for transcontinental services. The plane cruised faster and had better overall performance than the 049 Constellation. Like the 049, the DC-6 required a third crew member on the flight deck, the flight engineer. Sometimes called the "Straight Six," the last of 86 built, was sold to Braniff Airways in

A Douglas DC-6 in its _First Wind_ heyday with the United Airlines fleet. (Wikimedia Commons, Robert J. Bosler CC BY-SA 3.0)

November 1951. Other orders went to both U.S. and international airlines including American, National, Delta, Pan American Grace (Panagra), and Sabena.

Early on the "Straight" DC-6 had a couple of setbacks including a fiery crash killing 52 passengers and another fiery emergency landing (most survived), both caused by a fuel dump exit port spitting fuel into a misplaced combustion heater intake position on the outside of the fuselage. The DC-6 was grounded for a few months while this intake was relocated, preventing further problems. These incidents did not impact DC-6 sales, unlike the Martin 202 wing failure setback. An inflight wing separation apparently had a worse public perception than a mere inflight fire. Approximately 176 Straight Six DC-6s were ultimately built before the next model.

The DC-6A was a stretched freighter version that first flew in September 1949. It had wide freight doors added to the front and rear fuselage on the left side, and a reinforced cargo floor. With gross weight increased to 107,000 pounds and a 5-foot fuselage stretch, it could carry a payload of 30,000 pounds with its uprated R-2800 CB-16 or CB-17 engines developing 2,400 and 2,500 horsepower respectively on takeoff with water-alcohol injection. Some were built as convertible -6Cs, and many -6As were converted to -6C standards, which is similar to the C-118. Military sales comprised 166 out of the 240 DC-6A/Cs produced starting in 1951. The military planes used the -54W version of the R-2800, which was the military equivalent of the 2,500 horsepower commercial CB-17. Seventy-four commercial DC-6A/Cs were delivered to initial operators such as Slick Airways, Belgian Air Force, Canadian Pacific, Pan American, United,

American, Flying Tiger Line, KLM, and Trans Caribbean until production ceased in 1958 with the last delivery in 1959.

The DC-6B was the pure passenger equivalent to the DC-6A/C which first flew in February 1951. There were no wide cargo doors nor a reinforced cargo floor, and the -6B had a capacity of 60 to just over 100 passengers depending on the passenger layout. Douglas built 288 of these that went to 32 airlines in 20 countries. Both transcontinental and over-ocean variants were built, with maximum gross weights of 100,000 and 107,000 pounds respectively. However, the over-ocean planes rarely could make westbound trans-Atlantic crossings against prevailing headwinds without a fuel stop at Gander, Newfoundland. Until production ceased in late 1958 the DC-6B was delivered to most recognized major airlines of the time including non-U.S. carriers (a notable exception was TWA which used only Constellations and Super Constellations), and many replaced their earlier Constellation fleets with -6Bs.

Widely considered the most efficient, reliable, and successful piston propliner ever to plow through the skies, the stretched DC-6A/B variants recorded the best airline operating economics in its class, for both passenger and pure freight operations. When retired by the major airlines during the 1960s, remaining passenger DC-6s flew A-lister celebrities, rock bands, corporate groups, travel clubs, offshore platform crews, and sports teams to venues all over the world. Passengers considered the plane smooth, quiet, and comfortable. We will see later that a direct descendant airline of Mark Aero—owned by Mark Morris—flew the very *last revenue passenger* DC-6 flight in 1980.

Some straight DC-6s and many -6Bs were converted to freighters over the years as the majors discarded them during the 1960s. During the *Second Wind* era, the DC-6 remained popular with both reputable and not-so-reputable, large and small commercial cargo operators, many never getting off the ground so to speak—with some operators lasting only a few days, and then others lasting for a decade, or two. During this same era, beat-up cargo DC-6s acquired a dubious reputation for flying illegal narcotics to the U.S. out of Latin America, often in exchange for arms back in. Most *Second Wind* DC-6 operators tried to be above board, providing services somewhere between the legal extremes. DC-6 freight operations were dwindling but still going strong into the 1990s, with less than a handful *still* flying freight and diesel fuel north out of Anchorage, Alaska to remote arctic mines and outposts where there are no roads. This will likely not be for long due to the increasing scarcity of 100 LL (Low Lead) avgas.

CHAPTER 11

Box Canyon Loophole

In the pre-deregulation environment of the 1960s and '70s, the Civil Aeronautics Board (CAB), established in 1938, regulated the economics of commercial aviation in the U.S. It blessed and certified proposed air routes, and approved passenger fares and cargo rates. It supervised the financial health of airlines, particularly for proposed upstarts (most could never get past the proposal stage under CAB rules), as well as the competition between them, and assisted the State Department in working with foreign governments to facilitate international transportation. The CAB was at first also responsible for all aspects of air safety.

The Federal Aviation Act of 1958 provided for the creation of the Federal Aviation Administration (FAA), which now governs and manages Air Traffic Control (ATC), as well as safety requirements, standards, and regulations for licensing pilots and crews, mechanics, and ground servicing crews. These were former CAB responsibilities. The FAA also regulates the testing requirements for new aircraft designs and certifies the final production of such aircraft, as well as the operating limitations of such aircraft. Its ATC role is the most publicly visible one and certainly one of the most important.

In the *old* regulated airline era, when you hear about regulations such as FAR Part 91, 121, and 135 you are hearing about FAA operating regulations as granted to operators under CAB governance. Those *Parts* do not govern pilot training or qualification regulations. In essence, Part 121 contains the strictest regulations governing the *commercial operation* of large transport-category aircraft. Part 135 is less strict governing mostly commercial charter air taxi operations of small aircraft. In 1981 (post-deregulation) Part 125 later came into effect allowing various degrees of so-called *private* operations with large transport category aircraft, otherwise operated under Part 91. Part 91 is the least restrictive, covering *private operations* of general aviation aircraft—which during the *Second Wind* was fraught with loopholes that allowed what were really "commercial" operations to be cleverly disguised as "private." Another regulatory body, the National Transportation Safety Board (NTSB) which was created in 1967, investigates accidents from all modes of commercial transportation including aviation and makes recommendations to the FAA based on the findings of such investigations. I would start becoming somewhat familiar with this regulatory stuff at age 15 because of a single airline disaster that set me off at a young age, but I cannot claim to be even close to an expert on this very convoluted and ever-changing aviation regulatory environment. But at least you now have a basic framework.

In the fall of 1970, I start my sophomore year at Kirkwood High School in St. Louis County. A few neighborhood mothers from ours and neighboring streets, including my mom, decide to form a carpool of three moms and three station wagons, running three days per week so the affected five kids, including me, wouldn't have to walk or ride bikes two miles to school every single day (why that concerned the mothers I don't know). Kirkwood School District doesn't have school buses yet as is the case with a large percentage of districts nationwide. The kids in our carpool either are too young to drive like me or don't have access to their parents' automobiles.

There are four guys including me, and one hot, blue-jeaned blonde girl named Kaye in our carpool. She is a year ahead of me and a rebellious teenage girl. When her mother is driving, she constantly disses her right in front of us all. Kaye's mom doesn't seem interested in defending herself, she just takes it with silence. During our morning rides, "Top 40" songs that are playing on the radio include "Lola," "My Sweet Lord," and "Knock'n On My Back Door,"—familiar half-century old classics today. During this fall, hard rockers Janis Joplin and Jimi Hendrix both die of drug overdoses, and both are 27 years old. They are the very first inductees of Rock N Roll's infamous "27 Club," and the legendary rocker Jim Morrison would join this macabre club the following year.

One day when one of the mothers was to drive, her station wagon was in the shop, so we all cram into a much smaller sedan. Kaye was always the last one picked up on the route, and I was second to last. But this time there is no place for her to sit in the little sedan except on my lap. I had become very interested in girls from a distance starting quite a few years earlier, but this particular carpool ride greatly intensifies this interest—even though I'm not particularly attracted to Kaye if only for her strange adolescent personality. As a result, I decided I will join extracurricular clubs and play sports at school to meet normal girls.

So, I join the Kirkwood wrestling team (no girls there) and a couple of after-school clubs. Since I am taking my second year of German class, one of these is the German Club. For some reason, I don't interact much with German Club girls, but I do want to become conversant in German because my late grandfather on my mom's side spoke it fluently and taught it to high schoolers, and I am intrigued with my plastic models of the World War II Messerschmitt and Focke-Wulf fighters that I had built. I like to associate these models with the gruff sound of the language spoken by real German pilots.

We have a German Club meeting after school on the cool, clear crisp Friday, October 2, 1970. My mom picks me up in the evening after the meeting and on the radio there is a horrible news bulletin that an airliner had just crashed in the Colorado Rockies, killing half of the Wichita State football team. There was a rash of bad jetliner crashes during these years, and I think *heck, another 727 or DC-9 "down."* Soon, I'm surprised to learn that the aircraft that crashed was not a modern jetliner, but a Martin 404. What?

The next morning on Saturday, I hear the whine of R-2800s climbing to the east, so I grab my binoculars and run out to my front yard. It's got that "green Ozark trim," so it's probably that Martin 404 dad and I saw parked at Mark Aero two months earlier in the VW Squareback. Years later, I find this Mark Aero 404 is the *sister ship* to the one that just crashed in Colorado. Both started life with Eastern airlines and were both retired from scheduled service by Ozark Airlines during 1967 when they were sent to the Las Vegas desert and stored by Fairchild in trade for their new F-227 turboprops. The FAA registrations of these two planes are no more than a digit apart.

There was another Martin 404 on the same football charter for a total of two planes. The single DC-6 Wichita State was supposed to lease for the whole team was damaged in an Oklahoma City thunderstorm. So, the two trips originated from Wichita, Kansas, and were to terminate at Logan Utah. There was a planned refueling stop at Denver's Stapleton Airport, which is over 5,000 feet above sea level. After refueling, the other 404 crew flew the original flight plan out of Denver—flying north along the eastern edge of the Rocky Mountain range, then turning west over lower mountains to arrive at Logan. The ill-fated plane did *not* follow the plan. The only thing they had in common on his 80-passenger trip was that both planes were flown under visual flight rules, or "VFR," which was common then but rarely allowed in today's commercial air traffic environment.

The two crewmen of the ill-fated aircraft were low-timers in the 404 with fewer than 153 hours in the 404 between them, and only one, the pilot-in-command, was type rated in the aircraft—but he was occupying the "wrong seat"—the right one. At the ill-advised insistence of the non-type-rated copilot—sitting in the left seat—the plane deviated from the original flight plan. How bizarre, the second-in-command forcing the pilot-in-command to take what was later determined to be an *overweight* 404 on a "scenic route" of rapidly rising terrain, directly toward the highest part of the mountain range, 12,000 feet at Continental Divide, 70 miles west of Denver. They slowly climbed *inside* the long, rapidly-rising gorge called Eagle Pass at low altitude to give the football passengers "a view of the fall colors and ski resorts" along the gorge. Soon, there was as much terrestrial scenery *above* them as *below*.

The few surviving football players noticed the pine trees and ground inching up towards them to the point where they could "shoot rabbits from the plane," as the left-seater stupidly forged ahead into the narrowing blind canyon bounded by the Continental Divide. The 404 was trapped—it couldn't climb and couldn't turn, and that was it. The surviving passengers felt on-and-off episodes of violent wing-stall buffeting starting a few minutes before impact. In a vain last-second attempt to rightfully exert his pilot-in-command authority, 27-year-old 404 type-rated Danny Crocker grabbed his yoke and yelled at non-type-rated left-seater Ron Skipper, "*I've got it.*" Only a second too late. Thirty-two out of the forty passengers perished on a steep wooded slope of Mt. Trelease just short of the Eisenhower tunnel then under construction. Nearly half the Wichita State football team perished, but not suddenly. The majority survived the impact but were too dazed to navigate their way out of the plane before a flash fire engulfed them—yes, *Tiger on a Leash*.

Over the next few days, I save newspaper clippings about this crash and am somewhat disturbed. Informed witnesses say they heard backfires as the plane flew overhead near Georgetown and Silver Plume, including "unspent fuel coming out the exhaust." There is a

A faded-through newspaper clipping of NTSB workers in Denver hosing down the two R-2800 C-Series engines of the ill-fated Wichita State Martin 404 the day after it crashed just short of the Continental Divide. From the minute I first saw this image, it burned itself into my head for good.

newspaper photo of the sister ship that brought in the surviving half of the football team, parked at Logan Airport with a five-gallon can sitting under the engine. The photo caption says, "*It's leaking gasoline from an engine into a can, but the airport manager said that's not unusual for a 20-year-old plane*." What a casual analysis!

Prevailing *early* speculation was that the 404 experienced mechanical problems due to poor maintenance, but later that was shown not to be the case. The cause was determined to be pilot error, including poor last-minute flight planning caused by sudden deviation from the original plan, and an overgrossed aircraft weight condition at a high density altitude. The plane was 5,000 pounds heavier than it was supposed to be. The confusing and overly-lenient FAA regulations then in force contributed to this accident.

The charter arrangement made with Wichita State was convoluted if not dangerous, and sickeningly common for small charter operators under the 1970 regulatory environment. In November 1969, a company called Golden Eagle Aviation was formed in Oklahoma City. They leased out flight crews to customers, including captains, first officers, flight engineers, and flight attendants. Customers such as sports teams, rock bands, and convention groups were *unknowingly* utilizing a vast number of low-time, poorly maintained, and cheap propliners. Jack Richards Aircraft Company, also of Oklahoma City, was also involved big-time. They were a "used propliner" dealer/broker with a large pool of them for sale. While in inventory, these aircraft would be flown under short-term leases to keep the cash flow going until a firm buyer could be found. This was *standard practice* during these *Second Wind*.

The problem was that any half-reputable airline *holding itself out* as a nonscheduled group charter operator of large transports (that is a "non-common carrier") should have, at a minimum, an FAR Part 121 Commercial Operator certificate—so that the "operator" would be *clearly defined*. So, the first question was, *who* was the operator here? Golden Eagle, Jack Richards, or Wichita State? The Martin 404 capacities were 44 passengers or a payload of 11,700 pounds, putting it in the "large transport" category. Meeting Part 121 standards for large transports, at any tier level, was and is prohibitively cumbersome and expensive for small hand-to-mouth charter operators that need the capacity of larger aircraft. This is not to mention the regular FAA scrutiny and mountains of paperwork that Part 121 operators endure—and that Part 91 operators *do not*.

Golden Eagle contracted with its customer, Wichita State University Athletic Department to fly football team members for the 1970 football season, not unlike a "general contractor" arrangement in the construction industry. It leased its employee/crews to fly the 404s on both flights, and pulled in "good neighbor" Jack Richards Aircraft to provide the aircraft, which was then leased to Wichita State as part of the charter package. In doing this, and within the completely legal FAA rules in force, Wichita State was designated as the "aircraft operator" by leasing this aircraft—making them responsible for the preflight maintenance, crew qualifications, and liability, even though they didn't know squat about aviation or running airlines. But the Wichita State athletic department didn't heed the fine print and thought they were "just chartering airplanes." Was Wichita State a legitimate aircraft operator? Clearly not!

Thus, making Wichita State the operator essentially turned a commercial operation into a "private" one under the minimally restrictive and less costly FAR Part 91 rules which govern non-commercial or private general aviation operations. This was no different than if Wichita State was merely a private pilot flying a light Cessna on a pleasure flight, but renting the plane from an FBO. And this loophole means more profit for Golden Eagle and Jack Richards—the real owners and operators.

Inexperience coupled with lax regulations tends to breed carelessness, conflict of interest, and downright sloppiness. The 27-year-old captain and pilot-in-command of the ill-fated and overloaded flight, Danny Crocker, was an A&P mechanic and type rated in the 404, DC-6, and other propliners. With only 123 hours of pilot-in-command on the 404, he was also the *employee* of the *non-type rated* First Officer Ron Skipper, 31, who in turn *was the owner* of Golden Eagle Aviation with only 30 hours in the right seat of the 404. Today, company boss and non-rated Skipper was calling the shots on his modified flight plan, so he grabbed the normal pilot-in-command's left seat to "command" the flight, against the advice of the younger Crocker who was now just along for the ride.

Danny Crocker, and a young female flight attendant (who was only a week out of training), were crushed to death on impact. Ironically, Skipper, the instigator of all this, escaped with his life and survived years of litigation, only to continue his flying career. This Wichita State crash was only the *beginning* of the FAA tightening crew requirements for Part 91 operations of large aircraft—and an eventual clarification that *any* Part 91 "operator" had to possess the aviation knowledge, experience, and appropriate certifications and ratings to serve in such capacity. Due to normal bureaucratic red tape, implementation of these changes regarding the "private" operation of large transport-category aircraft would take years—as the abuse continued.

CHAPTER 12

Air Travel Club

The concept of the air travel club grew out of that swollen glut of cheap, low-time, "throwaway" propliners starting in the mid-1960s. This represented an unlimited pool of flying clubhouses just waiting to happen. The first air travel club was formed in 1964 with a Washington D.C.-based club that acquired a Douglas DC-7 to form one that would be classified as not-for-profit for IRS and other regulatory purposes. Other travel clubs with similar aircraft began to sprout. Each would start with a promoter who would acquire a large aircraft, then organize the non-profit travel club corporation to sell to or lease that aircraft. These clubs had catchy names like "Voyager 1000," "World Samplers," "Air Venturers," "Denver Ports-of-Call," "Voyager," "Wings Away," "All Seasons," and "Air Trav-A-Lairs." They flew every heavy propliner from Convairliners and Martinliners to big DC-6s, DC-7s, and Lockheed Super Constellations, as well as those first-generation Lockheed L-188 Electra turboprops, and eventually first-generation Boeing 720 and Douglas DC-8 jet transports.

Members joined a club for a minimal up-front fee of say around $100 for either an "individual" or "family" membership, renewable annually with a modest annual fee of, say $25. Then trips would be organized to destinations such as the Caribbean, Mexico, Las Vegas, and other Continental U.S. destinations, Hawaii, and Europe, and those who signed for the trip shared in the expenses of operating the aircraft. The "shared expenses" fell below major airline ticket prices along the same routes. And while these travel clubs were touted as affordable, deep-discount vacation travel vehicles, their upscale clientele also enjoyed the *bragging rights* of being a *big airplane owner* and *exclusive travel club member* at cocktail parties. Hotel accommodation and ground transportation were provided on each trip, and traveling passengers often had access to an onboard concierge.

As far as the FAA and CAB were concerned, these air travel clubs were classified as private clubs, later termed "affinity groups," much like a small group of general aviation pilots forming a partnership to own a light plane such as a 120 horsepower Cessna 172 to be legally operated under Part 91—which specified no crew qualifications or mechanical standards. But the average travel club, as outlined, owned and operated one or more large transport category piston aircraft along with the infinite mechanical complexities that came with them. These second-hand planes were originally in great shape, having just been retired by the major airlines that had operated and maintained their equipment by the book. Initially, most travel clubs had no alternative but to fly these large planes using the Part 91 loophole described in the previous chapter. But they liked that because they were not under regulatory scrutiny and did not need to bear the associated expenses of a 121 operator. And, the owning of an air travel club was probably seen as an entry point for former civilian and military pilots to get into the airline business through the back door without initially having to deal with Part 121. Things changed in 1968 as we shall see, but first, we will share a typical story involving a Part 91 travel club operation circa 1966 which is baffling—at least for me.

So, here we have a relatively complex and unforgiving heavy-piston transport operation—with a plane that starts in relatively good shape—that becomes part of a "private club" transaction in 1967, allowing it to become a Part 91 operation. We note that the extent of Part 91 regulatory enforcement is *nearly nothing!* The *worst* might be a short, unannounced, and informal "ramp check" by the FAA (checking for proper licenses and registrations) that might happen at your home airfield every five years if that. They do not "look under the hood" of any airplane, question or scrutinize your operation such as where and/or how often you fly it, or for whom. There are no associated inconveniences such as "minimum crew qualifications," "maintenance requirements," or "operating requirements" to speak of.

With that in mind, here we have a well-known aviation author whom I have respected, unwittingly illustrating this regulatory laxness to an incredible degree in a book he wrote during the late-1960s. He describes that he is a newly-minted 18-year-old private pilot with around 100 hours in just one airplane, the single-engine Cessna 150 *trainer*. He had been doing odd jobs around the Dallas airport for the previous several years to pay for his flying lessons and is known

A Lockheed L-1649A Starliner Constellation, the most sophisticated long-range piston propliner ever built. With a newly minted private pilot's license in 1967 and less than 100 hours in a 100 horsepower Cessna 150 trainer, you too could be a legal copilot on one of these 13,600 horsepower ex-TWA piston *Aerial Leviathans*, under the absurdly lax Part 91 regulations of the 1960s, even if you didn't have a clue about its complex systems or flying characteristics. (Wikimedia Commons, NACA/NASA)

by most who worked there, including tower personnel, pilots, fixed base administrators, and mechanics. This is a typical young pilot's story.

He goes on to describe a morning when he gawks at a newly-formed travel club's Lockheed L-1649A Starliner Constellation sitting on a Dallas Ft. Worth (DFW) airport ramp. It is an ex-TWA plane that had flown several million miles all over the world. The piston-powered Starliner was the most advanced, highly sophisticated, powerful, and overly complex propliner ever built, developing 13,600 horsepower on takeoff. The kid and soon-to-be aviation author strike a conversation with its captain and flight engineer who are discussing fueling. The kid mentions he has a newly-minted private pilot's license. After congratulating the kid, the captain tells him they are preparing for a "proving flight" to Oklahoma City, then to Wichita Falls, and back. On board will be "several passengers" who are "travel club executives" who "want to check out their new flying clubhouse." The pilot also tells the teenager that they are "short a co-pilot today" and would he be interested in "filling in." How would any teenage, 100-hour single-engine, non-instrument rated, non-commercial private pilot answer a question like that? In the book he states, ". . . *since I was a private pilot, I was all that was necessary to legalize the jaunt.*"

The pilot and flight engineer go through a "46-item checklist" and the new first officer kid in the right seat jokingly states that the only item he recognized was "seat belt lights—ON." He also described some of the non-essential banterings between the pilot and the flight engineer during some of the critical phases of flight. During the max power takeoff roll, the teenage copilot is told to hold the yoke forward while the pilot worked the tiller "until the three rudders become effective." Gee—what if this green kid we just met *freezes up* on takeoff roll? Let me get this straight. A kid who has never flown anything bigger than a 1,600-pound Cessna 150 is now grasping the yoke of a 160,000-pound Starliner Constellation. Student pilot *freeze-ups* are not uncommon, and the strength of Hercules cannot "unfreeze" these bad situations. Later in the flight, the teenage copilot is also given some of the ATC communication duties (maybe not a problem), and also is "given the yoke" for a while during cruise flight (also maybe not a problem).

They land at Oklahoma City (OKC) and then "take on two more passengers" for the leg to Wichita Falls. From there our boy-copilot "calls his mom" saying he'd be late for dinner. His dad, a fully seasoned and famous airline pilot/author dad grabs the phone and our 18-year-old explains his situation. Dad fully understands and approves of the situation as he had "been through that drill" himself while growing up. At the conclusion of the final return leg to Dallas, our boy-copilot is "given the landing" of this monster aircraft at DFW (certainly not a light traffic environment), with the captain on his yoke making "subtle corrections." Again, the panicked "freeze up" scenario comes to mind.

So that's the way it was in 1967—one cannot blame the teenage author or his airline pilot/author dad for being lax about things because those were the *norms* then. It should also be pointed out that no club passengers or crew were known to be injured or killed in a Part 91 travel club operation. However, in 1968 the FAA decided to semi-legitimize these clubs, so they carved out a new regulation. This was *FAR Part 123 Certificate and Operations: Air Travel Clubs Using Large Airplanes.* This brought travel club safety, maintenance, and crew qualification standards up closer to Part 121, but didn't address economic considerations like route structuring and fees. This is because travel clubs were still considered private carriage of affinity groups and not common carriers. But contrary to private carriage Part 91and non-common carrier Part 121 rules, it was implied that private travel clubs were *allowed to advertise* for memberships and *sell individual tickets* to any member of the so-called private club like a commercial common carrier, so they did. The FAA didn't care much about this because they considered air travel club operations an insignificant drop in the ocean of airline operations, and they were not-for-profit on top of that. Their big planes flew sporadically, infrequently, and on a different route each time. But as we will see in a later chapter, some took the advertising issue *way* into the gray area. The undefined line between *social club* versus *certificated air carrier* would determine the fate of the entire air travel club industry.

Most established travel clubs upgraded to and complied with Part 123, and the popularity of this concept exploded with approximately *thirty* new travel clubs formed immediately after Part 123 became effective in 1968. And one of these was called *Pegasus Club* which was headquartered in St. Louis.

CHAPTER 13

Gramps Crashes the Gate

My paternal grandfather Reed (Gramps) was a cool guy, and grandma was a close second from that standpoint. She provided anything and everything my mom and dad would regularly deny, mainly all the on-demand junk food we would ever want. While growing up my parents shipped my little brother Jeff and me off to their white, one-story, asbestos-paneled house on any weekend they had a night out, which was often. We have so much fun there that by 1970 we spend weekends there as teenagers even though we are old enough not to need babysitters anymore.

Their modest house is on three acres in the otherwise dense St. Louis suburb of Rock Hill. Gramps has only half of a right hand consisting of the two smaller end fingers and one thumb, the whole assembly looking more like a lobster's claw than a human hand. He also has a glass eye. Gramps was sixteen in 1912 when he was hunting quail with his dad and uncles near Eldon, Missouri when his 12-gauge discharged while he was scaling a fence, blowing a hole in his hand, with just enough stray shot to puree his left eye. He almost died from shock on the 100-mile Rock Island train ride home to St. Louis for medical attention. There was no morphine on this long, torturous trip. If this mishap didn't happen, I suppose with two intact hands he could have died on the World War I Western Front where his brother Jason went five years later. Jason survived that, and we used to play with his old brittle gas mask that Gramps kept in his basement.

Gramps is a semi-gearhead and outboard motor race-boat builder which greatly influenced my mindset. He teaches me how internal-combustion piston engines work, which sparks my fiery fascination with these engines. He lets my brother, cousins and me run around his field in a dangerous riding lawn mower pulling a cart. Hit the *wrong lever* and three sets of sharp blades start whirring with five of us kids on the apparatus. On several occasions, we roll this assembly over (the blades were disengaged), with all of us kids laughing like hell, including Gramps.

When grandma and Gramps were raising my dad, and beyond that, after I was born, Gramps designed and built some pretty slick wooden race-boat hydroplanes and runabouts, about seven of these machines in all, most of them with driver-only passenger capacity. He put a "Quincy Looper" modified 10 horsepower Mercury Hurricane 10 outboard motor of 1950 vintage on the transom of these boats that now probably developed nearly 20 horsepower. When he sold an existing boat, he built a new one in its place and transferred this same Mercury outboard to the new transom. Gramps needed a place to run his boat, so we would all stay at several of the old mom-and-pop fishing resorts on the Niangua Arm of the Lake of the Ozarks, including one called Pikey's Beach. Gramps's little racers hauled ass at a moderate 45 miles per hour, but their micro-size made it feel like you were doing 150. My parents let me start driving these boats *solo* when I turned 10 years old. A decade later, my mom and dad built their own lake house not far upstream from Pikey's Beach. That's where our family's lake legacy and "race boat" mentality came from, and why dad had all those high-performance custom-built machines over the years.

Back in St. Louis, my interest in aviation is exploding as I am not always around boats. I can't drive cars when I am 15, so I have Gramps do it for me when I want to go to the airport to look at airplanes on the ramp, and in particular, propliners. On some days when dad drops me off at Gramps' house, both grandparents are already waiting in their car, all warmed up, playfully bitching about "having to go to that *damn airport* again." My Christian mom and dad do not like any profanity at all, and neither does my grandma, but Gramps always says it's perfectly all right to say "damn" or "hell" when you need to, *"but no other cuss word."* I always direct him to the Banshee Road parking lot adjacent to the Mark Aero ramp on the northwest corner. There are several DC-3s in faded Ozark livery, some with exposed engines and missing outer wing panels. I now notice at least two other ex-Ozark Martinliners had made the Mark Aero ramp home, for a total of three. I'm always hoping to see one start-up, taxi out, take off, or taxi in, but never do. At this point, I still never think to bring a camera, and probably don't own one yet anyway. Besides, that annoying chain link fence is in the way of most good photo opportunities.

About this time is when I start noticing all those USAF piston Convairs flying east-west over my house out of Scott Air Force Base. One day in March 1971 my brother Jeff and I get into Gramps' car for another airport run and I decide to "mix it up." I instruct him to take us eastward across the river over to Scott, which is much farther away than Lambert. As cool Gramps always does, he complies and we cross the Jefferson Barracks Bridge over the Mississippi and head toward Belleville, Illinois. Now I will see if all those Convairs come from Scott.

We get to the big "Welcome to Scott Air Force Base" billboard at the entrance of the base, and we drive down a long, straight road that widens at a checkpoint structure. A menacing-looking uniformed guard with a square jaw, a big machine gun, and wearing a brown beret walks out of the gated glassed guardhouse, mechanically pushing forward his hand for us to *"HALT."* I nervously tell Gramps that *we don't really have to go here, let's just turn around.* Gramps tells me to *just hang on* as he rolls down the window at the guard's hand motion. Before the guard says anything, Gramps points his lobster claw back toward us brothers, *"they just want to go in and have a look around."* The expressionless guard waves us in as the striped gate goes up, saying, *"Go on in, have fun."* I am in stunned disbelief. Wow! What just happened? We're in—just like that! These days it is not possible to enter a military base under these circumstances without a military pass and a lot of paperwork that shows a "damn good reason."

We drive to the massive main hangar with a thick concrete front "keystone" above the large hangar door. Two piston Convair C-131 Samaritan twins are sitting right outside the hangar, literally in our face as I've never seen, with their respective fat big three-blade propellers. They have the familiar "red cross" on the tail that I had seen with my binoculars on the overflights, and a blue strip also on each tail with the white letters "MAC." Above the passenger windows, it says "Military Airlift Command" in official-looking letters. The Convair has long, clean engine nacelles, without the giant air scoops, exhaust stacks, and cowl flaps found on its Martin 404 peer. On the Convairs, most of that is flush with, or inside the cowl panels and invisible. The exhaust dumps are at the very trailing edge of the nacelle and wing, with the venturi effect of the overwing exhaust augmenter tubes serving to pull cooling air through the engines.

Walking inside the open hangar I am further rewarded—there are at least *two more* identical C-131 Samaritans sitting inside. All these planes of the 375th Aeromedical Airlift Squadron are *clean*, virtually spit-shined, and almost new compared to the faded and chipped, sometimes dirty and unmarked civilian propliners I'd seen on the Mark Aero ramp. I've never been *so close* to a propliner, but don't know that the Samaritans I'm looking at are well into the process of a methodical retirement from the Air Force. I don't know that in four years all these perfectly good planes will have been relegated to the desert storage area at Davis Monthan Air Force Base near Tucson, Arizona. They will be replaced by C-9 Nightingales, a military DC-9 jet transport.

In early 1971 I never though I would get this close to a 375th Convair C-131B Samaritan (a miltary version of the commercial Convair 240 airliner). Before our unannounced visit to Scott AFB in March of that year, the Samaritans seemed little more than toys flying high over my house. I shot this in 1987 at the Pima Air Museum in Tucscon, Arizona, long after the Samaritan fleet had been turned into cookware.

which will blend with the airline movements and I will not be able to discern a 375th flyover again.

We walk up to the nearest C-131 and smell oil and grease long before we get close to it. Naturally, the first thing I do is walk up to the nearest engine nacelle, which is painted light grey, and then up to the prop dome and peer between the large paddle blades inside the tight open-face cowling. It is jam-packed with large, dirty grey trash-can-sized finned cylinder jugs, and the smell of the old metal and oil/grease mixture is now stronger. I see oil stains on the lower parts of the engine nacelles and the tarmac below them. I scoop some up with my index finger and smell it. It becomes spiritual. Weird—yes—but it is what it is. I can't believe that I'm touching the *actual* planes I've been seeing over my house.

Convertible cabin interior setup for a Convair C-131 Samaritan. Before the massive base closures of the 1990s (Scott was never one of them), there was a large demand for these 375th medivac aircraft domestically, and Scott AFB was the headquarters. Soldiers based in the continental US regularly sustained injuries and otherwise got sick during training and maneuvers, even though it was not wartime combat. The more serious cases had to be transported by these dedicated aircraft to hospitals scattered all over the U.S. with the appropriate specialties to address their specific situation. (Wikimedia Commons, USAF)

The Convair entry door is on the right side of the fuselage behind the flight deck and it's *open*, and the built-in entry steps are *extended*. Of course, we climb the steps into the plane. It has a full passenger complement of grayish seats, facing backward, complete with that musty dark interior, with the slightly musty-oily smell of old fabric and a thousand other materials so common to these large old planes. These are quick-disconnect seats that can be replaced with stretchers or removed for cargo. I realize how close this dingy interior is to how Pat Lane described the interior of the Pegasus DC-6 to me a few months before.

I stick my head right into the flight deck in awe and weasel my way onto the left seat. The cockpit seems small, cramped, and filled with more instruments, switches, levers, knobs, and controls than I could understand or manage at my age. Between the pilots' seats, there is a center pedestal shaped like a barrel on its side, with the throttle, mixture, and propeller controls. The windscreens surrounding the flight deck look purposeful and are surprisingly in your face, with big, mechanical-looking rain wipers positioned motionlessly on the front panes. A uniformed, unconcerned ground crewman on the hangar floor smiles and waves up to kid stranger "me" sitting in the cockpit. I proudly wave back.

There are also two large four-engine transports parked deeper inside the hangar, a C-54 (military DC-4) and a C-118 (military DC-6). At this point, I'm able to distinguish between the two. They are both in Air Force colors similar to the Convairs, and the C-118 has that red cross painted on its tail, along with the other MAC markings seen on the Convairs.

Imposing view of Douglas VC-118 R-2800 engine installations similar to the those of the medivac C-118 we inspected at Scott AFB. This was my field of vision as I moved the propeller blades with my bare hands (see paragraph below). This happens to be a shot the first Air Force One for President John F. Kennedy that I took in 1987 at the Pima Air Museum.

We can only inspect this spit-shined C-118 close-up from the outside, as the plane is buttoned up. I walk up to the #2 engine nacelle first, which has air scoops, cowl flaps, and exhaust stacks almost like the Martinliners. That aside, it's the very same 2,500 horsepower R-2800 C-Series engine (a military -54W) mounted in the C-131s we just inspected, but with the standard "unstreamlined" cowling. The shiny chromed three-blade props have a smart red and white trim pained on the squared tips, and the blades converge at the prop domes inside shiny silver bullet-like spinners. I can see my clear reflection on the spinners and on any part of this plane from my vantage point. I grab one of the paddle blades and can easily move the prop. Why is it so effortless to move? I wag the prop several inches back and forth with no resistance to speak of. With that big engine, I expected the prop to be as immovable as an oceanliner's propeller. In retrospect, I wasn't moving it enough to reach the compression stroke of the next piston.

Under each engine nacelle of the C-118 are large plastic mats to capture the copious oil and grease normally dripping from the engines. There are pools of oil on the mats, so I find some restroom towels and soak up this "spiritual oil" as a souvenir. Again, that may be getting a little too serious, but the fact is that's what I do. I keep the sacred oil-soaked paper towels for years but lose track of them at some point.

Behind the pilot's side window on this C-118, and slightly below is a colorful rectangle "quilt" made up of many flag decals, totaling about three feet tall by two feet wide, representing the flags of all the countries that this particular plane had visited. It reminds me of the Johnny Cash song that goes, *"I've Been Everywhere, Man!"* I notice the South Vietnamese flag in the rectangle. The United States is still 4 years away from losing that war.

Our next move is to wander outside the east hanger door. I cannot remember seeing this elephant of a plane when we first arrive—I know it had to be there—but now there it is, a spanking new widebody Lockheed C-5A Galaxy parked right there on the other side of the hangar! In early 1971 this is a *very big deal* as the plane had been flying with the Air Force for only a few months. We approach its front at the bulbous nose. It starts out looking humongous, but as we get closer it seems to get a little smaller—some sort of spatial illusion. There is rope surrounding this particular plane—probably the Air Force doesn't want random civilians like us tinkering with their new C-5As. Obsolete piston transports?—*No problem!* There are smartly uniformed Air Force officers, perhaps the crew, in front of it who seem to have no concern about our mulling around. The big fan blades the size of a barn door are rotating freely in the wind within their respective cowl rings, and make squeaking noises like a Kansas prairie windmill. This aircraft had just replaced all the Air Force's giant C-133 Cargomaster turboprops and would soon do the same for the surviving piston C-124 Globemaster IIs. On rare occasions I do spot C-124s flying over my house, sometimes to/from Scott. However, I never see a C-133 Cargomaster.

This was an up-close-and-personal day with propliners I'd never experienced before. I tell Gramps w*hat a DAMN good day—thanks a million*! I know he's fully aware that I'm fluent in other cuss words besides "damn" and "hell."

A C-9 Nightengale "gate guardian" at Scott AFB, Illinois in 2020. It is a military variant of the commercial McDonnell-Douglas DC-9-30. When these fully replaced the Convair C-131 Samaritans and C-118s in the mid-1970s, I never noticed 375th traffic over my house after the conversion to jets. This is because these C-9's fully blended in with generic commercial airline jet traffic.

CHAPTER 14

A DC-7 Unlimited Racer?

In May 1971 dad takes my brother Jeff and me to another airshow. It's across the river at a reliever airport in Illinois then called Alton Civic Memorial Airport, just northwest of Scott Air Force Base. It is the second show here in less than a year that we attended here, which were both organized by airshow promoter Leo "Baron" Volkmer. These shows have a major impact on my ongoing quest for knowledge on heavy piston aviation and its manifestation in propliners. While there are static vintage warbird displays galore, the main attraction for this 1971 show is that this venue is the finish line for an unlimited aircraft 500-mile cross-country race that originates in Milwaukee. Modified World War II unlimited warbird racing is a growing sport again after petering out in Cleveland in 1949 due to serious accidents, and since 1964 there have been a growing number of closed-circuit race venues all over the country such as Reno, Mojave, and Cape May, as well as many straight-line cross-country races like this one. Many of these racers are powered by engines that are used in propliners, such as the R-2800 and R-3350, as well as Rolls Royce V-12 Merlins (often used on Canadian and European propliner aircraft).

Famed World War II fighter pilot, test pilot, and airshow performer Bob Hoover does his famous Shrike Commander (Aero Commander 500S) routine at the September 1970 air gathering at Alton Civic Memorial airport. He performed at the May 1971 show too. The "Aero" part of the corporate name "Mark Aero" reflects when the company was one of only 5 Aero Commander dealers early on. (John J. Reed home movie frame)

Everybody who is anybody in World War II combat aviation culture and unlimited air racing is at this show from the four corners of the earth and anyone in the crowd who wants to mingle with these famous aces can. World War II combat heroes such as these mean very little to the general populace today. One reason is that modern military technology has made air-to-air combat *so obsolete* that many people barely know what aerial combat is! Hence, there are no more enduring legends like the air combat heroes that attended this show.

But there today is Peter Townsend, fighter pilot hero of the Battle of Britain (not the singer with the Who). He had been popular in the tabloids for his dating Princess Margaret—a big *no-no* for a commoner like him, despite his risking his life for the Queen. Some people, including my dad, go overboard to label him as a "playboy," but to me, that takes it a bit too far—he is a hero and that is it. Also here is the legendary German World War II fighter ace Erich Hartmann, the all-time highest scoring ace with 352 kills in his Messerschmitt Bf-109 F and G fighters.

Erich Hartmann leaning against a very rare Messerschmitt Me-108 light plane used to train German fighter pilots. He is being interviewed at Alton Civic Airport by a U.S. Air Force officer for their archives. Hartmann was best known for combat over the eastern front in his Messerschmitt Bf 109G he named "Usch." During this period, I have am obsessed with German World War II fighter aircraft and their aces such as Hartmann and Gunther Rall, probably due to my being always being #1 on the grade curve in my high school German classes without even trying. Photo taken at Alton Civic Memorial Airport, September 1970, during the first Baron Volkmer airshow held there. Hartmann also attended the second show in May 1971. (John J. Reed).

Bob Hoover is there with his P-51 and Rockwell Commander acts. In his book *Forever Flying* which was published in the 1990s, Hoover refers to this very airshow as the most fun and memorable one for him *ever*. Paul Poberezny, founder of the Experimental Aircraft Association (EAA) taxis up in his one-of-a-kind P-64, which was essentially a retractable-gear North American AT6 with a larger Wright R-1820 engine in it. The airshow announcer says that Paul's nickname is "Poopdeck" and he jokes that not long ago Poopdeck bellied in this rare P-64 when he forgot to lower its landing gear.

Then the crowd is called to silence shortly before the line of unlimited race pilot heroes scream through the finish line at 400 miles per hour along the north-south runway, mostly in single file. I do not remember the winner, but this race included popular pilots such as Clay Lacy in his purple #64 "Snoopy" P-51 Mustang racer that was the current Reno Champion, Sherm Cooper in his highly modified Bristol-Centaurus powered Hawker Sea Fury "Miss Merced," Gunther Baltz in his red and white F8F bearcat, along with Hayden Baillie in another Sea Fury. Some of the pilots participating in today's race would die in air crashes within the next couple of years.

It is here that I am reintroduced to the sounds of these big idling heavy aircraft engines up close as the racers all taxi in right by our faces after the race finish—before this, I had only *vague* memories of Constellations and DC-6s pulling up at Lambert so many years previous. This reintroduction includes the R-2800 C-series engine powering the F8F, similar to those mounted on the Convairliners, Martinliners, and DC-6s, and the R-3350 in a Douglas Skyraider, the core engine for the DC-7s, Constellations and Super Constellations. I'm taken in by the deep-bass throbbing of the engines and the sweet smell of the exhaust plumes rocketing out of the individual exhaust stacks in timed precision. I am less impressed with the sounds of the Rolls-Royce V-12 Merlins on the North American P-51 Mustang and Supermarine Mk.VIII Spitfire. To me, the

EAA Founder Paul "Poopdeck" Poberezny climbs down from his one-of-a-kind North American P-64 at Alton Civic Memorial Airport in May 1971. The airshow announcer joked that Poberezny had earlier bellied this plane in because he forgot to lower the landing gear on the "rarest airplane in existence." In recent years the EAA has restored this plane to its former flying condition after being static for many years. It is now seen at EAA events all over. (John J. Reed)

Merlin sounds like a light aircraft "flat-six" engine on steroids, which doesn't quite project the presence of an 18-cylinder radial like the R-2800. While all this seems silly, it is all about sensations for me.

Jeff and I mingle with the aviators, while dad fades back with his movie camera. We walk up to Sherm Cooper next to his modified Sea Fury and get his autograph on our popcorn box flaps. He looks more like a cross between a mafia kingpin and a dime store hood, with slicked back curly black hair, a white shirt with a gold necklace on exposed chest hairs, with his tight black pants, and pointy black leather shoes. He doesn't look like a race pilot or who just flew a 500-mile cross-country race. He's not too personable, but that's alright with us—he is an accomplished unlimited race pilot and we are just fine with the autographed popcorn boxes. Cooper would die in the crash of a high-performance Pitts Special aerobatic biplane less than a year after this airshow. To this day I reminisce about our crossing paths with this "mafia hood" pilot.

A crowd starts gathering in front of the Spitfire that is at the show. My brother and I muscle in. Erich Hartmann is "trying out" the Spitfire cockpit as bushy-haired Peter Townsend and airshow promoter Baron Volkmer look on. We are right there when the press cameras are clicking all over the three war legends next to us. A few days later that photo shows up in the St. Louis Globe-Democrat newspaper.

Two high school classmates of mine, the Garlich brothers, are indirectly tied to this airshow. I had classes with the younger one, but we are just acqquiaintances. One of my other Kirkwood High School classmates and close friend, David Troupis, did hang out with them. Their dad, Bob Garlich, was a P-51 ground strafer ace in Europe during World War II—as opposed to an aerial ace like Eric Hartmann. However, ground strafing was equally dangerous. Bob owns and manages

Slicked-up Sherm Cooper checking the shiny prop on his highly modified Hawker Sea Fury "Miss Merced" at Alton Civic Memorial Airport, May 1971. The plane had been modified a few years earlier by Mike Carroll, who in 1968 was killed while testing another unlimited racer. Carroll replaced the standard cockpit canopy with a tiny, aerodynamic canopy only slightly larger than the pilot's head. It's powered by a stock British 18-cylinder Bristol Centaurus sleeve-valve double-row radial engine that develops horsepower somewhere between an R-2800 and R-3350. (John J. Reed home movie frame)

Sherm Cooper's autograph that was obtained by my brother Jeff. I got one too but have since lost it. Cooper was the ultimate "impersonal autographer"—no "best wishes Jeff" or anything like that. Tragically, Cooper would die in a Pitts Special aerobatic plane only months after we got our autographs—I did like this mysterious pilot—he seemed to be a real stud like James Dean.

Garlich Printing which prints FAA sectional maps for private pilots. On one of the evenings during airshow weekend, Bill and his wife host dinner for *both* Erich Hartmann *and* Bob Hoover at their Kirkwood home. Dave is invited and attends. Years later, Bob Garlich was interviewed in at least one P-51 documentary that appeared on A&E, and he is also featured in one or more of the many P-51 books out there.

More recently just before his passing, Dave Troupis gave me a worn-out book from his library called *Luftwaffe Aircraft and Aces* by Edward T. Maloney. On page 12 there's a photo and blurb on German ace Erich Hartmann. That page is autographed, "*To David—Erich Hartmann*" which was signed that night at the Kirkwood dinner.

Erich Hartmann, Peter Townsend, and Sherm Cooper aside, I'm *most* interested in meeting Clay Lacy—unlimited air racer, airline pilot, aviation and airline photographer, and Hollywood aerial filming cinematographer. Weeks earlier I read in *Air Progress* Magazine that in late 1970 he raced an ex-American Airlines DC-7B at the closed-circuit Mojave California 1000 air race against single-engine unlimited fighter aircraft. This captures my attention. Surprisingly, the -7B came in sixth out of a field of 20 and was more maneuverable around the pylons than some of the

Race finisher Gunther Baltz taxiing in his F8F Bearcat. The overall dark color on the plane is bright red, with gold trim. It's powered by a Pratt & Whitney R-2800 C-Series engine similar to that which powered the Martin 404 and Douglas DC-6. The main difference is that the Bearcat (as well as the earlier Hellcat and Vought Corsair World War II fighters) utilized a two-stage single-speed geared supercharger rather than the single-stage two-speed geared superchargers used in the transports. This gave the fighters better performance at high-engagement altitudes. This airshow caused me to realize the technical connection between World War II fighters and the postwar heavy-recip transports. This did nothing but fire my imagination regarding the current-day piston transport operations out of **Mark Aero**. (John J. Reed home movie frame)

My friend Dave Troupis' autographed page in his 1960s-era book on Luftwaffe aces. Dave was lucky enough to have dinner with both Erich Hartmann and Bob Hoover at Bob Garlich's home in Kirkwood, Missouri.

competing warbirds. Allen Paulsen—who later founded Gulfstream Aerospace (long since the largest producer of high-end corporate jets) was Lacy's co-pilot for this race. However, in 1971 Paulsen is the largest propliner broker/dealer/refurbisher in the universe. He owns California Airmotive, which had purchased every one of TWA's Martin 404s for resale when they were retired in 1961. Now, he had accumulated the *largest ever* inventories of used propliners, particularly Super Constellations, Douglas DC-6s, and -7s. Ironically, Allen Paulson started his life out making ends meet on a dairy farm, just like Joe Morris.

Lacy taxis his purple Mustang Racer, #64 *Snoopy* right by us after the race, just before Sherm Cooper, Gunther Baltz and Hayden Baille did (I don't remember for sure but I think Lacy won this race). I find the light purple color of the plane a little strange, but there's a story behind that. Just like the Morrises, Allen Paulsen wanted to start airlines using his propliner assets. He'd planned a shuttle service between Los Angeles and Honolulu using three Lockheed Super Constellations in his inventory and his wife wanted to paint them a festive color that would appeal to vacationers, so he bought thousands of gallons of purple paint for the job. Paulsen found it too cumbersome under the existing regulatory framework to obtain his operating certificate from the CAB (much more of this to come) and his Hawaii service never got off the ground, so he was stuck with all the purple paint. He and partner Clay Lacy started painting as much of their inventory as possible purple, including P-51 #64 *Snoopy*.

Clay Lacy taxis his purple P-51 Mustang racer #64 "Snoopy" at Alton Civic after completing the Milwaukee 500 unlimited cross-country race in May 1971. Lacy and Snoopy won the 1970 Unlimited Class at the Reno Air Races so my dad was filming the current champion. The Mustang is powered by The Rolls-Royce V-1650 Merlin V-12 engine. I wished Lacy would have raced his DC-7B at this event—expensive but would make more sense for a straight-line cross-country race rather than flying the circles of a closed-circuit pylon course. Still, I was happy to settle for the purple Mustang. (John J. Reed home movie frame)

After Lacy parks #64 *Snoopy*, my brother and I corner him in the pavilion. He looks like the stereotypical professional motorsports racer— young and tall with a full head of thick black hair, in a pristine white jumpsuit uniform with aviation competition patches all over. His uniform looks like it was just picked up from the dry cleaners. I expect him to be doused in sweat after the high-speed Milwaukee to St. Louis run, but just like Sherm Cooper, he doesn't exhibit even a drop.

Before I can speak up brother Jeff jumps in to ask Lacy about his DC-7 racer. Lacy, in a very enthusiastic and polite manner, replies, "*Actually, the DC-7 is very fast and is a great racer. We had a lot of fun with it, and look forward to racing it again in San Diego this summer!*" Referring to his P-51, he autographs my popcorn container flap, "*To John—best wishes, Clay Lacy & Snoopy #64.*" He signs Jeff's popcorn box a little differently (see photo below). Lacy and Paulson's logically named their DC-7B "Super Snoopy," which was also Race #64. During this era, cartoonist Charles Schultz and his "Snoopy versus the Red Baron" theme is embedded in popular culture and is a recurring theme at this and most other airshows. He and Lacy are good friends.

I can't believe it, we just had a conversation with a *real propliner pilot* who flew them for thousands of hours with United Airlines. For the next 1000-mile closed-circuit race scheduled in two months near San Diego, Lacy would enter the DC-7B again, Lockheed test pilot Herman "Fish" Salmon would enter an L-1049G Super Constellation, with Allen Paulson defecting to that team as co-pilot. We will have a lot more on "Fish" later.

Just before the San Diego race, the other race pilots flying the traditional modified single-engine fighters protested and threatened a boycott—propliner wake turbulence was rightly considered a hazard to the smaller racers. In a gentlemanly manner, both propliner teams conceded and sat the race out, but that did not detract from a post-race evening of drinking and partying for all at the Hotel Del Coronado.

A frame from dad's close-up footage of Clay Lacy removing items from the rear cockpit of his purple P-51 Mustang racer #64 "Snoopy." The rear cockpit also carried his stuffed Snoopy mascot that was with Lacy on every flight. Lacy's friend and Snoopy's creator Charles Schultz loved the idea. As you can see, my brother Jeff kept track of his "popcorn box" autograph to this day. I long misplaced mine, which had a different greeting (see text above). (John J. Reed home movie frame)

This Alton Civic airshow and our brief encounter with Clay Lacy intensify my desire to seek out more activity at the Mark Aero perimeter of Lambert. The Bearcats and the Corsairs I got to see at the show are powered by *propliner engines*. During and after this great show I become more motivated and somehow just *have* to see heavy-recip transports operating *up close* instead of way overhead.

    . Unlimited racing and most other classes of air racing are not part of airshows today. The exception is the dwindling Reno Air Race event each September, a tradition that was "re-started" in 1964 with the help of Clay Lacy himself. Yes, with today's airshows there are great military and vintage warbird flybys, aerobatic routines, great static displays, and "STEM" booths (Science, Technology, Engineering, Math). STEM booths try their darndest to get school kids to be interested in aerospace—but it's like pulling teeth. In my generation, STEM booths were unnecessary—*every boy* of my generation built and often flew model airplanes, and many such "boys" like me still do. That resulted in a large pool of pilots, aero-engineers, and mechanics for several decades—and that has since dried up. And the larger-than-life air war heroes? Nowhere to be found—they have all passed on. After he had to stop doing airshows, Bob Hoover is on record stating that *this* May 1971 event at Alton Civic Memorial Airport was his "*most memorable airshow ever.*" It was mine too.

CHAPTER 15

A Motorcycle Outside the Fence

Starting in the late summer of 1971 I begin using two pieces of "high tech" to enhance my regular field trips to the Mark Aero perimeter. First of all, I receive my driver's license in early 1971 and shortly thereafter inherit a Yamaha DT-250 Enduro dirt/road motorcycle from our lake fleet to give me unlimited mobility. I also gain second-hand access to a good 35-millimeter Pentax camera. Grandma and Gramps are no longer required for these airport trips, but they sometimes drive me for old time's sake.

I make my first motorcycle/camera trip up Lindbergh Boulevard to the airport on a seasonally chilly, low-overcast Labor Day weekend in September 1971. I feel in control as the 250 cc two-stroke engine whisks me through the gray, cold mist.

As I approach the airport from the southeast I notice a huge straight line of simultaneous strobe flashes in the mist. These are the Runway 12R lead-in towers that cross Lindbergh Boulevard which I drive right under. These flashes are not really simultaneous, but the "fireball" lead-in lights where each strobe flash is offset with the next one by milliseconds, originating with the strobe further from the runway and ending with the strobe nearest the threshold. The Mark Aero hangars come into view around a slight bend in the road on the top of a rise—and then a Martin 404 comes into view. It is parked on the far side just in front of some McDonnell Douglas buildings, with its nose facing me. Parked right next to it is a Ford 4-AT Trimotor.

The 404 is now smartly painted with a multi-colored blue stripe along its cabin windows, and a navy blue "meatball" painted on its tail with an aqua blue form of a big flying swallow superimposed on it. Over the top of the cabin windows in a blue script, it says "Interstate." While I don't know it just yet, there are now three Interstate Airmotive Martin 404s that are on call at this ramp: N471M, N473M, and N471M. N473M had been acquired from Jack Richards Aviation of Oklahoma City (remember them?), and the other two from Fairchild Hiller in Las Vegas, Nevada. All three were 1967 trades by Ozark Airlines for new Fairchild F-227 twin turboprops.

I recognize the Trimotor as the one that participated in a small airshow at Spirit of St. Louis Airport that dad and I attended the weekend before. It was giving rides for $5 per passenger and our neighbor Jay Henges told me he rode in it during that show. I remember little else about that show except it was very hot with high humidity, causing a green hot air balloon in the show not to be able to inflate. It just rolled around on the ground like a lazy elephant as the burner roared incessantly. I don't know how its pilot prevented that balloon fabric from bursting into flames during this clumsy operation. There was also a radio control (RC) aircraft demonstration, and one of the demonstrators was Al Signorino, flying the novelty plane he designed and built himself. It looked like a flying doghouse, complete with yes—you guessed it—the Snoopy dog pilot and control stick on the roof, just like in the cartoons. It's *Snoopy and the Red Baron* all over again. I could not know that 3 years later, Signorino would teach me to fly hang gliders off the 250-foot lead mine chat dumps at Flat River, south of St. Louis.

I park my motorcycle outside Mark Aero's chain link perimeter and photograph the 404 and

Interstate Airmotive Martin 404 in early September 1971 on the Mark Aero ramp. Registration is not visible but it is either N465M, N471M or N473M. The Ford 4-AT Trimotor next to it had participated in a small airshow at Spirit of St. Louis Airport a few days earlier. McDonnell Douglas buildings form the background.

Martin 404 right-side (#2) power package—a Pratt & Whitney R-2800 CB-16. It developed 2,400 hp with water-alcohol injection on takeoff. This is a later version of the same engine that powered the highly modified (as well as stock) unlimited F8F Bearcat fighter air racers I experienced at the Alton Civic Airshow the previous May.

Trimotor together. I look to my right and am surprised at what I see right next to me, something I had almost forgotten about over the past 2 years. It's a DC-6 with the word "Pegasus" painted over the cabin windows! I snap a photo of N90710 *fairly close*. It turns out this is the very same plane I had seen at Spirit Airport in August 1969. This time it wasn't in all bare metal but was painted up with a white top and vertical fin and nice blue trim. Each engine cowling is painted in this blue and white. The vertical tail has a blue elliptical globe on it with a winged Pegasus horse superimposed in the middle of it. As mentioned, I had learned from Pat Lane that this is a travel club, but I still don't know who is involved.

During the previous year, I had seen and logged several Interstate Airmotive Martin 404s flying over my house, coming and going, high and low. I even caught them at a distance taxiing, taking off, and landing, from inside the sterile environment of Lambert's main terminal. At full takeoff power at rotation, the loudly singing Martinliners shake the entire terminal. I also log several overflights of the Pegasus DC-6 over my home and high school. Through later research I isolate two of these sightings as departures for club trips to Atlanta and New Orleans.

Pegasus Club DC-6 N90710 in early September 1971 on the Mark Aero ramp. This is the first time I had seen it in 2 years when it was sitting at its hangar in basic natural metal at the National Air Races at Spirit of St. Louis Airport in August 1969 (see photo page31). It had since been repainted into this white and light blue-trim scheme.

In the months to come my motorcycle and I continue making trips to the Mark Aero facilities to get photos from behind that annoying chain link fence. I would lose quite a few of these photos over the years but some survived. One plane that shows up on their ramp in July 1972 is th ex-American Airlines DC-6 N90729 with the name "All Seasons," a now-defunct travel club (see photos below and Chapter 17). This would become the second Pegasus fleet DC-6 and would be repainted in Pegasus livery nearly identical to the first one.

That same day in July, I get multiple close-up shots of another DC-6, right at the fence. This plane looks so exhaust-stained and dirty that I assume it's *run out* and *about to be scrapped*. However, looks are deceiving, especially with aircraft. Its left wing extends over the fence and I can stand under it view the fine the details of its aluminum skin and aileron hinges, including

Front view of the former All Season Travel Club DC-6 N9729 on Mark Aero Ramp in July 1972, just weeks after its arrival. It will soon be the second and last DC-6 to join the Pegasus Club Fleet along with the original N90710 I'd first seen in 1969 at Spirit of St. Louis Airport.

individual rivets. It's N37570 acquired by Mark Aero from the now defunct Air Trav-A-Lairs travel club. I could not know it is about to start a different, varied career with the Mark Aero entities, and also could not know that after that it would *still* be operating with an outfit named Universal Airlines *28 years later,* past the year 2000. So much for my perceived imminent one-way trip to the boneyard.

On another day I arrive on my motorcycle and see an R-1830 running on a test stand at the far eastern end of the ramp. It is churning madly at what seems to be an above-idle or mid-throttle setting. This is probably the break-in run of a DC-3 engine that had just been overhauled. I do not see anyone nearby supervising the run, but this may have been because my distant vantage point. Otherwise, I had still not witnessed any human activity on this ramp.

As mentioned in the Introduction the first-generation Lockheed L-188 Electra four-engine turboprop was a contemporary of the heavy-recips. It had a brief life with the majors (except for Eastern who flew it on its east coast shuttle until 1977). Allen Paulsen's company, American Jet (which was the successor to his California Airmotive) converted many passenger Electras into freighters. I recorded a lot of Electra overflights, and both passenger and cargo Electras were turned around at Mark Aero. In July 1972 I photograph an L-188 parked in front of the Old Terminal, now part of the Mark Aero complex, then serving as Lambert's International Terminal. In small letters, it says "McCulloch" on the fuselage.

During this timeframe operator McCulloch Properties flies several L-188 Electras. This airline was initially a captive to its vacation real estate concern selling properties mainly in the western US around Havasu, Tahoe, and Las Vegas, but they are also advertising lakefront properties at Lake of the Ozarks near our lake house, as well as their vacation home developments in Arkansas. In 1971 it assumed the operating certificate of the defunct Vance International Airlines, conducting ad hoc passenger charters and military contract work, diversifying its operations. I see a full-page ad from a *St. Louis Post Dispatch* newspaper featuring a whisking L-188 Electra caricature artwork urging people to sign up for free tours to McCulloch's Lake of the Ozarks properties. Because of their newly acquired Part 121 operating certificate, McCulloch also flies general charters in the U.S. and Europe.

My July 9, 1972 photograph is of a McCulloch Electra that is flying *The Rolling Stones* on their U.S.Tour that year, complete with their familiar "lips and tongue" logo painted next to the forward door. Their Electra is parked in front of the Old Terminal (then leased by Mark Aero) on

Photo crops of a dirty DC-6B N37570, formerly with Air Trav-A Liars in July 1972 at the Mark Aero ramp at Lambert. It was so dirty I thought it was about to be scrapped. I soon find that "dirty" has little to do with its mechanical condition or airframe hours. This particular plane would have the longest and most varied history with Mark Aero-related entities until around 1981 and would fly with other operators well past the Millenium (see also the photo in Chapter 17).

the day the *Stones* will be playing in St. Louis. I always thought it would have been funny if the first human being I ever saw walking on the Mark Aero ramp was Mick Jagger.

A few weeks later when I pull up to the Mark Aero International Terminal there is a huge Boeing 707 jet parked in front of it, with "Luftwaffe" painted above its passenger doors, and it's marked in the expected places with the familiar German iron crosses. Germany is buying F4 Phantom II fighters from McDonnell Douglas, and the well-known World War II German ace Gunther Rall (one of the great German World War II aces that were not at last year's Alton Civic airshow) is now Inspector of the German Air Force. He and his entourage regularly stop at St. Louis to inspect the production lines and to meet with top McDonnell Douglas executives. These days, most international, military, private, and charter traffic transfers take place at the Mark Aero

Lockheed L-188 Electra N6118A of McCulloch Airlines on the Mark Aero International Terminal (Old Terminal) ramp on July 9, 1972. Note *The Rolling Stones* "lips and tongue" logo next to the passenger entrance. The man climbing the steps is not Mick Jagger, however, but at least a rare sign of life on the ramp. The *Stones* were on their 1972 U.S. tour and playing at the St. Louis Kiel Auditorium that evening. Another client of McCulloch's was Elvis Presley. McCulloch ceased operations in 1979.

Old Terminal (then serving as Lambert's International Terminal), not at the newer, main terminal.

One late Sunday afternoon in the early fall, grandma, Gramps and I decide to drive to Mark Aero, if only just to relive memories. We get there just before a light rain shower and parked in front of the old International Terminal is one of those United States Navy Douglas C-118s that I often see flying over my house, deplaining a bunch of those Navy reservists from weekend duty at NAS Millington, Tennessee. The reservists don't hang around. They walk into the terminal, say their goodbyes and quickly disburse to enjoy what little is left of their weekend. We walk into the dimly lit facility and it's now deserted and eerie. There is not even one soul behind the glass counter windows. We walk out the back and down some shallow steps toward the apron and the parked C-118 where we cannot even find a single crewman. It is though a ghost ship had just landed.

It begins to rain, and next to the steps stands an outside weather station, with a squeaky annemometer, thermometer, barometer, and weathervane among other instruments. It's a mechanical curiosity that looks like an upside-down steampunk ceiling decoration designed by some wacky artist—who uses this contraption? Is this rusty weather machine where our local TV stations get their weather readings "from Lambert" on the ten o'clock local news each night?

The brief disembarking Navy reservists are the first real sign of "life" I see at Mark Aero after two years of visits, even though they disbursed like Zombies. For me it remains a ghost town of parked aircraft every time.

Poor quality photo reproduction of the Mark Aero facilities in the early 1970s including the the two historic Navy hangars, looking *north*. Two parked Martin 404s are seen in the center of the frame and at the bottom are two PBY's, presumably earlier associated with Edgar M. Queeny. The billboard above the left hangar, right at the Banshee Road "boomarang" curve, was a McDonnell-Douglas ad for its new F-15. This billboard with essentially the same ad remains intact in 2022. (US Congressional Record as provided by Joseph E. Morris)

Looking *south* right down the center line of Banshee Road in the early 1970s. Lindbergh Boulevard is the parallel road to the right. On the lower left is the historic west Navy hangar. On the left is a parked Martin 404. Just above and to the right of that is the historic and original Old Terminal of Lambert. Just to the south of the Old Terminal are two other hangars leased by Mark Aero housing the engine shops. I would ride my motorcycle north on Lindberg Boulevard, approaching the scene from the upper right. I would enter the crossover to Banshee Road, turn left and park at the chain link fence along the row of light planes to "spy" on things. (US Congressional Record as provided by Joseph E. Morris)

CHAPTER 16

Pegasus

On July 8, 1967, Douglas DC6 N90710 became part of Joe Morris's Mark Aero's fleet in its original passenger configuration. Original owner American Airlines traded in the plane for a jetliner in February 1966. While Joe purchased this DC-6 from intermediary Miami Aviation Corporation, a month later in August1967 he transferred it over to a brand-new nonprofit organization he founded which he named Pegasus Club. This seems to be Joe's first large flagship-sized four-engine airliner to appear on his roster.

Joe was plugged into all people and things aviation, and he was likely aware that the FAA was in the process of crafting FAR Part 123 that would carve out a regulatory niche for the recent air travel club phenomenon. Joe probably figured if he, Mark Aero, and its employees got air travel club experience, it could only help serve as a stepping stone to enter into the traditional airline business at some point. Joe was also by necessity well connected with St. Louis high society and their cocktail-talk tendencies.

He had long associations with CEOs such as Edgar Queeny of Monsanto, Ed Phelps of Peabody Coal (later Peabody Holding), and other corporate hitters and their high-powered board members, as well as with all the local banking and legal firepower he needed to run a large, risk-intensive operation like Mark Aero. Joe likely mingled among and became well known to many of the St. Louis suburban elite. Almost like shooting fish in a barrel—and the perfect storm to get the big airplane experience beyond air-taxi and light planes. It would also be a geographic monopoly—travel clubs had to be localized. And if Pegasus Club didn't serve the St. Louis departure point for affluent vacationers, someone else would. Besides, travel clubs were the "thing" and they were beginning to spring up everywhere to make use of the major overabundance of discarded, cheap, low-time obsolete propliners.

Even though this was a deep-discount travel scheme for members, Pegasus Club members could brag that they were part of an exclusive club that "owned an airliner" that flew to leisure destinations "all over the world." Never mind that your "airliner" was an old hand-me-down crock—you didn't need to mention that anyway. If you did, it was probably better than 50-50 odds that the impressed listener pictured a jetliner and did not know that a DC-6 had propellers.

Air travel clubs had regional membership by necessity—Pegasus eventually drew from a 250-mile radius from St. Louis. Longer-distance travel to a departure airport sort of defeats the purpose. Assuming an average of one couple and one child per family, you only needed around 25 family memberships to reasonably fill a DC-6 way past breakeven for a trip. Reach a certain minimum universe of members, set up some nice destinations with group hotel rates and you're off.

Mark Morris stated that to the best of his recollection members paid a one-time fee of $1,000 to "own" a share of the plane, in a closed subscription. That seems a little steep compared to other air travel club pricing structures. This may, however, have been a wise move, keeping memberships "closed" would keep the club "exclusive" as well as keep them away from FAA and

CAB bloodhounds. The only other charge was the per-mile rate for each trip.

Pegasus' DC-6 was crewed and maintained by Mark Aero personnel. As mentioned, club members then shared the cost on any planned trip they signed up for, and apparently, those travel costs were way cheaper than using a traditional travel company package with the scheduled airlines. Once Part 123 became effective in 1968, Pegasus Club started booking and flying trips. In the months to come, a DC-7 would be added to the Pegasus fleet and by 1972 that other "All Seasons" DC-6 was added.

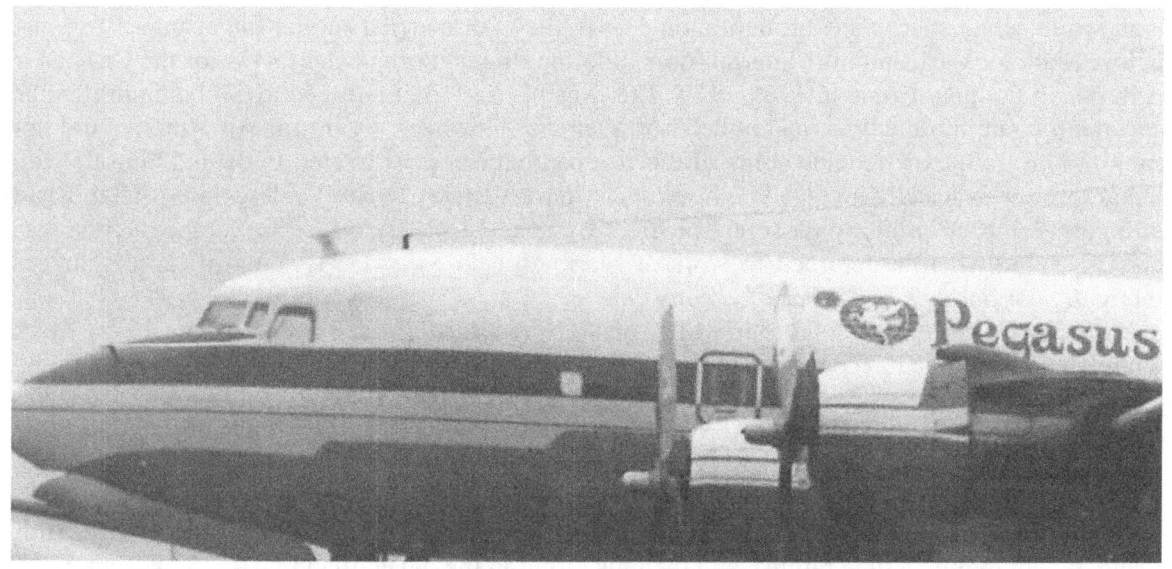

Want to brag about your "own" airliner on the cocktail circuit? Join Pegasus Club. This is the plane I spotted at Spirit of St. Louis airport two years earlier when it was in bare metal and also in the air over St. Louis County several times in this early-1970s timeframe—on both inbound and outbound on member voyages.

Time has erased the details on most of the Pegasus trips taken, but most of them seemed to be within North America. Destinations included places like Tampa, New Orleans, Chicago, and Atlanta, as well as the Caribbean, Mexico, and Costa Rica. Trips were scheduled by the president and vice president of the club, with details worked out by other administrators.

In 1968 Mark Morris passed his first officer check for the DC-6/7 in check plane N90710, the club DC-6 to FAR 123 standards, which are fairly close to FAR 121. This was not a type rating for a DC-6, but a right-seat qualification to fly co-pilot—now requiring "slightly" more qualifications than a few hours in a Cessna 150 trainer. He would get his actual DC-6 type rating (to fly left-seat pilot-in-command) a few years later. Joe was giving Mark's check ride with an FAA observer who was, in turn, giving Joe *his* check ride to become an FAA check airman for the DC-6 and DC-7.

Shortly thereafter that same year Mark flew his first run as a DC-6 first officer on a club trip from St. Louis to Tampa, Florida. The flight engineer on that flight was family friend Bob Werner, co-founder of Remmert-Werner. Mark looked like a young uniformed greenhorn with epaulets, barely out of his teens. However, with his rapid accumulation of his multi-engine and commercial flight time he was a tad bit more qualified for the four-engine right seat than our newly-minted teenage Cessna 150 pilot in Chapter 12. During Mark's layover in Tampa, a crewmember dared him to approach an attractive young woman at the hotel pool who was traveling with her Pegasus member parents. Upon his slightly nervous introduction she thought he looked too young to be in the front office of the big airliner she was on, but she accepted when he asked her to dinner that evening.

To Mark's surprise, Susan turned out to be a whopping 4 years older than him. She lived in Kansas City working for Hallmark Cards as an upper management graphics designer. They would soon go on short midnight dates when Mark's weekly mail flights arrived at Kansas City Downtown Airport from St. Louis, mainly just talking on the ramp while he unloaded and loaded mail while eating snacks she brought along. Still, they got married sooner rather than later, just before Mark took a 12-month "intermission" piloting Pilatus Porters and C-47s for the CIA's Air America in Southeast Asia in 1969-1970. This was his best alternative to avoid being drafted as an infantryman into the "rice paddy hell" of Vietnam. However, flying for Air America did not exempt him from experiencing some of the rice paddy horrors of having to defend himself with lethal force. This usually involved being shot down over enemy territory a few times. All this had a lingering impact on his "philosophy of life." By necessity Mark's stint in Southeast Asia was classified, but when he returned to work at Mark Aero in early 1971, some of the employees thought, *poor daddy's boy is back from his time off.*

After his Southeast Asia tour while mentally readjusting back home in late 1971, Mark completed his degree in economics at the University of Missouri St. Louis (UMSL) while flying charters and corporate runs three nights per week all over the Midwest. A few years later was made chief corporate pilot at Mark Aero. Also, he started flying Pegasus Club jaunts again as first officer, and later, after a grueling checkride from dad check airman Joe, he got his DC-6 captain type rating, while racking up time as a leased pilot for Interstate Airmotive flying their DC-3s.

By this time Mark also got checked out in the small twin turboprop Mitsubishi MU-2 (this plane did not require a type rating), and then his rating in the deHavilland DH-125 twin-jet, both

Mitsubishi MU-2. (Wikimedia Commons, Alan Labeda GFDL 1.2)

corporate hot-rods. He also received his Airline Transport Pilot (ATP) rating in the deHavilland around this time. Mark Aero flew 4 MU-2s and 2 DH-125s and a rare Hansa Jet on corporate charters.

Experienced pilots loved the MU-2—it flew like a jet fighter. This means it was a "hot" machine with a poor safety record. Because its maximum gross takeoff weight was far less than 12,500 pounds, a type rating was not necessary to fly it—if you were multi-engine rated just get a check out with a qualified flight instructor. It had a very high wing-loading and therefore flew at faster speeds in all regimes and had twitchy flight characteristics including high stall speeds compared to the average light piston twin, resulting in less-experienced pilots auguring them in with disturbing frequency. As a result, some countries, particularly in Europe, required a type rating to fly this plane despite its low weight. It was powered by two Garret AirResearch TPE331 turboprops developing around 775 shaft hp each. Mark Aero regularly flew these on corporate runs in the early 1970s.

On one corporate MU-2 flight to Columbia, Missouri, Mark recounts a harrowing nose gear jam on the descent to landing, coupled with super-bad winter weather that was moving in. The manual lowering mechanism was *badly* jammed. These snowballing circumstances (no pun intended) required him to divert *way* out of the way to Nashville, Tennessee while he was on the radio with the Mitsubishi manufacturers rep to troubleshoot the problem. After juggling the aircraft systems and otherwise trying everything under the sun to no avail—and running low on fuel—he made a successful emergency gear-up landing at Nashville International, which required one engine to be feathered and the other to be cut just before touchdown to prevent the propeller blades from shearing and slicing into the passenger cabin, the latter of which would result in the shredding to pieces of the executive softies on the inside. Mark was now "hero of the day" and got plenty of local media coverage.

Mark co-piloted or piloted around 15 DC-6 Pegasus trips starting in the late 1960s and resuming in the early 1970s. However, he was also checked out as first officer in the Boeing 720 but says didn't fly it on trips. There is evidence that the Pegasus Club DC-6s were later leased to Mark Aero for large corporate charters operated by them after they received their Part 121 Commercial Operator's certificate in 1972—the logical next step out of the travel club syndrome.

CHAPTER 17

Time for a Real Airline

Interstate Airmotive was founded by two St. Louis executives, Ken Teasdale, a partner with the St. Louis law firm of Armstrong Teasdale, and James O. Holton, Jr., President of Citizens National Bank in St. Louis County and the Holton Insurance Companies. Interstate's origins and/or exact date of founding are unclear, but in 1970 they touted themselves as the *"Oldest Charter Service Company at Lambert Field,"* which suggests their origins could have dated back to the Remmert-Werner days. In the mid-1960s they were flying "single-entity" charter operations with a DC-3 and a much smaller Beechcraft D-18, but also owned or had access to the Lockheed Lodestar which had a passenger capacity falling between the two planes. Then in 1967, they acquired an even *larger* passenger transport, Martin 404 N471M.

At some point this airline was able to secure a *restricted* Part 121(b) Supplemental Carrier certificate (in appropriate places we will explain our 121(a), (b), and (c) categories we use for simplicity), meaning they could advertise, but their operations were restricted to charter only and *no trip segments could be longer than 250 miles*. From St. Louis, it meant that the airline had to make at least one stop on a trip to Chicago, Cincinnati, or Memphis, and two stops on the way to Denver, even though their planes had the range to make all those trips nonstop under typical load factors. It's extremely hard to make a profit when having to make all those unnecessary stops. Because of this, it is not surprising that Interstate was the very last airline to fly with this limited certificate. Nonetheless, they acquired two additional Martin 404s, N465M and N473M in 1970.

All three Martinliners were former Ozark aircraft pulled from that very same storage apron near Las Vegas as the ill-fated Wichita State plane. When Interstate acquired them they were still in Ozark colors (with the "Ozark" name rubbed out), complete with the three green "swallows" on the tail. N471M was later painted in a generic Interstate Airmotive scheme, but in 1970 all three 404s received a more artistic bluish "Interstate" scheme, even retaining an aesthetic form of a single swallow within a large blue roundel on the tail. The three Martinliners would be on-and-off fixtures on the Mark Aero ramp and over St. Louis until at least 1975.

Interstate leased its crews, including pilots and flight attendants, from Mark Aero, who also performed all other support services such as ticketing, fueling, scheduling, and maintenance for the airline making it an important customer at the time. Mark Morris cut his teeth in large transport category aircraft by flying Interstate's DC-3 along with the smaller Lodestar, starting around 1968 when he was only 20 years old, but he never flew the Martins under Interstate's original ownership. Interstate Airmotive secured seasonal and long-term charter contracts with specific groups needing on-demand air transportation, such as entertainment, collegiate, athletic, and corporate groups.

A 1970 Yellow Pages advertisement placed by Interstate Airmotive touted that they specialized in low-cost air charters for up to 50 people for groups, organizations, and athletic teams. They also touted they could provide ambulance, air cargo, and aerial photography. The ad showcased a photo of their Martin 404 in its earlier paint scheme, saying it could carry 44 people, and went on to mention that its DC-3s could carry 26 and it's Beech D-18 could seat eight.

A 1970 St. Louis Yellow Pages ad for Interstate Airmotive.

The ad further stated that Interstate employed professional pilots that were airline transport pilot (ATP) rated, and that they had all-weather capability and full service 24 hours a day. It also touted that Interstate provided sales, rentals, and flight instruction, which must have been referrals to the Mark Aero entities with which they were affiliated.

In 1972 Mark Aero acquired its Part 121(c) Commercial Operator certificate at considerable cost, allowing charters to anywhere in large transport category aircraft, not just within a restrictive 250-mile radius like Interstate. However, the "(c)" meant that they could not in any way advertise or hold themselves out to the public. They were allowed to be an unscheduled contract carrier only.

In early 1972, it became clear that Interstate would never make money and it voluntarily ceased operations on July 4, 1972. Joe Morris then acquired the assets of Interstate, including its trade name, its "restricted (b)" operating certificate, and the equipment, all of which was financed by original owner Jim Holton at Citizens National Bank, and put the aircraft under their new Mark Aero certificate. However, they could still fly the planes, or "piggyback" under the old Interstate Part 121(b) range-limited certificate, and as a result, they formed a new subsidiary called Mark Aero Supplemental Carriers, to service any current or future Part 121 operations. The same Mark Aero crews leased to the former Interstate would now be on call for Mark Aero only. The "new"

Interstate Airmotive Martin 404 on the Mark Aero ramp in July 1972, shortly after Interstate's dissolution. Under Mark Aero, it would still fly charters into 1973 in Interstate colors (navy blue and aqua blue) under the old certificate, strictly to fulfill outstanding contractual obligations.

Interstate, now operating under the "Mark Aero" brand, sometimes used the old restricted certificate strictly to fulfill remaining Interstate contracts under the original ownership. Such residual operations were with university athletic departments and were all fulfilled by late 1973.

For the record, at that time the chief pilot for Mark Aero was Frederick A. Leidner, Jr., and had been leased to Interstate Airmotive since 1967. He was also their check pilot and ground instructor for both the DC-3 and Martin 404, and after the demise of Interstate in July 1972 he, along with most other Interstate crews flew exclusively with Mark Aero before moving on. Under Mark Aero's new ownership, Mark Morris began building up time on the Martins as first officer/copilot. But during this period things were getting worse financially. First quarter 1972 profits for Mark Aero were $70,000. For the same quarter of 1973, they experienced *losses* of $108,000. Mark Aero was *always* strapped for cash and the loss trend was accelerating downward.

Robert J. (Bob) Stevenson was another colorful character with the Mark Aero team and its successors for many years, though he was never an owner or board member. Nonetheless, he was highly qualified with in-depth airline experience. Joe hired him as Mark Aero's director of operations as their business shifted toward airline operations. They had become good friends many years back when they teamed up to organize several airlines in the northwest, including Pacific Northern. Stevenson was an Army Air Corps aviator in World War II and trained pilots in North Africa, Europe, and India until the war's end. He then became a bush pilot in Alaska before his involvement in organizing several airlines in the northwest, including Northern Consolidated where he was chief pilot and later VP-operations and treasurer. He was also in charge of writing all manuals and maintenance schedules.

In 1957 Stevenson formed Arctic Air Cargo which delivered bulk fuel oil to Arctic Distant Early Warning Network (DEW Line) construction sites as the Cold War with the Soviet Union was reaching a fever pitch. When the Dew Line was complete Stevenson formed CAL-NAT

Airways in California, a company that specialized in modifying and operating heavy aircraft into tankers for fighting forest fires. CAL-NAT thrived through the 1960s into the 1970s, and Stevenson developed several aircraft tanker firefighting techniques that remain even today as standards with the U.S. Forest Service firebombing contractors.

CAL-NAT specialized in the conversion of surplus F7F Tigercat twin-engine fighter aircraft that appeared at the end of World War II for the Navy. They proved unsuitable for carrier operations and were not used in the war, so they were transferred to the land-based Marines. The Marines used them in the temporary postwar occupation of China and then in the early 1950s as successful ground attack aircraft during the Korean War, before being stricken from military use for good. With a crew of only one or two (the pilot and sometimes the radar "guy in back"), the Tigercats were powered by 2,100 horsepower R-2800 C-Series engines that were the core engines used in the Martin 404s, the Convairliners, and the DC-6 series, except *without* the water injection to boost takeoff power for the airliners. Two such powerplants seemed to be a lot of engine for a single-pilot fighter, but despite that, the aircraft was reported to be forgiving and pleasant to fly.

CAL-NAT modified their surplus F7F Tigercats with 800-gallon fire retardant tanks and they proved to be efficient firefighters before larger heavy piston aircraft began to dominate the fire tanker world. A respectable number F7Fs were saved and are flying today with private owners and on the airshow circuit in original military configurations and colors. *All* are former CAL-NAT fire tankers. Were it not for Bob Stevenson and CAL-NAT, it is conceivable that *no* F7F Tigercats

F7F-3 Tigercat flying restoration I photographed at Kalamazoo, Michigan in 1988. That is a lot of power for a one-man prop-driven fighter. It was then owned and flown by the Kalamazoo Air Zoo. Several Tigercats fly in airshows today on the shoulders of Bob Stevenson and CAL-NAT and the aircraft has a good safety record.

would be flying today.

In 1971, Mark Aero became the sole tenant of the historic 100,000-square-foot Old Terminal at Lambert Field, adjacent to their hangars. They renovated the building for $100,000 to convert it into a U.S. Customs area and international passenger terminal under Bureau of Customs specifications. The US Bureau of Customs had now begun to use this renovated building to process all international flights into Lambert, so it is now dubbed as Lambert's "International Terminal." Mark Aero was beginning to claw its way toward an expanded role at Lambert.

In 1972 Joe Morris came upon an opportunity. The tiny Caribbean Island of St. Lucia, far down the West Indies island chain, did not have access to conveniently *scheduled* airline services. This would be Mark Aero's first shot at a *scheduled* airline. Tourists came to St. Lucia from Europe, Canada, and some from the U.S. but did not have an efficient way of hopping between the many islands in the West Indies chain. Also, scheduled operations from St. Lucia fell under the British Civil Aeronautics Authority (CAA) out of its Antiqua Island outpost, the next largest island just north of there. The British CAA certificate was less expensive and troublesome to obtain than a U.S. Part 121(a) scheduled airline certificate. However, Antigua CAA personnel were fairly lax at getting around the islands to "enforce things."

Joe owned a 51% controlling interest in startup St. Lucia Airways, so he sent Mark's brother with his family down to the island to establish operations, starting with the passenger flagship ex-Air-Trav-A-Lairs DC-6B N37570. This was that "dirty" plane I had photographed a few weeks earlier in the summer of 1972. The plane was still registered to Mark Aero, even though it was thought that a St. Lucia registration had superseded it—unknowingly the U.S. registration was never dropped. A DC-3 and two other light twin aircraft were also part of the fleet. Services commenced, but once the airline was up-and-running Mark's brother and family came back to St. Louis for other assigned duties. That was a mistake, as this put St. Lucia Airways on "autopilot."

But in late 1972, Joe sent Mark south to St. Lucia to *"check things out and move things along and report back."* Mark was shocked at what he found. The DC-6B flights were almost always overloaded. Instead of 105 maximum (coach) passengers plus luggage, it was typically 125 or *more* passengers plus luggage. Passengers filled all the seats, and the aisle was *packed* with standing passengers holding onto plastic "bus straps" screwed into the ceiling, something you'd normally see in some third-world island nation (like this one?). The DC-6 flights were very short between the islands, often 20 minutes or less, so President and Captain "Red" Mettric (Mark Morris cannot remember the exact spelling of his last name) rationalized he could get away with more passengers because of minimal fuel requirements. The DC-6 was designed to fly on medium- to long-haul routes of 250 to 1,000 miles or more but was *not stressed* for high puddle jumping cycles like this, especially when overweight.

This overload habit was very bad, compounded by the fact that the main active runway at St. Lucia had a mountain obstacle, where the over-grossed plane had to *always* execute an aggressive bank after rotation to avoid impact with lush green-foliaged granite. The not-so-uncommon hiccup by any one of the four big piston engines on takeoff would have a high likelihood of ending in disaster. Yet the British CAA in Antigua didn't have a clue about any of this as they rarely bothered them, and Red told Mark they always announced any visits far in advance. Upon hearing back from Mark, Joe appointed Mark as the chief pilot (at only 25 years old) and he was quick to remedy this disaster waiting to happen by forcing *increased* DC-6B flight frequency to relieve the overloads. This cut into profit margins and therefore the St. Lucia government's take, which made the local authorities unhappy. Even though Mark was type rated in the DC-3 and not the DC-6, both British and U.S. air regulations did not require a chief pilot to be type rated in all the aircraft that a particular airline flew. Actually, a type rating is required in only of the aircraft types that a particular airline flies in order for a line pilot to be designated as the chief pilot.

As was true for some Caribbean nations during this period, St. Lucia had a problem with corruption and on/off political instability. The year 1973 was an "on" year in St. Lucia and during a resultant coup all of St. Lucia Airway's operations were embargoed and its aircraft impounded and *chained* to the runway. Uniformed guards with machine guns were stationed in and around the control tower and around the aircraft and airport perimeter. Mark reported this to Joe, who hightailed down to St. Lucia in record time. Joe sure as hell wanted to get his damn airplanes back. Citizens National Bank, the small suburban St. Louis bank that bankrolled much of Mark Aero's fleet over the years, including N36570, wanted it back too.

DC-6B N37570 in July 1972 (see the previous chapter) on the Mark Aero ramp at Lambert just before assignment to St. Lucia Airways in the Caribbean. When I took this photo, I thought the plane was so dirty and neglected-looking it was about to be scrapped. It started its life with United Airlines and was acquired by Alpha Aviation/Mark Aero from the defunct Air-Trav-A-Lairs travel club in May 1972. Under Mark Aero and affiliate Alpha Aviation, and also under on-and-off lease terms with then Peabody Coal CEO Edwin R. Phelps, it flew for St. Lucia Airways and a subsequent Mark Aero-related airline (covered later). This DC-6 was historic in that it was the last one in the world to operate in revenue passenger service. N37570 went through numerous owners after Phelps and Mark Aero and was still flying after the turn of the new millennium, only to belly land in Alaska a few years later after the crew failed to lower the gear. That was nearly four decades after this photo of my presumed "junk" airplane was taken! Nobody was hurt, but the plane was scrapped on site.

Then Joe had a bright idea. He'd tell the armed guards that the DC-6 and DC-3 needed to do full engine runups every few days to prevent mechanical atrophy during inactivity, or the planes would be rendered useless. This was not really true as the planes were capable of sitting for several months before requiring any attention. But the guards went along and Joe and Mark made a point of running the engines of both aircraft in the pitch blackness of midnight on the appointed days until the guards became complacent. Joe typically ran up the DC-6, and Mark the DC-3. They also purchased a big set of mechanical chain cutters and hid them in the aircraft before one of the runups. Since the highest value asset was the DC-6B, it would need to be rescued first. While a flight engineer was required for a DC-6 under normal operating circumstances other than a licensed ferry flight, this was an "illegal" ferry flight, so who needs the flight engineer!

During one runup both Joe and Mark were on the flight deck. When the takeoff checklist was complete, Mark climbed out of the flight deck hatch using the escape rope, cut the chains, and climbed back in. Joe gunned the four engines on the 95,000-pound plane, made a ninety-degree bat turn onto the active runway, then took the four throttles to the max power takeoff gate at 10,000 takeoff power with all water-alcohol boosters on. They had a smooth liftoff and a relaxing 2 1/2-hour flight to American territory—San Juan, Puerto Rico—where they were arrested and thrown into jail for "stealing a plane."

It was in the Puerto Rican jailhouse that Joe found out Mark had failed to drop the U.S. registration on both the -6 and the -3, meaning they were both dually registered. Joe scolded his son for being so careless, but in the same breath, he congratulated him for the oversight. It turned out that the U.S. registration would prevail on U.S. soil (San Juan), so they were released from jail and returned to their plane.

Joe told Mark to find an idle DC-6 crew to help him fly -570 up to Miami. But Joe set his sights back on St. Lucia. He was *going back in* to "steal" his DC-3. Mark thought this was crazy, telling his dad he would be machine gunned on sight. Joe rationalized that the guards would never expect the "DC-6 bandits" to return to the scene of the crime. So Mark gave up and located some parked DC-6s on the apron while Joe caught a scheduled flight back to St. Lucia. Near the parked DC-6s Mark found an idle crew twiddling their thumbs just waiting for their next job. He paid them to help him ferry -570 back to Miami and then purchased their return airline tickets to San Juan.

True to his logic, back in St. Lucia Joe was somehow able to approach his DC-3 without raising suspicions, but he did not know its fuel tanks were near empty. After the Morris team escaped with their DC-6B, the rebel guards drained the DC-3 tanks, which is possibly why they ignored Joe's approach. Joe jumped into the cockpit and blasted off anyway on residual fuel, barely making it to nearby Martinique for gas. He touched down just after one engine failed, with the other one cutting out on rollout—only the soft sound of rolling rubber tires could be heard as it came to a stop. He refueled and island-hopped the DC-3 up to Miami, meeting Mark there for drinks. Welcome to the airline business.

CHAPTER 18

Roberto Clemente

The following is an account of an event that happened just before the Morris/St. Lucia caper that highlights the devastating consequences of the shoddy operating practices that characterized many fly-by-night propliner operators in the *Second Wind* era. On December 23, 1972, a major earthquake hit the politically unstable country of Nicaragua in Central America, killing approximately 5,000 people. Just two months prior, Puerto Rican Roberto Clemente, the National League baseball legend with the Pittsburgh Pirates, had coached the Puerto Rico team at the Baseball World Cup hosted by Nicaragua. Clemente was a 15-time All-Star and had just collected his 3,000th hit with the Pirates in September, becoming the 11th professional baseball player to do so. He also had two World Series rings with the Pirates. Clemente was a folk hero of sorts in Nicaragua and during his time coaching there he developed a deep affection for its people.

On New Year's Eve, 1972 I'm getting ready for a party with my high school church group, which includes my girlfriend Patty—which is one of the reasons I go to the group in the first place. I see a special news bulletin on TV that Roberto Clemente had just perished in a plane crash just off San Juan, Puerto Rico. Damn! A baseball All-Star in the prime of his career! I'd seen him on TV and at Busch Stadium against the Cardinals several times and always liked him. The first thing I think is that he probably died in some fancy corporate jet, or a Boeing 727 or Douglas DC-9, "like any of the rest of us would." No, it is reported that he was in an old, beat-up DC-7 freighter. What? A wealthy, affluent National League All-Star perishing in an old piece-of-junk DC-7?

After the earthquake, Clemente decided he wanted to help. In the days after the quake, he bankrolled three planes and a boat to Nicaragua with relief cargoes. He later found out that all had been confiscated by the Nicaraguan military who had in turn profiteered off the illegally diverted shipments. He decided that if he sponsored a large planeload and then personally accompanied the flight to Managua—and personally supervised the delivery of the goods to their intended recipients—the resultant publicity would cause the military to back off and leave the shipment alone.

Unfortunately, he put his trust in a fly-by-night operation called American Air Express Leasing headquartered at Isla Verde Airport near San Juan. Clemente couldn't be expected to know (or wasn't concerned about) their corner-cutting reputation. It was a one-man-one-plane show, owned by a 27-year-old named Arthur Rivera. Rivera had just purchased U.S. registered DC-7CF ("F" = Freighter conversion) N500AE which would be ideal for Clemente's planned trip.

The plane had not been flown for months and during a runup and ramp repositioning in November, the number two and three propellers strike some ground equipment causing the violent sudden stoppage of both engines. This is a strange combination of engines for abrupt stoppage because these are the inboard engines with the widest distance between each other, with the fuselage between them. The ground person taxiing the aircraft must have had way too much rum to perform a feat like that. When a sudden stoppage happens on a heavy radial engine, it needs to be replaced immediately—no questions asked—so the affected engine can be torn down, magnafluxed, rebuilt, or otherwise junked. Despite this, the mechanics on the plane simply replace both damaged propellers, perform runups on both affected engines, shrug their shoulders, and sign off on leaving both engines in place. Yes, Rivera had previously told them to *"try and keep it as simple as possible."*

A Douglas DC-7CF freighter similar to the ill-fated one that American Air Express Leasing (AAEL) was operating. This one is unloading at St. Maarten and was operated by Trans-Air-Link (TAL) out of Miami during the 1980s and early 1990s. TAL was no slipshod corner-cutter operation like AAEL and many others.

An experienced freelance heavy piston transport pilot named Jerry Hill is hired to command Clemente's flight. He has thousands of hours in DC-4s, -6s, and -7s with type ratings in each (the -6 and -7 share the same rating). He also has thousands of hours with the U.S. Air Force in the far larger and more complex four-engine R-4360 powered Douglas C-124 Globemaster II heavy transport. The crew makeup just goes downhill from here. The first officer is none other than Rivera himself who is type-rated in a much smaller DC-3, but *not* in the DC-6/7 or any large four-engine recip. The flight engineer is Francisco Matias, who is a moonlighting mechanic with little to no experience as an onboard operating flight engineer. Additionally, this hodgepodge crew that covered the entire spectrum of qualification levels had *never flown with each other before*—not good considering the vital importance of coordinated teamwork flying large transport category aircraft.

Before its 9:20 PM takeoff on December 31, the plane is loaded with 38,300 pounds of relief cargo and 32,800 pounds of fuel, giving it more than enough fuel for the round trip, but causing it to be approximately 4,200 pounds over the plane's maximum gross takeoff weight of 144,750 pounds. Considering the fuel burn, this would cause the landing weight at the destination to be 134,700 pounds or 25,700 pounds over its maximum allowable landing weight of 109,000 pounds. Joining the three required crew members and Clemente on this flight was his associate, Angel Lozano.

Engine runup is satisfactory and the fully loaded plane with the five souls on board taxis into position on runway 7 at 9:20 PM local time for its 1,420-mile, 4-hour flight to the southwest.

The weather had started to clear but it is a moonless night with scattered clouds in haze, making it charcoal black outside. The ocean horizon is not discernable at all, so the climbout and perhaps the rest of the flight are essentially on instruments with minimal external visual reference. The takeoff roll is unusually long and the engine exhaust ports are flaming excessively and getting worse by the second. Turbo-Compounds always had spectacular exhaust flames on takeoff, but not quite like this.

The plane breaks ground just short of the runway's end but barely gains altitude as it skims over the ocean, with witnesses saying it was never higher than around 100 feet. It looks like the engines are badly over-boosted just to get off the ground, an absolute no-no with the temperamental R-3350 Turbo-Compound. Still not gaining altitude, Captain Hill begins executing a left turn to the north, where the tower receives a transmission from him that he's immediately returning to the airport. The DC-7CF is way over the allowable landing weight and it would take at least 20 minutes for Hill to dump enough fuel to reach that weight. He'd have no more than one minute left to dump the fuel, which was impossible. Landing weight is now irrelevant.

Immediately after Hill's announcement, the number two engine explodes *internally* with a spectacular fireball. All 16 connecting rods—*and* the 2 robust master rods—are severed from the crankshaft and twisted in all directions, ripping the rest of the engine internals to pieces. Then number three engine loses most of its power. These are the ground-damaged engines that were not changed per Rivera's polite request. The engine explosion cut the control boost hydraulics that the pilot needed to control the aircraft and there was not even close to enough remaining engine power to maintain flight. To make things worse, Hill is likely disoriented by the confusion of this rapid-fire emergency and lack of ground references. Before hitting the water, a *major explosion* is noted by some witnesses. The fuel mist trailing the plane from the dumping goes off in a powerful thermobaric fireball, destroying much of the fuselage before the chunks of the airplane impact the ocean. Its many scattered pieces sink 100 feet to the ocean floor 1 ½ mile out from shore. Call me "stupid" but I'm willing to bet everything I own that there are no *"Emergency Procedures for a Thermobaric Ignition Event"* in any heavy-recip pilot operations manual.

Most of the plane is recovered by salvage crews over the next 4 weeks. The remaining chunk of the fuselage had been crushed and severed, the wings and tail were in pieces and separated from the fuselage, and all four engines were even separated from the airframe, scattered about. The word "violent" is too mild to describe this crash. The *Tiger on a Leash* lashes out again, this time mauling Roberto Clemente, his buddy, and three crew members to pieces in a matter of seconds.

CHAPTER 19

What's Going On?

I ride my motorcycle up Lindbergh on the coldest and dreariest of winter days. It's January 1973, about the time the divers are recovering Clemente's DC-7 pieces from the ocean floor. I'm freezing. The wind penetrates my gloves and my fingertips are on the verge of total numbness. My Yamaha bike continues to hum away with purpose, unaffected by the cold. I'm a senior at Kirkwood High and my girlfriend Patty has just completed her first college semester at William Woods in Fulton, Missouri. She neither likes motorcycles nor cold, nor old airplanes for that matter. I think her protective parents don't want her on the back of my motorcycle, period. I'm on my own, as I always am on these periodic trips to Mark Aero just to see what I can find.

Then an unusual surprise. The ramp is now *full* of parked Martin 404s randomly positioned on the ramp. I count 4 "new" ones I'd never seen before, for a total of seven Martinliners on the ramp at once including the 3 Interstate Airmotive planes. The new ones had been retired from Piedmont Airlines only three years previous. They have faded navy blue trim with two navy blue stripes across the vertical tail. It turns out this is the livery of that airline, but the airline's identity above the cabin windows had been rubbed out. It looks to me like someone is trying to start a new airline. All four of them were originally configured for TWA with no weather radar at the nose and featuring the red rotating beacon on top of the fuselage instead of the tail, among other nuances.

Weeks later I'm getting ready for school one February morning when rapidly approaching R-2800s have me running outside. Climbing out right over our house, one of the blue-trimmed Pegasus DC-6s is roaring over. I later find that the destination of this trip is New Orleans. In theory, that makes sense, Mardi Gras is in full swing.

This Pegasus overflight reminds me that I want to check the Mark Aero ramp again. Upon arrival I notice the ex-Piedmont 404s had been repositioned from my first visit—not particularly unusual. Whoops, one of them has both engines removed and the nose is held down with ropes and cement-filled 55-gallon drums. The firewalls have loose hose fittings, pipes, and wires sticking out the front and they seem to be burnt or oil stained. This may have been due to an engine overhaul in progress, but who knows? As usual, I see no human activity on the ramp. The other three ex-Piedmont 404s still seem intact. Eventually, two are sold to other operators (one based at Mark Aero) and two would be cannibalized on-site. However, evidence shows that Mark Aero may have operated at least three of them for short periods beforehand as we shall see.

One day in March I'm at gym class at Kirkwood High School and we're playing "flag football" on one of the fields. During one of the plays a Pegasus DC-6 roars over, a near repeat of last month. I am the only one who looks up and I am accused of daydreaming on the field. This time Pegasus is off to Atlanta as I would find out later. I wonder why a bunch of rich people would take a vacation to Atlanta in March. One of those life's mysteries where only God and those people in that plane know at this point.

In the last week of that month, our family goes to the lake for the weekend, which is

Ex-Piedmont Martin 404 N462M, without airline titles, in 1970. This is exactly what the four ex-Piedmont Airlines Martin 404s that arrived at the Lambert Mark Aero Facilities in late 1972 and early 1973 looked like. The only difference was that the Mark Aero ones were TWA-configured, but this one is former Eastern Airlines (rotating beacon on top of tail fin instead of on fuselage and pointed radar nose). The Mark Aero arrivals were N40402, -408, -410, and -414. Over time two of these were refurbished (-408 and -410) and sold to private operators. At least three of them had been operated by Mark Aero or Alpha Aviation for a time before being stored, cannibalized, or broken up. One of the junk hulks (-414) ultimately became a fire dump practice plane for airport fire crews and was an eyesore on the west side of Lambert well into the 1990s. Before being acquired by Piedmont in early 1965, -402 was leased by the British Invasion rock band The Dave Clark Five (The DC5) from East Coast Flying Service for the band's 1964 U.S. tour. (Wikimedia Commons, RuthAS CC BY-SA 3.0)

unseasonably warm and muggy. Not much to do at the lake for an 18-year-old that time of year, so I walk to the point of our peninsula and stare across the water at the tall hills on the east shore—I've since forgotten my purpose for doing that. I soon hear the thunder of R-3350 Turbo-Compounds approaching from the south. It's a low-flying twin-boom twin-engine Air Force C-119G Flying Boxcar, heading northeast right over the lake, just like the one I saw at the Spirit air races 4 years ago. Then only 3 minutes later another one right behind it approaches and flies over as well. I hope they might be setting up to land at nearby Lee C. Fine Airport. As some nasty storm clouds begin brewing, I jump on my dad's Honda 500 motorcycle to start a 40-mile round trip, starting down highway 5 into Camdenton, then north on highway 54 and over to 42 heading east to the airport, which has the 6,500-foot runway 4-22 in the middle of the Lake of the Ozarks State Park.

I ride up the wooded hill and reach the airport on top of a plateau. Not a single C-119. What? Instead, there is a lonely Martin 404 still in Interstate Airmotive colors parked right next to the chain link perimeter fence! There are no other planes around and no people or activity either. I am suddenly confronted with the closest shot of a Martin 404 ever—right in my face. I reach for my camera to get some shots, then feel like one of those skydivers who jumps out of an airplane after forgetting to strap on his chute (well, not quite that bad!). No camera and here I am alone nose-to-nose with a big Interstate Martin 404! I just stare back at it and take it in for a few minutes. The clouds are darkening and thunder is intensifying and the wind gusts are picking up. I hear something small squeaking back and forth, coming from the 404 fuselage like a small open hatch swinging in the wind or a loose cowl flap. I have no idea what that is. One more look and I better get out of here. On the way back I am drenched by a violent thunderstorm, with lightning and major thunder claps striking all around me, with the motorcycle sometimes hydroplaning dangerously. By the time I get back to the lake house, the temperature had dropped some thirty degrees or so and I am drenched and shivering all over. All this for a damn "memory"—no photos!

Fuzzy background blow-up shot of part of one of the ex-TWA/Piedmont Martin 404s (which is missing its rudder) on Mark Aero ramp, summer 1973. This is the only surviving photo I have of any of the four ex-Piedmont 404s that showed up here in 1972-73. There is an outside chance this *may* be N40402 which was years previously leased by the rock group *The Dave Clark Five* (DC5) during their first US tour May-December, 1964, as operated by East Coast Flying Service. DC5 played at St. Louis Kiel Opera House that December 1st so it might have been parked on this very same ramp on that date, almost nine years earlier. After the 1964 tour, the plane was sold to Piedmont Airlines and flew with them until March 1971. If this is that plane, Mark Aero had already furloughed it from flying status at the time I took this photo, then scrapped in July 1976. In the meantime, it may have been flown intermittently by Mark Aero. Note the vertical stabilizer of one of the three Interstate 404s behind it. Also note the arched Lambert main terminal in the far background.

It is years later when I find that Interstate Airmotive had ceased operations 9 months before my encounter at Lee C. Fine airport. Remember, during this timeframe, Mark Aero is attempting to establish an airline or airlines, especially to employ its Martinliners, and had been in talks with St. Louis media magnate Ted Koplar in an attempt to set up a scheduled airline between St. Louis and the Lake of the Ozarks (that did not happen). The Koplars developed and owned the popular Four Seasons Resort on the south side of the lake's Horseshoe Bend and were also the largest holder of raw acreage on the lake. They owned the non-network affiliated KPLR TV Channel 11 in St. Louis. KPLR TV did a lot of different kinds of local TV programming but while I was growing up I religiously watched *Captain 11* after school. It was hosted by an "old guy" (Harry Fender) playing the part of a 19th-century riverboat captain with a studio audience of schoolchildren. Their main feature included a couple of hours of *The Three Stooges* shorts that I watched diligently each afternoon during all those years. All thanks to Ted Koplar, who was considered by the community a really good guy.

Was this 404 here in March 1973 to show off Mark Aero's equipment to the Koplar group, or was it just some sort of group charter? Mark Morris tells me that it's hard to tell—Mark Aero was doing a lot of charters to the lake at that time using all their equipment. Customers certainly included the Koplar family, but also major St. Louis corporations, mayoral entourages, and even Jimmy Hoffa's attorney Morris Shenker (see Chapter 6).

Pegasus DC-6 N90710 on Mark Aero ramp with an Interstate Airmotive Martin 404, summer 1972. The easternmost ex-Navy hangar is in the upper photo—it's one of two of the first buildings erected at Lambert in the early 1920s. The other Navy hanger with "Mark Aero" signage is out of view to the left. This is the only "clear" photo of one of the old ex-Navy hangars that I retained.

CHAPTER 20

Top of the Food Chain

At the very top are the major U.S. airlines we're all familiar with, formerly known as "trunk" or "first-tier" airlines. These were the big guys and this discussion describes the *old* regulatory framework before airline deregulation hit in 1978. The big guys, along with the smaller local service airlines described below were all *scheduled* common carriers and were generally required to fly their scheduled routes as authorized under their certificates of public convenience and necessity, regardless of load factor. Allowable fares and route assignments were set by the federal government, mainly through the CAB. These scheduled carriers were able to solicit the general public (that is, individuals) to use their services through advertising and other marketing means. Today's surviving legacy U.S.-flagged post-deregulation survivors include Delta, United, American, Alaska, and Hawaiian. Because Mark Aero operated mainly in the U.S. environment, we concern ourselves with the U.S.- registered airlines only. All operate under FAR Part 121(a) of the old federal air regulations, which was the most protected subpart of 121. Part 121 had (and has) several subsections and certification levels for airlines under its purview. These have evolved over the years, particularly with airline industry deregulation after 1978. Our discussions here involves pre-deregulation rules that were in place in Mark Aero's era. For simplicity and convenience, we divide Part 121 into three relevant buckets, 121(a), 121(b), and 121(c) which have been alluded to earlier. Each bucket will be more clearly defined and clarified as we move along in our discussions.

The Civil Aeronautics Board (CAB) was created under the Civil Aeronautics Act of 1938 and was the rule-making and enforcement arm of all federal air regulations, including safety, training, air traffic control (ATC), and accident investigation. At this point, we should make it clear that the CAB had jurisdiction over *interstate* traffic, *not intrastate* (operations originating and concluding within a single state's boundaries) the latter of which would be governed by state and local transportation authorities and local governments. As the result of a highly publicized 1956 midair collision over the Grand Canyon involving a TWA Super Constellation and a United DC-7, the Federal Aviation Administration (FAA) was formed in 1958 to take over the air safety, training, and ATC functions from the CAB, who retained control over certification, routes, pricing, and accident investigation. In 1967, the CAB's accident investigation role would be turned over to the newly-formed National Transportation Safety Board (NTSB), which handles these investigations to this day.

There were many other legacy trunk airlines formed in the 1920s and 1930s that have either since died (such as Pan Am, Braniff, and Eastern) or absorbed (such as TWA, Northwest, and Continental) into what ultimately became today's surviving big three—Delta, United and American. Before the Airline Deregulation Act of 1978, airlines operated in a completely different regulatory environment than today.

Fare setting was almost like a guaranteed "cost plus" arrangement where route traffic demand and operating costs were analyzed while adding an average 10% profit margin in the fare structure (which could still vary all over the place based on normal traffic fluctuations). The number of required scheduled flights on that route was calculated and a lucky airline or two would be assigned to exclusively handle all the traffic. Thus, the major airlines had their routes and pricing guaranteed. All other existing airlines and any proposed new entrants were locked out on that route (back then "new entrant" = "almost impossible"). Therefore, most of the competition between the major airlines was greatly reduced or eliminated, allowing airline managements to comfortably focus on managing their routes and their overall business models. Saying that this was a cozy situation between the airlines and the federal and local governments would be an understatement.

Traditionally, the major airlines served the best and most lucrative national and international markets, consisting of the major population centers. These airlines wanted nothing to do with Meridian, Mississippi, Liberal, Kansas, or Marion, Illinois, unless someone else could deliver those passengers to the big population centers they served. The majors with their lobbying power would "bury" anybody threatening their lucrative routes or desired expansion into other big markets.

This leads us to the next layer or second-tier of scheduled airline service that evolved since World War II that was once called the "feeder" airline system and later the "local service" system. These served the smaller communities and were common carriers operating under Part 121(a), just like the majors. They brought their small-town passengers to and from the major population centers mostly to feed traffic to the major airlines but also flew routes *between* small communities that the majors would not touch. The CAB sanctioned these airlines so that unserved communities could have airline service despite unfavorable economics.

From 1945 to 1955, twenty experimental local service airlines were issued *temporary* certificates of "public convenience and necessity" to fly services in the Continental U.S. The certificates were just that—temporary—to be renewed every three years so that the participants could prove their fitness, willingness, and ability to safely and efficiently conduct such operations. Unfortunately, few if any of the small markets they served could make money due to short-legged routes and resultant high cycle frequency. But the federal government thought it important that smaller communities be served, so all local service airlines received mail subsidies from the U.S. Post Office and certain CAB agencies. The most common equipment utilized was second-hand DC-3s (trade-ins from the majors who were moving to better equipment) or the thousands of converted military C-47s which had flooded the market after World War II.

In 1955 President Eisenhower gave the 13 surviving locals permanent 121(a) certificates that would not have to be renewed. Airlines receiving permanent certificates included names such as Ozark, Piedmont, Southern, Allegheny, and Mohawk. But shortly thereafter Eisenhower signed The Federal Aid Highway Act of 1956, creating the Interstate Highway System which over time helped defeat the purpose. The highway system virtually guaranteed the locals would *never* make a profit on most of their routes without subsidies, contrary to the government's growth projections. But the government gradually awarded longer, more profitable routes to the locals so they could reduce subsidy requirements as part of the government's fiscal conservatism during the economic downturn of 1957-58. This prompted small airlines to gradually phase out their used DC-3s in favor of larger, more modern, and comfortable piston Martin and Convairliners. As we moved into the 1960s they began putting turbine equipment such as Fairchild F-27s, F-227s, Convair 580s, and even Douglas DC-9 and Boeing 737 jets into service.

With the jets, most of the locals further expanded their networks and stage lengths, at which time many no longer needed subsidies because of the longer, more profitable routes served.

Several expanded their route systems with minimal restraint after the airlines were deregulated starting in 1978, described in detail later. The "locals" now became the "regionals," abandoning their originally intended small markets, thrusting many communities back into zero airline service status. A few of the regionals such as Ozark became so large it was difficult to tell them apart from the majors, who eventually absorbed most of them.

Part 135 Air Taxi operators of smaller aircraft began to fill in some of this small market void. This can be considered the third level of airline passenger service. These air taxis could not fly large transport category aircraft like the DC-3, so each aircraft operated under 135 had limited passenger or cargo capacity using lighter planes weighing in at below 12,500 pounds maximum gross weight, such as the Beechcraft Super 18 or Cessna 414. Most flew "on demand" or charter services, but some were also "semi-scheduled" operations even though they were *not* common carriers. Despite that, they could "hold themselves out to the public" and advertise their services. Air taxis operated under more lax rules and were truly at the bottom of the airline food chain. Early on they did not receive as much public acceptance because the planes were "little planes with egg beater propellers," and many of the air taxis were undercapitalized and unreliable with a short lifespan. Part 135 flight cancellations were frequent due to all that and considering their equipment was far from being all-weather capable.

While all the original local service airlines are long gone today, this local system evolved over time and still exists in various forms post-1978 deregulation, with the most recognizable manifestation today being the "commuter" airlines operating newer "right-sized" twin turboprops and twinjets, which began "code-sharing" routes with the majors using common branding and ticketing. Now, even the majors such as United, American, and Delta have their own regional operations (they may not always refer to the term "regional") using appropriate equipment such as the smaller "regional jets" which are a step above corporate jets in size.

Briefly jumping forward, after 2001, another, tier of the air taxi industry evolved called the Small Aircraft Transportation System or SATS, resulting from joint research by the FAA and NASA. After 9/11 the resultant Patriot Act, Homeland Security and TSA security, large airports became congested. A solution for this was to develop, under Part 135, a system to help relieve this congestion by diverting some of this traffic away from large airports over to underutilized small general aviation airports using small general aviation aircraft. SATS services began in 2005. SATS flights are limited to aircraft with gross takeoff weights of under 19,000 pounds with nine or fewer passengers.

Going back to when the Airline Deregulation Act was signed in October 1978 by President Jimmy Carter, the longstanding comfortable paradigms were busted and all hell broke loose for the high-cost major and regional operators. The protective rules and regulations of the CAB, including those regarding route assignments and fare pricing, were phased out over the next few years. Free market principles took over—there were no more pricing or route restrictions on any airline. Now the established airlines had to figure out how to compete with non-union upstarts who paid their pilots half the salaries negotiated by the unions. As we will see, it was Mark Morris who helped spearhead that deregulation effort in an uphill battle to convince the airlines and the government to embrace deregulation, eventually making most of the CAB's major functions irrelevant.

So, during this early post-deregulation period, uncertainty ruled and many of the majors and regionals could not accurately forecast their operations under free-market rules. To help deal with this uncertainty, CEO Robert Crandall at American Airlines developed the "hub and spoke" system for *passenger* operations which much of the industry soon followed. However, it was overnight package carrier Federal Express that first implemented this kind of route structure years earlier with their Memphis hub. Crandall also started a phenomenon more famously known as the "frequent flyer' loyalty program which is a key competitive element with the big carriers today. However, none of these long-term solutions stopped the immediate uncertainty in the first years of deregulation.

To make things worse, a multi-year double-dip recession hit starting in 1980 just as 20 new airline entrants began to spring up. Because these were mostly non-union, semi-controllable fixed costs were lower and used airplane prices were low as well, giving then new entrants a very low barrier to entry and cost structure. In his book *Flying too Close to the Sun*, author Sveinn Vidar Gudmundsson refers to this as the *first wave* of new entrants that occurred after the Airline Deregulation Act of 1978, of which over 90% failed within three years. Post-deregulation, only one of the four smaller existing *intrastate* (non-CAB regulated) operators survived with its identity as an *interstate* new entrant, using an innovative customer-centric business model. That is today's Southwest Airlines. The other three, PSA, Air California, and Air Florida have long since merged and lost their identities. None of this *first wave* of pure startups survive today.

The airline business is strange in that it is not a manufacturing industry, but a service industry that is *highly* capital intensive like a manufacturer, with very high fixed and semi-fixed costs (i.e.: interest expense on debt, employee costs, etc.). This makes an airline more like a utility (also a service industry) rather than say, an insurance company which is a more traditional service company that does not require heavy capital outlay per dollar of revenue.

Because people tend to use the same amount of electricity whether rates go up or down (note that utility rates remain highly regulated), pricing for the electric utility industry is said to be "inelastic" under most circumstances, and utilities can operate much more consistently over their fixed cost breakeven point. Airlines, on the other hand, have two distinct kinds of customers: Business travelers and pleasure travelers. Business customers represent the more inelastic component of the airline industry just like the utility, but pleasure (discretionary) travelers represent the elastic component—they are very price sensitive, directly impacting leisure travel volume. This makes managing the economics of airlines, including breakeven over fixed costs, much more difficult than those of the electric utilities.

Because of their outrageous capital intensity (and high labor costs before deregulation), breakeven aircraft load factors are high, averaging around 65-70%. The main variables that determine this, among many others, include route distance, fuel costs, and passenger capacity of the aircraft in question. When the overall economy goes down the tubes, breakeven load factors go up because airlines have to lower fares to try and regain leisure travelers. However, pleasure traveler volume is often not recovered to the extent that prices are dropped, especially with the higher breakeven load factor, causing this unique problem for the airlines.

Airline price sensitivity and therefore demand is more elastic overall than with electric utilities, causing a fluctuating breakeven load factor target. This causes the industry to "go to hell and back" every decade or two with economic downturns and with volatile swings in fuel costs (and these days, pandemics). It is a miracle that anyone in this industry survives for any length of time and history has shown that most cannot. Unlike utilities, there still are other, though less attractive, alternatives for airline customers, such as automobiles and to a much smaller extent trains and buses for the non-business crowd, or old-fashioned teleconferencing or the trendy Zoom for the business market. On the other hand, there are few other practical alternatives for customers of electric utilities when rates go up, and rate decreases do not move the demand needle very much either.

CHAPTER 21

The Cleanup Crew

Another class of airline operation evolved under Part 121. This was called the limited service or the "non-sked" airline, redesignated "supplemental" airline in the early 1960s. These were still common carriers but had authority under what could be called Part 121(b) which restricted them on the routes, operating geography, and frequencies they could fly but they could also have both domestic and international authority. Supplementals were generally "on-demand" carriers for both passengers and cargo and usually not timetable-scheduled like the majors, but some routes were on "semi schedules." Like the majors, supplementals could hold themselves out to the general public and advertise. Normally, a flight under 121(b) would be scheduled by the operator *only* when the plane was booked above the breakeven load factor—something the majors could not do.

This type of airline filled in the gaps or *supplemented* the major scheduled airlines with irregular, or on-demand charter services using similarly large transport aircraft. Like Part 121(a) operators, the 121(b) Supplementals were considered common carriers needing a certificate of public convenience and necessity, but there were severe geographic restrictions on their certificates. Supplementals, while considered common carriers, typically worked with various groups or organizations under contract—either written or verbal, on an on-demand basis. Nothing much came of this level of airline operation until after World War II when suddenly there was a glut of experienced combat pilots looking for civilian work, combined with a glut of low-time surplus aircraft, primarily military C-47 (DC-3) transports, that could be easily converted for commercial work.

As air travel exploded after the war, approximately 140 supplementals popped up in the early postwar years, operating both nationally and internationally, with many of the undercapitalized fly-by-nighters weeded out fairly quickly. The survivors were the true innovators in air travel. They pioneered a wide variety of low-cost, specialized transportation services such as all coach and all cargo flights (the majors later copied this). At first, the supplementals flew mostly passengers, but as time went on they expanded into lucrative cargo operations as icing on the cake. This much later evolved into sweetheart military logistics contracts that eventually became their bread and butter under the "LogAir" moniker. Because of their on-demand nature, the supplemental airlines were more profitable than the scheduled airlines, once averaging 95% load factors compared to a typical average of 65% to 70% for the scheduled airlines. The less innovative scheduled majors were not happy about this and they complained to their partner, the federal government and the CAB, who listened and complied.

As the supplementals matured they discarded their old C-47s and DC-3s to move into second-hand DC-6s and -7s, Constellations and Super Constellations, L-188 Electras, Convairs, and Martinliners. They flew these propliner types well into the jet age, even after many of the majors had fully converted to turbine equipment. Into the late 1960s and 1970s, the supplementals naturally moved into second-hand first-generation DC-8, 707, and 727 jets, with a few of the larger operators phasing in all widebody types such as the 747, DC-10, and L-1011, with some even ordering new jets from the factory. When a passenger was on a supplemental charter, he/she could barely tell the difference between that and flying on a scheduled flight of one of the Part 121(a) majors. Most passenger operations were all coach and the majors reacted by increasing their coach capacities.

Since their inception supplemental airline operations went through two distinct eras—pre-1978 (pre-deregulation) and post-1978 (deregulation). The supplemental players in these two eras were almost mutually exclusive. What we have been describing up to now is the pre-1978 era, characterized by route and fare restrictions. Some of the more common names of this era were Flying Tiger Line, American Flyers Line, Capital International Airways, Evergreen International (formerly Johnson Flying Service), Intermountain, Fleming International, Modern Air Transport, Overseas National, Riddle/Airlift International, Saturn Airways, Seaboard World, Slick Airways, Southern Air Transport, Standard Airways, Trans International Airlines (TIA), Transocean, and World Airways. These supplementals all flew both domestically and internationally. Evergreen, Intermountain, Saturn, and Southern Air Transport flew so much LogAir business (with so much ownership traced to the CIA that they were considered CIA "proprietaries"). A few, such as Transocean, disappeared from the scene early on (Pan Am and the federal government killed Transocean in 1960 when they tried to purchase new Boeing 707 jetliners), and others, such as Evergreen, Southern Air Transport, and Trans International Airlines (under the new name TransAmerica) lasted into the post-1978 era before fading away.

During most of this first era, the supplementals served primarily two types of customer categories: Leisure and the military. Travel agencies and tour operators relied heavily on them. These involved all-inclusive packages covering transportation, hotel, and entertainment, under the tight regulation of the CAB and other federal agencies. As mentioned, route authority for each supplemental was strictly granted by the CAB. Aircraft and crew proficiency regulations under Part 121(b) supplementals were in some ways more complex and stricter than Part 121(a) and many of the highly-scrutinized supplementals had a better reputation for safety as a result. Supplemental fares were 20%-50% lower than the scheduled airlines on the same routes but the level of service seemed to be about the same—which irked the majors.

The military category of services was extremely lucrative as well. LogAir contracts provided considerable additional airlift capacity to the Department of Defense (DoD), Military Air Transport Service (after 1966 the Military Airlift Command), and the CIA. The supplementals were invaluable to all branches of the military during the era of the cold war and the proxy wars including Korea and Vietnam. They toed the line for logistics in those two wars as in both cases the military didn't have the necessary airlift capability to prosecute those wars, even when including all the capacity they used on the major airlines. For more than 30 years these LogAir operations regularly involved flights into the middle world's hotspots, where crews sometimes had to wear helmets and flak suits. Supplementals still do this, but not under LogAir which no longer exists.

During the late 1960s, the Vietnam War resulted in a doubling of Department of Defense (DoD) revenues for the supplementals, where combat zone flying peaked. Some crews cherished the adventure of their jobs and enjoyed the stigma of being characterized as "mavericks." These crews could visit the entire world in a single month, unlike the crews of major airlines who, for the most part, were "eternally stuck" on one route. Other side benefits for these crews included long leisurely layovers in places like Tahiti, Paris, or Monaco.

Crews on supplemental flights had much broader responsibilities compared to those on scheduled flights. Supplementals usually didn't have access to the same ground support services as the majors so pilots, mechanics, and flight attendants had to be multi-taskers similar to most of today's corporate jet flight crews. They often had to perform dispatching, fueling, loading, and unloading and had to arrange for food service themselves. Flight engineers had to also be licensed A&P mechanics so they could sign off on their own maintenance work in the field to make an aircraft operable, or at least legal for the next leg.

Other types of service were provided by smaller supplementals whose 121(b) certificates contained greater restrictions on operating geography. These included "single-entity" charters for organizations like sports teams, rock bands, entertainers, associations, and corporate groups (see Chapter 17 on Interstate Airmotive).

Then there was the Part 121(c) Commercial Operator certificate. Operators under this authority were *not* considered common carriers—nor supplementals—but purely "private" commercial carriers (or "true" contract carriers). They could fly large transport category aircraft commercially but could not hold themselves out to the public or advertise in any way, even in the Yellow Pages. They often required CAB exemptions to make certain trips—a real pain. In the mid-1970s most of the Morris airline operations fell under 121(c). Mark Morris states, *"We would risk being shut down even if we printed our airlines' names on a pencil."* As we saw in Chapters 12 and 16, "affinity" group heavy piston operators such as travel clubs operated mostly under Part 91 in the early days (virtually no regulation) and later fell under Part 123 and a high degree of regulation (like Pegasus), which was enacted in 1968 and stricken in 1983 (explained later). In both cases, they were *not* common carriers but *were* allowed to advertise for cost-sharing groups (club membership) rather than for individual flights and fares. Some of them opted to go to the expense of obtaining a 121(b) certificate, generally ruining the economics of a travel club.

The often-struggling major airlines did not appreciate the resounding successes of the supplementals. They weren't jealous—they just didn't want them to be in business, period, whether in competition with them or not. Over time their ally, the CAB, allowed the majors to expand services to a point where they siphoned off many of the charter services that were the exclusive purview of the supplementals. As the majors grew, the increasingly "Catch 22" nature of regulations leveled on supplementals slowly reversed their growth to a point that by the late 1960s there were only 13 of them remaining. Also, in economic downturns, the federal government would *bail out* any distressed major, but *shut down* any distressed supplemental, despite their often superior safety records. The end of the Vietnam War and the resultant permanent drop-off in DoD LogAir contracts, coupled with a deep recession of 1974-1975 and exploding fuel costs caused the number of supplementals to dwindle to only *six* by 1977.

The onset of deregulation in 1978 was too late to help the six remaining legacy supplementals. Many new competitors started trickling in during the first couple of decades of this post-deregulation era. Why? Barriers to entry fell—no more restrictions on routes or fares. A few of the legacy supplementals vainly attempted to ramp up their fleets and operating scope. World Airways survived as the only *passenger* legacy supplemental, and legacy cargo supplementals such as Evergreen, Rich International, Arrow Air, Southern, and Zantop survived a bit longer in the freight realm as well. However, none of them *thrived* past 1978, especially when in 1992 the Department of Defense dropped *all* LogAir contracts in favor of switching to a combination of major scheduled airlines and trucking companies. This helped cause the few remaining legacy supplementals to gradually fall off the edge of the earth.

Under post-deregulation, three different categories of Part 121 operations evolved. What follows here is necessarily developed in greater detail later, but we need to introduce post-deregulation concepts now. *Today* (that means *not* in the days of Mark Aero) an airline might be approved for one or more of these three categories, depending on meeting differing requirements. These are "domestic," (scheduled passenger or cargo), "flag," (international scheduled or cargo), and "supplemental" (domestic and international charter) operations. In the simplest form, a "domestic" operation is where the departure and destination are both within the United States, either interstate or intrastate. A "flag" operation is between the U.S. and a foreign country or possession, or between two foreign countries, or between the lower 48 states and either Alaska or Hawaii, or between Alaska and Hawaii. A "supplemental" operation is a non-scheduled or *charter* operation between any two points.

These three categories apply to passenger, cargo, and mixed operations. To be clear, it is the *individual flights* that are now so categorized—not necessarily the airline itself—though such airline would first need the overarching *operations specifications* to perform a flight in one or more of these three categories. That means if a carrier with all three *operations specifications* flies a *flag* or a *supplemental* mission without meeting the specific regulatory requirements of those categories on the proposed route(s), those flights would be illegal. So, each flight is legalized, released and operated according to the category of flight.

Today, most major and many mid-sized scheduled airlines can and do meet *operations specifications* for all three categories even though they may not fly in every category at any given time. In essence, this regulatory structure greatly lowers barriers to entry, particularly on the regulatory capital investment sides. A new entrant can now more easily obtain blanket *operations specifications* for all three categories before proving financial viability or taking delivery of aircraft (unlike pre-deregulation). It can then start operating charters right away (helping to cover initial fixed costs) until enough capital is raised (a time-consuming process) to obtain the necessary ticketing and gate infrastructure needed to begin scheduled operations. This will bear itself out in later chapters.

As we mentioned, after deregulation, many *new* supplementals arrived on the scene. Undercapitalized fly-by-nighters also reappeared in droves as they had in the early postwar years, with some of them not lasting a day and most lasting only a few weeks or months. Examples of "non-fly-by-nighters" that operated post-deregulation (many using heavy-recips) included Trans Continental, the "new" Universal, and Kitty Hawk (general cargo and auto parts), Bellamy-Lawson, Trans-Air-Link, and Everts Air (remote area cargo servicing). Others included major jetliner operators like American Trans Air (they started as a travel club to later become a supplemental), Atlas Air, and Kalitta. These are just examples and are by no means an exhaustive list. The new supplementals mentioned here also flew *scheduled* domestic and flag operations. Just because they were formed post-deregulation does not mean life was easy. There are regular failures, with American Trans Air on that list.

The days of the 121(c) Commercial Operator are gone, being supplanted by Part 125 which was enacted in 1981. To a small extent, the Part 91 problem still exists in the pure turbine age, even with the advent of the more restrictive Part 125 for private carriage using larger aircraft. Unlike those operating under the current Part 121, Part 125 operators are still not common carriers, just like under the former Part 121(c). One of the major market niches that keep these smaller operators alive today is the transport of general staples and other cargos to remote populations in the Caribbean, northern Canada, and northern Alaska who lack ground route connections and/or transportation services.

While on relative terms things seem to have "stabilized" for the airline industry, the cycle repeats. And the industry remains anything but stable in the long run, as will always be the case at any point in time.

CHAPTER 22

Jumping Through Hoops

Standard Airways, Inc. had operated as a domestic and international supplemental air carrier of passengers and cargo since 1945 under various CAB regulations and in the end held a Part 121(b) Supplemental certificate to operate specific routes from within the U.S. to the Caribbean, Mexico, and Canada. In September 1969, Standard filed a petition under Chapter 10 bankruptcy. A judge then suspended Standard's authority in July 1970. As will be recalled, in the previous chapter we mention Standard as one of the major legacy supplementals.

Since the bankruptcy judge was first appointed in 1969, nine entities had submitted proposals to purchase Standard for all or part of its authority. Many tried more than once, but all such attempts had since been aborted. The only asset any of these suiters wanted was the 121(b) certificate which was easier to "piggyback transfer" than to build from scratch. Mark Aero had a 121(c) Commercial Operator certificate to fly transport category aircraft but wanted 121(b) supplemental authority which would allow it to advertise and greatly expand its airline operations. This fully explains why in early 1973 I first spotted the four "brand new" ex-Piedmont Martin 404s parked on the Mark Aero ramp.

Mark Aero presented a modest proposal to the CAB for the rehabilitation of Standard starting with the sale of small charters using their fleet of heavy-recips. According to Joe Morris, such charter groups were not currently being served on Standard's former operating routes by the certificated carriers. It was perceived that demand was not being satisfied under the "convenience" part of the "public convenience and necessity' benchmark because of the small sizes of the chartering groups and the remote locations of many of their origins and/or destinations. Many of the prospects Mark Aero proposed to serve had 65 mph intercity buses and automobiles as their only choices. Under the certificate, Standard's rates were competitive between many point pairs with regular schedule fares and even scheduled airline incentive fares, which were of severely limited availability. Moreover, under Mark Aero, Standard would propose services not provided for some of these markets, such as keeping aircraft *with* the charter groups throughout an entire multi-destination tour. That would be economical because operational breakeven would already be at very low load factors, meaning service could be provided to multiple remote points without the need to arrange expensive repositioning and empty backhaul flights with the same or different aircraft.

Toward that end, Joe Morris/Mark Aero attempted to acquire Standard in 1972 for its certificate only. While Mark Aero's proposal represented the last best hope for Standard's creditors who had been left hanging over the previous 3 years. Unfortunately, Standard's certificate was revoked and Joe Morris's acquisition was denied in August 1973 by the same hostile administrative law judge who had earlier suspended the certificate in 1970. Luckily, Mark Aero had acquired a stopgap contract under its 121(c) authority to keep their Martinliners (and employees) busy for at least 5 months out of the year. We cover this in Chapter 25.

Joe Morris proposed to transfer a DC-6 and five Martin 404s—a mix of both the more active ex-Interstate 404s and the "newer" ex-Piedmont aircraft—over to Standard upon approval of the acquisition. This would be his best option to keep these assets utilized more consistently on numerous routes not currently authorized for Mark Aero, as its certificate would avoid the costly need for Mark Aero to file for endless CAB exemptions to make trips. It was contemplated that Mark Aero would have an 84% stake in Standard and would manage it, and Charlotte Aircraft Corp. would be a passive minority investor with the remaining 16%. Charlotte's consideration would be an assignment of its $180,000 claim against Standard to Mark Aero and Mark Aero would also be the guarantor of Standard's $300,000 note to the trustee-in-bankruptcy.

Under Mark Aero, the new Standard Airways would obviously seek restoration of its authority to Canada, Mexico, and the Caribbean. Operations would be headquartered at its St. Louis base and later satellite hubs would be established in Houston, Texas, and on the West Coast. In the first year of operation, which was contemplated to start on January 1, 1974—and each year thereafter—$60,000 or 40% of Standard's profits, whichever was greater would be paid on the $300,000 debt to the trustee-in-bankruptcy, until paid in full.

Mark Aero claimed that with its existing and available contracts, Standard's first year of operating profits would be $500,000 on revenues of $2.7 million. Domestic passenger services would account for 42% of the business, domestic and international cargo operations, 28%; passenger operations from the U.S. to the Caribbean and Mexico, 15%; and U.S. to Canada passenger operations, 15%. "Single-entity" charters would be the primary type of trip. One of Mark Aero's contracts to be transferred to Standard was a new "semi-scheduled" weekly Martin 404 round trip charter between the U.S. and Mexico that was to begin in May 1973. Residual ex-Interstate Airmotive charter contracts that were being flown under Mark Aero's restrictive supplemental Part 121(b) certificate could also be rolled into Standard and possibly expanded.

In support of all this analysis, it became clear to both Mark Aero and the federal regulators that a market existed for small, 40-80 seat propliner charters of all types throughout the various areas of Standard's present authority and much of this was untapped. Joe Morris maintained that had a staff that was ready, willing, able, and fully experienced to run such piston aircraft operations, and that proposed operations were soundly based and adequately financed assuring that Standard would at least come into compliance with all applicable regulations after approval. The creditors of the former Standard had good reason to approve the acquisition, which would provide them with far greater recovery potential and even upside prospects after that. But in the end, the court's answer was still "no." Case closed.

In December of 1973, Mark Aero filed a motion to reopen the Standard case. But the regulators and judges continued to drag their feet, inappropriately maintaining that *jet* equipment should be used on those routes and that Mark Aero was not equipped to run a jet airline. One might ask *since when* was a technical decision on equipment type part of this court's purview in this case? This stupid argument was presented even though there remained several Part 121(b) charter and 121(a) scheduled airlines then economically employing significant fleets of "old fashioned" propliner equipment, including passenger 404s—particularly in the southeast.

They did not consider that a large scheduled regional airline, Southern Airways, a 121(a) operator, was still profitably running up to 15 "obsolete" piston Martin 404s on dozens of its shorter runs in the southeast, and ironically, it was common knowledge that their passengers *liked* and even *preferred* them. Then out of nowhere, the CAB made an arbitrary ruling that all supplemental certificates which were dormant for over 3 years would be permanently canceled and could not be "piggybacked" to another airline. "End of conversation," as they say, just in time for Christmas. The scheduled Martinliner round trips to Mexico did not materialize either.

CHAPTER 23

More Bad Stuff, More Revelations

On July 23, 1973, Ozark Airlines has its only fatal crash, almost in my "back yard." It proves to be the worst aviation disaster in St. Louis history. On the clear evening of the day before—just before sunset—I'm with my high school church group at our west county outside retreat at Sunday evening "vespers" services singing contemporary "Jesus songs." As we sing a contemporary hymn containing the refrain "*I wish we'd all been ready*," I look to the east and see an Ozark Airlines Fairchild F-227B twin turboprop (the type of aircraft for which Ozark traded its Martin 404 fleet 6 years earlier) climbing out in the distance heading southeast—like toward Nashville. The F-227B is powered by two Rolls-Royce Dart turboprops of 2,300 shaft horsepower each.

Early the next evening, Flight 809, also an F-227B is on final approach at Lambert-St. Louis International on its scheduled flight from Marion, Illinois, after originating from Nashville. The F-227B In the final flight segment, it flies into zero-visibility and then a torrential thunderstorm cell hits severe turbulence and then encounters a microburst as it transitions to a short final for runway 30L at Lambert. It slams into a wooded area just west of the University of Missouri (UMSL) St. Louis campus. Thirty-eight out of the 44 occupants perish. Reportedly a passenger who happened to be a dog survived, but the onboard dog may have been just a rumor. At the time of the crash, my brother Jeff and my dad are at my cousin's motorcycle shop on nearby St. Charles Rock Road. During the relentless downpours, they hear what seems to be hundreds of sirens from all points of the compass around them, near and far. "*Man,*" Jeff thinks, "*something super bad must have just happened.*" Within an hour we all know why.

A makeshift morgue is set up at County Hospital in Clayton. That creeps me out as big crashes like this only happen in other cities, not here. In the past I had visited sick relatives at this hospital and now it's a gory collection place for pieces of freshly-dead people. People who had seen my vespers sunset the evening before and got up this morning and put their shoes on, just like me—but they just couldn't quite make it to dinner tonight. Coincidentally, Eddie Rickenbacker, the legendary World War I ace and first helmsman of Eastern Airlines, also dies earlier today—at least he gets to die of regular old age and in one piece.

In the coming weeks I would see the wreckage of this F-227B, just haphazardly piled onto the apron at Young Aviation in the southeast quadrant of Lambert, in full view of all who drive by it along I-70. Why didn't they just hide this sickening junk pile somewhere else? It doesn't remain there for long. I always wonder if the F227 I saw flying outbound the evening before at the vespers service was the same plane.

On a more pleasant note, a month later my girlfriend Patty and I are attending a festival at Creve Coeur Lake Park, which is hugged by a curve in the Missouri River around 6 miles southwest of Lambert. I randomly glance at the sky over the lake to the southwest. I immediately lock on to the head-on profile of a lone four-engine craft, a DC-6, in the distance with landing lights glaring, in a 3-degree descent profile, and heading right toward us. It makes several small banking corrections as it roars overhead at the low-power approach setting. It's Pegasus again, on

An Ozark Airlines Fairchild F-227B similar to the one that crashed on approach to Lambert on July 23, 1973, killing 38 on board. It was powered by two 2,300 shaft horsepower Rolls-Royce Dart turboprops. (Wikimedia Commons, RuthAS CC BY 3.0)

its final approach to Runway 6 at Lambert, probably just off the Maryland Heights VOR final approach fix. I never find out the nature of this particular Pegasus operation and never again see another Pegasus Club aircraft either on the ground or in the air.

It's fall 1973 and I am enduring my first college semester at DePauw University in Greencastle, Indiana. Directly overhead is northeast-southwest Victor Airway 14-15, one of the legs between Indianapolis and St. Louis. I am awakened some nights by the sounds of R-3350s and R-2800s passing overhead at medium altitude. These are mostly DC-6s, DC-7s, and, on at least one occasion, a Super Constellation. I also hear a few C-46s as well as Convairliners. As you can guess, by now I know the subtle sound variances between the various heavy-recip aircraft. I hear—but it's late at night and I never see. These are all likely cargo aircraft running just-in-time auto parts from Detroit and Indianapolis to auto factories in St. Louis or Kansas City.

During Thanksgiving 1973 I am home for the long weekend and mom asks me to pick up dad at Lambert after one of his business trips. She knows she can assign me to an airport job without any guff from me. I'm a bit early so I go to the airport restaurant for a soda while I am waiting for dad's arrival. The lounge has a panoramic view of all runways and taxiways, and it is a nice clear late fall evening with a slight haze, perhaps only an hour before sunset. The wind is from the west and I notice a Martin 404 holding short at midfield for runway 30R, the parallel runway furthest from the main terminal. It is not a blue-trimmed Interstate 404 like I'd seen last March at the lake, instead, it's all white with mustard yellow and red trim along the windows that blend to look orange. There are the letters "MA" on the vertical tail, surrounded by a circle that has a break on the right side. It taxis into position and I immediately observe the propellers speed up at full power, and the 404 lifts off, the singing R-2800s subtly vibrating the panoramic airport lounge windows. That's that, it's gone I surmise until minutes later when I look to the east I see it on final approach to the same runway it took off from. It lands, back taxis to its original midfield position, and takes off again. It turns out I know this plane—it just recently "changed clothes" with a different paint job. But at this point, my personal Martin 404 airshow is over as I need to get over to the gate to get my dad.

What I witness is one of two (out of three) former Interstate Airmotive Martins, either N465M or N473M. These were the ones they acquired in 1970, and I am not yet aware they are now seasonally active d/b/a Mark Aero between summer shuttle seasons between Minneapolis

Ex-Interstate Martin N473M, probably at Minneapolis, which started flying under Mark Aero's certificate circa 1973-74. The painted trim was changed to mustard yellow and red by mid-1973 (my mind was fooled to make it appear "orange") and I caught this plane (or identically painted N465M) doing takeoffs and landings at Lambert in November 1973. Years later I find this St. Louis sighting was probably a month after Mark Aero's first summer flying seasons for sportsmen between Minneapolis and Reindeer Lake Saskatchewan, as conducted by Mark Aero under Part 121(c). (Jerry Riebold)

and a posh fishing resort deep in the arctic Canadian wilderness. The planes spend their off-season in St. Louis for annual maintenance and are used for other charter work. That explains what I saw. It was either a currency or training flight or a maintenance check operation. Let's see, this new tail logo "MA surrounded by a broken circle" could mean "Mark Aero." The broken circle, however, could also be interpreted as a "C." So, does this logo stand for "Mark Aero" or something like, for instance, "MAC?" Maybe either or *both*. Yes, it's both. A new iteration of Mark Aero's Part 121 supplemental airlines is in the making and Mark Morris's wife and graphics designer Susan designed the dual-purpose tail logo. I learned decades later that at this time, Joe and Mark were attempting to start a shuttle service between St. Louis and Kansas City using the three ex-Interstate Martinliners—Missouri Commuter Airlines (MAC) as we will cover. But in the meantime, the Martins were flying on the Mark Aero (MA) Part 121(c) Commercial Operator certificate to utilize the airplanes.

Fast forward three weeks. It's only one week before I leave DePauw for Christmas break. I don't tell dad I transferred myself to the University of Missouri—Columbia (Mizzou). DePauw is a liberal arts school and Mizzou has a real business curriculum, plus 24,000 more possibilities for friendships than DePauw has, and a boatload of my high school friends are there. Also, Patty

This is the tail of N473M still in "original owner" Interstate Airmotive of navy blue and aqua blue that I spotted *for the last time* in March 1973 at the Lee C. Fine Airport that serves the Lake of the Ozarks. It would be re-painted in new colors sometime between March and November of that year.

This is the *same tail* in colors I first spotted 8 months later in November 1973 while it was doing takeoffs and landings at Lambert, with an "MA" or "MAC" logo (depending on which airline the plane would ultimately be flying for). Window "cheat line" trim is mustard yellow and red which blends to look "orange." This new paint job would be retained on the 404s and a fleet of DC-6s with a major offspring airline founded by Mark Morris in about three years. This new livery was designed by Mark's wife Susan. (Jerry Riebold)

would now be only 20 motorcycle miles away because she was attending William Woods College in nearby Fulton. Of course, I have to tell dad at some point, so I rationalize that I'm saving him a bundle of money, but he thinks I am making this move to be "cozy" with Patty. That was a consideration—but only part of the reason. Anyway, there are 10,000 more coed opportunities at Mizzou than at DePauw and I break up with Patty within months after transferring, so dad's theory didn't quite materialize.

However, getting back to my last days at DePauw before Christmas break, I rely on my day-late issues of *The St. Louis Globe-Democrat* subscription my parents got me so I can keep up with what is going on at home. I see a large display ad in one issue for *Pegasus Club*. It is for an upcoming open house—and this is the only Pegasus advertisement I had ever seen. It boasts its two DC-6s that would be available for open house tours, plus their "new" four-engine Boeing 720 Intercontinental jet that would be the feature display at the upcoming member recruiting event. The ad had a photo of the 720 only—not the DC-6s. It touted some of the trips that members had been on in previous years, including the ones to New Orleans and Atlanta ones that flew over me earlier that year. The ad made it look like those past trips were on the 720 jetliner only.

At the time I see this Pegasus ad I don't know that the novel air travel club industry is in the midst of a rapidly tightening *death spiral*. The CAB had just won a lawsuit against the largest air travel club in the U.S., Voyager 1000 out of Indianapolis. At the time, Voyager 1000's fleet consisted of two Lockheed L-188 Electras, two Douglas DC-7s, two Martin 404s as well as a Boeing 720 Intercontinental jet (just like Pegasus).

Voyager 1000 was one of the first air travel clubs to appear in the mid-1960s and the most successful one. They began operating under Part 91 but became a Part 123 operator (like Pegasus) immediately upon its enactment in 1968. However, by the early 1970s the CAB didn't like Voyager 1000 or any travel club anymore. That's probably because the major airlines finally made it clear they didn't like air travel clubs, period.

Voyager 1000 was a bright "on the radar screen" target because it was the *biggest*—the juggernaut of air travel clubs. They did mass-market advertising to the public to solicit members. They also published trips, flight times, and ticket prices that probably reached more non-members than members. They advertised in Time Magazine and Travel Weekly and ran high-frequency regional newspaper ads and TV commercials in respectable metropolitan markets such as Indianapolis, Cincinnati, Terre Haute, and Evansville. They reached major college markets like Purdue, DePauw, Ball State, and Indiana University. There were feature articles in all kinds of high-circulation magazines. Voyager 1000 gave open houses with aircraft tours in those metropolitan areas so that the public could "*see and hear the Voyager 1000 story.*" For a mere $100 initiation fee for a family membership (less for the individual) and a $25 per year membership renewal, you were "in." By 1971, this air travel club had 14,500 single and family memberships, allowing 43,000 people to fly on their trips. Its flights were almost always filled to capacity—something the major airlines did not appreciate. In essence, the CAB charged that Voyager was actually "*holding itself out*" and "*operating illegally as a common carrier*" without any such authority. Voyager 1000 advertised upcoming trips—a gray area for sure.

Voyager 1000 managers maintained they were merely a large social club that happened to fly large airplanes on private flights as one aspect in carrying out its many socialite-oriented programs—and not a common carrier airline. They had all types of social gatherings that did not involve airplanes and members shared a close bond. The CAB did not buy this. They maintained that all the gatherings were travel-themed promotions to the *general public* based upon planned, upcoming vacation trips using airplanes.

The CAB won the case and forced Voyager 1000 to "cease and desist" in March 1973. Voyager 1000 lost its court appeal that November and remained shut down for good. A final attempt to restart operations under a more CAB-compatible business model fell on deaf ears and that was it. There were subsequent attempts to modify Part 123 to clarify the vague advertising rules for travel clubs, allowing advertising for members but not to the general public for trips, flight schedules, or flight details. Again, deaf ears. From then on, with this precedent, the FAA and CAB began stepping up their harassment of Pegasus and the other travel clubs and the clubs began to drop like flies, just as the major airlines (and their travel agencies) hoped. The CAB and FAA were always ready and willing to do their dirty work.

Pegasus lasted into 1974, but the fuel shortages and the deep recession later that year is likely what finished them. Pegasus' two DC-6s were sold during 1975 (the 720 jet probably earlier) and FAR Part 123 was finally rescinded for good on January 1, 1983, long after the travel clubs faded away. Despite this weird government crackdown, there are no known serious crashes, injuries, or deaths resulting from Part 123 or Part 91 travel club operations—which probably just a matter of the industry's small scale more than anything else. The saga of the air travel clubs is a clear example of a single oligopoly defeating the essence of capitalism and free enterprise to preserve its interests. The two Pegasus DC-6s, including the one I first saw at Spirit Airport in August 1969 that started it all for me, were cannibalized and scrapped only months after they were sold.

There is something else that captures my attention besides the Pegasus ad while reading that same *Globe-Democrat* issue at DePauw. Its front-page headline calls attention to the crash of a Lockheed L-1049H Super Constellation freighter just east of Miami International Airport, killing three crewmen and six on the ground. At the northwest "Corrosion Corner" ramp area of the airport the Constellation had been packed to the roof with Canadian Christmas tree bundles (but not over-grossed by weight) bound for Caracas, Venezuela, but the ensuing investigation showed that the heavier bundles were inadvertently placed *aft*. There was a long delay caused by minor mechanical and other problems, so the flammable trees had to be watered down with a hose inside the *hot* cargo hold during the wait. An invisible pool of water had developed under the trees. It was surmised that upon takeoff rotation, the water immediately flowed to the rear and the trees slipped back with the flow causing a fatal aft center of gravity condition—there were no cargo restraints and none were required under the governing FAA rules governing this particular flight which, as you probably guessed, was to be flown under Part 91.

On takeoff roll, the plane rotated prematurely up to a horrific 30-degree pitch according to witnesses and the engine power could not sustain the near stall condition. The plane never climbed over about 120 feet as it arced over the eastern perimeter of the airport at full power trying to hang on its props, then slammed in a fireball into a residential area. The National Transportation Safety Board (NTSB) found some toxicology problems with the pilot (carbon monoxide from chain smoking and overexposure to aircraft ramp exhaust) and flight engineer (blood alcohol). The first officer had never flown in a Super Constellation under newer (stricter) rules in place governing second-in-command qualifications. These were contributing factors, but not the major ones according to the NTSB. The big factor was improper aft loading (by weight), aggravated by the pool of water that collected in the rear of the plane. There were minor mechanical infractions that were discovered, but surprisingly all four engines were found to be mechanically sound.

The fatalities were instantaneous and the plane and several houses and vehicles were vaporized. Yes, it was one of those Part 91 operations where an account of the loading distribution was *not required* and there was that normal squabble over "who the operator was"—the freight forwarder or the owner, Aircraft Pool Leasing. Aircraft Pool conceded to be "operator" just this one time. While the NTSB said this squabble was not a factor, that silly argument seems to find its way into all Part 91 heavy-recip accidents—past, present, and future. But once again, a trainwreck of adverse circumstances all at once allowed the *Tiger* to break loose from its *Leash* and rip its masters to shreds. If it's not a thermobaric explosion, it's a "rushing pool of water and sliding Christmas trees." What else can go wrong?

While reading this article on the Super Constellation crash I recall another crash six months earlier in June. A Skyways International Douglas DC-7C freighter operating under Part 91 was on a westbound climbout from the same airport, Miami International --the opposite direction from the Christmas Tree Constellation takeoff—and then slammed into, and was swallowed by, the Everglades. It was caused by a combination of an engine fire, radio receiver failure, and resultant inability to receive ATC vectors around one of the worst "Level 5" thunderstorms ever recorded in the area—all at once in a nice neat little package, almost complete with a bow. Most of the wreckage was forever entombed in the muck of the Everglades and only a few "water craters" could be seen in the swamp foliage from the air. I know—the *Tiger on a Leash* again. All three crewmembers perished and only a small fraction of the wreckage was recovered. Yes, that's what else could go wrong—is that all? Let's see, is there anything else?

Let's look at three well-documented accounts described in a great book by Brett Lane, *A Cargo Pilot's Life: Tales from Corrosion Corner*, which I highly recommended. How about an old cargo DC-6 that is loaded with 4,000 pounds more freight than the allowable 26,000 pounds for this worn-out crock? Suppose it is taking off from Guatemala City airport with a field elevation of almost a mile high, meaning it's surrounded by "thin" air, and one engine backfires only once on rotation but the improperly-armed auto-feather feature automatically feathers that prop at the worst possible time. Assume the overloaded 105,000-pound plane stalls at the far edge of the plateau and crashes into the middle of Guatemala City just below, killing all three crew and around 25 other innocents on the ground. Well, that did happen, what could go wrong?

These old DC-6s with their slightly weakened multiple-overhauled R-2800s were cleared for a 26,000-pound payload at that high field elevation, but some operators wanted to advertise loads of *"30,000 pounds out of Guatemala City."* Crews either complied or lost their jobs. The "legal loophole" to achieve this was to arm the "auto-feather" feature on takeoff which would allow for the 4,000 extra pounds of payload according to the original DC-6 manuals. But things weren't "original" anymore with DC-6s. Auto-feather was designed to automatically feather a propeller at the first sign of a backfire, relieving the crew of the distraction of doing this manually in what is otherwise an emergency. This was fine in the 1950s when the engines were fresh and new and rarely backfired on takeoff with their *moderate* passenger loads of say 18,000 pounds with baggage. If a rare backfire occurred on this typical takeoff—especially in "normal density" air nearer to sea level—the plane could become comfortably airborne on *three engines* after the armed auto-feather feathered the propeller.

Widely-spaced backfires on takeoff happened more frequently with old, worn-out engines found on old DC-6 freighters, but left alone chances are they too would clear out before rotation allowing a normal takeoff. Therefore, in modern *freight* operations, during the *Second Wind,* it was considered best that the auto-feather be *disengaged* during takeoff, requiring a slightly reduced freight load in a really old plane—preventing the unintended automatic incapacitation of the offending engine.

Contrary to this, *arming* the auto-feather in an old freighter "allowed" the operators to boast a 30,000-pound payload out of Guatemala City, instead of the slightly reduced 26,000 pounds.

The backfire sequence at Guatemala City would have likely cleared *without* auto-feather and the overloaded plane might have been happily on its way. Instead, the autofeather shut down the offending engine, and three of them at full power could not get a 30,000 payload into the air. Even better—don't overload your plane at high-density-altitude Guatemala City under any circumstances.

Anything else? Lane describes how an old overloaded DC-6 freighter flight from El Salvador to New Orleans runs out of gas a couple of hundred miles short of the destination, but "safely" pancakes into a lowland area only to hit a solid levee, killing all three crewmen sitting up front, including one of his best friends. Old DC-6 fuel gauges were notoriously inaccurate at best and inoperative at worst—and that was expensive to fix and "keep fixed," so many freight operators didn't. So, the standard procedure was to open all the over-wing fuel caps and manually "stick" the tanks with a simple measuring stick as part of any preflight check to verify the fuel level before departure—*reliable* panel gauges *or not*. The pilot in this levee crash, who often bragged about his superior fuel management skills, did not have the tanks manually checked this time and it just so happened that the fuel truck put in 17% less fuel than the flight plan required—with not-so-great results.

How about this one. Lane once again describes one of those big piston Boeing C-97s (former KC-97 tankers) operating commercial freight out of Miami was loaded to the gills with horses in Mexico City, which is located 7,000 feet above sea level—resulting in even "thinner" air than at the Guatemala City airport. Avgas is substantially cheaper in Mexico City than in Miami, so the pilot decides to play "corporate hero" and fill the C-97's tanks to capacity with cheaper gas, greatly overloading it. Just after takeoff, the landing gear refuses to retract, causing a tremendous drag on this otherwise heavy and drag-prone airplane that is struggling to climb. Climb it cannot, so it careens into a *heavily populated* area bursting into flames, resulting in heavy human (and horse) carnage all over the crash site. The "corporate brown-noser" crew is miraculously able to walk away.

OK, you get the picture, there are a million and one sets of random or negligent circumstances that can unleash the heavy-recip *Tiger*. Badly stressed engines that should be replaced. Sliding Christmas trees. A Level 5 thunderstorm, a flaming engine, and a failed radio all at once. Too *much* fuel. Too *little* fuel. Simply arming auto-feather when you *should not*. Where does it all end?

The Miami Super Constellation Christmas tree crash happened on December 15, 1973, just before midnight. My overriding question is: *Don't most people already have their Christmas trees set up at home by this date? Why do the Venezuelans need a "Super Constellation load" of trees just 10 days before Christmas—that will still take a few more days to get to the end-user— at a time when most tree lots are throwing their scraggly inventory remnants into the wood chipper?* These kinds of strange, inconsistent, and unexplainable event sequences always seemed to surface at Corrosion Corner and almost everywhere else these old heavy-recips operated.

CHAPTER 24

Works on Paper

Starting in late 1972, Joe had another iron in the fire to hedge his bet on Standard at Mark's suggestion. They had to keep those irons hot. Joe's extensive business contacts led him to an underserved *intrastate* commuter market opportunity between St. Louis and Kansas City. Mark Aero startup affiliate Missouri Air Commuter (MAC) had acquired its authority from the FAA to operate a scheduled common carrier *intrastate* Martin 404 service under a FAR Part 121.7 Intrastate Commuter Airline certificate which was a simpler proposition as the CAB is not involved. The proposed airline's operating boundaries would be strictly within the State of Missouri. Operating approvals would be made by the state and local authorities and the FAA—and the CAB would have no say whatsoever.

However, that meant that in the air, you could not even have a wing tip penetrate the boundary of another state for even one second, so Kansas would be *the* state that would make MAC vulnerable to an accidental incursion. This is because the endpoint airport to be utilized by MAC was to be the Kansas City Municipal Airport (MKC), later known as the Charles B. Wheeler Downtown Airport—Kansas City, also called the Kansas City Downtown Airport. Until 1972 this was Kansas City's main airport, which was right on the Kansas border at the Missouri River. In addition to not requiring the entanglement of CAB approval, MAC would be able to *advertise*. So, a proposed scheduled shuttle between this major city pair *within* Missouri seemed to be an obvious "end-run" for a second attempt at a domestic scheduled airline.

However, two other stakeholders, both *interstate* airlines under CAB jurisdiction, were providing scheduled nonstop service on this route. These were TWA with its older generation short DC-9-10s and Frontier Airlines, with its Convair 580 turboprop twins (which was slightly larger and definitely faster than the Martin 404). Ozark Airlines was not as much of a factor at that time as it was puddle jumping several stops across the state between those two points—but they would put their two cents in. Joe and Mark concluded that entry into this market would not siphon passengers from any of these airlines, but would mostly compete with bus lines, passenger rail, and automobiles, which was the same argument they used for Standard. In making his preliminary preparations for regulatory approval, they proposed using five Martin 404s and possibly later a DC-6, which all could be easily brought up to requirements. Mark Morris would run the airline.

Joe's main argument centered around the building of Kansas City's massive new major airport 25 miles northwest of downtown Kansas City, Kansas City International (KCI) which was completed in 1972 using land that TWA previously bought up and sold to the city. This replaced the easy-access Kansas City Downtown Airport (MKC) located *immediately north* of that same downtown just across the winding Missouri River. The other factor was Mark Aero's International Terminal (Lambert's Old Terminal) was right off Lindbergh Boulevard, which was an *easily accessible* north-south artery in St. Louis County. The International Terminal had an adjacent open parking lot just to the west. Walk in, walk out just like at a shopping center. There were none of the logistical inconveniences that characterized Lambert's larger main terminal on the south side and its complicated multi-level parking lot that took time, effort, and money to get in and out.

Using these two easy-access endpoints would save commuter passengers several transit hours compared to using the main terminals of Lambert and KCI, which TWA and Frontier had to use. There was a lot of same-day round trip business traffic between this city pair, and with Joe Morris's new airline using the old MKC near downtown, a business person could have breakfast at home in St. Louis, get to a 10:30 AM business meeting in Kansas City and be back in St. Louis in time for dinner. Not so with TWA or Frontier using the new KCI. Get up at 5:00 AM, snarf down a quick breakfast before the family gets up and get home by 11:30 PM or later.

Joe and Mark identified other compelling economic considerations that favored a new commuter shuttle service. First of all, driving an automobile point-to-point between St. Louis and Kansas City on I-70 took about 4 hours. Flying TWA or Frontier, including processing the passenger at either of the main terminals at St. Louis and Kansas City plus a 45-minute (or more) total ground commute time would take about 3 hours, or just one hour less than driving, at a much greater expense. Doing the same trip with MAC Martin 404 service between Mark Aero's International Terminal and Kansas City Municipal downtown would take 1 to 1 ½ hours, at only a slightly greater expense than driving the 4 hours.

There was also that world energy crisis in progress which was getting more severe by the day. The Arabs embargoed petroleum shipments to the U.S. in retaliation for its support of Israel in the October 1973 war with Syria and Egypt. Fuel prices were going through the roof and there were long lines of automobiles at the gas station. Interstate highway speed limits were reduced to 55 miles per hour from the customary 70 to conserve national fuel supplies. This energy crisis caused the curtailment of TWA and Frontier flights between St. Louis and Kansas City due to falling demand and tight fuel allocations, while Greyhound bus traffic between St. Louis and KC had increased proportionately. This meant the market served by these two airlines was underserved. In addition, the capacity-limited air taxi/commuter services were *expanding* as the Federal regulators allocated these carriers all the aviation fuel they needed, at the expense of trunk carriers. Why? Because lighter aircraft used a fraction of the fuel and stage lengths were shorter. MAC would fall into this category because it would not be a Part 121(a) operator, and on top of that the Martin 404 burned much less fuel than a DC-9 or a Convair 580. Also, MAC would carry point-to-point commuter traffic, not the "through traffic" that TWA and Frontier usually carried. It looked like MAC was in the right place at the right time.

Joe and Mark would successfully work through MAC's regulatory loose ends over the next two years, but this badly drained their family resources. They and their team successfully jumped through all the hoops thrown at them. First, they successfully established that their proposal was a matter of "public convenience and necessity." Then, it was able to prove to the FAA and the Missouri Utilities Board that MAC was ready, willing, and able to operate a scheduled Part 121.7 Intrastate Commuter Airline serving these two large metro areas and had met other standard Part 121 financial requirements, resulting in the awarding of its certificate. It had five Martinliners and a DC-6 that were either certified or could be certified to the required standard very quickly. Also available were 30 trained and certified personnel who were currently underutilized and waiting to get going, from pilots to flight attendants, to airframe and powerplant mechanics, to ground crew. And, of course, there would also be no problem obtaining fuel in the wake of the energy crisis, as a commuter airline would not be subject to fuel allocation.

An exception was also obtained to allow MAC to operate as a commercial airline at the recently abandoned MKC, which was now serving only general aviation. A potential hurdle was, starting with the 1972 opening of KCI, a 20-year prohibition of scheduled airline operations out of this old downtown airport that the affected airlines (mostly the majors) *signed on to*—but MAC was not a party to that agreement. The 20-year rule was a necessary covenant to induce investment banking firm E.F. Hutton to float the $400 million bond issue to build KCI. In addition, the required security plans for both the St. Louis International Terminal and Kansas City Municipal gates were paid for by Mark Aero which the FAA helped develop and then pre-approved (involving mainly a high-security fence around the airport perimeter). The MAC plans even exceeded the security standards than found at many major airports which were often given a "pass" on falling short of full compliance.

A Martin 404 sits on the very spot where the contemplated Missouri Air Commuter (MAC) orange-liveried 404s would board and deplane passengers at the old Kansas City Downtown Airport.

Mark and Joe also did numerous flight demonstrations with the Martinliners at MKC to prove they could operate them near the Kansas border without breaching that border. MAC would be flying between two federally funded airports and asserted that meeting all these requirements gave it the right to operate at and between these two airports. Also, MAC would not require government subsidies for the proposed operations, and not a penny of MAC's costs would be borne by the respective city governments. While Mark Aero had invested $400,000 in startup costs for both MAC and the stillborn acquisition of Standard, things were at least looking up for MAC.

CHAPTER 25

Canadian Wilderness and Heating Oil

At first, it seemed the four ex-Piedmont Aircraft now parked at Mark Aero came from a major aircraft broker Charlotte Air Services in North Carolina. Many of Piedmont's discarded 404s came through there after being retired in 1969, and Joe Morris had developed a good relationship with the Buckley and Cardwell families who owned and ran it. However, all four of the Mark Aero arrivals appeared to have come from other sources, one of them possibly directly from Piedmont. It seems these four aircraft were acquired as a hedge of sorts for any combination of things to come, either as spares support or to remain in one piece for potential service.

It appears Joe Morris was working on Standard and Missouri Air Commuter around the time the ex-Piedmont aircraft arrived, but an immediate "filler" opportunity presented itself as Joe fought with regulators on these longer-term ventures. This quasi-scheduled opportunity could be fulfilled under Mark Aero's Part 121 (c) Commercial Operator authority. In early 1973 Northwest Orient Airlines had secured a contract to provide a passenger shuttle service between Minneapolis and a posh sport fisherman's resort known as the Reindeer Lodge at Reindeer Lake, Saskatchewan, way up in the Yukon just west of Hudson Bay. This resort was and remains a highly popular summer destination for affluent sportsmen. The problem was that the destination runway was unpaved with loose gravel and too short. The smallest plane in Northwest's jet fleet, the Douglas DC-9 twin jet, could not land there.

Mark Aero just happened to have underutilized equipment that could land there so Northwest assigned them the contract to provide this charter service with all its Martinliners and employ the flight attendants and mechanics who were now badly underutilized with the shutdown of Interstate. This charter Canadian shuttle was highly seasonal, from June through October only, but would entail a fairly tight weekly shuttle schedule, involving 6 to 8 round trips using 3 active planes and 10 pilots. The seven months of winter were impossible, if not deadly in this remote area. While this was only a seasonal money maker, this shuttle bolstered Mark Aero's cash flow.

The 3 ex-Interstate Martins, N465M., N471M, and N473M, handled the bulk of the shuttle work over the three seasons—1973 through 1975. Mark Morris states he selected these as being in the best-known condition as he had seen them torn down for "wing pulls" several times. One Martin would sometimes be set aside for spares a few months at a time, only to be reassembled for continued service—a very normal and common practice when juggling capacity. These 3 Martins were later rotated into another contract job in the southern U.S., as discussed later.

Mark Morris maintains that *seven* Martins were put on this service, but looking at ownership records it seems unlikely they all flew during each season. Ex-Piedmont Martin N40402 once the Dave Clark Five tour aircraft, was likely never put into service by Mark Aero because it was partially cannibalized shortly after delivery and then scrapped 3 years later. Of the other 3 ex-Piedmont aircraft, registration records show that N40408 may have flown the 1973 season only, N40410 could have flown the 1973 and 1974 seasons only—if leased back from Red Baron Charter who owned it since March 1973. N40414 probably flew for all 3 seasons—1973, 1974,

Provisions waiting for loading aboard Mark Aero Martin N473M at Minneapolis before departure on a twice-weekly (per aircraft) 945-mile passenger shuttle due north to Reindeer Lake in Saskatchewan. Is the tail logo denoting MA for Mark Aero or MAC for Missouri Air Commuter? That depends on how concurrent litigation would turn out. (Jerry Riebold)

and 1975. That one was owned by Alpha Aviation the whole time and withdrawn from use in 1976 to become the Lambert fire service practice hulk. However, this accounts for only 6 of the 7 planes Mark said flew the shuttle service. What about the seventh? There was also another TWA-configured 404 that entered the fleet, N40436 which could have also flown all 3 seasons if leased from Alpha Aviation for the first two seasons and then leased from transferee-owner Mark Morris for the final 1975 season. It was not part of the ex-Piedmont acquisition. More on N40436 later.

Minneapolis would be the logical operating base for the Reindeer Lake shuttle and St. Louis would be the maintenance base for the Martins, where they would be maintained for other contract work during the off-season. The first shuttle season would start in June 1973, so my sighting that November at Lambert during Thanksgiving break was one of the 3 ex-Interstate Martins on the seasonal break after the first shuttle season.

The 945-mile shuttle route would normally require a refueling top-off at Winnipeg going up and at a town called Flin Flon on the return trip (about 180 miles south of Reindeer Lake) as flights were fully loaded. In the first season, 1973, Joe assigned Mark to Minneapolis to coordinate things and Mark would also serve initially as a Martin 404 first officer the first year. The problem was that to serve as captain Mark first needed to be type-rated on the plane in the midst of being busy with all his other duties up there. Here we find that Mark is a real practical joker.

It just so happened that one of the Martinliners was due for a "wing pull" to check for cracks and corrosion of the 13 wing bolt attachments that secured each outer wing panel, which attached just outboard of each engine nacelle. This was a periodic procedure required by the FAA on all operating Martin 202s and 404s. This preventative check schedule likely originated years earlier with the Northwest 202 inflight wing separation over Winona, Minnesota in 1948, killing all on board. Since initiating this check requirement, no Martin had since suffered a wing separation.

This work had to be done at Mark Aero in St. Louis, and for various reasons, a few pilots and flight attendants deadheaded on this ferry flight down to headquarters. Even though this was not a revenue flight, two purportedly attractive flight attendants were assigned to work the flight, though this was not a requirement. The flight attendants and passengers were told that Mark would be in the left seat working on his 202/404 type rating and not to be surprised if the aircraft experienced a few sudden movements, deviations, or minor departures from normal cruise flight. The passengers (who were all airline professionals) were in a jovial mood and told the training captain—Dave Barnholtz—to "*have at it, we'll all be partying back here.*" Mark would occupy the right seat and Barnholtz the left for this training session.

During the preflight-planning session, Mark suggested to Mark Aero then Chief Pilot Bud Phillips and Barnholtz that they do an inflight prank on the two "working" flight attendants. As expected, all three agreed, which was designed to throw the attendants into a tizzy. Bud would ride—and party—with the passengers, and Barnholtz would provide an obnoxious distraction by "acting cool" with a potent Dominican cigar, filling the cabin and flight deck with smoke—the kind of smoke most women hate. Mark would sneak onboard an airsickness bag filled with warm and thick, lumpy potato and ham soup, as well as a container of water to be used later in simulating profuse sweating from his scalp, face, neck, and chest. One can probably figure out where this is headed.

With passengers settled in, Mark, Bud, and Dave with his lit cigar climbed up the Martin's built-in ventral stairway and walked through the half-full cabin. The working flight attendants got mad at Dave telling him to put the cigar out. He just sneered and brushed them off. Mark made a fake comment within earshot of the flight attendants that he was "*quite nervous*" and "*not feeling so hot.*" Bud reacted unsympathetically, nudging Mark into the cockpit, telling him to "*calm down, man up—and don't screw up!*" while Dave unapologetically puffed on his cigar—acting like a big shot who was going to give Mark the roughest time of his life on the flight deck.

Once established in cruise flight, Dave rang the attendant call bell several times and the two women climbed the two short steps and opened the cockpit door. The flight deck was filled with cigar smoke and Dave was puffing away more than ever. Mark's eyes were closed, head down and he was moaning and drenched in fake sweat all over his head and shirt. Dave told the girls that "*Mark isn't doing well so can you bring in some damp washcloths and check back on us every 5-10 minutes?*" The girls became livid about the cigar smoke and little else, but as instructed they did check back several times over the next 30 minutes. Mark explains it best as to what happened next:

I take the ham and potato soup and half the barf bag on the yoke and the instrument panel. Dave gets on the passenger address system and tells the gals to quickly come to the cockpit. They open up the door and look on and I'm wrenching into the barf bag, with the ham and potato soup all over my face. Dave is still puffing away on the cigar. I finally stop my fake puking and Dave asks if I am done. I say yes - I think I'm done puking - he then grabs the barf bag from me - looks into the bag and puts his fingers into the bag and gets a handful of the soup and says, "Not too bad!" With that, the blonde who is standing behind the brunette turns nauseous and feints into the small crew luggage hold. So, the blonde is now

Captain Mark Morris, 26, commands the Martin 404 shuttle flight for the nearly 1,000 miles to Reindeer Lake during the summer of 1974. Flight time between Winnipeg and the Arctic Lodge was normally 6 hours. (Jerry Riebold).

Captain Morris is not "working the GPS"—that was not yet invented. He's doing manual en route nav calculations on one of those simple "Bomar Brain" type calculators that became a technological rage of the early 1970s. They did + - x / and little else but were considered the coolest thing since sliced bread. (Jerry Riebold)

feeling sick and the brunette is now yelling at Dave about how sick of a person he is. I then grab the bag away from Dave and tell him "that's mine" and he's is yelling at me to back off and that he is the captain, etc. The brunette is now looking at us saying we are both sickos and she is never coming back to this cockpit again.

While the FAA would come down hard on such distracting inflight cockpit antics today, this type of behavior was across-the-board "customary" back then. This story circulated throughout Mark Aero and other flight crew operations centers, and it took a while before the tricked flight attendants would fly with either Mark or Dave again. That aside, Mark did get his Martin 202/404 type rating but flew as first officer on the Reindeer Lake shuttle for the remainder of the 1973 season, moving up to captain for the subsequent 1974 and 1975 seasons.

Around this time, Jerry Riebold, an up-and-coming Mark Aero flight instructor turned line pilot with a newly-minted airline transport rating (ATP), would be the next to be type-rated on the Martin 404. He was promoted to first officer on this shuttle for the 1974 season, where he became a Martin captain the following year. Jerry states:

The Martin 404 was extremely heavy on the controls much more so than its peer aircraft [twin Convair], *even with its hydraulic boost. This is partially due to its fierce wing dihedral which fights to keep the wings level, resisting pilot input. For the 404 type rating, a candidate had to demonstrate he was capable of flying and landing the plane without control boost—a nearly impossible task.*

Martin 404 First Officer Jerry Riebold scans the panel on the way to Reindeer Lake in the summer of 1974. In a couple more years he would become Mark Morris's chief pilot for his new airline to be covered in later chapters. The Martin was Jerry's first heavy transport category type rating. (Jerry Riebold)

In addition, the Martin 404s had a dismal climb rate by any standard. Mark Morris maintained that on good days it could climb at only 300 feet per minute. Now that's the definition of "dismal."

The Reindeer Lake route was over extremely desolate and hazardous wilderness littered with vast finger lakes that all looked the same. The lake itself had 2,500 square miles of water, was 140 miles long, and had 5,000 islands. This made air navigation by pilotage (that is, flying with reference to ground landmarks only) nearly impossible. Landmarks consisted of positive recognition of various lakes and shorelines along the route. Electronic navigational aid coverage was sparse, coupled with the extreme northern latitude magnetic variation that rendered primary navigation equipment (directional gyro as manually reset using the magnetic compass) nearly useless as the accurate re-setting of a gyro compass was nearly impossible and all of this was done in conjunction with winds-aloft *estimate* report—and the clock. There was no such thing as "GPS" in the early 1970s. To make matters worse, the destination runway was a barely discernable narrow gravel strip only 4,500 feet long, barely long enough to handle a loaded Martin.

Martin 404 First Officer Jerry Riebold jokes around with the flight attendant. "OK, enough pictures!" (Jerry Riebold)

On the way up, the last useable navaid was a VOR located at that small town called Flin Flon, which was around 180 miles due south of Reindeer Lake. It had a 150-mile VHF range, which is typical for a VOR, but it left the last 30 or so miles to Reindeer Lake without a course indication. So, when passing over Flin Flon, pilots tracked the appropriate VOR radial outbound that represented a straight-line course to the final destination. They had 150 miles of "positive tracking" off of the VOR to get the wind drift angle correct on that particular course and then when the VOR signal was lost, they just held that heading (which included the predetermined wind drift angle) and used pilotage (looking for ground references or landmarks) for the last 30 miles. When the ADF (Automatic Direction Finder) picked up the Lynn Lake NDB (Non-directional beacon) with the needle registering 90 degrees to the left they simply had to fly straight for only 10 or so miles to the strip. It worked every time, but there was no room for screw-ups. In poor visibility conditions one wouldn't want to get lost over this geography—only to run out of gas over the most inaccessible and inhospitable terrain in the world. That is if one of the vast lakes making up a large percentage of the "ground" doesn't find you first. On the return trip, navigating inbound from Reindeer Lake to the Flin Flon airport for fuel top-off was easy. Point the nose south to a 300-mile target only 30 miles away (150-mile VOR radius times two). If you miss a Flin Flon VOR radial intercept, you are in the wrong career.

Toward the end of Jerry's *first* five-hour flight on the shuttle as a first officer, Captain Dave Barnholtz ordered him to initiate the descent. At the end of the descent when they leveled off near pattern altitude, Jerry could discern nothing ahead of the windscreen except for the generic wilderness he'd been staring at for hours. Dave then told Jerry to "begin final descent" and started calling out landing flap settings and then gear. The inhospitable terrain got uncomfortably closer and closer, but even at the "gear down" command, Jerry saw nothing but forest and lakes in front of him. No airport, no runway, very low, and headed *down*. *"Where is it?" "Right there." "Right where?" "Right there at eleven O'clock right here, just a few clicks above the nose." "I still don't see it!" "Look where I'm pointing, it's right in front of you." "What?—THAT'S IT?!"*

What Jerry saw was *not* the approach end of a wide concrete runway at an international airport with bright lead-in lights. It was a narrow, short gravel road cut out of a forested island in the middle of a huge, "fingery" lake stretching all over the place as far as the eye could see. He could not see any lodge, buildings, or signs of any civilization nearby. In a cloud of dust, the

Martin 404 on final approach for the diminutive Reindeer Lake runway 7-25 gravel airstrip near the center of this photo just behind the group of 3 small islands. This is the "needle in the haystack" destination at the end of every exhausting outbound shuttle flight. This strip was only 4,500 feet long—barely enough for a fully-loaded (often overloaded) Martin. (Jerry Riebold)

Martin settled right on the gravel runway threshold and Dave called for reverse props, rapidly decelerating the plane, generating a violent dust plume in front of them. The rollout used up all the 4,500 feet of runway and they turned around and taxied back to a single unpaved apron that had no terminal building or *any* building. Just trees. Also, the Reindeer Lodge itself was not located on this airstrip island. Customers had to board houseboat ferries for a 7-mile trip to the lodge island itself.

Takeoff was another matter and also used all the runway. The airplane was always loaded to the gills often slightly exceeding allowable full gross weight and required the activation of water/alcohol injection to generate maximum power at 2,400 hp, which is also called "wet" power. That keeps the engines from literally "exploding" while under the heat of max takeoff power. Jerry Riebold stated that there was a large soft patch midway down the runway that temporarily scrubbed takeoff roll speed, which didn't help things out at all.

During this first season, Mark's mind was not just on shuttle operations. As part of the job, pilots had considerable downtime between and during flight assignments, doing a bit of fishing and thinking. To fill downtime, charter pilots often dream of starting side businesses and in some cases, the pilot-turned-entrepreneur could *eventually* make more money on the side than his primary job as a pilot. However, because a pilot's true love was flying, he could have the best of both worlds. Mark was no exception and his long entrepreneurship career was partially nurtured during his Reindeer Lake downtime. He planned and started business partnerships with in-laws and friends, involving a waterbed retailer, "unbranded" oil distribution, and even the invention and manufacture of practice gadgets for golfers. Despite this, you just can't think about your future *all the time* during layovers. Mark Aero flight crews enjoyed serious partying that included the "native hospitality" during their extended stays at Reindeer Lodge.

Landing rollout from Jerry's perspective in the Martin 404 right seat. It's sand, dirt, dust, and gravel everywhere. Not a good combination for a jet engine, but doable for piston power with smaller, filtered air intakes. (Jerry Riebold)

Touted as a fishing resort, the Reindeer Lodge was much more. It could better be classified as a "no-wives retreat" or a rich boys club of sorts, that also provided booze, gambling, and even "female companionship"—all three of which were illegal in at least that part of Saskatchewan. It's no surprise that the Arctic Lodge was under mob control at that time (it no longer is) but surely Mark Aero personnel couldn't help but suspect this even though they never got any formal confirmation. The Canadian Mounties often did spot-check surprise visits at the lodge, arriving in one of their pontoon-equipped de Havilland Twin-Otter turboprops.

The lodge personnel, who were mostly enterprising Blackfoot Indians who were native to the area, had set it up such that the gambling tables could be "cleaned up" in three minutes and the bar and alcohol hidden under the floor with a giant trap door when they heard the sound of the approaching Twin Otter containing the Mounties.

Especially when they were intoxicated, a very few of the native Indians still had "white man animosities" that came out as though it was still 1876 at the Little Bighorn. It wasn't safe to stroll

Eager sportsman just after deplaning at Reindeer Lake. Fishing, hunting, partying, and girls to hang out with for the next week or two. (Jerry Riebold)

too far from the lodge at night due to the possibility of a flying arrow (it happened to Mark), though there is no evidence of anyone being seriously injured from that. The natives were also good at stealing boats from the lodge, which they used to get around the various islands before winter set in and in late spring. A guard with a shotgun often had to fire warning shots from the pier to get the offending natives to turn around and go home. They could also get very jealous if Mark Aero personnel got too chatty with their particular "off-limits" girls and on one occasion both Mark and Jerry found themselves in headlocks with knives at their throats, requiring some quick thinking.

Winter on Reindeer Lake is deadly harsh—only the Blackfeet were hardened enough to survive it each year. Temperatures of forty below and blizzards galore are the norm. Mark Aero had to *always* get everyone out of there by late October, or they could be trapped and frozen to death should their Martin 404 become *suddenly* encased in ice and snow before a planned final seasonal departure.

Mark relates that at the end of the 1974 season the resort manager insisted he would stay for the winter. He lived in Minneapolis and always went home in October, but still for some insane reason wanted to "experience a winter" at the lodge at some point. Since his wife had unfortunately died only months before, he thought now was the time to do it. This drove Mark nuts as they frantically summoned the passengers and loaded the plane early in an attempt to beat the first winter storm which was forecasted to be a whopper—but there was nothing he could do to get the manager to take the flight. If the manager didn't go, he would have no way out until 8 months later in June of the following year. The manager told Mark he had enough food and fuel to endure the worst. So, Mark and Jerry were forced to fly the last flight out without him. However, Jerry did not actually know it was the wish of the resort manager to stay—he thought the manager was just "slow." So, the consummate joker Mark Morris played along with this, pretending that the resort manager was just late for "scheduled departure" and led Jerry to believe that he, in his sole discretion, decided to leave without him to avoid an oncoming winter storm. At that point, Jerry was furious at Mark that he would do such a thing and leave a man to freeze to death.

Passengers mull around under the Martinliner's inner wing at destination Reindeer Lake while awaiting the unloading of supplies and luggage. The man in the middle with his back to the camera is famed Minnesota Vikings coach Bud Grant. He was a regular at Reindeer Lake, along with several of his players. Mark says that Bud liked to ride on the flight deck with the pilots. Furthest to the right is "cigar-smoking" pilot Dave Barnholtz. Interestingly, Barnholz worked for Ron Skipper at Golden Eagle Aviation at the time of the Wichita State crash in Colorado and was therefore a peer of pilot Danny Crocker who was killed in that crash. Jerry Riebold maintains that Dave was one of the best pilots he ever knew and one of his best friends. Barnholz "strapped on" every plane he flew like a tailored suit and otherwise flew it like it was part of him—even on initial familiarization flights. He would eventually become Peabody Holdings' first chief pilot when they took their flight department in-house, and later he would conservative radio talk show host Rush Limbaugh's first chief pilot for his "EIB One" corporate jet. (Jerry Riebold).

The following June when Mark and Jerry flew the first flight in, they found the manager in a plush lounge chair in front of the huge hearth, mummified and stiff as a board. Everything else in the room was just as Mark and Jerry had remembered it eight months before. When they tried to move the body, the manager's fingers and hands snapped right off—time out! It was later determined it wasn't the weather that got him—he had an apparent heart attack 8 months earlier, probably close to the very same day Mark and Jerry last saw him before that final flight out. At that point, Jerry called Mark a "murderer." Mark had to fess up, and Jerry realized the joke was on "him." With this unfortunate incident, a "Mr. Moretti" became the interim manager of the lodge for the new season. One must wonder what organization he belonged to.

The crew's Reindeer Lake cabin quarters had a partition separating the male bunks from the female flight attendant section. Each section had a wood stove for heating. Summer night temperatures got down into the thirties each night, so the wood stoves were fired up in the early evenings. Cans of used motor oil were used as a fire starter but had to be applied sparingly to work properly. After the stoves were lit, mixed-company pajama drinking parties were the norm before lights out. One of these nights was Jerry's birthday, so that party would be special.

Before the party started, Mark was firing up the "girls' stove" while Jerry tended to the "boys' stove" at which time Mark heard a mild explosion. Jerry's can of oil blew up and singed his hands and eyebrows. Eventually, they got both stoves working and the birthday party commenced in the men's quarters—Jerry's burns were annoying but not too bad. Then that stove went out due to damp wood. Mark threw on more logs and began the starter ritual with the motor oil. Violent flames erupted from the stove and propagated backward into the oil container Mark was holding, setting his T-shirt on fire. He burst out of the cabin door in flames, full speed ahead, running 50 yards straight for the frigid lake, flailing his arms about his torso, with Jerry following

Runway 7-25 as seen from the Martin just after takeoff from the Reindeer Lake airstrip. The climbing Martin has just turned 180 degrees to downwind for the return to Winnipeg and then Minneapolis. What you see is lingering "takeoff dust" thrown up by the powerful 2,400 horsepower R2800 CB16 radial engines generating full "wet" power with their gigantic Hamilton Standard paddle-blade props. (Jerry Riebold)

behind him beating on Mark's flaming back, all the way to the lake where they both jumped in. A couple of their passengers were outside nearby, when one exclaimed, *"Wasn't that our pilot on fire who just ran by?"* Another answered, *"Yeah, and the copilot right behind him."*

When the two pilots got back to the smoke and soot-filled cabin, they were relieved that their flight attendant co-partier had put the fire out with blankets. Her pajamas and face were black and sooty and Mark and Jerry were all wet with smoke-stenched sludge, with gaping holes in Jerry's T-shirt. Both their hands were swollen and blistered. After trying to figure out what just happened, they began laughing at their dumb luck—nobody got burned alive and their quarters didn't burn down. Mr. Moretti then walked in, exclaiming, *"Boy, you three have a twisted idea on how to party!"* He went to the infirmary supply room and brought back some liquid Novocain and bandage wraps and the party resumed with a fresh bottle of scotch.

It was a rogue Blackfoot who diluted the motor oil with the right amount of gasoline to make it hard to smell. First, a flying arrow past your head, and now this. Flying the Martin 404 out of Reindeer Lake with two pairs of *heavily bandaged* hands proved challenging.

One of Mark's major entrepreneurial ventures was in full swing during his Reindeer Lake years. At the urging of his father-in-law, he and his brother-in-law formed Spiegel Oil in June 1973 to get into unbranded oil distribution. This was four months before the October Arab Oil Embargo. Spiegel Oil would distribute oil mainly to commercial accounts such as construction companies but also had a small retail heating oil delivery service. At that time, there were still thousands of homes in the St. Louis area that used heating oil in the winter, but that market was rapidly declining. Mark was able to marshal resources, including an agreement with an owner of tank wagons to serve the retail operations. Mark replicated the Spiegel business model in Kansas City by starting another distribution company called Arrow Oil.

During the Arab oil shock, the Federal Energy Office (FEO) placed regulatory pricing caps in an attempt to curb exploding oil prices. Against the advice of his father-in-law, Mark was unusually aggressive in his profit margin request and negotiation with oil companies and asked for three times the "normal" profit margin at $0.13 per gallon versus the normal $0.04 per gallon. He got it with no resistance. Before the embargo, he had also negotiated an outsized allocation from Gulf Oil at normal market prices, locking in fat profit margins over the next two years.

According to Mark, he had his two oil businesses set up such that they would virtually run themselves day-to-day. Well not quite, as we will find out—he needed and got an efficient administrator to do this as we will see. That said, it appears that at only 25 years old, Mark may have become one of those pilots that made more "on the side" than with his primary flying job, which he loved the most.

That was good for Mark Morris because Mark Aero and affiliates were becoming strapped for cash as Joe tried to implement the Standard and Missouri Air Commuter expansions, and the Reindeer Lake shuttle would see its third and final season in 1975. Securing a first officer slot with the majors was not working well for Mark either, even though just after his Air America service in Southeast Asia he landed a short stint as a flight engineer on United's first 747 under work rules that would keep him as an engineer forever, so he quit.

But now in 1973, there was a glut of pilot candidates, particularly Vietnam veterans and furloughed commercial pilots flooding personnel departments of the fuel-strapped majors. Mark was fully qualified and primed to start with Delta Airlines which was ready to hire him, but an easy-to-correct bureaucratic screw-up busted his planets out of alignment like a cue ball. The bureaucrats refused to reverse their admitted stupid mistake—end of conversation. Tough luck reigns in the airline business and always will.

CHAPTER 26

Spooks at the Door

Missouri Air Commuter—MAC— was ready to go. Then, out of nowhere, a guy named McClure—FAA Chief of the St. Louis Air Carrier District Offices (ACDO)—inexplicably reneged on the pre-approved security plans that they and Mark Aero had developed for MAC. He now required that the plan had to be first presented to the Director of Aviation for Kansas City (with jurisdiction over both MKC and KCI) before they could re-approve it. There was a huge undercurrent behind all this: TWA had its operations base at the new KCI and had almost unilateral influence over their Director of Aviation. At one hearing, the TWA attorney threatened the calling of an $842,000 loan TWA made to Kansas City if the city accepted the FAA-approved Mark Aero's security plan. That loan was most likely "seller financing" for when the city purchased the land for KCI from TWA years earlier.

That Kansas City Director of Aviation was initially enthusiastic about MAC (before TWA stepped in) and had then promised to cooperate with the Morrises to the fullest. However, after the FAA's change of heart because of city politics (and in cooperation with McClure in St. Louis), the Director began avoiding calls from Joe and Mark wo finally barged into the Director's office. They were told to stand down because they were way over their heads and people could die, *"so please leave my office."* It soon became clear that Frontier Airlines, which currently operated Convair 580s on MAC's proposed route across the state, was in on this too. It was TWA, Frontier and the City of Kansas City who had pressured the Director to oppose the reopening of Kansas City Municipal to commercial operations and not to submit the MAC security plan. All of the sudden, Kansas City's city council was thrown into the mix and was now required to approve the MAC plans as well—a typical case of changing the rules in the middle of the game. Even the Morris Kansas City outside counsel, a senior partner with a prestigious Kansas City law firm, was told to stop representing them or the firm would lose all their business from Hallmark Cards and other major Kansas City firms.

The City Attorney who was also an initial supporter of MAC was also compelled to change his tune. He purportedly accepted a $10,000 bribe from TWA to reverse his stance, which he did, as well as to deliver a letter to sway the city councilman who had the swing vote on the MAC issue. The Morrises were then forced to sue the Director of Aviation and the City, which were now both refusing to negotiate. The Director was subpoenaed and then shortly thereafter was found floating in the Missouri river "totally dead," under mysterious circumstances. On top of that, both Joe and Mark were being "tailed" and their homes in St. Louis were being surveilled.

Then, out of nowhere, another set of underworld figures came to the aid of the Morrises. They were aligned with the Kansas City cab drivers union and wanted an exclusive on cab services for MAC passengers. After a few "secret meetings in dark alleys," as Mark put it, Joe and Mark had no problem with that and the union began providing "complementary" armed protective services from the shadows who were tailing them. The union also claimed that it would pull strings within the City Council for them to turn things around. Assurances were provided that with City

Council approval, MAC would go through and could begin operations.

This gave the Morrises renewed vigor in their battles with TWA and Frontier, and with their lawsuit against Kansas City. They would charge that the two airlines violated the Sherman Act, which prohibited restraint of trade and monopolies. This expensive battle went on for months well into 1974, causing MAC to miss its planned startup date of January 1 of that year. The opposition used lame arguments against MAC—there was the familiar claim that MAC's use of obsolete propeller equipment wouldn't be accepted by the public (then what's the competitive worry?). They didn't either know or care that several local service airlines were still flying Martinliners all over the southeastern U.S. without passenger complaints. Then they opined that the Martin 404s would compete directly with Frontier's more advanced Convair 580s (so what was the concern about the alleged lack of public acceptance of the Martins—wouldn't they fly Frontier's Convair turboprops instead?). The Martin was slower than the Convair 580, but it also burned 30% less fuel on the St. Louis—Kansas City route. Did they think the energy crisis wasn't that big of a problem after all? The court's analysis was full of hypocrisy with nitpicking seemingly way beyond their purview—all the way down to evaluating and analyzing the aircraft types on the route, grabbing at anything to stop MAC in its tracks. The only relevant issues were transit time, endpoint convenience, and fuel conservation.

The Morrises reiterated that the real competition would be buses, automobiles, and trains. According to Joe, it was like the two major airlines were saying *"even though we cannot fulfill the public need, we are against anyone else doing it."* The same argument that the majors seemed to use against all the supplementals and proposed new entrants. Despite this, Mark and Joe were getting close, but the swing vote Kansas City councilman said he would vote against approval. St. Louis FAA Chief McClure had no problem with this.

It was rumored that the cab union "reps" protecting the Morrises were about to put a hit out on the dissenting councilman, which alarmed Joe and Mark who wanted no part of that—they took some "steps" in hopes of thwarting this. Despite that, the endangered councilman made a deal with the cab union that it would obtain an exclusive for TWA ground transportation in and out of the new KCI. The cab union now "miraculously" didn't need MAC so they reneged on their handshake deal with the Morrises and that was that. The Kansas City Judge then dismissed Mark Aero's case against the city. As Mark Morris had stated many times, *"in the airline business you never know whether anyone is your friend or your enemy."* During all this, Mark became president of MAC and began flying limited capacity MAC services using Mitsubishi MU-2s under their Part 135 Air Taxi certificate, which did not need a security plan. This proved to be a dysfunctional solution and would last only three months.

At this point, Joe Morris made the tough decision to hang it up. He had been diagnosed with colon cancer in 1974. According to Joe, the failed Standard bid, the stillborn Missouri Air Commuter, coupled with the hefty lawsuit expenses and a recession, *"were the basic causes of my family and I being completely wiped out."* The Mark Aero board of directors held meetings at his hospital bedside to determine what to do with the business.

While an interim corporate general manager was put into place, on loan from a major international consulting firm. He was said to be an arrogant, narcissistic bean-counter with zero practical experience in anything tangible and who did not get along with Mark Aero employees. He just made things worse. It was decided that Mark would now be leading the company, which was not Mark's first choice, as he thought his brother had more specific management experience there. Mark still just wanted to be an airline pilot with the majors, but he reluctantly took the helm

What might have been? A former Systems International Airways Martin 404 against the backdrop of the old Kansas City Municipal terminal building in December 1990, exactly where MAC Martin flights from St. Louis would have terminated. This plane had just been flown in from Florida for refurbishment by the airline preservation group Save A Connie, now the Airline History Museum in Kansas City.

of Mark Aero. Fortunately, after two major surgeries, Joe fully recovered later in 1975. Out of the blue Joe then instructed Mark to methodically liquidate Mark Aero. And that is what Mark worked on for the remainder of the year. This process caused him to gain a tremendous amount of legal and financial structuring experience in the process, which he referred to as *"the hardest job I ever did."* That experience would in some ways change the direction of his later life. But now he would just figure out how to continue flying and would gain that and much more than he could imagine from his current circumstances, at only 26 years old.

Joe, after having lost everything, including his wife who had just divorced him, went off to St. Lucia in early 1975 to see if he could restart things there as the politics down there had calmed. He brought with him the same DC-6B he and Mark had rescued from there 18 months earlier, N37570, which was the one I thought was headed for the scrap heap in the summer of 1972. A revived St. Lucia operation proved futile and would last for only a few months. By the end of 1975, Joe and N37570 came back, but as a result of the airline liquidation, it was sold to aviation-minded Peabody Coal CEO Ed Phelps, former Navy pilot and longtime friend of Joe's. This plane would soon play an even more important role with the Morrises.

In an attempt to recoup something from the Standard and MAC debacles, Mark Aero filed an anti-trust lawsuit against TWA on December 1, 1975. This would drag on for a couple of years to no avail, gaining zero traction. By now it was clear that the Morris's arch-enemy *number one* was the neanderthal federal air bureaucracy in a highly regulated winner-loser, oligopolistic environment. This terrible relationship would only get worse. There was one small consolation prize for the Morrises as a result of all this. Joe and Mark were able to secure Mr. McClure's reassignment away from the St. Louis ACDO as a result of his handling of the MAC debacle.

CHAPTER 27

Winds of Change

Back-tracking to the late spring of 1973—a few months before I ship off to college—I continue my sporadic excursions to the northwest corner of Lambert and Mark Aero. I notice a Convair 440 being serviced by them out in the open with propellers removed, cowling panels open and engines exposed. As usual, there are *no people* on the ramp. This is N4826C which started life with Delta Airlines and is now owned by Florida Aircraft Leasing as a converted freighter and is being leased to Dow Jones & Company. What? The big Wall Street publisher? After this initial encounter, I notice it flying in and out of both Lambert and nearby Spirit Airport for at least the next decade. As late as 1982 I get up close to this red-trimmed airplane on the tarmac at Spirit of St. Louis with its huge overhead cargo door wide open. It is oily, greasy and all scratched up, especially around the engine nacelles. In small black letters, it says "Dow Jones & Company" under the flight deck windows. It turns out Dow Jones had been leasing eight of these, strategically based throughout the U. S. for the distribution of daily regional issues of *The Wall Street Journal (WSJ)*.

Convair N4826C was based in St. Louis and used for the distribution of the *WSJ Midwest Regional Edition* which was printed in Highland, Illinois, right across the Mississippi. Early each morning these eight 440s headed out on their respective "paper routes" all over the

Dow Jones & Company Convair 440 N4826C freighter undergoing maintenance at Mark Aero in the late spring of 1973, trimmed in red with a black stripe below the window line. At the time I took this photo, Joe and Mark Morris were no doubt getting ready for the first season of the Reindeer Lake Martin 404 shuttle out of Minneapolis. Note the tailfin of one of Mark Aero's ex-Piedmont Martin 404s behind the 440. Twenty-three years later in 1996, this Convair crashed into the Caribbean with a subsequent cargo operator. The octogenarian pilot was lost but thankfully the copilot survived. Note the tail of one of the ex-Piedmont 404s behind it.

U.S. to their regional drop-off points. Then the "paperboy" trucks took over from there for delivery to newsstands and post offices. I find it strange that all those WSJ issues read by business executives (and later, me) are delivered by World War II era R-2800 C-Series power in the age of jetliners, flights to the moon, and space shuttles. Delivering a massive 10,000-pound planeload of intangible information every night in heavy machines powered by big old World War II aircraft engines seems as archaic as the Wells Fargo stagecoach or the Pony Express. Fast forward to today and its internet and electronic funds—not much newsprint-and-ink or canceled check tonnage is needed these days to get information into people's brains or money into their bank accounts.

These 440s remained in service with Dow Jones into the 1990s, at which time they reverted to the lessor. N4826C went through several more owners before crashing into the Caribbean in 1996, killing the 84-year-old pilot. Luckily the copilot got out.

Later in the summer, I notice changes with a couple of the ex-Piedmont Martin 404s I first noticed on the Mark Aero ramp around January 1973. N40402 (the *Dave Clark 5* plane) is now rudderless and cannibalized. N40410 had been sold to Red Baron Charter Co., headquartered in nearby Clayton, Missouri but it is said that the plane was mostly flown privately. Red Baron Charter was owned by Robert Baskewitz who was a bottler for Anheuser-Busch, and the "Red Baron" name was a play on his initials "R.B." (the *Snoopy & the Red Baron* theme was obviously still popular in 1973). The Piedmont trim pattern remained, but the color had been changed from dark blue to bright red and the aircraft appeared to clean up pretty well.

My Mark Aero 404 runway sighing at Lambert in November 1973 (from the airport restaurant) was my last sighting of any of the "original three" ex-Interstate Martin 404s I had tracked since 1970. Out-of-state jobs, such as Reindeer Lake, probably accounted for this. With

Ex-TWA/Piedmont Martin 404 N40410 was refurbished by Mark Aero on its ramp in the summer of 1973 while with Red Baron Charter of Clayton, Missouri (a large St. Louis suburban business center). This operation was owned by Robert Baskewitz, a close friend of the Anheuser-Busch family, but the plane was flown mostly for private use. The Baskewitz family also founded and owned the popular Daniele Hotel in Clayton. The Piedmont trim remains except the color is now bright red instead of dark blue. In 1975 it was acquired by Joe Simkins of Tiffany Industries and remained on the premises until sold in early 1979. It crashed in Bolivia in late 1979 with 10 fatalities while flying with CAMBA Bolivia. Note the Lambert main terminal in the background on the left.

Interstate, they sat around a lot at Lambert. With Mark Aero, they were much more active, though *elsewhere*—but still not active enough. By December 1973, Mark Aero was in ever-deepening financial distress. So, to raise cash they sold those three Martinliners to a Dr. Harold Steck, a "rich dentist" in need of tax depreciation. He leased it back to Mark Aero and possibly others, a common practice of the day when the huge Investment Tax Credit (ITC) write-off was available for such capital purchases (now long gone). However, these "investment airplanes" often did not pan out too well from an operating cash flow standpoint and Dr. Steck's deal did not work out well for him either. This was due to the failed MAC startup and continued underutilization of the aircraft. The seasonal Reindeer Lake contract alone simply could not put food on the table all year round, but Joe began rotating the planes down to the Paul Fournet FBO in Lafayette, Louisiana on a new contracts serving the petroleum industry. In the meantime, the relationship with Dr. Steck continued to sour.

It's a few days before the 1975 Thanksgiving break at Mizzou in Columbia, Missouri. I'm after a girl named Sherry so I take her to dinner at Earnie's in downtown Columbia. Sherry lives in Florissant, just north of Lambert. The theme inside this art-deco diner, which featured white-block architecture and a glass block entry foyer, is the famous comic character detective "Dick Tracy." Dick and the other characters, including criminal characters such as "Itchy," are painted all over the upper walls, complete with the trademark wrist walkie-talkie communicators. These are shown with small lightning bolts shooting out of them to signify communication. This was a fun retro-diner atmosphere that retrieved my long-forgotten memories of Dick Tracy cartoons when I was a kid.

Sherry and I had a good dinner and ice cream at our high-top table near the counter. Then she asks me if I want to come over to her house while we are both at home during Thanksgiving break. That's a good sign, so I have no problem with that. We agree on a time for the Friday after Thanksgiving and she writes down directions to her house on a napkin. It leads me north on Lindbergh right past Mark Aero. But I forget to have her write down her phone number.

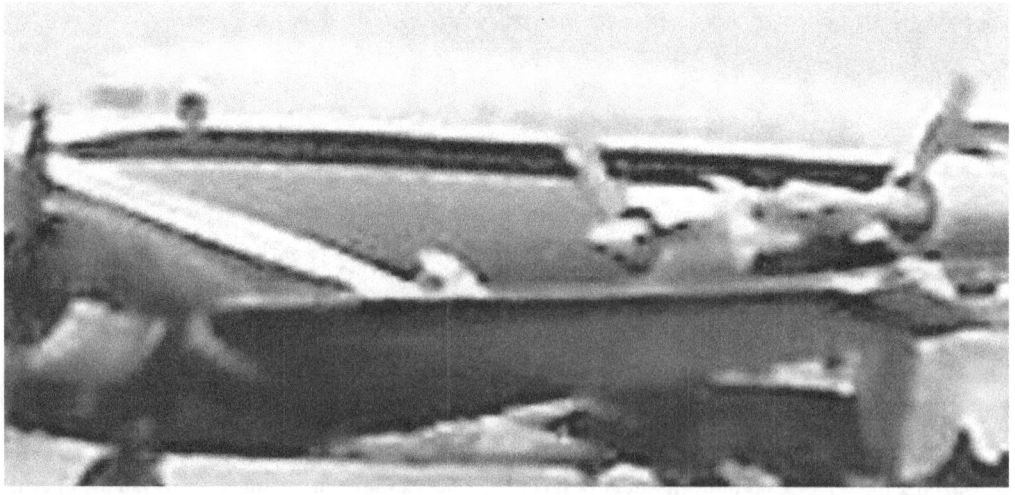

A random, poorly composed close-up I took on the Mark Aero ramp in April 1973. In the foreground is a Beech Super 18 like the Ralston plane my dad regularly flew in a few years earlier. Behind it is an unidentified transient DC-6A (or a freight-converted -6B). It has dark blue trim along the window line and the lower fuselage is painted in a strange light aqua blue.

It's bone-chilling cold, low gray overcast, a typical November Friday. I'm not on my motorcycle this time but am driving my red Mazda to Sherry's house. I'm running a little late and when I pop around the curve, there sits a sharp-looking Martin 404, right there at the fence along Banshee Road, engine cowl panels removed, pointing north at the hangars. For sure, I don't bring my camera again and do not immediately know which 404 this is, but it has a light bluish trim I'd not seen on any Martinliner on this ramp, with bluish triangle shapes on the tail. I'm wanting to stop, but have to keep going while taking note of something else I've rarely seen. There is human activity around the plane. It looks like something is about to happen—but I must reluctantly drive on.

When I get to Sherry's house at the appointed time she invites me in as I anticipate her plans for my visit. The first thing she asks me to do is to turn around and go home—*"I'm so sorry!"* Man am I confused. She says her grandmother lives with her parents here. They are both out and grandma just got sick "within the hour." She could not reach me because she didn't have my home phone number, and I didn't have hers to confirm things (remember, only landlines then). Her excuse sounds remotely plausible but I think she just made up this "sick grandma" story. There was no way I could just tear through her house to find the invisible grandmother if any. So, from then on out I lose interest in pursuing things further.

The good news is I can now head back down to Mark Aero and see what's going on with that light-blue trimmed 404. When I get there, both props are churning while the R-2800C engines are madly idling, belching thick smoke everywhere. After five years I finally see one running on the ground! There is a sizeable ground team staring at it and then it begins a slow taxi toward the hangar, stopping well short of the hangar door as my heart pounds. Wonders never cease. There is activity—complete with actual people—on the Mark Aero ramp! Then the engines are shut down and it's towed into the hangar as the group follows it, so I continue my drive home. I can now only speculate on which Martin 404 this plane was, but it was not one of those 4 ex-Piedmont planes that arrived here 3 years earlier, nor one of the 3 ex-Interstate planes. It was that "mystery" Martinliner, now registered directly to Mark Morris, that had been on the Reindeer Lake shuttle for all three seasons (see Chapter 25, page 152).

So now we have positively identified 8 Martinliners that were associated with Mark Aero. Seven of them were operated by them at various times, and one was cannibalized outright for spares. One of the active Martins was withdrawn from service in 1976 and cannibalized down to the hulk to become the Lambert "fire dump" plane.

A few years after that, Mark Morris purchased several "pre-owned" Boeing 727-100 jetliners from Piedmont Airlines for his new airline fleet (discussed in later chapters). At that time, the CEO of Piedmont was aware of that lingering, highly visible Martinliner eyesore in *Piedmont colors* sitting on the west side of Lambert and the rough public image it may have projected. The CEO half-joked that he wanted Mark to immediately rub out the Piedmont colors on the new jetliners and *"please keep them out of those Lambert fire dumps!"*

Years after my late-1975 round-trip to Sherry's house, I find that Mark Aero, as part of its public relations programs, may have occasionally hosted trade school students on its premises. In 1984 a friend named Randy Ezell told me he was one of those students. We were drinking beers evening on my apartment balcony and he brings this up as a Convair 240 flies overhead, which he says he recognizes. He says during his trade school days he shadowed Mark Aero mechanics working on all the planes and he got to *"start the big radials"* and *"taxi those Martins and Convairs"* under the supervision of Mark Aero personnel. I'd known Randy for years and he never mentioned this to me until that anonymous Convair flew over.

So, trade-school activity *may* have been what I was witnessing with the Martin 404 on that late November day in 1975—just a guess—but the number of people around the plane, coupled with their group behavior, would suggest it could have been some kind of instructional event. As it turns out Mark Aero was only one month away from *complete shutdown* and maybe this session was to fulfill a remaining obligation.

After years of occasional contemplation, I think I may have identified this "instructional Martin 404." In Chapter 25 we mention Martin 404 N40436 (an ex-TWA ship like the four ex-Piedmont planes) had been owned by Alpha Aviation and then transferred to Mark Morris in February 1975. Because of the light blue trim on this Martin—including light blue isosceles triangles shapes on each side of the vertical tail—from photographic evidence I think N40436 may very well have been the plane I witnessed. As we stated in a previous chapter, it's plausible that this one too could have flown all three Reindeer Lake seasons in addition to the ex-Piedmont fire dump plane, N40414. The point of all this is that Mark Morris has repeatedly told me that Mark Aero had "seven Martin 404s" on the Reindeer Lake contract. That may have been so, but not all at the same time! To that he agreed—we were both juggling our memories going back 50 years.

In any case, on that cold, overcast November day in 1975, the "Phoenix" was beginning to rise out of the ashes, right before my eyes as we shall see. I just didn't know it.

CHAPTER 28

Shamrock Props

Since I'm mostly away from home, I'm not able to swing by the Mark Aero ramp very much during my Mizzou college years from 1974-1977. I'm unaware that Mark Aero had gone out of business as of January 1976, despite the "Mark Aero" name that remains over the hangar doors. One time in my Columbia dormitory my friends and I were sitting around and I see an article in the Globe-Democrat about severe storms that blasted through St. Louis. It mentions that several DC-6s at the northwest corner of Lambert were blown out of their chalks during the storm and banged into each other in a minor pile-up with minimal damage. I mentioned this to some of my friends who surprise me when I find they are familiar with those DC-6s parked at the northwest corner of Lambert.

When I am home on some weekends and breaks I notice World War II-era Curtis C-46 freighters over St. Louis County from 1975 through 1977. These big twins are powered by earlier R-2800s B-Series engines (see Chapter 5), which look and sound different than C-Series engines on the Martinliners, Convairs, and Douglas's. The B-Series growled, and ran rougher, and at slower RPMs than C-Series engines. As mentioned earlier, the C-Series was a significant redesign with better internal harmonics, balancing, and cooling, causing it to be the most reliable 18-cylinder radial ever produced. In truth there was little difference in RPM settings between the two engines, it's just that the B-Series *seemed* to turn slower. I don't know who is flying these C-46s, and when I catch them on the former Mark Aero ramp they are unmarked, with white tops and green trim. There are also green "shamrock" logos near the nose of each plane under the flight deck side windows. As I find out years later, these planes are—or were—in the fleet of the mysterious "Shamrock Airlines."

Around this time, my Mizzou roommate Tom Noonan and I informally befriend an Iranian student named Amir, while taking our regular evening coffee breaks from studying at the student union. Amir is personable but not particularly good-looking. He always wears his dirty denim jacket and he doesn't smell like he showers much. He also makes it clear he hates the leader of his country, the Shah of Iran, who is an American ally. That aside, for some reason Amir thinks we have the magic touch with American women (maybe Tom does, but I don't), and that we can therefore get him laid. Neither of us wants to recommend him to anybody, but we always play along and tell him we are working on it.

One day he struts into the student union proudly beaming, telling us he got laid last night. We are baffled as to how he accomplished this and we privately decide we do not want to meet this girl he hooked up with. On top of his great feat, Amir is doubly excited about tomorrow's planned demonstration against the Shah by most or all of Mizzou's Iranian students. Over the next few weeks, they are all over campus, in lines along the sidewalks, complete with cardboard anti-Shah signs painted in "blood" and bags over their head—I guess they don't want to be identified. Also, a lot of pro-Palestinian and Iranian propaganda flyers that justify revenge and terrorist acts against the West are floating around everywhere, including on bulletin boards and in the Mizzou libraries. This is an early taste of rotten things to come out of Iran and the Middle East. I translate their definition of "terrorism" as a justification to kill "me." Tom and I then try to distance ourselves from our "amigo" Amir, but we can never seem to get him to go away. More on Amir later.

One morning in the summer of 1977 I am drawn out to our front lawn by the forceful growling of an approaching C-46 from the north heading south. It is very low, it seems even below the 500-foot minimum that must be maintained over persons and property, and clearly under the Lambert terminal control area (TCA)—why? I don't know. It just about takes my head off as it flies over my front yard, then makes a steep bank on a seventy-degree turn to the east. Wow! Then I look onto the street and see our aging, rather quiet bachelor neighbor, Bob McClure, on his morning walk also staring at the plane. I yell, *"C-46?"* He replies, *"Yes."* He would know—he was in the US Army Air Force during World War II, and his brother, Charlie, was the navigator on the B-25 named "The Ruptured Duck" on the Doolittle Tokyo raid. Both of his shoulder blades were broken when they crash-landed in China. Charlie's character is featured in the movie *Thirty Seconds Over Tokyo*, as played by actor Don DeFore who also played the character "Thorny" in *The Adventures of Ozzie and Harriet*.

Shamrock flew other propliners along with the C-46s. I regularly spot a similarly painted DC-6B on the ramp as well. It has a large Shamrock roundel on its vertical tail and it says "Shamrock" over the green trim over the cabin windows. The plane looks like it came right out of Ireland, but it is dirty. The fuselage behind the wings has black oil splotches down the sides, as does the tail fin. The engine nacelles are covered in black soot that streaks back to the trailing edges. This plane looks like it had received quite a workout, just like when I first saw DC-6B N37570 (Air Trav-A-Lairs) in the summer of 1972. It turns out this ex-Shamrock DC-6B was being leased by that "Rising Phoenix" alluded to in the previous chapter, as we will see.

A lucky but far-away shot of a Trans Continental (ex-Shamrock) C-46 freighter chugging over my St. Louis County house heading southeast in August 1976. I took this photo exactly one year before Bob McClure and I spotted what was possibly the same plane over our neighborhood "a bit too low" in August 1977. This plane is probably N1259N which is now C-GTPO and still flying freight in northern Canada with Buffalo Airways. Only about 3-4 of these are still airworthy. All now fly near the Arctic Circle, but probably not for long.

Many years later I find that Shamrock Airlines was a "CIA proprietary" company operating to all points in the western hemisphere out of San Juan, Puerto Rico. They flew cargo for the military-industrial complex for the U.S. Air Force and the CIA like its peers but also general cargo like everyone else. During this era, the Caribbean and Latin America were politically unstable as the Morrises found out with St. Lucia Airways. There have always been rumors that CIA proprietaries flew drugs, arms, currency, and other contraband to appease general third-world populations and friendly militias at big profit margins "for the greater good." In some cases, this might have been true, but my mind goes wild, imagining that Shamrock was flying in drugs and guns inbound to the St. Louis area mob syndicates, who were especially powerful during the 1970s. But Shamrock had been shut down since 1974 and was no longer operating the DC-6B nor the C-46s when I was seeing them. So what's the deal? It turns out that all these planes had been leased or sold to someone else, but the Shamrock paint schemes remained mostly intact—a rule, and not an exception during the *Second Wind* era.

The so-called "Shamrock" C-46s I witnessed were with a small startup fleet for Trans Continental Airlines out of the Detroit area, which later became a big DC-6B freighter and Convair

Ex-Shamrock C-46 freighter N1259N on the former Mark Aero ramp in June 1977, only a few feet north of the Old Terminal. The trim is green. Note the barely visible Shamrock logo under the pilot's side window, as well as the remnants of the larger logo on the tail. It is flying for startup Trans Continental Airlines, hauling auto components out of Detroit which were destined for St. Louis assembly plants. Many other cities throughout the US were also so served. Trans Continental would later fly nicely painted DC-6A and -6B freighters, and later, piston Convairs. This is the C-46 that would a month later buzz low over my parents' house, almost shattering my mom's china. Believe it or not, as of this writing, this C-46 is still flying freight in the Canadian arctic as C-GTPO with Buffalo Airways out of Yellowknife Northwest Territories, but with stronger forged C-Series cylinder jugs replacing the original cast B-Series cylinders which are nearly impossible to come by these days. This plane started life with the USAAF during World War II, then flew with Flying Tiger Line until 1957, and went through several other owner/operators including F.A. Conner and Ortner before its time with Shamrock and Trans Continental. I believe this is one of only two C-46s I ever witnessed in revenue operations, spotting it many times over my home from 1975 well into 1977.

operator. They were hauling just-in-time "hot-shot" auto components destined for the several auto assembly plants located in the St. Louis area, including the sole assembly plant for the Chevrolet Corvette. Auto parts handling would explode on the ex-Mark Aero ramp over the next few years, which we will cover in detail.

By June 1977 I find the former Mark Aero facilities are morphing into an unkempt hodgepodge of rusting support equipment and other junk, forming the backdrop for an occasional unmarked and faded propliner sitting here and there. The facilities would soon be tidied up and become more active in coming years to due to that Rising Phoenix we've been mentioning. When I photograph C46 N125N (see photo previous page), I catch two other DC-6s parked there. These were both ex-military C-118s and I can't tell whether they are about to be junked or not. The U.S. military markings had been blotched out, but the basic overall faded military schemes remained. Along with the dirty Shamrock DC-6B I'd earlier spotted on this apron, I don't yet know that these two C-118s are manifestations of that Rising Phoenix.

CHAPTER 29

Checkride Time

Jerry Riebold, who cut his transport-category teeth flying the Martin 404s on the Reindeer Lake runs, describes his nerve-wracking type check ride in the much larger 50-ton four-engine heavy-piston DC-6B circa 1976 when he was 27 years old. This was a near replay of Mark Morris's rough experience getting *his* DC-6 type rating only months earlier. As Jerry states:

My DC-6/7 type rating ride was with Joe Morris in the right seat and Lou Salmons the FAA Southern District check airman working the engineer panel. The flight plan was MSY to MSY [that is, flying from, and later shooting approaches at, New Orleans International Airport]. *The check airman (Lou) made me re-do the 2-engine out on one side approach because I "cheated" (his words) because I flew the approach at VMC +30* [Minimum Controllable Airspeed + 30 Knots] *with #3 and #4 engines idled, which is what any sane person would do with an entire side out, while looking for an appropriate 10,000-foot runway.*

They made me do the next one with #1 and #2 at zero thrust, leaving only the critical engines #3 and #4 at my command [given the direction of prop rotation these are the worst engines to be doing *all the work* in such an emergency] *and then told me to attempt to fly the ILS at VMC. I had to get Joe Morris to hold full aileron and I locked my leg onto the right rudder and holding on to the armrest to get me more leverage. My thigh muscle burned so badly I thought my trousers would catch on fire. They deliberately took me to the verge of losing full rudder control, but Joe maintained his expert "feel" for it to keep us out of disaster. On about one mile final when I figured we would crash land someplace near the Hilton Hotel across the street from MSY Lou give me my motors back and we make a normal landing.*

I thought I busted the ride for sure. Both Joe and the Lou burst out laughing because it was a surprise baptism by fire for the new kid. I now knew what a near aerodynamic upset felt like in a heavy transport. I could hardly get out the seat because my leg hurt so bad and Lou told me, "Don't ever fly this airplane any slower than VMC +5 and add 10 knots for each engine out." Lesson learned—and felt.

To his dismay and supercharged relief, Jerry passed his DC-6 check ride from hell. While fairly normal check ride procedure then, by today's standards this was a dangerous operation that would no longer be practiced due to advances in simulator technology (and no more DC-6s). The check plane was none other than passenger-configured N37570, that dirty/oily former Air Trav-A-Liars plane I photographed in July 1972 on the Mark Aero ramp (see photos, Chapters 15 and 17). The plane had just completed its second—and last—stint with St. Lucia Airways, which had been fully nationalized, thus sealing this airline's permanent demise. It was now on a tax lease from airplane investor Edwin Phelps. Who was the lessee? It was Mark's new "Rising Phoenix" corporation he registered as "Petroleum Air Transport, Inc." and N37570 was its first DC-6. I later find this is the mysterious place where the ex-Interstate Martins wound up. In due course, Mark would promote Jerry Riebold to chief pilot of his new airline, who started with Mark Aero only a few years earlier as a primary flight instructor at Mark Aero. Because Mark needed good pilots *now*, he pulled Jerry off the instructor line to train as a line pilot for the big iron (Jerry thought this was way too premature, but he'd take it.). In Mark's words:

Jerry, by far, was the best chief pilot an airline could have. He was a stickler for following the regulations, knew them as well as the back of his hand. And he even led the charge to change about 11 federal FAA regulations - by far he knew the aircraft super well—better than anyone alive—and was a great manager of pilots and flight attendants. He didn't put up with mediocrity and would come down on a pilot if he did something stupid (which as a fellow pilot I can say there are a lot of stupid pilots out there). Overall I would put Riebold as the best overall management pilot I have ever had in any of my airlines [Petroleum Air Transport and future airlines] . . . *and I've had some great ones but Jerry was the best. He was the only senior manager I had that I didn't have to check up on. When he took a task on it was always done right, and on time.*

This new airline was a specialty contract carrier that transported offshore oil services crews for weekly change-outs all around the Gulf of Mexico and the Caribbean. Their typical destinations outside the U.S. included Mexico and Baja, Central and South America, with four Martin 404s in its initial fleet (the three ex-Interstate planes plus N40436—the "Sherry" plane—that had the blue trim and triangles on the tail). Back in St. Louis, all of Mark Aero's previous St. Louis fueling and servicing operations for transient and locally based airlines had been turned over to Lambert FBO Midcoast Aviation (later Airport Terminal Services or ATS). Even though

Peabody Coal CEO Edwin R. Phelps at a White House dinner with President Gerald R. Ford in 1975. Phelps had just presented Ford with an ornamental clock mounted in a block of coal. Phelps was a former Naval aviator and unapologetic aviation advocate and close friend of the Morris family. He was also owner/lessor (on-and-off) of passenger DC-6B N37570 that the Morrises operated for their various airlines from 1975 to 1981. (White House photo)

Petroleum Air Transport was based in Lafayette, Louisiana, the company's future opportunities would soon have it take over the ex-Navy hangars and the 52 acres of tarmac previously leased to Mark Aero. This would not, however, include the historic Old Terminal that was slated to be razed. While John Tucker of Midcoast had a reasonably good relationship with the Morrises, he wasn't happy about them retaining the use of all that space because he wanted it for his expansion goals. He would get it in due course.

For some background, Petroleum Air Transport's predecessor was the Lafayette Division of Mark Aero which had been started by Joe sometime in 1975 under Mark Aero's Part 121(c) Commercial Operator certificate, during the final Reindeer Lake shuttle season. This new operation was to provide some cash flow while Mark Aero was being liquidated. Joe, who was on his road to recovery from his cancer, had landed several contracts with some major oil exploration companies to shuttle offshore platform workers, and could therefore keep Martins busy year-round. This was an opportunistic move as the current rise in world crude oil prices meant more drilling activity.

In addition to Mark's liquidation assignment, Joe sent Mark to Lafayette to take charge of flight operations, adding to the persistent strain on his long-distance marriage to Susan. Unfortunately, while managing the division, Mark reported directly to that bean-counting corporate general manager put there by Mark Aero's board. The bureaucrat rejected most of Mark's recommendations to get the Lafayette Division running smoothly, growing, and diversified, but this bean counter was finally canned on December 31, 1975, the day Mark Aero shut down for good.

Because cash had been tight long before the Lafayette Division was started, we mentioned that Joe had sold the three Martinliners to that dentist, Dr. Harold Steck who leased them back to Mark Aero. But as time went on Steck could not make his airplane mortgage payments to Citizens National Bank because Mark Aero was slow on its lease payments, which were piling up in arrears. Joe, however, had a very good relationship with the president of Citizens, Cathy Mullen.

By mid-1975, Mark had been able to stash away considerable profits from his Spiegel and Arrow oil operations. After consulting with Thom Fields, Mark Aero's (and Ozark Airline's) attorney, Mark decided to buy out, reorganize and incorporate Joe's Lafayette division. By transferring Mark Aero's existing three ex-Interstate Martins plus the other one he owned outright, plus the contracts in place, as well as the former Mark Aero employees, they were able to piggyback Mark Aero's 121(c) Commercial Operating certificate over to the new Petroleum Air Transport. The bona fide operation was already there, so it was hardly more than changing the name on the certificate. However, as of the company's January 1, 1976 start date (the first day after Mark Aero's doors were closed for good), the 404 fleet had not yet been yet transferred to the new company because of the problematic lease arrangement with Dr. Steck, and for some reason Mark's 404 (N40436) wasn't ready either (Also, the Phelps passenger DC-6 was still in St. Lucia and not in the mix yet). This was a problem that needed a quick solution to allow the piggybacking of the certificate so operations could continue uninterrupted. In Mark's words:

My dad had to get a life insurance policy on the three aircraft Dr. Steck had, as Mark Aero was the lessee. Later in 1974 when we were in a recession and Dad was recovering after complications from his cancer, Dr. Steck would call me every few weeks to see what stage of cancer he was in. After almost a year, Dad was re-staged as Stage 3 and Steck was yelling at me because he thought for sure Dad was going to expire and he would only get enough money out of the life insurance policy to pay off his mortgages at Citizens

National Bank in Maplewood and not recover any equity value for the planes.

Cathy Mullen, the bank's president had a good relationship with my dad, so when I needed the Martins to get the certificate transferred to start Petroleum Air Transport, I asked her if she could finance them, but Dr. Steck wanted $120,000 each. It was overpriced but I was coming up on deadlines with FAA on showing I had at least one Martin on contract for certification reasons. Cathy sent a letter to Steck saying she was going to foreclose, sell the aircraft for spare parts and he would be at least $100,000 short, maybe $150,000.

He owed $80,000 against each one. I called Dr. Steck shortly after I knew he had received Cathy's letter, and told him I was about to cut a deal to buy a few other Martins from another company and wished him good luck. That said, I got Dr. Steck's aircraft purchased for me by simply assuming his notes to Citizens Bank for $80,000 each.

Mark got a 10-year term on these reissued loans with zero down payment, so Petroleum Air Transport then got the Mark Aero Commercial Operator certificate piggybacked and was on its way. A new airline was born, initially headquartered in the upstairs back office of Citizens Bank.

Citizens National Bank (CNB), the small suburban bank that bankrolled the Morris aviation enterprises for many years as a result of the James O. Holton, Jr. relationship. It still occupies its longtime headquarters building at Manchester Road and Oakview Terrace in Maplewood (St. Louis County), Missouri, where Petroleum Air Transport had its original offices in the rear of the building where the second story protrudes.

CHAPTER 30

School is *Out*—And Reality is *In*

I graduate from Mizzou in August 1977. I was supposed to graduate in May, but I'm two credit hours short. I have to go back to Columbia in June to get those two credits by taking a tennis class in order to be awarded my BSBA degree in Marketing—the soft road compared to my original accounting major—just to *get me out of school*. I had tried to finish out at the University of Missouri St. Louis (UMSL), but the silly rule was that you must get your last credits at the specific Missouri campus awarding your degree. So, in Columbia, I stay in a beat-up, mold-filled apartment located in a damp creek valley just south of my high-rise dorm, Hatch Hall, where I had just finished a great social life over the previous 2 ½ years. But now it's lonely at Mizzou playing tennis in the summer with the equally unmotivated students in our small tennis class. There was hardly a soul around this giant campus like a neutron bomb went off and put me in the Twilight Zone. However, I need to graduate—bittersweet anticlimax or not.

I'm renting with three of my college motorcycle buddies, all of them seniors too, who also fell short on credits last May. They get bored *fast* with this summer situation just as I am, but they soon take it a step further and drop out of summer classes deciding to just finish in December. It takes them just a couple of hours for them to pack up for a motorcycle run to California—the preferred destination for Mizzou dropouts in those days. I now have the entire apartment to myself because I just want to get it over with. I leave their unmade beds in place and leave their Farah Fawcett and Bob Seeger posters tacked onto the wall and watch *The Gong Show* in the afternoon, which is so stupid you can't stop watching it. At least I go home every weekend to see my soon-to-be fiancée Cindy. We had started dating at Mizzou just 6 months prior. She was in my Class of '73 at Kirkwood High, and she graduated on time in May with her liberal arts degree. I'm envious that she had just landed a good public relations job working for the top bureaucrats at the South County headquarters of the St. Louis County Parks and Recreation Department, while I have zero leads in securing my first full-time job.

In my apartment solitude, and with my lightest academic load ever, I have ample time to remain up to speed on the *Second Wind* propliner world. During the second week of July, I catch a disturbing article in the *St. Louis Globe-Democrat* where one of my dorm buddies, Rick Stoff, has just landed a job as a reporter. The day before—just before midnight on July 6—there had been a fatal crash of a Lockheed L-188 Electra turboprop freighter on takeoff from Lambert, after several aborted attempts. It's Fleming International N280F on an attempted backhaul to Detroit after a hot-shot auto parts run for the St. Louis assembly plants. The number three propeller hub was acting up, making random un-commanded blade pitch adjustments. On previously aborted takeoff attempts, that powerplant would not put out full power because of this prop discrepancy. On an Electra, a propeller hub assembly is said to be more complicated than the engine itself, and some general field mechanics made several vain attempts to address the issue after each aborted takeoff (likely without the proper tools). Finally, the pilot and his two crewmen voted to perform an *"all or nothing"* takeoff on runway 30L. Remember, *"it probably won't happen this time."*

The takeoff wound up on the "*nothing*" side of the equation. Well into the roll, number three lost power and it is thought that the propeller went into reverse. Just after liftoff the aircraft careened to the right and cartwheeled into the ground bursting into flames, instantly snuffing out all three of the "voting" crewmen. I guess a "pure democracy" is not always right. The flaming pieces and parts all came to rest just southeast of the now abandoned Old Terminal, near the former site of the original Remmert-Werner facilities, just a stone's throw south of where I photographed the ex-Shamrock C-46 only four weeks earlier (see pages 172 and 173). I remember the newspaper photo of the aftermath, consisting of unrecognizably burnt aircraft remains with a couple of the fully separated 4-blade propellers lying there all twisted and bent up. Despite its generally good reputation, Fleming did have a sporadic history of FAA compliance problems which was not unusual for *Second Wind* freight carriers.

Later in the month, on another quiet evening of solitude, I am sitting on my unmade floor mattress thumbing through a 7-month-old issue of *Time* magazine while watching the TV show *Baa Baa Black Sheep*, a series on the renowned World War II Corsair squadron in the Pacific starring Cliff Robertson. I naturally get stuck on an article that has a photo of a DC-6 on the ground entitled "Pity Those Who Take Pot Luck." Federal agents had received tips that this aircraft movement would originate in Colombia, South America. It was reported that the plane was bankrolled by the New York mob and would be loaded to the gills with 25,000 pounds of marijuana with a street value of $16 million to some unknown destination in the northeast. This was rumored to be the largest shipment of pot ever to be flown into the U.S. to date, and several stakeouts were conducted at remote airports along the east coast in anticipation of the movement, but no DC-6 landed anywhere.

Finally, in late December a US Customs surveillance plane intercepted a *"mysterious DC-6 high over Key West"* and tracked it up the coast, warning the authorities. It landed in the pitch black at a remote Mount Pocono airfield in Pennsylvania at 1:00 AM. It came to a stop at the end of its landing roll as its four engines shut down. Nothing happened for 15 minutes. Then, unloading began. After half of the cargo was loaded into vans, the feds stormed out of the brush and captured the crew, handlers, and lookouts without a struggle. This sent the New York mob reeling. I stupidly ask myself, why does an iconic plane like a DC-6 turn to a life of crime? Then I remember that *"guns don't kill people, people kill people."* It logically follows that *airplanes don't make illegal flights, people do.* But among elements of the spoon-fed public, these old pieces of flying junk were the actual criminals. All of them—BAD. Never mind that only 20 years earlier they were a crowd-pleasing Sunday afternoon airport terrace attraction for all ages.

Mark Morris adds an interesting twist to this story. Joe once told him that the president and DC-6 captain of St. Lucia Airways, "Red" Mettric (the DC-6 "over-loader" who we met earlier), could not find a job after the second shutdown of that airline in 1976. So, Red went to prison for getting caught flying a drug-loaded DC-6 into the U.S. from Bogota, Colombia up the east coast "headed in the direction of Boston." This was at the exact same time that the "Pot Air Lines DC-6" was busted in Pennsylvania in 1976 per the *Time* article. Was this the same guy who was piloting the DC-6 in that article? That does fit like that pair of broken-in cowboy boots, but we cannot know for sure.

After finally getting my college degree in August, it takes me three months to land my first full-time job, an industrial sales position. Cindy has that nice office job in South County while my time remains flexible. On August 16, 1977, I wait in my Mazda to pick her up from work at around 5:30 PM, leaving the car radio on low volume. I guess her car was in the shop. My eyes are attracted to an approaching sound in the southern sky where I witness something I'd never

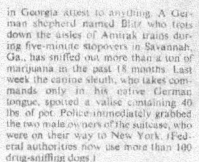

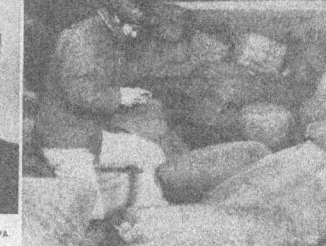

"Pot Air Lines DC-6" article in a December 1976 issue of Time Magazine. DC-6s, -7s, Lockheed Constellations and Super Constellations, Curtiss C-46s, and Convair 240/340/440s became the "equipment of choice" by the big drug syndicates in the U.S. and Latin America in the late '70s and into the '80s, starting about the time of this big drug bust. Piston propliners were numerous and cheap with high-cargo capacity—and *expendable*, just like the pilots who insanely chose this line of work. Back then, this is *exactly* what the general public thought of whenever the topic of "those old propeller planes" came up (rarely).

seen. A four-engine de Havilland Heron flies low overhead toward Lambert in a seemingly shallow descent. It's an unusual British light plane, but a "big" one, with *four* Lycoming O-540 flat-six engines hung on the wings that at some point replaced the original British Gipsy Queen inverted-six engines. This 1950s-era plane carries 14 passengers, and a few of these re-engined ones are still in service. As it recedes to the north there is a shocking news bulletin declaring that Elvis Presley is dead.

That's probably the reason why I remember this Heron overflight, and over the coming months I would regularly see it coming in at exactly 5:30 PM each evening, often framed by the sunset on my way home from my first full-time job. I find this all-yellow plane is part of the SEMO (Southeast Missouri) Airways commuter fleet headquartered a hundred miles south of here

You sure don't see these anymore. The re-engined de Havilland Heron commuter plane—the four-engine propliner with that "light plane" feeling. SEMO Airlines flew these into St. Louis and other Midwest destinations for a short time during the mid-1970s. Their Herons were powered by four Lycoming O-540 flat-six engines developing 290 hp each. Its original engines were 250 hp de Havilland Gipsy Queen 30 Mk.2 inverted 6-cylinder inline engines. (Wikimedia Commons, RuthAS CC BY 3.0)

in Cape Girardeau. Several years later in 1981 I would land my rented Gulfstream American Tiger at the Poplar Bluff Airport in southeast Missouri on a work assignment and would catch one of these yellow Herons parked right there, ripe for a close inspection (though for insurance purposes my company didn't allow the use of private aircraft for work, I sometimes broke the rule). The Heron looked larger than I expected. It's sitting there intact like it is ready to go, but closer inspection reveals a faded, scratched-up machine that looks like it had been through hell, with stop-drilled cracks everywhere around the aluminum engine nacelle panels. After a little research, I find that SEMO Airways had long since ceased operations.

Two months after Elvis died, another tragedy hits the Rock n Roll world. It involves the southern rock band Lynyrd Skynyrd, one of my college favorites and a favorite of most of my peers. They are at the height of their most successful concert tour ever when they board a Convair 240 at Greenville, South Carolina for a leg to Baton Rouge, Louisiana for a concert at Louisiana State University (LSU). The owner of the aircraft is corner-cutting L&J Company and the lessee is Lynyrd Skynyrd Productions, Inc. On the previous leg from Lakeland, Florida, band and support members were horrified by not-so-normal 10-foot exhaust flames shooting out of the right (#2) engine nacelle on takeoff. The crew said "not-to-worry," they'd have it fixed in Baton Rouge. After their engagement at Greenville, several band members had normal premonitions about the worst and didn't want to re-board. But "get-there-itis" combined with "it-won't-happen-to-me-this-time-itis" won out and they all stepped aboard. It is rumored that the flight department of the rock band Aerosmith had turned down this plane and crew only days before due to their scheduler's safety concerns.

There was one CB-16 and one CB-17 engine mounted on the plane, which is not necessarily bad. But the "flaming" right R-2800 engine had been running "hot and rough" for weeks and had to be flown in the "auto-rich" mixture setting to smooth it out and cool it down. This increased its fuel consumption by 14%, but the pilots really did have "good intentions" of having this fixed once chalked down at Baton Rouge. Why just now? Why not earlier?

Close to the destination near Gillsburg, Mississippi both engines quit within a minute of each other due to complete fuel exhaustion. After an engineless, difficult-to-handle descent, it pancaked into a wooded area, shredding the aircraft to pieces—with no post-crash fire (obviously—no fuel). The engines remained intact. Six out of the 26 onboard perished on impact, including the two pilots and the lead singer and founder of the band, Ronnie Van Zant, as well as guitarist Steve Gaines and his backup singer sister Cassie, as well as assistant road man Dean Kilpatrick. The other 20 passengers, who were all support personnel for the band survived with serious injuries, many sustaining permanent disabilities. The NTSB cited several contributing factors to the crash including "poor preflight planning" by the leased pilots, "careless and negligent fuel management" including reliance on faulty fuel gauges, and "failure to manually 'stick' the wing tanks" during preflight (just how did they confirm that?), and "prolonged operation with an engine anomaly that caused substantially increased fuel consumption."

Now the "broken record" part. While *not considered a direct cause of the crash*, this was another of those sloppy but perfectly legal Part 91 "commercial" operations pretending to be a private one, where the lessee, Lynyrd Skynyrd Productions, Inc. was deemed the "operator." Lynyrd Skynyrd Productions, which was understandably uninformed on things aeronautical, did not read the fine print in the lease agreement that they *"have paramount and complete responsibility for the supervision and direction of the flight crew."* Additionally, the pilot had only 62 hours in the Convair 240, and the copilot 32 hours—remember, specific crew qualifications don's matter under Part 91. I was as disgusted with this crash as I was with the Wichita State

Convair 240 similar to the ill-fated Lynard Skynyrd Convair N55YM. A rough running engine sucking excess fuel, negligent fuel management by otherwise complacent pilots, and one of those smoke-and-mirrors "Part 91 Loophole" operations spelled disaster. The NTSB report said that though this was a Part 91 operation, that was not a major factor in the crash. I think it was. As we've mentioned before, the 240 was Convair's competitive counterpart to the Martin 404. (Logawi at English Wikimedia CC BY 2.5)

Famed victims of the "Part 91 Loophole." Lynyrd Skynyrd was one of the most popular rock bands on almost every college campus in the mid-1970s when I was attending Mizzou. It was a complete shock to me and my peers when they went down in "a plane." Band members killed in the Convair 240 crash included Ronnie Van Zant (arms crossed) and guitarist Steve Gaines (front, second from right). Backup singer Cassie Gaines and assistant road manager Dean Kilpatrick also perished but are not pictured. (Wikimedia Commons, MCA Records)

Martin 404 crash of 7 years earlier that had an even worse outcome.

A few weeks later in November 1977 I finally land a sales engineer job at a Kansas City-based company called Industrial Bearing and Transmission (IBT). For the next 5 years, I work out of St. Louis and cover the southern half of the St. Louis metropolitan area and most of southeastern Missouri. The people at IBT are great to work with, and I largely attribute it to them for helping mold me at least into something at least half-successful. But my dad, who notices me tracking well with IBT, starts charging me rent to incentivize me to leave the nest, so I get an apartment in the same complex as Cindy's place in Creve Coeur, just a few miles southwest of Lambert airport. My new apartment has a great balcony that faces north toward Lambert Airport, only 5 miles away.

I sell all types of mounted and unmounted industrial bearings, speed reducers (essentially industrial gearboxes), electric motors from fractional horsepower up to a couple of thousand horsepower for steel mills, variable-speed electronic motor controls, V-Belts, chain drives, gaskets, lubricants, conveyor systems and industrial hose to every conceivable type of manufacturing operation in my territory. I call on purchasing agents, engineers, and maintenance departments. I enjoy designing industrial power trains using our cherrypicked SKUs to tailor mechanical and electrical power transmission system solutions for our customers. To me, it is like playing with tinker toys or an erector set.

On the negative side, our home phone numbers are printed on our business cards so we can respond to "after-hours" and weekend industrial breakdowns. More often than I like I am rudely awakened by my ringing landline in the middle of the night and forced to get up, get dressed, and solve customer problems at their plant. These plants are sometimes located in the worst parts of town, and the situation might be outdoors on top of a cement elevator tower in heavy rain or a blizzard on, say, Christmas Eve.

IBT has a rule that all outside salespeople like me must wear suits and ties every day (except for the aforementioned midnight emergencies), so we'd appear a "stand out" compared to most other industrial salespeople. The rationale for salesmen "dressing down" in this industry is so that they aren't perceived as "city slickers" by their similarly dressed-down customers. We also have to take a customer to lunch every day, and in those days business lunches involve beer and martinis. We are tacitly expected to "keep up" with customer lunchtime drinking—which characterized almost all of them. It's hard to believe it bothered almost nobody that many of our drinking customers were around dangerous heavy machinery all day. For one of my cement plant customers, I bring in a case of beer late every other Friday afternoon and drink with them—that is all I need to do for them, no sales pitches, no nothing—and they order from me like crazy to become one of my "top five."

There I am, for the next 5 years crawling around dirty factories all dressed up in my fancy Jos. A. Banks business suits and ties. I spend every day sweating inside my suit in iron foundries, steel mills, railyards, grain elevators, chemical plants, machine shops, food processors, quarries, construction sites, cement plants, and everything in between. In this business, one learns very quickly to tuck your tie deep into your shirt when around such facilities (or wear a fake "quick disconnect" tie) lest it gets caught in a drive chain, rotating shaft, V-belt, or gear reducer. Instant strangulations, broken necks, and decapitations were not uncommon for dressed-up people like me in this line of work.

Early on this proves to be the perfect first job for a semi-gearhead like me, and I'm finding all this dovetails well with my pursuit of understanding both wartime and postwar heavy piston radial engine technology, as well as gas turbine technology. I don't mind at all that I am required to attend numerous industrial schools and seminars on our products. My knowledge and understanding of the universal principles of horsepower, torque, thrust, and basic thermodynamics grow exponentially. I become proficient in my knowledge of spur, helical, planetary, and spur-planetary gearbox systems with multiple reduction stages—just like those found on the big piston radial engines and turboprops which by necessity had to reduce propeller RPMs to half or less of engine crankshaft speed for big piston engines, that is, a 2:1 reduction, or one-tenth (10:1 reduction) for a turboprop.

My work at IBT incentivizes me to become more knowledgeable on the workings and evolution of every U.S.-built postwar heavy piston radial aircraft engine from the Wright R-1820 to the monster Pratt & Whitney R-4360 and also on their complex constant speed propellers they turned, and everything in between. I continue to accumulate a personal library of books and manuals on all this, mixed in with my volumes of manuals for electro-mechanical, materials handling, and lubricant products that we sell at IBT.

Simply put, my vocation and avocation feed on each other and leverage my enthusiasm for life. It turns out that my marketing degree doesn't turn out quite so "soft" after all. At least I'm not fighting for retail shelf space for health and beauty aids, which is where degreed marketing majors typically wind up in the 1970s (Yes, to cover my bases I did interview with, got job offers from, and turned down those opportunities).

CHAPTER 31

A Different Concept

Near my IBT office in Hanley Industrial Court, there is a company called Cupples Products which manufactures high-rise window frames for new skyscraper projects all over the world. They are a good customer of mine for flange bearings and pillow block bearings and are known for their central roles in the construction of the World Trade Center and the iconic Cadet's Chapel on the campus of the U.S. Air Force Academy. For years Cupples wind-tested these robust frames with a curious contraption—an R-2800 B-Series powered World War II Vought F4U-1 Corsair. The rear fuselage had been chopped off just behind the cockpit and its outer wing panels were also removed. This airplane-turned-wind machine was secured by a special frame, among other unusual cowling modifications that kept the engine cool during high power operations. Its last flight was with the Navy in 1958 when it was flown into Lambert by a reservist, where it was promptly towed over to the factory 20 miles south on Hanley Road. It was in all-natural metal with no markings.

I'm stopped in my tracks several times when I see some random employee climb into the cockpit to handle the complexities of firing up the 2.000 horsepower R-2800 B-Series engine for a wind test session. When the employee hits about half throttle after a long warmup, other workers shoot jets of water from fire hoses into the propeller blades creating a violently wet, hurricane-force maelstrom. I find it fun and interesting to watch, but it's not so pleasant for the small retail businesses across the street who are always taking legal action against Cupples due to the noise, vibration, and merchandise walking off their shelves and breaking. Cupples has to later move the contraption to the other side of its complex away from its business neighbors, and they then paint it light blue and even put some crude "Navy" markings on it—something tells me they were attached to this machine for which there were few alternatives if any. For decades warbird collectors from all over made offers to buy the chopped Corsair, but Cupples would never sell. With the worldwide decline in high-rise expansion projects and changes in window technology, the company eventually ceased operations and was liquidated in the 1990s. A California warbird collector finally got possession of the Corsair for a massive rebuild to flying condition, which has been a work-in-process for at least two decades. While it is slowly morphing back into an intact Corsair once again, it remains to be seen whether it will fly again.

Before and during my early time with IBT and working with Cupples there was a young freight-only airline making its initial footprints on the domestic scene. The company was called Federal Express. The world was just a few years into the dawn of the door-to-door overnight package industry, which was first conceived and brought to reality (especially internationally) by a company called DHL (Dalsey, Hillblom, Lynn) back in 1969. But DHL had no dedicated aircraft fleet. It outsourced all its courier transportation—including air service—making it by far the largest worldwide overnight courier. Federal Express came along with different ideas. Its founder and CEO, Fred Smith wanted to do this with an in-house aircraft fleet from the get-go, giving the company more control. Smith was well on his way to *creating new domestic airline markets*, something the FAA, CAB, and the established airlines *did not* want. On the other hand, DHL's business model fit the established airline system like a glove. The airlines loved DHL because they greatly profited from it as we shall see later. To further realize and grow his new concept, Smith had to almost single-handedly *change* the airline industry rules as it pertained to hauling cargo which started with that legendary college term paper of his that did anything but dazzle his professor.

In 1971 Smith registered Federal Express with the CAB as a Part 135 Air Taxi Operator—the best he could come up with within the existing regulatory framework. As an interstate airline, they could only fly small aircraft with a gross weight of under 12,500 pounds to any destination in the U.S. The problem was that rapidly-growing Federal Express had to order 32 Dassault Falcon 20 *corporate jet* freighter conversions to meet its projections. While it is a relatively small aircraft, the maximum gross weight of the Falcon was just over 28,000 pounds, which was much heavier than allowed under the Part 135 certificate, so Federal Express had to obtain a Certificate of Public Convenience and Necessity *exemption* for each route applied for. This would be an onerous administrative mess and paralyze growth. A true overnight package operation would have to fly many more routes every 24 hours than a single passenger airline on established routes. Being just a 135 Air Taxi operator would not work.

Late in 1971 and into 1972, Smith fought the CAB tooth and nail to increase the weight limits for an air taxi operation by amending Part 298 of FAR Part 135. In July 1972 the CAB increased the air taxi passenger and payload restriction to 30 passengers and 7,500 pounds, respectively, which was thankfully higher than the Falcon 20 capacity. After raising $90 million in venture capital Federal Express finally began operations in March of 1973 with the Falcons and within a year it was servicing 25 cities while burning through the venture capital proceeds. So, he was working with General Dynamics in St. Louis and others for more capital but they ultimately pulled out. However, Smith pulled a rabbit out of his hat and raised around $60 million more in venture capital from other sources—which when combined with his first deal left Federal Express with the most venture capital financing on the books to date. That's nothing when compared to deals that are done today.

In 1976 I see TV ads featuring the Federal Express Falcon jets lined up on the tarmac with their catchy Federal Express purple, red, and white paint jobs—the first time I become aware of this unusual airline. Here I learn that late at night every 24 hours, the fleet of *little* Falcons *all* descended into their Memphis hub from all points of the compass to unload inbound packages and then load outbound ones, then departing outbound to all points of the compass in the early morning for delivery. To me, doing this with little Falcons seemed like digging a house foundation with a teaspoon. At the time, I did not know that this was the first "hub and spoke" route system, which would be adopted by the major passenger airlines years later after the Airline Deregulation Act of 1978.

By 1975—the year before the Falcon TV ads—the modified air taxi rules that Smith worked so hard to achieve became useless again. Federal Express needed bigger planes. They applied for a specific exemption to operate first-generation DC-9 freighters that would increase payload to 15,000 pounds. They were denied after every major U.S. airline objected, even though Federal Express could prove a strong and growing demand for their services. Smith was eventually able to pull it off, but this would take a few years.

Smith's primary approach to employing larger aircraft was to convince regulators to *separate pure cargo operations* from the onerous regulatory structure which was geared toward passenger operations in the first place. He began work on this on January 1, 1976, with the start of the new congressional session. The timing may have been good because Congress was beginning to warm up to the concept of *comprehensive* airline deregulation. However, the world's largest pure cargo airline, Flying Tiger Line out of Los Angeles, vehemently objected to carving pure cargo operations out of the regulatory structure (which protected them as a long-established airline on the "big" routes such as LA to Chicago or San Francisco to New York). As well, the Teamsters union opposed *any* deregulation—and to rub salt in the wound, Federal Express was non-union. So, by the end of 1976 Smith's legislative proposal was rejected.

The first Federal Express Dassault Falcon 20 jet freighter is seen on display at the Steven F. Udvar-Hazy Center, Smithsonian Institution, in Washington D.C. In 1976 several of these planes were featured in a TV ad campaign. I thought they had a good concept, but I asked myself, *why aren't they using bigger planes?* I think my question may have been one intended purpose of their ads. (Wikimedia Commons, RadioFan CC BY-SA 3.0)

At the beginning of the 1977 Congressional session, Smith was back. He continued an aggressive media campaign with reporters, business groups, and customers, claiming the opposite of what most airlines have always sought—government protection. He stated, *"The government doesn't have to give us a thing—it just has to get out of our way."* Later in the year both the Senate and the House were looking at bills that would allow Federal Express to fly larger aircraft and use more efficient fixed pricing versus the customary distance/volume pricing, and receive exemptions from the CAB as necessary for growth. All this was still totally opposed by the airlines including Flying Tiger Line, but Smith, his employees, and his attorneys persisted.

Despite this, in the summer of 1977, I notice Federal Express is using larger planes than the Falcons even though the separate cargo rules had not been carved out yet. I repeatedly observe a

Federal Express flight out of Lambert St. Louis International passing overhead on the way to Memphis each evening at 11:00 PM. But it's not a Falcon—it's a big, old piston DC-3 flying nightly runs for Federal Express under contract. These were not "feeder" runs, but direct runs to Memphis. The DC-3 is dimensionally larger than the Falcon 20, with a slightly higher maximum payload. I never found out who that DC-3 subcontractor was, but Federal Express used a lot of subcontractors using all types of aircraft and still does. Of course, if this 11:00 PM nightly run was done with a jet, I would have never noticed.

President Jimmy Carter had taken office earlier in the year and was the "go along with it" champion of deregulation of the transportation industry, including the airlines. Smith was able to change the minds of several congressmen and even Flying Tiger Line (but not the Teamsters). In late 1977, Carter finally signed the transportation bill to first deregulate air cargo, allowing Federal Express to expand with larger aircraft to enter the big time. They began flying converted secondhand Boeing 727-100 freighters. Carter's full deregulation of the entire airline industry would follow that year after considerable help from the fired-up Mark Morris, as we'll see in later chapters. Interestingly, in 1989, Federal Express would acquire its former nemesis, Flying Tiger Line, to enhance its earlier half-baked entry into international markets in1984. During the 1990s the company would also change its name to FedEx, as that was how most of its customers already referred to them. Also, the word "Federal" probably did not sit well with its new international customers. The rest of FedEx's evolution, and its life-changing innovations beyond aviation that went with it, are expansive and would fill volumes—which it has. For our purposes, this early summary of Federal Express lays our foundation for later chapters so it ends here.

While Federal Express is breaking out during the late 1970s, the pop culture craze is "disco dancing," which I hate. My now fiancée Cindy, however, is obsessed with it and even becomes a studio dance instructor and gives disco dance "demonstrations" at area shopping malls. I never understand the point of these demonstrations, exactly who bankrolls them, or just who is supposed to benefit. As her fiancée, she begs me to be her dance partner in all this, but as a non-exhibitionist, I want no part of it. She goes off the deep end and flatly cancels our engagement in mid-1978 in favor of a John Travolta look-alike named "Rodney," who has puffed-out "disco hair" and no evidence of sideburns—typical then. In my mind, I call him the "disco dirtbag." Best this happens now rather than when it's too late, so back to the drawing board.

Ironically, still hitting the disco bars with my buddies is a partial antidote for my "anti-disco breakup" (does that make any sense at all?). I know that *disco* is the repeated brunt of jokes these days—and it has been for decades—but like it or not, back then a single guy could not escape its misery. However, another thing helps offset the downer. I am *still* checking out the old Mark Aero ramp from time to time, which is an added diversion. I start noticing some interesting changes that, unbeknownst to me, would later *greatly* impact the overnight courier industry. To hell with fiancées. They can wait.

CHAPTER 32

Rising Phoenix Slammed

As the year 1976 progressed, Mark's specialty passenger airline was doing well. Under the new Petroleum Air Transport, he was able to retain his dad's oil services contracts and even pull in some bigger contract customers including Zapata (the George H.W. Bush family), Shell Oil, Marathon, Odeco, and Global Marine. The three Martin 404s were fully utilized, and passenger DC-6 N37570 was soon leased back from Ed Phelps and put into service to bolster the Martinliner fleet which would be historic. It is here that N37570 would be the *very last DC-6* to operate in *passenger* service. The other Martin, N40436, which was owned by Mark and was the first one transferred to Petroleum Air Transport in January 1976, was sold later that year. Again, that was the "Sherry" plane I had seen idling and taxiing on the ramp in November 1975.

Full utilization is something the other three ex-Interstate Martins had not seen since many owners ago—probably since their earliest operations with Eastern Airlines. Petroleum Air Transport's main routes originated along the U.S. gulf coast from Tallahassee, Florida to Houston and Corpus Christi Texas, along the Caribbean shores of Mexico Central and South America, facilitating offshore oil crew changeouts twice weekly under most contracts. These "carpooling" operations were during weekdays only, with departure just after sunrise to the various oil crew changeout points surrounding the gulf. Outbound oil crews would then board helicopters operated by separate companies to be transported to and from the offshore rigs, and Petroleum Air Transport flew the returning crews back to the same points in the U.S.

While Mark at first just wanted to be an airline pilot and not a businessman, he got to be an airline pilot because now he *was* a businessman. He was Petroleum Air's sole owner, CEO, President, operations manager, line captain and mechanic—unheard of in the industry. And on top of that, he still owned and operated the largest oil distribution businesses in Missouri that enabled the formation of Petroleum Air Transport in the first place. The only thing he had to sell was his MGB sports car but overall, he felt satisfaction in keeping his dad's aviation legacy alive while simultaneously keeping him employed.

All the moving parts worked well together because of his highly effective, long-time executive assistant, Patti Finot. She was good at going the extra mile day in and day out and could tackle multiple assignments where she had no previous experience. Mark required her to wear many hats just like he and all his employees. So, part of her job description was that she would have to serve as a flight attendant—without knowing at first that she had a slight fear of flying. Mark explains:

When I hired Patti I had gone through what seemed to be dozens of exec assistants. I fired most within days of hiring them. Someone said I should interview this person – so met Patti at the bar at Cheshire Inn . . . During the interview I told her that I would expect her to be qualified in most jobs as I was a mechanic, a line pilot, knew accounting, negotiated all insurance and fuel purchasing and she would also need working knowledge of all these areas plus the oil business as I had the largest unbranded oil business in Missouri. I told her that was mandatory- she said she would agree to all of that. Five hours later I stood up to leave and it was hard to stand - she said "bye" and to call her to let her know. She had a drink or two of scotch more than me - and I had too many and she drank me almost literally under the table . . . I got my bearings lined up and hurried out to catch up with her in the parking lot. Told her I would hire her but she would have to become a flight attendant. She said she liked flying and would accept the position. Six months after she started she was down in Lafayette Louisiana taking her first IOE flight [Initial Operating Experience check flight] and I was the captain. It was about 5 AM in the morning and she was sitting on a bench inside the fire fence at the airport. I came up to her and asked her how she was doing. I knew it would be tough on her as when I told her she needed to go to flight attendant training she then admitted she was terrified of flying- I asked her why she said she "liked" flying and she said "to get the job" and she figured she could convince me she didn't need to be a flight attendant. Well, here it was in the wee morning and the sun wasn't even thinking about coming up. There she was in uniform—scared to death—and when I asked her how she was doing—well if looks could kill I would have died a thousand deaths from her stare . . . she never answered that question even to this day.

One of Petroleum Air Transport's key operating areas was Central America, particularly Guatemala. Mark learned of political instability in that area and asked Patti to research it. Mark was not happy to learn that there were ongoing military skirmishes in Central America between Belize, a traditionally British territory, and Spanish-settled Guatemala. The Spanish insisted that in addition to Guatemala, Belize was *its* territory and did not belong to the British. The U.S. had a history of siding with the Brits in virtually all post-colonial uprisings, and this was no exception. One of the ports that Petroleum Air Transport served was Puerto Barrios, Guatemala which was not on the American side. They risked aircraft impoundment or worse at any time, but Mark had been through it all at St. Lucia. On approaches into Guatemala, their aircraft were often the targets of small arms fire, and allied British destroyers patrolling offshore would sometimes point their big anti-aircraft guns at them. With every arrival of a Martin 404 or the DC-6 at Puerto Barrios, armed soldiers would enter and inspect the aircraft, looking for an excuse to seize it.

Petroleum Air's situation was further aggravated by the CIA. It seems since his days in Southeast Asia flying for Air America, Mark remained on their "list." Before one of the early 404 flights to Puerto Barrios, a CIA agent visited Mark at Lafayette headquarters and gave him a small camera. The agent asked him to exercise caution and discreetly photograph anything and everything that "looked military" at the Puerto Barrios airport, inside and out if possible. The airport was a suspected staging area for military equipment, arms, and munitions, and the CIA wanted further intelligence. At considerable risk, Mark complied, taking photos of crates of these war materials inside a large hangar, almost getting caught red-handed. The CIA acted appreciatively and did not bother him anymore.

Around this time, Mark bought out his brother-in-law's 50% share in Spiegel Oil. He was getting tired of listening to advice from his father-in-law—the one who prompted Mark to start this business in the first place. Mark brought in a new partner named "Garry" who, over time, became a worse partner than his brother-in-law. Garry was a successful attorney who was looking for something else to do. He turned out to be a loose cannon who was making bad decisions without Mark's knowledge while he was busy with Petroleum Air Transport. As it turned out,

Petroleum Air Transport A&P mechanics tweak the number two R-2800 CB-16 on one of the ex-Interstate Martinliners. Petroleum Air maintained this same mustard yellow/red paint scheme that was first applied here in mid-1973 when operated by Mark Aero on the Reindeer Lake shuttle. The mechanic on the right was a Latino with the surname "Castro"—one of the best. He often served as the translator on airplane trips to Central and South America. A year or two later, I'd swear I'd seen him—shirtless in the middle of a hot summer—tweaking idling engines of the expanded Petroleum Air DC-6 fleet on the ex-Mark Aero ramp at Lambert. (Jerry Riebold)

Garry had various unethical tendencies that Mark wanted nothing to do with. Garry also wanted to expand and diversify Spiegel at a rate that would spread things too thin putting its profits at risk. On a planning trip in Aspen, Colorado, Mark and Garry had a violent falling out (don't ask) and they finally agreed that Garry would buy Mark out, which he did. Speigel slowly went downhill from there, which is another story.

On the other hand Petroleum Air Transport was doing fine but its operations were unfairly limited by the FAA Southern District. Under Part 121(c) the airline could only perform services for groups under blanket contracts, but to make matters worse, in the Southern District they could not exceed *ten* such open contracts in any given year. Also, remember that as a 121(c) operator they were not allowed to advertise their name—"*not even on a pencil.*" This stymied the company's growth, sparking a fight with the FAA and CAB, much like what Fred Smith went through for Federal Express.

Other FAA districts allowed a greater number of open contracts, and there was no consistency between these districts. The Miami District allowed up to 350 contracts in a given year for Part 121(c) carriers, hence the unrestrained growth of heavy-recip operators at Miami International Airport's "Corrosion Corner" and the Caribbean during the 1970s and 1980s. On the other hand, Part 121(c) carriers in the FAA Southern District seemed to be bound by an arbitrary straightjacket. But many of Petroleum Air's competitors in the Southern District were *not so limited*. Many of them thrived and grew faster than Petroleum Air Transport. Here we go again— they were able to take advantage of our old nemesis, the longstanding Part 91 Loophole. Under Part 91 they could directly compete with Petroleum Air—with a lease or transfer ownership of the equipment to the customer for *a single round trip* and a *rented crew*. Lack of even minimal maintenance, operational rules, or crew qualifications permitted a very low-cost structure and big profits. One of these Part 91 operators out of Miami flew around eight L-188 Electra turboprops on these one-time per-trip leases. They had a few hundred blanket contracts and no FAA to breathe down their necks, other than infrequent "ramp checks" which were worthless. The owners were also closely linked to President Jimmy Carter, so they were not typical fly-by-nighters either.

In response to this lopsided competition, Mark helped organize and was then elected vice-chairman of the Commercial Air Carrier Association (CACA), a lobbying group all Part 121(c) commercial operators (over 40 of them). Besides Petroleum Air Transport, some of the big players in this group were Bird Air, Fleming International, Trans Continental and Zantop (which had lost its preferred 121(b) Supplemental Carrier status and "demoted" to Part 121(c) Commercial Operator due to its being acquired by Universal Airlines and then going bankrupt).

CACA was formed to try and standardize things among and between the FAA districts. Several meetings were conducted jointly with the FAA and the Bureau of Operating Rights of the CAB, a more moderating force. Good in theory, not in practice. Instead, the FAA brought in the Enforcement Bureau of the CAB, a biased group in favor of the major scheduled airlines. To make matters worse, the opposing team was chaired by Mark Aero's "old FAA friend" Mr. McClure.

Petroleum Air Transport DC-6 freighter parked at an unidentified winter location, but possibly at the ex-Mark Aero ramp looking southwest. It is in its new mustard yellow and red paint scheme. (Jerry Riebold)

Yes—the same McClure who killed MAC a few years earlier. He rose from the dead and weaseled his way to become *national* head of all FAA ACDOs after being fired from the St. Louis office. McClure sure had a chip on his shoulder for Joe Morris and prided himself in helping to put Mark Aero out of business.

It is no surprise, these meetings got nowhere. Mark's counsel, Thom Fields, could not tame Mark's occasionally explosive episodes in the meetings. His fact-laden outbursts just served to piss off the bureaucrats and cause them to double down. Mark then laid down the argument of the competing Part 91 operators in the district. McClure denied they had any authority over Part 91 general aviation. What? Mark then said if that were the case, in order to compete he would proceed

View of #4 engine from a Petroleum Air Transport DC-6B over the coastal bayous of the Gulf of Mexico. This is passenger N37570, the keystone fixture throughout the life of Petroleum Air Transport (see photos pages 109 and 121). (Jerry Riebold)

to convert Petroleum Air into a Part 91 operation just like President Jimmy Carter's buddies who were flying Electras out of Miami. McClure fumed, saying that he would shut Petroleum Air Transport down if he did that. All the carriers in the room half-joked that they were being blindly led into the proverbial gas chambers. Meeting over.

In subsequent weeks the FAA then rewarded Mark and Petroleum Air with a deluge of harassment. Their inspectors began riding the jumpseats of Petroleum Air flights and incessantly inspecting all their equipment until Thom Fields got a successful cease-and-desist order against the FAA. This got nasty ole McClure a reprimand and he was later sent packing for good (for the second time due to the Morrises). Petroleum Air Transport later got its sought-after relief from the ten contract limit.

Around this time, the well-known economist, free-enterprise advocate, and *CAB head* Alfred Kahn learned of Mark's work with CACA and asked to see him. With that meeting, Kahn enlisted Mark's help in exploring an airline deregulation initiative that would later garner the support of Senators Ted Kennedy and Howard Cannon. So, Petroleum Air Transport was becoming a catalyst, and this was the beginning of Mark's role in deregulating the airline industry. And Alfred Kahn would later earn the informal title of "The Father of Airline Deregulation."

CHAPTER 33

An Upward Change in Direction

As the late 1970s wore on, Petroleum Air Transport rebranded itself as "PAT Air," (Petroleum Air Transport) for a logical reason as we will see. And this would be the reason why I *later* witnessed a growing number of shiny "orange" DC-6s in St. Louis with "PAT Air" painted on them. While being slammed by the FAA, Mark Morris was approached by Bob Stevenson, their longtime partner with Joe and Mark. Sometime during 1976, Bob acquired an idle DC-6A freighter (registered N44DG) and was looking to utilize it. He approached Mark who told him that Petroleum Air Transport *did not need* a freighter—they were a passenger carrier. This did not stop Bob—he had a slick idea up his sleeve. He introduced Mark to Dave Clark of Auto Air Cargo (AAC), headquartered at Willow Run Airport in Ypsilanti, a suburb of Detroit, Michigan which was a big freight hub airport for the auto industry. AAC was *the* airfreight consolidator for this industry and had exclusives with Ford, GM, Chrysler, and American Motors.

Through its contracts with all but one of the Ypsilanti big auto parts air carriers, AAC divvied out hot shot "just-in-time" (JIT) auto components and machine parts to each airline, who in turn flew the parts to airports near auto assembly plants all over the U.S. From the airports the cargoes would be trucked to the nearby plants. This allowed them to keep a minimal assembly part inventory, a practice that was part of a broader philosophy introduced years earlier in Japan with the Toyota Motor Company. These JIT airlines operated old fleets of heavy-recips, typically DC-6s, C-46s, and piston Convairs, but also a growing number of Lockheed Electra turboprop freighters and later DC-8 jets. Destinations were normally within two hours of Detroit, representing the largest concentration of auto assembly plants, but deliveries could be made anywhere in the U.S., Canada, and Mexico. St. Louis was one of the largest destinations with three assembly plants (later four). All the carriers delivered to the ex-Mark Aero ramp on the northwest corner of Lambert and later Spirit of St. Louis Airport as the GM Wentzville plant went online in 1983. Chicago, Kansas City, Cleveland, and Cincinnati were the other major destinations out of the Detroit area.

After delivering parts at Lambert, the propliners were then fueled and turned around with backhaul cargo when possible. Most of these operators also had LogAir contracts and flew general cargo in and out as well. Early on, much of this heavy-recip fleet had been dirty, oily, faded, and unmarked, or in the colors of previous owners, and the flight crews were often dressed like hippies in tee shirts, ratty tennis shoes, and jeans. This would later change as a result of Mark's introduction to Dave Clark.

Zantop, Trans Continental, Petroleum Air, and Fleming were the bigger airline names in this business at the time. Dave worked with Mark who was awarded a big piece of the pie (Zantop did not yet work for AAC due to recertification problems after a bankruptcy reorganization) and in no time Petroleum Air Transport suddenly found itself a "freight dog" operation in the JIT auto business in addition to its passenger operations—so, tricky Bob Stevenson got his intended lessee for his DC-6 freighter N44DG. Mark had entered one of the most lucrative cargo transport

Two ex-military C-118s (DC-6s) freighters at the former Mark Aero ramp in front of McDonnell Douglas manufacturing facilities on June 6, 1977. When I took these photos I had no information on the ownership or status of these aircraft. It turns out these freighters were being leased to Petroleum Air Transport from Plymouth Air Leasing (Detroit) —ex-USAF N3426F (top) and ex-USN N3645F (early Navy designation R6D-1), under the guise of a new add-on business segment for Petroleum Air Transport—"just-in-time" (JIT) auto assembly parts. These represent two of the company's Plymouth leased DC-6 freighters. The third one from Plymouth was ex-Shamrock N630NA (see photo below) and still in Shamrock green colors and titles. At the time of these photos, the other freighter being leased by Petroleum Air was N44DG from Bob Stevenson, for a total of 4 freighters (plus passenger DC-6B N34570 at Lafayette, LA for a total of 5 DC-6s in all). Soon there would be a growing number of private investor-owned DC-6 freighters coming into the fleet at a rapid pace. This new business segment resulted from a relationship Mark Morris developed with Dave Clark of Auto Air Cargo (AAC), the big air freight consolidator for Ford, GM, Chrysler, and American Motors out of Detroit to auto assembly plants all over the U.S.

business segments ever to exist and he was in a near panic to expand his DC-6 fleet. But this time he needed freighters for auto parts, not passenger planes for oil exploration. Per Clark's insistence, Petroleum Air's auto business would involve two hubs— Detroit and St. Louis. This made St.

Louis the only air auto parts hub *outside* of Detroit and from these two hubs Petroleum Air Transport would ultimately serve approximately 20 endpoint destinations. As was customary in this business, Petroleum Air was paid on a per-mile basis, not by weight. The customer would pay the same whether it was an emergency 1,000-pound load or a normal 26,000-pound load. There was some cyclicality associated with the business where perhaps 50% of the fleet could be found concentrated at the hubs most of the year, or hardly any planes at the hubs during the busy summer plant model changeover season. Each day about half of Petroleum Air's fleet overnighted at points outside Ypsilanti and St. Louis. Planes would depart a hub between 10:00 PM and dawn, and, if lucky, return with backhauls in broad daylight the next day. However, based on cargo movement patterns, both auto and non-auto, flights could occur at any time.

Petroleum Air's oil services passenger activity would still concentrate in New Iberia and Lafayette Louisiana. It turns out that the Petroleum Air activity I would witness at St. Louis over the next few years was related solely to this new auto parts freight segment. I had no idea there was an original passenger operation in the south that started it all, despite my earlier familiarity with the individual passenger planes that made up that southern fleet (the three ex-Interstate Martin 404s and DC-6 N37570). I didn't know where those familiar planes had gone.

Ex-Shamrock Airlines DC-6B N630A markings as it appeared in early 1977 when it was one of three DC-6 freighters being leased to Petroleum Air Transport from Plymouth Leasing. They began using this plane in the summer of 1976 (2 years after Shamrock purportedly ceased operations) and purchased it outright in late 1979. Chief Pilot Jerry Riebold said all the pilots liked flying -30A because of its "slick" flight director.

Petroleum Air was suddenly short of DC-6s and needed to add a lot of them quickly as the automotive industry was booming out of control. So Mark pulled a rabbit out of his hat by courting wealthy individuals—doctors, lawyers, and CEOs—to enter into tax leases with generous ITC credits by acquiring DC-6s and leasing them back to Petroleum Air. Even Dave Clark got involved the Petroleum Air's DC-6 leasebacks, as did their (and Ozark's) counsel, Thom Fields, who eventually owned *six* of them. By 1979, Petroleum Air Transport would purchase at least 13 of the intermediary-leased DC-6s outright, with another 12 remaining on lease mostly with these individuals needing tax shelter, for a total fleet of approximately 25 aircraft—making Petroleum

Air the *largest DC-6 airline* in the *Second Wind* era and an uncharacteristically profitable one.

So, this new auto business segment is why Mark changed the name of Petroleum Air Transport to the PAT Air anacronym to better align their brand. This is what Federal Express did seven years later by changing its name to "FedEx." PAT Air was the name painted in orange over the window line on all the later planes I saw.

All fleet aircraft additions would get in the queue for a repaint in the consistent mustard yellow/red (orange) trim scheme, including Susan Morris's new, artistic orange "sunset meatball" logo on the vertical tail, as well as the orange name lettering over the fuselage window line. This is the paint scheme (except for the "meatball") that originated on the 404s during the Mark Aero/MAC/Reindeer Lake era. Additionally, PAT Air crews wore freshly-pressed professional uniforms with shoulder epaulets like the major airline crews. Also, each plane was washed at least once per week. This contrasted with the other Ypsilanti JIT fleets were at first made up of a hodgepodge of dirty, junky-looking heavy-iron, most *without* their identities painted on them and where the crews normally dressed in T-shirts, jeans and worn tennis shoes.

Dave Clark and PAT Air's competing JIT airlines thought the money-saving junky appearance was just fine as they were not in the public eye. Dave queried Mark why he would go to the great expense of needlessly painting up his airplanes and dressing up his crews. But Clark and the others ate their words when the big-four auto executives announced they were going to do a formal, military-style ramp inspection at Ypsilanti. Clark *ordered* Mark to fly a large number of his painted DC-6s, along with his dressed-up crews, to Ypsilanti for the inspection. That started a panicked trend where the larger JIT airlines professionalized their images like PAT Air.

By the time Petroleum Air Transport opened for business on the first day of 1976, it had been able to lease the 52 acres of the old Mark Aero ramp space and the two Navy hangers from the City of St. Louis. As previously mentioned, while John Tucker of Midcoast now occupied much of the ramp space at Lambert, he was not happy that PAT Air got this lease despite having the fueling contract. This wasn't the last time the Morrises had disagreements with Tucker, despite their overall amicable relationship with him that included bouts of drinking and partying together.

Also, the new airline could not utilize the historic Old Terminal building, which was no longer serving as Lambert's International Terminal—that was moved over to the main terminal with TWA's massive concourse expansions. This old building was earmarked for demolition to make room for "future airport expansion," despite this acreage not having been "expanded upon" until at least two decades after its 1979 demolition. With the hangar and ramp leases, PAT Air added in-house engine and avionics shops inside the old Navy hangars, which continued to be run by Bob Stevenson, who also supervised all ground activity. Also, Mark Morris even hired Joe as general manager at PAT Air.

The *transient* auto parts and general cargo propliner movements (meaning PAT Air competitors), including ground support and fueling, were handled by Midcoast Aviation. This was later handled by Midcoast's newly-formed subsidiary Airport Terminal Services (ATS), beginning around 1981. Midcoast/ATS comprised about 70% of the support business on this premises while PAT Air was operating there. Despite all these changes, the Mark Aero names were still in place over the hangar doors in large letters. It looked to me that the same Mark Aero was still in business at the northwest corner of Lambert, but it wasn't. It was a different operation with all the same characters!

Since the Old Terminal could not be occupied, PAT Air's St. Louis administrative offices first consisted of a couple of trailers on the ramp, which grew to at least 10 trailers by 1979. PAT Air was charging along like gangbusters, all due to a kid in his mid-20s. Mark successfully tackled the complexities of starting and running this big specialized airline with 50 employees—and still got to fly the planes as a fully qualified line pilot. He was innovative in keeping costs down and one example of that was his operational procedures for the DC-6A/B's R2800 CB 16/17, and CA18 engines. Due to worsening availability issues with these powerplants, slightly different commercial variants of this engine could be legally hung on a single four-engine aircraft—reducing downtime and keeping them flying. However, these were old, obsolete engines that had gone through multiple overhauls and re-borings since the 1940s. Tolerances were not as tight anymore and old overhauled engines were developing slightly less than the full-power they were designed for. Another problem was that higher performance number (P/N) avgas blends that the heavy-recips were designed around were becoming scarce. This required a default to the lowest P/N avgas, 100LL (Low Lead) which also incrementally reduced available power. With all that, irritating inflight mechanical problems became more common than during the *First Wind* heyday.

With average load weights and with at least three healthy engines, the DC-6 could still cruise along pretty well with its load without stressing the working engines. Therefore, when one engine started acting up or making the subtlest funny noises, Mark told Jerry to instruct his pilots to do an immediate precautionary feathering of the prop and engine shutdown, even though the engine could otherwise do its job. This would preclude the engine from "making metal"—the dreaded metal chips sometimes found in the oil sump that signify a badly damaged engine. The presence of metal chips would activate a "chip light" on the control panel. That meant the engine was likely near ruined and would require thousands of dollars to repair—that is if it *could* be repaired. With a precautionary shutdown before a chip light appeared or valves were swallowed, the problem could be addressed on the ground and remedied much more easily and cheaply.

All this explained why several of my sightings of overflying PAT Air DC-6s involved a single feathered propeller, making me think that PAT Air was cutting corners on maintenance (it wasn't). On top of this precautionary shutdown procedure, Patti Finot also initiated incentives that rewarded safe and economical on-time performance which apparently worked well. However, despite all safety precautions, things happened. Mark relates one harrowing engine experience flying a PAT Air DC-6:

I remember flying just 15,000 lbs. or so [about half the DC-6s load capacity] *into Ypsilanti. It was an early morning arrival around 6:30 AM and I had a green copilot and a very green engineer. En route we did a precautionary number 1 engine shutdown and then a number 2 shutdown before beginning our approach—no problem in a DC-6 half-loaded with engines on one side only, in this case, the right side. But then on final approach at the outer marker inbound number 4 blew its master rod cylinder. The only engine left was number 3 on approach with no time to restart numbers 1 and 2. My two rookies were going nuts ... after we got cleared for landing the tower saw our sputtering and smoking #4 engine and asked if we needed the crash truck. They could not see the left side where we had two other feathered propellers. My green co-pilot picked up the mic wanting to answer in the affirmative but I told him not to say anything and grabbed the mic from him and told tower, "No - we are fine." So, I just briefed the crew that we are landing no matter what. I made it clear to them that if we said we needed a crash truck we would be filling out paperwork for the next three days with the FAA and the local Fire Marshal. When we cleared the runway, tower could then see the other two very motionless engines and asked if those were failures on 1 and 2 as the props were both in the feathered position. I just told them that I was showing my green crew how easy it was going downhill in a DC-6 on just one engine but all was OK. As I was doing the final shutdown procedures my green engineer lost her lunch so to speak.*

Mark knew the risks well and had plenty of experience with them, both micro and macro. In the short run, he seemed to have the micro problems under control. It was the macro risks that kept him awake. Hyperinflation, *extreme* interest rates, and fuel prices were going through the roof. That temporarily helped the petroleum side of PAT Air, but made the auto side worse. This complex and bulging economic bubble seemed to be growing big and fast, and about to blow its stack like Mount St. Helens just did. PAT Air was directly exposed to two of the most highly cyclical industries, yet surprisingly, it was able to remain profitable when most airlines could not.

"Steam gauge" copilot front office of a PAT Air DC-6B viewed from the captain's seat. PAT Air kept its operations and appearances clean and professional despite its seriously obsolete aircraft fleet. At first, this was uncharacteristic of most of its peers during the *Second Wind* era. (Jerry Riebold)

One thing to help smooth some of this out was a holdover from Mark Aero, as PAT Air served as an outsourced corporate flight department with light piston aircraft and the DH-125 corporate jets. Post-Mark Aero, PAT Air retained this role for only one corporate customer, Ed Phelps' Peabody Holding. Jerry Riebold was doing some flying for Peabody in the light piston

Cessna 414 they were using, but Mark and later Jerry were both type-rated in the deHavilland DH-125 corporate twinjets under PAT Air's certificate, also utilized by Peabody. The DH-125s were the early -1AS models which were noisy "straight pipe" turbojets rather than newer, quieter, and more efficient turbofans. Both Mark and Jerry loved this plane despite the noise. Jerry stated that it flew around like a rocket. It went right where you pointed it, and was easy, responsive, and otherwise pleasant to fly compared to the massive heavy-piston clunkers.

Jerry had one huge phobia. He hated snakes, and both Lafayette and New Iberia, Louisiana had a lot of them. Not just your harmless garden snakes, but deadly poisonous rattlers that infest this part of the country. After heavy rains and accompanying floods that are common there, the rattlers could be seen on the ground everywhere—both dead and alive—and they even got into Jerry's apartment (which he shared with Joe, Mark, and others). Joe and Mark played tricks on Jerry with some of the dead ones. This put Jerry over the edge so he told Mark he did not want to fly out of Louisiana anymore (most PAT Air pilots rotated in and out of there). So, sometime in 1978 Mark reassigned Jerry exclusively to corporate flight duty out of St. Louis, flying the hot DH-125 twinjets on the Peabody account.

As Mark became more cognizant of PAT Air's overexposure to autos and petroleum, he began looking into still other alternative segments for his airline that would help stabilize his exposure and better utilize his DC-6s during the cyclical lows of the auto industry. The logical thing to do would be to diversify into a more stable segment—general cargo—and perhaps eventually into the emerging overnight package courier industry, which at the time was almost generically known as "Federal Express." He entered into a three-way joint venture with two freight forwarders out of Atlanta, leasing out PAT Air DC-6s and crews for these operations. The new operation would be called Profit by Air/Air Express International (AEI). The joint venture was run by Mark and he ran it in parallel with PAT Air. However, this operation was for general (heavier) cargo only—it didn't have enough capacity for overnight courier operations.

Eventually, Phelps took Peabody's corporate flight department in-house concurrently with their purchase of a Sabreliner corporate jet. Jerry came with the deal and got type rated in the Sabreliner. Peabody's mining activities were being emphasized outside of its main southern Illinois operations and more into West Virginia, Arizona and the Powder River Basin in Wyoming, requiring the improved performance, capacity, and range of jets, so the Cessna 414s didn't come with the deal. And years later Peabody would expand internationally, mainly into Australia and China. But in the meantime, Dave Barnholz became Peabody's first in-house chief pilot and Jerry assumed that role after Barnholz moved on—to eventually become radio talk show host Rush Limbaugh's first chief pilot. Jerry remained Peabody's chief pilot—overseeing its expanding corporate jet fleet—for well over two decades.

CHAPTER 34

Orange DC-6s Everywhere

After my canceled wedding engagement, I begin hanging out more with my old college friend Mike O'Brien, whose apartment is within walking distance of mine. He and I ride our motorcycles from bar to bar in St. Louis County looking for "action." Mike was one of those roommates during my summer school at Mizzou who fled to California for the rest of the summer of 1977. He was a junkyard automotive gearhead who collected, rebuilt, and sold cars, and he had uncharacteristically savvy social skills. He had torn down and built up auto and motorcycle engines in his 7th-floor dorm room just down the hall from me, during our regular semesters at Mizzou. He'd break the resident rules and haul parts and complete engines up and down the dorm elevator in a grocery cart. His room smelled like a machine shop, but this helped pay for his college education. Our elderly white-haired "house mother" never caught on to his system. A couple of years later out of school, we decided to earn our private pilots' licenses together. He would one day become Director of Marketing and Corporate Planning at Hyundai North America in California, after long stints moving up the ladder with Ford Motor Company, Nissan, and Toyota. In more recent years his employer news releases have touted that he was flying a vintage "French jet trainer"—most likely a Fouga CM.170 Magister—on the west coast airshow circuit.

Mike is one of those gifted people who can start with a paperclip and over time and after hundreds of trades wind up with a 10,000-square-foot mansion. Out of nowhere, he buys a 1966 Cessna 172 four-place airplane with a near run-out (and obsolete) Continental O-300 flat-six engine. We decide to take our flying lessons at a sleepy airport in West County called Creve Coeur Airport. It has a grass east-west runway (7-25), and a poorly maintained north-south gravel runway (16-34). It is run by Les Neuroth, a personable, white-haired, sixty-something guy who is rough around the edges and chain smoker of unfiltered cigarettes. Despite that, he lived into his late '90s, hanging out at the airport the whole time. As rough as he is on me in the cockpit, I have always considered Les a great teacher of fundamental airmanship.

I train in a 1969 Cessna 150 which is in great mechanical shape but is faded, scratched, and beat-up looking on the outside. Mike and I both hit it hard and obtain our private pilot licenses in November 1979 after four months of training. I am 24 years old, not 16 or 17 where most career pilots seem to start. Mike soon begins to trade his aircraft up in a string of transactions separated only by months, and I fly them all. He goes from the high-wing Cessna 172 to the low-wing Cherokee 140. In October 1980 I find a nice Cessna 177 Cardinal for him while on a business trip to Dexter Missouri. I inspect it and its maintenance logs, run it up, taxi it around, report back and then Mike tells me to place the deposit for him. That weekend we fly the Cherokee down to Dexter, pick up his Cardinal, and fly back home in formation for a while with me flying his Cherokee. He then regains his faster cruise speed and leaves me in the dust. That is a fun day I will always remember. Only months later he trades the Cardinal up to a Piper Twin Comanche. Before any training for his multi-engine rating, he buys it and flies it from Detroit to St. Louis

Yours truly in front of one of supplemental Transamerica's GE CF-6-powered Boeing 747-200s near the Midcoast Aviation ramp, late fall 1979. This was the successor company to legacy supplemental Trans International Airlines (TIA). Mike O'Brien shot this photo with my camera on one of our many aerial visits to Lambert while we practiced "dense traffic environment" flying. We took pride in "legally" holding up big TWA jetliners containing three hundred or more passengers, burning tons of fuel while holding short for our "proficiency" approaches in a 4-seat light plane. Not to mention, this was during a second energy crisis when fuel prices were through the roof and the airlines were bleeding money. Also, even as private pilots, we seemed to have free pedestrian reign around most major airport ramp areas except for the passenger gate zones and the military ANG ramps. The later imposition of stiff landing fees were extended to our Part 91 operations putting a halt to this abuse. If this were the post-911 era, we would have been thrown in jail or "shot on sight" for snooping around this 747.

through bad weather at night, without an instrument rating—not something I would try with such a lack required ratings. He then got his multi-engine rating and he let me fly his Twin Comanche around (with him in the right seat since I was not multi-engine rated). That airplane was more maneuverable than anything I'd yet to experience and sounded nice as well.

Mike can maintain all these aircraft himself (except for annual inspections)—always getting A& P mechanics to sign off on his work. I think he becomes the most knowledgeable non-A&P aircraft mechanic in the world. While Mike always "bought" aircraft, I always "rented," flying out of Creve Coeur, Arrowhead Airport, and later Spirit of St. Louis Airport. I moved into Gulfstream American Cheetahs and Tigers, Bellanca Citabrias, Cessna 172s and 172 RGs (retractable gear, constant speed prop), and Cessna 182 Turbo-Skylane RGs, and on New Year's Eve 1981 I obtained my instrument rating. In 1982 Mike moved to California to work for Nissan while continuing his aircraft trading process—soon trading up to Stearmans and AT-6s, and then up the ladder to his "French jet trainer" when he was with Hyundai.

During these early flying days, my apartment balcony conveniently faces north about 6 miles southwest of Lambert as previously mentioned. I can see a lot of low air traffic from there. I see and *hear* these orange-laced DC-6s flying overhead by day and *by night*. As mentioned in the previous chapter, I sometimes see them low overhead with a feathered propeller as they bank

PAT Air DC-6B in the snow, registration unknown, location uncertain but probably parked on the ex-Mark Aero ramp looking southwest. Most of PAT Air's fleet was eventually painted in this clean-looking standard scheme dating back to the Martin 404s of the Mark Aero Reindeer Lake days. (Jerry Riebold)

left for Runway 6, or on downwind for 30L. I then read a newspaper article about a PAT Air DC-6 skidding into an Ozark F-227 one night on an icy ramp at Chicago O'Hare, with substantial damage to both aircraft (more on that later). I mentally question again—*What is this airline PAT Air? Why am I witnessing an expanding 1950s piston airliner fleet in the established jet age?*

Mike is not particularly interested in old propliners like me. But now I can fly myself into Lambert allowing more up-close inspections. For whatever reason Lambert ground control does not let me taxi to and shut down at the former Mark Aero ramp—probably because it was a heavy freight transloading area—but occasionally I can catch and walk up to a parked PAT Air DC-6 at Sabreliner. It is fun to now be in the Lambert traffic pattern with Lockheed turboprop Electra freighters, Ozark F-227s and TWA 727s, and even Missouri ANG F4 Phantom II fighters. I feel like a "big shot" doing this—even causing big TWA 747s bound for Europe to hold short while I am on short final to runway 30L in a single-engine Gulfstream American Tiger. I'm just practicing! God knows how much that idling fuel burn costs them while waiting for one peon like me to land and taxi clear. Large airports would soon put a stop to this abuse by slapping the same landing fees on light aircraft that the big guys pay.

One day, I taxi onto the Sabreliner ramp and park right next to an *extremely rare* Vickers 810 Viscount four-engine turboprop with blue trim. On the fuselage just under the flight deck are the black stenciled gothic letters spelling out "Foreigner." Then a light bulb. I realize that I heard on the radio this rock group is playing at Kiel Auditorium tonight. I look into a passenger window

PAT Air Captain and Chief Pilot Jerry Riebold in his DC-6B left seat front office. (Jerry Riebold)

and think, *they were just in there, maybe only hours ago.* This is a Deja Vue of eight years earlier when at Mark Aero I stumbled onto the *Stones'* L-188 Electra at Mark Aero—another first-generation four-engine turboprop.

It is interesting to experience the steady buildup of these orange-trimmed "PAT Air" DC-6s at the ex-Mark Aero premises—sometimes four or five of them together with personnel scurrying all over. They are all *freighters*—and slick-looking machines that are no longer dressed in rags. I witness the runups of un-cowled engines, and shirtless mechanics lying prone on the nacelle behind an engine in the roily-hot summer air, making some sort of adjustment with a screwdriver or rachet. More recently, after seeing his photo (page 192), I swear that I recognize one of these mechanics as "Castro." This entire scene looks like a tightly-run airline that unapologetically flies outdated, classic aircraft—a major *Second Wind* airline in and of itself.

CHAPTER 35

Out of Nowhere

It's a fine Saturday afternoon in the fall of 1978 as I'm relaxing with a beer on my second-floor Creve Coeur apartment balcony. I'm counting on catching some vintage propliner traffic around Lambert, maybe some DC-6s. Within minutes I sense a deep guttural vibration to the west, getting louder. I instinctively look toward it and I see nothing but wings, engines, and three tails, very low, heading right toward me, then roaring right overhead, seemingly bypassing Lambert and heading east. Its engines sound a little rough and slightly out of sync. In a millisecond I recognize it as a Lockheed Super Constellation, an aircraft I haven't seen overhead in years. At this time and place, it can only be a civilian aircraft. It is dilapidated and seems to be hanging on its props, barely able to pull its way through the sky—as though it has one foot in the boneyard.

A beat-up three-tailed Lockheed L-1049 Super Constellation like this flies over my apartment balcony near St. Louis Lambert International Airport in the fall of 1978. It's almost hanging on its power, with out-of-sync chugging engines laboring profusely and props churning as it claws overhead. I almost expect random parts and slops of oil to rain down on me. This is the last Constellation I ever witness in possible revenue service.

I realize that at this time, Central American Airways (CAA) out of Kentucky is the only Midwestern operator of the Super Constellation, a single L-1049H freighter hauling auto parts. This company was a true, corner-cutting fly-by-nighter. With near certainty, I conclude this is a CAA overflight, as it has blue trim just like photos of the CAA aircraft I had seen. At the very same time, my future friend Doug Teel says he is in the middle of a training flight in his Cessna 172 over St. Charles, about 5 miles west of my apartment. As he and his instructor scan for traffic, they suddenly spot the Super Constellation right above them heading east, so close that they could feel the wing turbulence. After 18 months I would become reacquainted with what I think is this same dilapidated Super Constellation—in an unpleasant way.

Later in the year I read in the St. Louis Globe-Democrat about that PAT Air ground incident at Chicago O'Hare where one of their DC-6s slid on an icy ramp right into Ozark F-227, badly chewing up both aircraft. The DC-6 pilot was Sandy Thibault. Many years later both Jerry Riebold and Mark Morris tell me that this was a touchy situation. As it turns out, Thom Fields, general counsel for both Ozark Airlines and PAT Air (with Ozark Airline's CEO Ed Crane's permission), was the owner of the offending DC-6 which he leased to PAT Air. This mishap put everybody on the wrong side of an embarrassing state of affairs. Jerry tells me he had to immediately pull Thibault from the flight roster and give him a desk assignment, which caused him to quit. In Mark's words:

> *Thibault went on to start a DC 6 operation called Northern "something" . . . he was not a good driver. He had his accident a day before I was to close on the transfer of a few PAT Air DC-6s to DHL and his crash delayed the close a day or so . . . A super arrogant pilot with not much common sense.*

Transfer?

PAT Air DC-6B N37570 in flight. Sights like this continued regularly over St. Louis until late 1981 when the still-successful fleet was sold off and disbursed to the four corners of the earth forever. (Jerry Riebold)

DHL International GmbH (Dalsey, Hillblom, and Lynn) is currently the third largest overnight courier in the world, just behind FedEx and UPS, with an international fleet of modern jet freighters, from big wide bodies all the way down. Now a division of Deutsche Post DHL, it delivers perhaps 1.5 billion parcels worldwide each year. This German-owned company has its origins as an American corporation for its first 32 years of existence beginning in 1969. In its first ten years, it had achieved a thorough global expansion, becoming the largest overnight courier worldwide, *without a single fleet aircraft*. This was the beginning of the overnight courier business. Federal Express revolutionized starting 4 years later, but did not start it. And UPS was still traditional a door-to-door ground delivery service with a bunch of rusty brown delivery trucks and no planes.

In mid-1977, Mark Morris acquired a nice surplus U.S. Air Force VC-118 out of the Arizona storage to be added to the PAT Air DC-6 fleet. PAT Air needed to convert it to meet FAA standards for civilian cargo operations, so he delivered it to their maintenance and overhaul base in Tampa Florida which was able to do the conversion. It turned out that this VC-118 was thought to be a to be part of the John F. Kennedy presidential fleet which included his first Air Force One aircraft after his January 1961 inauguration. There were around 5 of these VC-118s in the Washington D.C. VIP fleet and Kennedy's Air Force One had been donated to the Pima Air Museum in 1978 (see photo page 95).

It turns out DHL operatives were eying this plane in the desert as well, but Mark acquired it before they could make an offer. So, DHL made an offer Mark couldn't refuse—he could easily find another DC-6 or ex-C-118. In the meantime, PAT Air continued with the conversion of the VC-118 to commercial standards for DHL. While Mark had received full payment (from somewhere) for the aircraft and conversion work, one day he found all the closing paperwork still on his desk consisting of all the sale documentation with DHL, including the aircraft title and registration papers. These documents should have been held in escrow until the sale was finalized, then delivered to the buyer at closing, but DHL never requested these documents.

Mark had not worked with DHL directly on this transaction, so he went to the World Aviation Directory to research them. It was there he found out they were an overnight air freight courier company whose founder/owner was Larry Hillblom based in San Francisco. Hillblom was a skinny unshaven hippie kind of guy who worked in jeans and cutoff sweatshirts, and he was known to sleep overnight under his desk. Mark phoned Hillblom to explain the situation and to request instructions for forwarding the paperwork. Hillblom was appreciative, and Mark queried him as to his experience operating those big old heavy-recips. Larry said that he acquired an unairworthy DC-3 and a couple of Beech 18s to be refurbished for the eventual expansion of his company into a new realm—a dedicated freight shuttle service between the Hawaiian Islands. Hillblom felt that demand might be so brisk that he needed larger planes such as the DC-6.

In retrospect, this local Hawaiian expansion did not seem in line with DHL's main international courier business strategy. It was more of a random opportunity. Like Federal Express, DHL transported light, time-sensitive documents exclusively and not heavier cargo. But as we mentioned, DHL did not have a commercial aircraft fleet. Instead, documents were packed into 70-pound bags, each of which was accompanied by a human courier who would purchase an airline ticket and check the bag to the overnight destination. In this way, DHL became the largest account for several major airlines as some widebody flights regularly had over 100 DHL courier-accompanied packages—with each 70-pound bag representing about $1,700 in revenue. To facilitate all this, DHL utilized its 180 sort centers worldwide. Well actually, these "sort centers" consisted of employees performing this task in their apartments and bungalows.

In the course of their conversations, Larry became impressed with Mark and PAT Air as one of the largest charter freight operations in the U.S. He told Mark he needed someone like him to start building a new in-house aircraft fleet, and that he would like to acquire PAT Air and its fleet as the launch platform. He offered Mark a job as president and chief operating officer of DHL and a residence in Honolulu he and his family could live. Mark was all ears. As far as he was concerned, this would provide a more stable home life. He could immediately wean himself away from his precarious exposure to the auto and petroleum industries in favor of the stability of the overnight courier business that he was already thinking about evolving into anyway. He could also get out from under PAT Air's debt with cash to spare and a stable income. On top of all that, this was an opportunity to run the flight operations of the largest overnight courier service in the world.

In September 1977 Mark flew out to San Francisco and accepted Hillblom's offer for the cash equity of PAT Air plus the assumption of debt, with a 6-month "back out" clause for the benefit of both parties. Mark was now President and Chief Operating Officer of DHL. PAT Air would retain its corporate identity operating certificate, branding, and management under the DHL umbrella, just as the fleet was being painted in the new orange-trim look. It was expected that the few PAT Air DC-6s flying the initial Hawaiian operations would be gradually transferred over to DHL. The three Martinliners were not transferred to DHL until March 1979 but were ferried to Hawaii beforehand (see the next chapter). So, by the time I saw the proliferation of orange-trimmed DC-6s at the former Mark Aero ramp and over my apartment in 1978, PAT Air was already under DHL ownership and control and no longer independent.

Mark made the mistake of wanting to "surprise" Susan and did not tell her until he got back to St. Louis. This infuriated her. She was not crazy about moving herself and their two boys to Hawaii and was upset about him not consulting with her first. She and the boys had strong family ties and social networks in St. Louis. This did not go over well with the extended family either, and Mark became an "in-law-outlaw." Job one after closing on DHL would be for him to immediately get a DC-6 and then the three Martin 404s over to Honolulu, *NOW*. There was an immediate opportunity to fly pallets of *Wall Street Journals* among the islands, just like the Dow Jones Convairs out of St. Louis. Hillblom was now wanting to ramp up for *both* a passenger and cargo shuttle service between the islands (not just cargo as originally intended) and felt he needed to strike while the iron was hot just as airline deregulation was kicking in. However, there were still obstacles. Two legacy all-jet operators had been doing just that for years. And we all now know how established airlines react to newcomers back then.

The first thing Mark did was to pick a "spare" DC-6 out of the PAT Air fleet to be quickly outfitted for a 2,500-mile transpacific delivery flight to Hawaii. However, this plane was only equipped with high-frequency (HF) and medium-frequency (MF) navigation (both non-precision navigation aids that are range limited and do not cover the full ocean route) and a standard VOR navigation radio (using very-high frequency or VHF) with a range out from the VOR station of only 150 miles or so. So, a long-range navigation LORAN radio was installed that could give them navigation fixes anywhere over the ocean. Mark recruited PAT Air's most experienced pilot in four-engine over-ocean flying to act as co-captain on the flight. As co-captains, both pilots had equal authority as pilot-in-command versus the single captain pilot-in-command and first officer. This arrangement risks a 50-50 stalemate in an emergency. Mark's co-captain was an experienced Super Constellation pilot who for years flew them for Bendix corporation in the South Pacific. A young woman named Janet was selected to serve as the flight engineer on the trip at her insistence. While a low-time PAT Air crew member, she was a "by the book" engine jockey with a reputation for working well with the aircrews. The plane needed to be delivered to Honolulu by the next Sunday, so they staged at Oakland the day before departure for a good night's rest.

Just before arrival at Oakland on Saturday, the mission-critical LORAN called it quits, and radio repair shops were not open on the weekend. So, they were stuck with no LORAN and a requirement that the DC-6 be delivered to Honolulu *that next day*. The co-captains decided to utilize the Oakland VOR as a "launch rail" that could take them on the proper westerly course up to 150 miles out, and then hold the same heading once the signal was out of range using less precise HF navigation to some point further out. Once HF signals were out of range they could just hold their established heading and follow jetliner contrails and monitor radio jetliner radio transmissions on one of three high-altitude jetway routes to Hawaii. The problem with "holding a heading" over the sameness of the ocean is that winds aloft are always changing and will imperceptibly take you off course, so following the jet contrails was important.

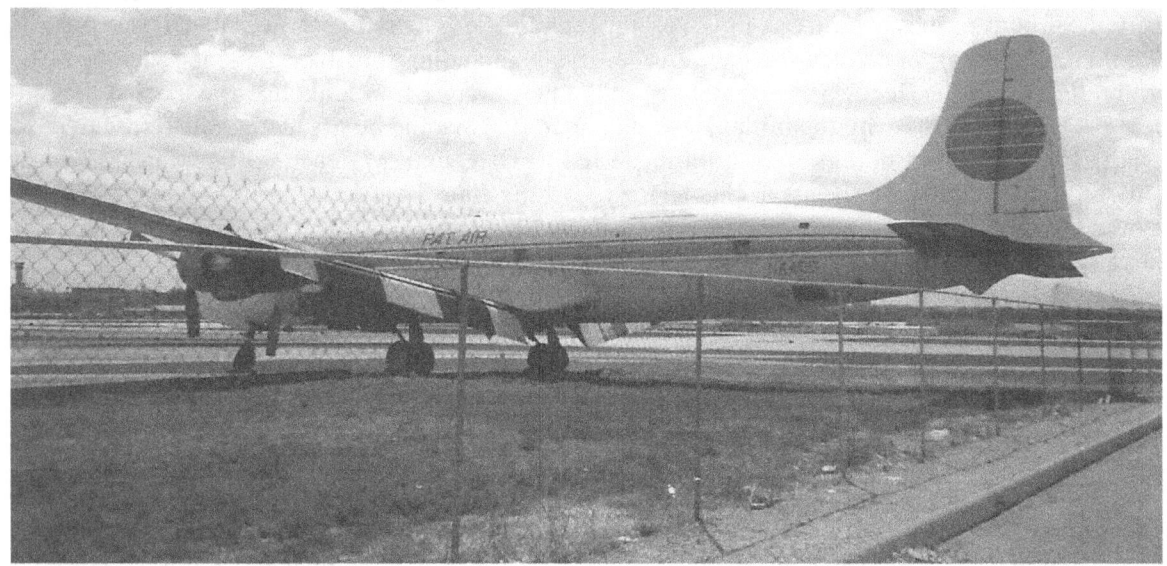

The *first* and the *last*. The very last remnant of a Mark Aero legacy is seen at Lambert's northwest corner in April 1987. This is ex-PAT Air N44DG more than 5 years after the company ceased operations under DHL (covered later). This plane was owned by Bob Stevenson. Mark Morris says it was the *very first* PAT Air DC-6 put into Detroit/St. Louis auto cargo service in late 1976 when Stevenson acquired the plane. It lingered here on the ramp long after PAT Air was dissolved and after Stevenson passed away. Here it sits in front of the approximate location of Lambert's historic Old Terminal which was demolished in 1979. Miami cargo operator F.A. Conner owned this aircraft at the time of this photo, after being sold out of Stevenson's estate. In 1991 I was flying the jump seat out of Miami on an island-hopping Trans-Air-Link DC-6A freighter when our first officer told me he ferried this aircraft out of St. Louis to F.A. Conner at Miami International's "Corrosion Corner" later in 1987. He had to make an unscheduled landing at Memphis International for engine repairs/replacement when a couple of the engines lost power. This plane would be put back into service with F.A. Conner and later others, spending most of it in Africa, probably Angola, before being broken up.

They departed early Sunday for the 11 ½ hour flight, but they almost didn't make it. The Oakland VOR station radial did establish them on the right course and heading including an approximate 4-degree drift adjustment to the right, before the anticipated loss of the VOR signal 150 miles out. As planned they then switched to the non-precision HF as the now primary navigation, but to cross-check this by following jetliner contrails on the San Francisco-Honolulu routes for most of the flight. It was planned that approximately 4 hours after passing through the equal time point (ETP), they would pick up the Oahu NDB (MF) and VOR (VHF) navigation stations a few hundred miles out and steer inbound. ETP is the point where half of the planned *flight time* is reached, rather than half the distance.

But things began to unravel. Only 15 minutes past ETP the number four engine started acting up and had to be shut down and feathered so it wouldn't catch fire. This slowed the plane down considerably, but the DC-6 was able to maintain altitude with its load of a few automobiles belonging to transferring PAT Air employees. To compound this problem, the atmospheric conditions were such that jetliners were not making contrails at their cruise altitudes. The only thing aircrew could do now was get on the emergency communications frequency, 121.5 MHz, and report their condition and estimated progress to overflying jetliners and surface ships—and otherwise fly by dead-reckoning (a crude and the least accurate way of maintaining course by holding a previously calculated heading with drift angle, while using the clock to establish ETA). Then, another problem arose. With only 3 engines running the ground speed (or "ocean speed" as the case may be) was reduced, causing their original ETA to become a moving target, that is, the ETA time was extended by default, requiring another round of quick calculations.

The now crippled and blind airplane was aiming for a needle-in-a-haystack over the near-infinite body of Pacific water. After a while, Mark's co-captain thought they were drifting too far south of Hawaii. But Mark's mental calculations and interpretation of the various strengths of jetliner transmissions on the three Jet Routes led him to believe that they were too far north of course. While going back and forth, they both realized that if they followed the advice of the one that was "wrong," they would all die. Here is where the 50-50 co-captain authority problem kicked in. Mark's co-captain established a new heading further north based on his educated calculation and gave the plane to Mark and told him he was going to take a nap—and *save me a few beers in case have to ditch in the middle of nowhere."* After the captain dozed off, Mark deliberately, but imperceptibly, steered the plane 90 degrees to the left (south) in what was hopefully a corrective heading adjustment. The co-captain woke up just as Mark was completing his opposite 90-degree right turn on the new westbound course after the near hour-long corrective heading, barking at Mark just short of thanking him for "killing them all." The DC-6 picked up the Oahu NDB at a point 100 miles *north* of Hawaii. This means that if Mark followed the captain's theory that they were headed too far south, they would have all been dead in the water halfway to Alaska, *along with a few beers.*

Upon landing in Honolulu 2 hours late, the tired DC-6 crew was confronted by some very mad FAA personnel. They charged that their plane had entered the Hawaii Air Defense Identification Zone (ADIZ) that surrounded Hawaii approximately 100 miles north of the civilian aircraft entry point—alerting air defenses (remember Pearl Harbor?). Mark had a lot of explaining to do as to *when* and where the LORAN and number 4 engine failed, which could impact the crew's future flight status. Fortunately, he convinced them by stretching the truth a bit, saying the LORAN quit just after the ETP point. And so ends the story of the delivery of DHL's very first operable "fleet plane" that morphed into today's worldwide DHL jet fleet. The several other ex-PAT Air DC-6 crossings to follow were uneventful.

Mark now had to figure out how to ferry PAT Air's three Martinliners to Hawaii. The problem was that each had a maximum range of only 1,000 miles, depending on load. That doesn't help when you need to make *three* 2,500-mile ferry trips over the Pacific.

CHAPTER 36

Transoceanic Martins? Again?

The last time Martin built a transoceanic transport was in the mid-1940s for the U.S. Navy. The main purpose of the JRM Mars seaplane was to fly Navy families and supplies between Oakland and Honolulu. Three out of the four produced were powered by 2,500 horsepower Curtiss-Wright R-3350s. The other was powered by 3,000 horsepower Pratt & Whitney R-4360 Wasp Majors. Retired by 1956, three were retained by a Canadian concern and converted to fire tankers and two of the survivors were utilized in this role with several operators until 2016 when Coulson Aviation retired them. The ultimate "static" fates of these giant seaplanes have yet to be determined—public interest and air museum space are scarce these days. Yet, they have been listed for sale for several years.

Martin JRM Mars seaplane in its heyday, flying Navy families between Oakland and Honolulu for a decade until 1956. This was the largest seaplane ever to enter regular service. (U.S. Navy)

The Martin 404 was "no Martin Mars." It wasn't designed to be anything remotely close. It was a very short-range "puddle jumping" airliner for use on overland routes. To get PAT Air's three Martin 404s across the Pacific to Hawaii, passenger seats had to be removed and ten temporary 200-gallon fuel tanks installed in their place, along with big auxiliary oil drums, one for each engine. That makes for one overloaded airplane. While the maximum gross takeoff weight for the Martin 404 was 44,900 pounds, the fully fueled aircraft with the temporary tanks would increase the takeoff weight to 51,600 pounds, making each plane 6,700 pounds overweight. With an FAA waiver, this would be legal only for a single specified ferry flight. The flight would have to be flown at METO power or Maximum Except Takeoff power. Takeoff power puts so much strain on the engines that it is allowed for only 5 minutes. METO is the first power reduction to about 93% of maximum where the engines can be run *continuously* without overheating—but still putting more stress on the engines than climb or cruise power. Normal cruise power is around 65% -70% of maximum takeoff power. Needless to say, a 12- hour over-ocean flight at METO renders additional wear on the engines and would not be recommended under normal circumstances.

Jerry Riebold thought Mark was insane to fly these short-haul Martins 2,500 miles over the ocean from Oakland California to Honolulu. He suggested that Mark just put the three planes on ocean barges *"like everyone else does."* Jerry was also concerned the Martins would run out of oil before running out of gas, even with the two temporary auxiliary oil drums in the cabin. Even though the odds are better that you won't lose an engine on a twin as compared to a four-engine aircraft, an overloaded Martin twin *could not maintain altitude* on one engine should that occur. That is, if an engine were lost over the ocean, it would have to ditch *somewhere* in the middle of *nowhere*. Just hit the waves at the "correct angle" as Mark's dad Joe would prescribe, but then wait to be consumed by the ocean to be lost forever.

Despite Jerry's barge idea, Mark got the FAA approval for the tank outfitting scheme which prompted him to go ahead with his original plans. In the spring of 1979, he asked Jerry to be his copilot on the first ferry flight. Jerry politely turned him down, so Mark recruited another copilot, as well as an observer-engineer/navigator and after careful preflight planning, they departed to the west from Oakland International on the first ferry flight to Hawaii into the early evening darkness. Their first challenge would be to fly through two storm fronts which were uneventful, but then around 3 hours out it was determined that the left auxiliary oil drum mounted in the cabin was not feeding into its main engine oil tank as the tank indicator was showing it was *down* to 5/8 full. Not good—it should stay full for the whole trip due to feeding from its respective auxiliary drum. It turned out that the auxiliary drum check valve on that side was installed *backward*, preventing this oil from getting to the engine. There was no inflight way to get to reverse this check valve. They had no choice but to immediately abort and turn around for Oakland, and that's exactly what they did.

So far so good, but visibility was near zero in absolute darkness as they passed back through the two weather fronts around midnight. At around 40 miles inbound to Oakland the *right engine* master rod blew (the one with good oil feed) and that prop had to be feathered. The *left* engine with the blocked oil feed was working just fine, thank you. But altitude could not be maintained if they wanted to maintain flying airspeed, so there was no way out but *down* at this point. By the time they were around 10 miles out of Oakland they were only 50 feet over the water, but they stopped sinking. Ground effect was buoying the wings at just above stall speed and Mark said the stall stick shaker on the control yoke was going crazy. If only he could maintain this one-engine ground effect configuration until he got to the Oakland runway threshold at the water's edge.

But there was another problem. There was a protruding dyke a few hundred yards before and perpendicular to the runway threshold. It was slightly higher than 50 feet over the water surface. They still had 2,000 gallons of explosive fuel in the wings and in the auxiliary tanks in the cabin, a recipe for disaster. The other two crewmen had been working the situation in the cabin when Mark barked over the intercom system for them to head for the very back of the cabin *immediately*—but they were ahead of him as they had *already scrambled to the back*!

Mark braced himself to go out with a bang in a ball of high-impact flames. But he tried one more thing. He lowered the nose to get a few more knots of airspeed, skimming the water's surface, and then pulled up. He cleared the dyke by inches and *just* made it to the runway threshold to grease the touchdown—and casually taxi onto the parking ramp on one engine. A pool of oil followed the path of the Martin from the touchdown point to the parking place. The master rod of the failed number two engine was protruding right through the engine cowl for everyone to see.

The three shaking crewmembers deplaned through the rear stair door and the first officer and navigator/engineer kissed the tarmac. Mark suggested they head right for the airport lounge for early-morning drinks. The problem with that was that his two crewmen were both recovering alcoholics and neither had a drink in over a decade. They both declined but Mark interrupted, *"Would you rather be alive and a regular alcoholic again, or a dead recovering alcoholic like you almost became tonight?"* All three went to the lounge and drank until just before sunrise.

In retrospect, *had* the mechanic installed both auxiliary oil check valves *correctly* before the aborted flight, Mark Morris and his other two crewmen *would* be dead. As mentioned, the engine that blew its master rod was the one that had the *correctly installed* check valve and the good engine that got them back to Oakland had the *reversed valve* and was not feeding that engine any auxiliary oil. So, if both valves were working correctly, the right engine would have still blown its master rod—only this time halfway across the Pacific—requiring an open-ocean ditching for sure. Fate has always played funny games like that with airplanes. Any way you look at it, the *Tiger on a Leash* turned viciously on Mark and almost nailed him and his crewmen—and this book would end right here.

After that harrowing, life-impacting experience, Mark decided to leave it to some of his other pilots who had previously volunteered for the job of ferrying the three Martinliners. They developed additional preflight procedures and tighter engine operating parameters and they were able to get all three Martins over to Honolulu without incident, with each flight taking around 13 ½ hours at the METO power setting. No pilot who desires a long life would make that his/her permanent job.

With the Martinliners in place, Mark began to set up the infrastructure required to operate an extremely short-hop island passenger shuttle. The two legacy competitors in Hawaii were already doing this with jet equipment, which, in truth, is an inefficient application for a jetliner. DHL would have a more cost-efficient operation with the old piston Martinliners. On a typical run between Honolulu and Maui, the Martins would be only 10 minutes slower than a jetliner—and they would fly lower so the passengers could savor the tropical scenery.

Soon, four additional ex-PAT Air DC-6 freighters were positioned in Honolulu to support the freight business, including the daily movement of newspapers, just like Dow Jones was doing with Convair 440's out of St. Louis. The DC-6 freighter fleet soon had a 10% share of the cargo market after Mark hired one of the competing airline's VP of cargo sales. The other two airlines didn't like this. One of them was flying DC-9 passenger/freight combis and older Lockheed L-188 Electras and was forced to retire the Electras due to the unwelcome competition. The Electras were sold and redeployed to Ypsilanti, Michigan on the JIT auto parts runs, most likely with Zantop.

In a near-repeat of what TWA did to the Morrises in the wake of stillborn Missouri Air Commuter 6 years earlier, one of the established competing airlines hired some mysterious Korean hit men to tail Mark. They shot up his MG sports car in his condo parking lot before he could get out of it, probably as a serious warning. Upon learning about this, Larry Hillblom didn't seem concerned—but it was doubly important to him that there was no "bad publicity," so this incident was not reported to the police. Through his newly-hired VP who knew the ropes, Mark got security guards from some Chinese syndicate, and the threatening actions stopped.

Mark was no stranger to this kind of harassment, even before the MAC incidents. When he was about 6-years-old he watched a group of gangsters working for the Pacific Northern airlines pilot union beat up his mom and dad. Yes, there was always this ugly side to the oligopolistic airlines in the era of regulation, which was rarely if ever visible to the travelling public. So, the DHL inter-island general cargo services continued for the time being.

While DHL had a growing worldwide overnight courier business, their entry into the Hawaiian passengers and cargo business *seemed* to be a non-strategic afterthought but was probably considered *part* of some prototype model for what they wanted to replicate worldwide. In addition to this, DHL wanted to start building an in-house fleet of aircraft like Federal Express for the overnight business but *also* wanted to grow general freight and passenger operations worldwide, requiring varied in-house fleets. That said, PAT Air's DC-6s and Martinliners were the *foundation* for DHL's international fleets we see today.

From his Honolulu office, Mark created a holding company for the air operations he was responsible for called DHL Air Group. Patti Finot moved to Honolulu to help set things up, working on pilot procedures and securing the necessary operating Part 121 certificates to operate scheduled airlines. The operating subsidiaries that Mark managed as president of that umbrella were as follows:

- PAT Air (specialty and general cargo in the US and Western Hemisphere)
- DHL Cargo Airlines (general cargo services between the Hawaiian Islands using DC-6s initially)
- DHL Airlines (scheduled intrastate passenger shuttle between the Hawaiian Islands using the three Martin 404s initially)
- DHL Airways (the *core business*—international scheduled overnight courier and freight *and passenger airline*, using an in-house jet fleet to transition away from third-party airlines).

This is a piece of history in its own right as this was the first holding company allowed to hold *multiple airlines* since the antitrust breakup of Boeing in 1934, which was the juggernaut aviation holding company with many airlines. These had to be combined and spun off, resulting in the birth of United Airlines. DHL's corporate structure was a direct result of Mark's deregulation work with CACA and Alfred Kahn, and later Senators Kennedy and Cannon, stemming from Petroleum Air Transport's fight with the FAA in securing more passenger contracts. The Airline Deregulation Act of 1978, with Mark's key input (discussed in greater detail later), allowed holding companies to own multiple airlines once again. For the next 15 years or so this Morris/DHL precedent was outlined in all prospectuses where post-deregulation airline holding companies and consolidations were formed. This would *not be the end* of Mark's work in refining post-deregulation rules and dealing with the CAB nemesis that held him and his father hostage for *years*.

Joe Morris would remain in St. Louis to manage the day-to-day operations of PAT Air under DHL as Mark's responsibilities with DHL broadened. Mark would remain president of PAT Air, but that was just a title. Joe, on the other hand, would be assisted by to old-reliable Bob Stevenson and another manager named Dave Ellis. Technically speaking, Mark Aero was in a way *still alive* in the late 1970s, but just in a different form. The difference was, Joe and the others were now reporting to *Mark* and not the other way around.

To put it mildly, DHL was biting off a lot, causing growing pains. Mark was soon made

CEO of DHL Airways which became the parent company of all DHL operations. And despite what Mark initially thought, managing the largest overnight courier in the world and its diversified airlines would not amount to that "stable desk job" he anticipated. He would be traveling the world now more than ever. Mark was in charge of 20,000 employees, and 140 sort centers (that would move out of those bungalows and apartment complexes) serving over 100 countries. This was *before* Federal Express began *any* international operations. Mark designed and implemented the worldwide operations that served as the foundation for what DHL is today.

Mark was able to convince Susan to move the family to Honolulu for a six-week trial period. After going through the trouble getting the Martins over to Hawaii and transplanting his family 4,500 miles from their St. Louis home, he had to go to Europe to set up DHL's operating stations there. When he got back to New York, he got a bit of bad news. Larry had suspended the startup of DHL Airlines and its Martin 404 shuttle service, only weeks after Mark spent well over $1 million of DHL's money to set everything up. The more appropriate word to use was "scuttled," and Mark was *pissed*. In essence, DHL's public relations department was worried about how the two established competitors on DHL's proposed interisland shuttle routes would react, maybe fearing for their own safety. Larry, without seemingly much thought, concurred with them hook, line, and sinker—and that was that. So, *passenger operations* were now stricken from DHLs long-range strategic plan.

The three ex-Interstate Martinliners just sat there deteriorating at Honolulu International for nearly 4 years. Finally, in 1983, all three, along with my memories and their rich *Second Wind* legacies out of St. Louis, Lafayette, and New Iberia, were unceremoniously *scrapped* on site. Never mind the crews that risked their lives (and the first crew that almost "bought it") to get these three airplanes to Hawaii in the first place.

During Mark's 4-year tenure in the early years of DHL he increased domestic revenue by 4 times, and international revenue by 6 times, increasing its international reach from a handful of countries to almost 150 countries worldwide.

CHAPTER 37

The Implosion

For Mark Morris, the year 1979 would go from bad to worse. His family came to Honolulu on a "trial basis," but Mark was out of the country most of the time. Communications among the worldwide field operations were deplorable, particularly financial communication that was needed for field office decision-making. None of the regional managers knew how the rest of the company was doing for benchmarking, much less the overall corporate strategy and their respective roles in it. Only Larry Hillblom knew the financials of DHL and he wanted to keep it that way no matter how big DHL got. At the time, DHL must have been the flattest corporate structure in existence, basically a collection of mildly loose cannons. Larry appointed Mark as chairman of a task force to see what could be done to remedy this situation. After many weeks of collaborative work with the group and the divisions which *had to involve financial data,* Larry just walked in one day and gathered all the task force workpapers, threw them in a dumpster, and burned them. Back to square one.

Susan and the two boys had just arrived at Honolulu airport with Mark escorting them from Los Angeles to Hawaii. Upon arrival, Mark was told to catch a flight *"in two hours"* to Hong Kong to meet DHL's Chief Financial Officer for International operations. Within weeks, Susan turned around, packed up the boys, and went home to St. Louis. When Mark got back to his office he found his divorce papers in his mail pile. During their 7-year marriage, Mark could never be around more than 5% of the time. That was probably worse than the average military marriage and it appeared that would continue indefinitely no matter what he tried. The divorce papers were not signed or executed and the couple remained married until re-filing in 2005. After 2005, Mark and Susan maintained an amicable friendship until she passed away in 2021.

One day in January 1979, Larry phoned Mark on one of Mark's rare days in the Honolulu office. He needed Mark at the DHL Tehran station immediately which was the most unstable and dangerous place in the world at that time. The Shah of Iran was in exile and western-hating extremists were now in control of Iran and going wild, executing anyone at random who was suspected of being a Shah sympathizer. This was the natural evolution of the same group I saw only two years earlier at Mizzou standing in long lines protesting the U.S. and the Shah. Our "old amigo" Amir could have possibly become one of these killer extremists if he wasn't first killed in the Iran-Iraq war of the 1980s. He had told Tom and I that military service would be required of him once he got his degree in the U.S. So in a small way I had experienced the beginning of this bizarre revolution just 2 years earlier, right here in the cornfields of the U.S. Midwest.

Mark arrived in Tehran from Hong Kong on a Pan Am Boeing 747, still not knowing the reason he was called there. He was then accosted as he came down the stairs of the 747 (no jetways then). They shoved him into a jeep which accelerated to an undisclosed location. They took him to an upper-floor room where he was shackled and pushed down onto a seat. Mark then saw Larry and DHL's head of international marketing just staring at him. They had been in this room for two days and there was a group of well-armed Iranians accompanying them. Mark concluded that

This DHL Boeing 737-300 sits on the tarmac outside my passenger window at what is now St. Louis Lambert International Airport as my wife Karen and I buckle in to leave for Las Vegas in 2019. Since DHL had long since been sold to Deutsche Post, a German company, they are not allowed to fly U.S. domestic services. This plane is operated by ABXs Air out of Wilmington, Ohio on behalf of DHL, and DHL makes up the bulk of ABX current operations. The origins of current-day ABX do trace right back to DHL—and Mark Morris—as discussed later in Chapter 55. DHL aircraft are now overall mustard yellow with red letters and trim. It is not a coincidence that this was the same color combination that was originated by Susan Morris on Mark Aero Martinliners and PAT DC-6s over 40 years earlier. DHL has long since settled in as the 3rd largest overnight courier freight company in the world, behind FedEx and UPS. In the years to come, Amazon Air may bump DHL to 4th place. DHL was the very first overnight courier company ever and the largest such operation in the early 1980s when Mark Morris was its CEO.

Larry called him over to this godforsaken place as a stalling tactic. The Iranians wanted Larry and the other executive to sign a document that stated DHL was a front for spy operations in Iran. If they didn't sign they would be shot. If they did sign they were told they would be escorted to the airport to catch a plane home—oh *really*?

The ring leader of the seven or so Iranians was a man named Mahmoud Ahmadinejad. He later would be elected the President of the Islamic Republic of Iran in 2005. Before mark was called there, Larry told his captors that he couldn't sign the papers without DHL's president and CEO (Mark Morris) being there to approve. Then, the three were led to a window to witness an execution by firing squad and told Mark Morris *"so you want to be next?"* The three captives agreed that their long-shot chances of survival would be to sign the papers, which they did and the Iranians left the room with glee about having obtained the signed confession. Mark never learned what the ultimate purpose of the signed confession was other than admitting they were "spies." Larry and Mark were allowed to head to the airport while for some reason the other executive ended up taking a mule across the mountains into Turkey. Larry got a seat on the packed Pan Am 747 to New York. He happened to be the largest shareholder in Pan Am at the time and a phone call to its CEO, William T. Seawell, got him that seat. Mark Morris *did not* get a seat and now had to think fast.

Earlier, on his way to Tehran from Hong Kong that led to all this, Mark had flown on the flight deck jump seat. In those days as long as a passenger was an aircrew he/she could ride jump seat if available. Due to the complexities of the Iranian revolution, now involving the installation of Ayatollah Khomeini as Iran's religious leader, the 747 hadn't moved since he got off the plane two days prior and the crew remembered Mark. Mark ended up talking to the senior captain on the flight who authorized him to fly the jump seat again.

On the way to New York Mark did some re-evaluating. He'd been working for DHL for only a few years which was supposed to be the answer to everything and instead it had wrecked his life. And now these people controlled his masterpiece, PAT Air, which he had built from the ground up back home. And despite the automotive downturn, PAT Air remained a *profitable* airline. In the meantime, amid this turmoil, PAT Air managers Joe Morris, Bob Stevenson, and Dave Ellis could not agree on a tactical framework for PAT Air going forward. Their working relationships became dysfunctional so Mark had to fire his dad, Joe. No hard feelings—it was all in the family and Joe understood!

Two years later in early 1981, Mark Morris resigned from DHL in hopes that he could now buy PAT Air back and rebuild it. There was a lot of legal maneuvering and in the end, Larry Hillblom declared that PAT Air's automotive and petroleum business was now nonstrategic for DHL, but he *still did not want Mark to have it back*. DHL proceeded to take some expensive actions such as stopping honoring contracts and draining the cash on hand. That allowed this profitable airline to declare Chapter 7 bankruptcy for a complete shutdown and liquidation. All aircraft were then returned to the lessors, sold, or moved to other divisions—mostly outside the contiguous 48 states. Even though Mark won the lawsuit to get his company back, DHL as a private company would not budge. Thus, the last great DC-6 airline on the face of the earth—a rare *profitable* one—withered to nothing in only six weeks.

Years later in May 1995 Larry Hillblom was killed in the South Pacific in the mysterious crash of a vintage seaplane. Five of his friends were on board. None of their remains were ever found. In the year 2000, DHL was sold to Deutsche Post (Now Deutsche Post DHL) and the newly combined operations of Deutsche Post DHL had over 540,000 employees with $76 billion (USD) in sales in 2020.

With the demise of PAT Air, the last passenger DC-6 N37570 and its 8-year history with Mark Aero and affiliates/successors were sold to Florida Air Leasing and converted to a freighter. From there its long life continued with several subsequent operators, winding up in Alaska with Universal Airlines in the early 2000s. It crash landed and was scrapped on site almost a decade later. The other PAT Air DC-6s were either scrapped on site in both Hawaii and at locations in the continental U.S. or lived a little longer with other cargo operators.

With the demise of PAT Air in 1981, Joe and Mark Morris exited the heavy-recip world for good and they were probably not too sentimental about it. One remnant lingered on at the northwest corner—that first DC-6 freighter N44DG owned by Bob Stevenson. It remained a fixture there in full, undisturbed PAT Air colors and markings until 1987 (see page 210). So, the "first" was also the "last," with the other 24 DC-6s in the former automotive fleet now long gone. It reminded me of one of those Japanese soldiers in the South Pacific islands who refused to believe the war was over. During most of those 6 years sitting idle at Lambert, this DC-6 straggler was owned by cargo operator F.A. Conner out of Miami International's Corrosion Corner. It was finally flown down to headquarters, but not arriving before another serious engine-out emergency just north of Memphis (the first was a 1981 fuel fire emergency that wound up at Alton Civic as described later) and then some extended downtime there. N44DG would fly for F.A. Conner and other cargo airlines for a few more years before being flown in Africa, most likely war-torn Angola, and then scrapped there. The other 24 DC-6s in the PAT Air fleet were long gone when I saw N44DG for the last time in April 1987, but a last one would still resurface right here in St. Louis only three months later as we shall see.

By 2018, DHL remained the third largest express and courier service provider behind number one FedEx and UPS. It moved nearly 37% of the world's parcel movements, now with annual revenues of over $75 billion. This is 67% higher than recent annual revenues for Delta Airlines— the world's largest passenger airline—of $45 billion. In the late 1970s and early 1980s, other freight forwarders and bulk cargo airlines began dabbling in or specializing in the overnight courier business using large first-generation airliners such as Douglas DC-8-60s and -70s, and Boeing 727s. These include Purolator Courier, Airborne Express, Burlington Air (BAX), Emory Worldwide. These have all been since absorbed by larger companies including FedEx, UPS and DHL so none remain intact. All this was influenced by the international overnight platform Mark Morris constructed between 1977 and 1981 while CEO of DHL. Mark considers DHL one of his major successes despite the personal hell it caused.

CHAPTER 38

Ancient Wings Overcast

Sometimes after finishing my last sales call of the day with IBT, I make the run the former Mark Aero ramp. PAT Air's numerous DC-6s are not the only big propliner freighters visiting the northwest corner of Lambert. There are cargo transients abound being serviced here. This propliner activity seems to be increasing to a level I had not seen since I was a child in the late 1950s. But these days it's for freight, not passengers.

One common sighting is the Zantop DC-6 A/B freighter. Zantop had a long history and is growing, but doesn't fly as many DC-6s as PAT Air does. But in this era, they are on their way to having the largest fleet of Lockheed L-188 Electra turboprops in the world for years to come. They also fly Rolls Royce Dart-powered Convair 640 twin-turboprop freighter conversions and are acquiring Douglas DC-8 jets freighters. They handle every kind of freight load imaginable, including general freight and military LogAir loads, but the Detroit to St. Louis run is almost exclusively JIT auto parts. The Zantop freighters usually sport red trim along the fuselage windows and window blanks, and another red stripe across the vertical tail. Many are unmarked, and others have "Zantop" or "Zantop International" titles over the red fuselage trim, and most of them are oily and dirty. I remember seeing an empty Zantop DC-6 taxi out of the northwest corner of Lambert with the number one propeller feathered and depart on runway 12R for a return flight to Detroit. Very typical.

A typically unmarked Zantop DC-6 A/B auto industry freighter on the ATS (former Mark Aero) tarmac in the fall of 1984. The trim is bright red. The last Zantop DC-6 I ever see operating out of here would be only one year later.

As I mentioned I had no ramp sightings of any of the 3 ex-Interstate Martin 404s since around late 1973. They were now operating out of Lafayette or Iberia, Louisiana, unbeknownst to me. The only Martins I now see at Lambert are the ex-Piedmont fire dump hulk sitting further south on the west side, and the more recent presence, the Tiffany Industries corporate Martin 404 N636X. CEO Joe Simpkins would base Tiffany N636X at Lambert until around 1982. The paint job was in pretty bad tones of brown and dark yellow "sunburst" design, and from interior photos,

I saw it looked like a senile grandmother was the decorator. After 1982 his ex-TWA Martinliner went through subsequent owners before being acquired by pilot entrepreneur Jeff Whitesell and restored as a flying exhibit on the west coast in a more palatable Pacific Coast Airlines livery. Ironically, it was back in 1978 that Jeff and his dad and brother had sold this plane to Simkins/Tiffany in the first place. Under Whitesell's second-time ownership it became the very last Martin 404 to fly, on February 28, 2008. It's currently stored intact in California (see photo page 73).

In the fall of 1978, I'm attending a Loctite seminar at Mansion House Center in downtown St. Louis. We're dismissed well before 5 o'clock and for a few moments, I stand on the sidewalk along North Broadway to get some "fresh air," or at least as fresh as you can get with the light stench of urban street sewer gas always present. I look to the south and see a *very low* DC-6 flying north right towards me, as though it is driving right up Broadway. It has a sinister-looking black nose that covers the flight deck windscreen, making it look like a bandit. A yellow and black stripe goes all the way down the window line to the tail. All in all, this plane looks pretty sharp as it roars by entering a shallow left turn, base to final, for one of the Runway 30 parallels at Lambert. This is my first sighting of a Trans Continental DC-6, one of the first ones acquired to complement their fleet of smaller ex-Shamrock C-46s.

A Trans Continental DC-6 A/B at Spirit of St. Louis Airport disgorges auto components about to be trucked 20 miles north up the highway to the new GM Wentzville auto assembly plant, in July 1985. The upper trim paint is tan-yellow, and the rest of the trim is black. In the early 1980s, Spirit Airport began supplanting the old Mark Aero ramp at Lambert as a transloading point for the JIT auto parts. This is because of its proximity to the new Wentzville plant, coupled with the gradual closing of all the other auto plants in St. Louis, including Ford Hazelwood, GM Goodfellow, and Chrysler Fenton. This DC-6 is in the same scheme I first saw on the DC-6 flying overhead while walking out of that Loctite seminar in 1978—see above narrative. (Douglas E. Teel)

For the next 7 years, I would see these clean-looking DC-6 "bandits" operating out of the northwest corner. These planes looked professional compared to the earlier unpainted C-46 fleet. On one occasion I see a full-blown, longhair "ground hippie" supervising the backhaul pallet loading of one of these -6s, who also oversees the securing of the cargo doors, and act as the fire-spotter during startup. As each prop on the left side turns, the pilot—who looks *just like* Clay Lacy circa 1971—sticks his head out his side window to visually monitor each engine start on the left. I then watch it taxi out to runway 24 for an immediate full-power takeoff and a slow climbing turn to the left. It arcs around the south end of Lambert and disappears to the northeast, on its way back to Detroit.

Now in late October 1979 when I'm two weeks away from getting my private pilot certificate and am sitting at a right window seat in an American Airlines 727-200 at Lambert, bound for Detroit. I'm going to Syracuse to visit my good friend and former college roommate Tom Noonan who is in his final year of law school. We are anticipating some fun college Halloween parties and flirting with women in costumes (with zero results). My plane is taxiing south of the main parallel runways heading northwest for takeoff on runway 12R when my window fills with a huge DC-6/C-118 with gear and flaps down, flaring way too high on touchdown, props whirling down to idle. Its high flare angle makes it look like it is going to hit its tail skid before the mains. It has its ex-military white fuselage top and tail with no window trim stripe, and in black letters above the window line, it says "PAT Air" which looks hastily stenciled in. The standard PAT Air paint job had not yet been applied. The DC-6 *slams* onto the runway, wings flexing a bit on impact, with the plane wagging slightly from side to side with the pilot's swift rudder corrections. Wow! I bet they pranged that one! I then watch it innocently taxi over to the PAT Air facilities at the northwest corner with all four propellers churning at idle, as though nothing had happened. Years later I'm told this "high-flare" landing profile was a not-so-uncommon occurrence with pilot trainees. While most PAT Air crews were seasoned high-time pilots, some were young, low time, and in a state of training and building hours. This DC-6 I witnessed was N1304S just returning from Florida, which began life with National Airlines in 1952 and was flown by Pan American for a while. Ultimately, it was written off due to a mishap in late 1989 while flying with freight hauler Aerial Transit out of Miami.

Eight months later the sweltering summer afternoon of June 22, 1980, is an otherwise nice clear day. My flying pal Mike O'Brien and I wing out to Sparta Illinois in his Cherokee 140 to visit the Sparta Sky Diving Club to see if we want to take this up at some point (we don't). On the return trip, I fly the plane for practice IFR under the hood (a shroud strapped to the head that blots outside reference) and then pause along our route to practice timed holding patterns over the Illinois farmland. At this very moment the same Super Constellation junkpile that I had described flying over my balcony in the fall of 1978, N74CA, "buys the farm." This happens on takeoff at the Columbus, Indiana Airport, killing two crewmen, just 200 miles east of our practice holding position.

Recall Herman "Fish" Salmon, the renowned Lockheed chief test pilot who entered his L-1049H Super Constellation to compete with Clay Lacy's DC-7 at the San Diego air races in 1971. This retired 66-year-old now happens to be the freelance pilot in command of this ill-fated ferry flight and is killed on impact, as was the flight engineer. The co-pilot, nicknamed "Scooter" who is Fish's son, and three passengers (the aircraft owner and two mechanics) survive. As a reminder, Fish was Lockheed's famous chief test pilot for all Constellation models and the Lockheed turboprop Electra, as well as the extremely hot Lockheed F-104 Starfighter jet fighter. Heaven forbid, if Fish had to die, it seems it should have been while testing a brand new F-104 in the 1950s, not while attempting to ferry a clapped-out 25-year-old Super Constellation in the 1980s.

What happened? For most of the time (after I saw this plane in 1978) it had been stored idle at Bakalar Airport in Columbus, Indiana. Its already deteriorated innards got worse, which *always* happens with long-inactive heavy iron. It had just been sold to a company called Aero Trader to be used for fish hauling between Alaska and the U.S. west coast. Fish and crew were hired by Aero Trader to "fix it up" and ferry the Super Constellation to Seattle. For weeks they inspected, tested, and replaced components and tested the engines. None of the engine tests went right, and at least one engine had to be changed. Overheating engines due to stuck oil cooler shutters, fowled plugs, unresponsive propeller control, and useless brakes were a problem. The 2,000 gallons of 100/130 octane aviation fuel, sitting in the wing tanks for almost two years, were never drained—just a few hundred gallons were added.

The plane's cargo hold was loaded to volume capacity with spare engines and parts, and their decision was made that they would depart the 6,500-foot runway on the sweltering 86-degree afternoon of the 22nd. After hitting speed V1 (commitment to flight), one by one *all* the engines lost power as the Super Constellation pitched up after rotation, lumbered past the end of the runway at a sickly high angle, tearing through power lines and poles, and slamming into a soybean field, only to skid into a thick grove of trees, shredding the aircraft into several pieces. Summer heat and humidity, plus a likely overgrossed airplane, plus sloppy "restoration" work and weakened and unreliable engines equaled unmitigated disaster, even for smart, conscientious people like famous Lockheed chief test pilots. Speculation was that the engineer's throttle locks vibrated loose causing the throttles to ease back with the vibration of full power, explaining the simultaneous power loss on all engines. And thus the demise of the very same beat-up Super Constellation I spotted over my apartment balcony almost 2 years previous.

Three months later, on a September Friday night Tom Noonan is in for the weekend and we go to the Rodeo Bar in St. Ann. This is a bar with the curious format of "country disco," which is located only a quarter mile or so beyond the departure end of Runway 24 at Lambert. To preserve this memory I committed it to paper the next day and filed it away:

Well, it's Tom's turn to drive on this dark Friday night. After cruising the parking lot for several minutes in his dilapidated, rusted-out white 1972 Ford Torino, we finally get a parking space. As we exit the car, a frightening, all-encompassing, disorienting roar vibrates my body and turns my head back and forth in a panicked frenzy, drawing my eyes skyward. Startled fear transitions into excitement as my brain translates the abrupt intrusion into meaning. Within milliseconds the starry canopy overhead is engulfed with the presence of a fire-breathing monster—a four-engine piston Douglas C-118 transport that CAN'T be more than 200 feet above us. This machine had just departed Lambert's Runway 24 in a shallow climb and gradual left turn south toward Memphis. We're drowned in the synchronized throbbing and harmonious drone of ten thousand horsepower of raw R-2800 energy turning four huge Hamilton Standard propellers. The sun-bright landing lights under the wing illuminate the madly churning propellers, the wings, and the fuselage underside. The letters "NAVY" on the left-wing underside are visible as this ancient aluminum dinosaur skims low, directly overhead if about to crush us all.

As this monster flying machine churned away to the southeast with red beacons alternately flashing, I could not keep my adrenalin levels in check, and all the people in the parking lot were stopped in their tracks and stricken just like me, looking UP. While surrounded by friends and nice-looking ladies for the rest of the evening, I wasn't thinking much about them. And they had already forgotten about "the monster flyover."

This was the Friday night Memphis/Millington NAS run for St. Louis Navy reservists, wheels-up for the weekend. I had not seen this operation in a couple of years, but this is the last such Navy Reserve movement I would ever see, sealing ten years of my witnessing Friday-Sunday shuttling of Naval Reservists in C-118s, C-54s, C-121s, and P2V Neptunes going into and out of Lambert—mostly in and out of the Mark Aero ramp.

Three months later on a Friday night in early December, Tom and I are back at, where else, the Rodeo Bar to celebrate his passing the Missouri Bar exam with some friends. Just as I'm about to leave after a long night of partying, I meet a personable and shapely blonde name Karen who is hanging out with her friends. It turns out she is a legal assistant who works for Peabody Holding. I get her phone number. Later, talking with Tom and me, she says she at one time worked for an attorney named Harvey Feldman in Clayton, who Tom knew. Later, Tom, a freshly-minted lawyer as of tonight, did some research for me and called Harvey. Harvey told him that Karen was the hardest working, most conscientious, and loyal legal assistant he ever had, "bar none." The fact that she was a very hard worker piques my interest.

The next day I call her and ask her for lunch. We go to Fourth and Pine downtown next to her office in the Marquette building (my investment banker dad worked in that building for years). We talk about the Rodeo Bar and she told me she almost stayed home that night because she was too tired. The other factor that might have prevented this lunch was that she was mad that I didn't buy her a drink that night—a dumb oversight on my part. A few days later I take her up in a Bellanca Citabria, flying in formation with Mike O'Brien and his 177 Cardinal. We wing due north up the Mississippi to Elsberry, Missouri where Karen's family river cabin is; what they call the "clubhouse." We circle the place at a low altitude so she can take photos while Mike keeps a loose formation, then we turn back south and stop for lunch at Alton Civic Airport. Later Karen tells me the Citabria adventure helped me to "reel her in." I'll admit it may have been the other way around.

Mr. "Fake Superhero Pilot" flying the Bellanca Citabria north towards Elsberry, Missouri, on his second date with his future wife, Karen Myers, who took this shot from the back seat. December 13, 1980.

Karen takes a shot of my "wingman," Mike O'Brien in his Cessna 177 Cardinal. We're over St. Charles County and the turn in the Mississippi River that bends from the east to the north matching our heading. We're on our way to fly her over her family's vacation river "clubhouse" near Elsberry, Missouri.

In future months I accompany Karen at several Peabody events and meet many of their people. Here I learn that Peabody has an in-house flight department with corporate jets. At the time I have no idea who Ed Phelps is or his relationship with Mark Aero and the Morrises. He had since retired as CEO of Peabody, but Karen had seen him visiting the office on several occasions. At the 1981 Peabody holiday party I'm introduced to one of Peabody's star pilots, Dick Horwitz, and we hit it off well. This Hawker 1000 jet jock treats me—a lowly private pilot that flies "little planes"—as an equal. Then Dick introduces me to Peabody's chief pilot who has a similarly welcoming disposition. His name is Jerry Riebold.

Karen in front of my rented Bellanca 7ECA Citabria on our second date on December 13, 1980, at Alton Civic Airport in Illinois (now St. Louis Regional Airport). We grab lunch at the airport diner with my pal Mike O'Brien who flew formation with us in his Cessna 177 Cardinal. Runway 29 was the active that day and there was a stiff 20-knot crosswind from the west-southwest that made me a bit nervous, but I was lucky enough to "grease it on"—one main wheel at a time—and impress the girl (that is, in my own mind). The girl probably didn't know the significance of negotiating a nasty direct crosswind in a light tail-dragging machine.

CHAPTER 39

My Best Shot

In early 1981, I have enough hours to accelerate my instrument rating. I move my training from the small, uncontrolled Creve Coeur and Arrowhead airports to Roederer Aviation at Spirit of St. Louis Airport to train in a controlled ATC environment (Spirit has a control tower and therefore is a "controlled" airport). I become good friends with the proprietors, Herb and son Bob Roederer. Herb was a former Northwest Orient DC-7C captain, so he had some stories for me. But we are in a deep recession and there is an air controller strike, so President Ronald Reagan fires the controllers to break the powerful PATCO (Professional Air Traffic Controllers Organization) union. So, we have skeleton crews of air controllers covering the airspace, consisting of a limited number of "rusty" supervisors. Departure times for IFR (instrument flight rules) flights have to be rationed into "departure slots." Tough luck if you are a minute late for your slot allocation due to a finicky instrument during preflight checks. Stress on the supervisor-controllers is incredible. Surprisingly, the temporary controllers are as accommodative as can be expected for pilots needing to train or stay current, so my instrument training moves forward, albeit at a slower pace.

I have a good instructor, Dave Meineke who is a young lad compared to me. Due to my job-related time constraints, I also have a few older fill-in instructors, including furloughed Ozark pilots. They have great stories about flying the DC-3s, Martin 404s, Convairs, Fairchild F-227s, and DC-9s. Some of the other students, both primary and advanced, don't show much interest in our conversations on dinosaur airplanes. I get along well with instructors and after a training session we often stop in at the airport pub called Blayney's for a beer to talk shop. One night at the pub the subject comes up of how to secure pilot jobs in this bad market.

PAT Air is not yet shut down but I know little regarding their current circumstances or ownership. One instructor says that PAT Air is seeking pilot trainees with instrument, commercial, and multi-engine ratings, and they can even "get on" with total flight time *"as low as 300 hours."* He says they *"hire a lot of women"* (even though there was no social mandate back then for the aviation industry to increase the hiring of women) but some of the trainees, both men, and women, had hinted they were *not happy* racking up hours in ancient DC-6s *"but will take anything at this point."* What? My ears perk up.

Rumor has it that some PAT Air trainees would rather be building time in new Beech King Airs twin turboprops, not big old DC-6 dinosaurs. In my dismay, I ask myself, *why a freakin' King Air 200 that carries only 9 passengers—and not a heavy DC-6 that can carry 90 people or 30,000 pounds of freight with incredibly complex engines that require infinitely more crew coordination, situational awareness, and responsibility?* To me, that was the dumbest and most senseless thing I ever heard to come out of a fledgling pilot's head. First, in Mark Morris's words:

As far as pilot recruits and the major airlines go, the heavyweights and transport airplanes were the biggest key for hiring pilots – the problem was with the fighter jocks from the military. They thought they were the best etc., but as the head of personnel told me at Delta Airlines that the 1,500-hour Air Force and Navy jocks flying the F-4s, etc., were useless to them. They would tell them to reenlist and get into the transports to learn crew coordination and how complex systems work with the larger transport aircraft. Jets are ten times easier as far as engines go and the landing and take-off speeds are about the same as the heavy-recip aircraft - so pilot hours in big airplanes are important. If you had a 3,000-hour transport pilot with time in 100,000-pound big recip aircraft it was much better than having a 3,000-hour pilot in the light corporate turbine aircraft [like the highly-revered Beech King Air]. *I don't think any of my co-executives in the airline business at that time would disagree.*

On the flip side is how the major airlines viewed heavy-recip crews flying out of Corrosion Corner at Miami International Airport. This place, comprising the northwest corner of the airport, was by far the *capital* of the *Second Wind* phenomenon for that entire era. No other place in the world came even close to this international bastion of heavy-recip operations during the *Second Wind*. This place also had an impossible-to-remove stigma of being the most lawless concentration of slipshod heavy-recip operations anywhere in the *universe*. Most of the Corrosion Corner operators in the 1980s were foreign-registered carriers (mainly Dominican) allowed to operate out of Miami under a FAR Part 129 exemption which excused them from most of the rules that the

Major airline HR departments in South Florida and Dallas in 1981:
"Heavy-recip jockeys out of Miami need not apply."

few U.S. registered heavy-recip carriers had to follow (namely Bellamy- Lawson d.b.a. Aerial Transit and Trans-Air-Link). Many U.S. crews flew for these 129 operators, *many of which were based in the U.S.* So, the major airline HR departments, particularly those of Eastern and American Airlines, were automatically biased against Corrosion Corner heavy-recip crews as lawless renegades, heavy drinkers, sloppy pilots, misfits, etc. If you flew around the Caribbean, Mexico, and South America, you were better off having flown light turboprop transports like King Airs, or even larger deHavilland Twin Otters, which represented *more reputable* carriers, at least in perception.

During one IFR training session, my instructor Dave asks me if I had seen the local TV news last night. I had not. Earlier that night a fully loaded and fueled PAT Air DC-6 took off from Lambert and the number three engine burst into flames on climb. It was the dreaded fuel fire. The crew hit the fire bottles and kept the plane straight, aiming for Alton Civic airport across the river for a successful straight-in emergency landing. Dave and I decide to go to Alton Civic for me to shoot approaches under the hood and then have a look at the crippled plane. There we see the flame-damaged DC-6 sitting on the ramp—N44DG (see photo page 210). It is scary to look at. The number three engine cowling and nacelle are charred black, and greasy gunk and debris sit in a nasty, irregular pool on the tarmac below it. We have no idea whether the fire bottles worked or not.

Boy did that look like a close call. A fuel fire emergency in a heavy-recip can result in the wing burning off within *minutes* if the fire bottles fail. Fifteen years later that would happen with a Northern Air Cargo DC-6 in Alaska, killing all on board. However, last night this crew was both skillful *and* lucky—looks a lot like *situational awareness* and *responsibility* to me. And here I am at Alton Civic, where I stood a full 10 years earlier at the great Baron Volkmer Airshows, and where I rubbed elbows with Clay Lacy, Eric Hartmann, Peter Townsend, Bob Hoover, and Sherm Cooper. And where I had my second-date lunch with Karen. But today I'm at the very same spot—this time looking at the sickening aftermath of a fire-damaged DC-6, where this *Tiger on a Leash* tried to kill its masters.

All the PAT Air talk at Blayney's may have just been unsubstantiated barroom hot air. But years later I learn PAT Air did hire low-time pilots as trainees. In listening to these conversations, I'm motivated to put my IFR training into overdrive—I already have more than 300 hours. I decide right there at Blayney's that I'll try and "get on" with PAT Air. I will call them up when I am nearer to the finish line with the alleged required minimal training, including my multi-engine rating and commercial certificate which I can do much more quickly than the instrument rating I'm working on now. I figure I can call them in just a few short months. In talking with Mark Morris decades later, he did say that at that point I did have enough pilot training momentum and enthusiasm to enter into discussions with PAT Air and start keeping them apprised of my progress.

But sometimes you need a break from job responsibilities, flight training, and bar talk. On a chilly, overcast morning in November 1981 I'm on my way to the lake to meet my family for a short autumn weekend in the country. Driving west down I-44 (old Route 66) one has to pass through the infamous "Devil's Elbow" section southeast of Rolla, Missouri. Devil's Elbow is a narrow, hilly, and winding stretch near the Big Piney River valley in the Ozarks known for its fatal automobile accidents—a true suicide stretch. I happen to look over to the eastbound lanes and cannot believe what I see chugging up the hill. It's a big flatbed rig and I glimpse at what I think is a pair of Douglas C-124 engine nacelles strapped on the trailer. There are big radial engines still inside the cowlings.

Just where are these nacelles are going? I rack this up as "interesting" but then forget about it. A week later I am passing by the former Mark Aero ramp on the way to an industrial customer and lo and behold, right there on the far northeast side of the ramp are those very same C-124 nacelles on pallets! As it turned out these were not C-124 nacelles, but those from a Convair C-131 pulled from the Arizona desert that look almost identical. So, this is now where all the aerial junk goes! Then I read an article in the *St. Louis Globe-Democrat* that there's a movie set encompassing several blocks in St. Louis city where a movie called *Escape from New York* is being filmed, including an airplane crash scene. It will star Kurt Russel, Ernest Borgnine, and Isaac Hayes.

Now things are making sense. I had heard the local talent company in St. Louis, Talent Plus, had been auditioning for "extras" for some big Hollywood movie and I did see hundreds of wannabes lined up for blocks. The plot of *Escape from New York* is set in post-apocalyptic New York City where it is now being loosely controlled by violent criminal anarchists (like now?). It turns out the Convair nacelles are to serve as part of the crash wreckage of "Air Force One" in the middle of the city, where the surviving President of the United States is pulled from the wreckage and kidnapped by the anarchists.

A few weeks pass and on New Year's Eve 1981 I pass my instrument checkride with FAA examiner Bob Burns. I do fine on the oral exam but it is low-overcast and windy today, so my checkride is in actual instrument meteorological conditions (IMC). We have a 200-foot ceiling, two-mile visibility spitting raindrops, and a choppy 25-knot direct crosswind burbling from the hills directly to the south of the Spirit approaches to Runway 7 (now Runway 8 after magnetic charts had been updated).

Whew!. I'm shaking when we taxi in and shut down and Burns doesn't hesitate to tell me that I "passed" the checkride. Relieved, I joked that it was amazing that he entrusted me to fly him through this wet, choppy, soupy mess. He retorted, *"Why would I cancel it? You did fine on the oral and I have no choice but to assume that if I'm going to give you the rating you should be qualified to fly in this mess. Dammit, I would have busted you on the spot if your CDI needle had drifted past one dot either way, or if you took more than ten seconds to check and correct your relative bearing on your NDB approaches in these bad crosswinds."* Wow, I just got my *instrument rating*, but just my luck. I had learned weeks earlier that PAT Air was all but gone—so I missed it by *"that much."* Now what? At least the New Year's Eve party Karen and I attended that evening in the basement of some north county Catholic church was secondary to my mental intoxication from my accomplishment—PAT Air or no PAT Air.

A few months into the new year Karen and I go to the premiere of *Escape from New York* at the Halls Ferry 6 Cinema in far north county, which is close to her apartment. This is the first and only premiere before general release. I joke with Karen, *"Wouldn't it be funny if Isaac Hayes, Kurt Russell, or one of those other stars shows up at this premiere?"* Sure enough, a few minutes later, a black stretch Cadillac limo with a large disco ball hanging from the rear-view mirror pulls up in front of us, with other limos behind it. A handler opens the rear door of the first limo and Isaac Hayes himself pops right out to everyone's disbelieving cheers. This was nothing but a wild premonition on my part as there had been *no announcement* that he would show up. I didn't know I was so clairvoyant about this, but it was, after all, *THE premiere showing.*

Smilin' Isaac with his shiny black bald head and his thick overdeveloped upper body walks through the lobby crowd right past Karen and me and sits down at a table for autographs. He is wearing a "wife-beater" black leather vest and pants with oversized metal chains. We don't bother to get an autograph—maybe we're thinking it's too crowded and we won't get seats together. His chains look familiar to me. Years earlier I was watching the Sammy Davis Show on TV where Hayes performed his Top 40 song "Shaft" wearing in a similar metal chain outfit. After the song and long applause, Sammy Davis thanked him for a great performance and credited Hayes' *fine wardrobe* to "Central Hardware"—not Macy's, Nieman Marcus or Saks Fifth Avenue.

We watch the movie, which was entertaining but many scenes are goofy by today's production standards. Right here on the big screen—in the middle of the urban crash scene—are the same two Convair nacelles that passed me in the opposite direction on I-44 and later spotted on the former Mark Aero ramp. Here see they used these *piston engine* power packages to mimic the *jet engines* of a *fictitious* jetliner type that could never pass as an "Air Force One" or any other jet. I realize that now in 1982, propliners are turning to junk at light speed and that kind of junk is perfect for sloppy movie props in disaster movies. Years later I buy the DVD only to realize how bad this film was. It wasn't a B-movie, but more like a "C-movie." Despite the poor quality of the film, the phrase *Escape from New York* seems to resurface in varied contexts within current popular culture.

With PAT Air gone in 1982, I begin spotting unmarked piston Convair freighters coming in and out of the northwest corner of Lambert, most looking shabby. Some are Trans Continental planes that have not been painted yet. Others are bottom-feeder airlines that always seem to surface when things are booming. The 1980-1982 economic downturn is in the rearview mirror and freighter activity which had dwindled to near zero is now picking up. Chrysler had re-invented its product line with the little "K-Car" that is supposed to compete with fuel-efficient subcompact Japanese cars. In the end, no way. These turn out to be boxy, tinny, "grandma-looking" cars that are embarrassing to be seen in. K-Cars are not around for long, but their chassis survives for decades as the basis for Lee Iacocca's revolutionary minivan. By 1984, inflation and rates begin deflating like air out of a balloon—this time for the long-haul thanks to Fed Chairman Paul Volker's back-breaking interest rate hikes.

During the summer of 1982, I regularly spend evenings at Karen's apartment in Hazelwood, which is only a couple miles from the threshold of runway 24 at Lambert. It is silent from that direction until around 10:00 PM each night. Then in the humid night air from over two miles away I start hearing—one after another—idling R-2800s soon cranking up to full takeoff power and thundering down runway 24 before circling wide to the north in their climbs. By the engine sound subtleties alone I can tell these are mostly piston Convairs with a few DC-6s mixed in. I tell Karen, *There goes another one headed back to Michigan.* This departure activity would sometimes keep me awake for an hour or two as though we were near some World War II bomber base at the beginning of a big mission. But this is mid-1982, not 1944. I tell Karen I'd like to fly in one of those old Convairs (or any heavy-recip) before it's too late. I know there is *no way* that's going to happen. But then, as they say, *"be careful what you wish for . . ."*

Fuzzy blowup shot of an unmarked Convair 240 freighter on a foggy day in October 1984. It's parked at the ATS former Mark Aero ramp in front of where the now "invisible" historic Old Terminal once stood. Behind it, Lambert Runway 30R fades into the background fog. The trim along the window line is a dark aqua blue. Around this time this plane may have been flying with Providence Airlines, a freight operator headquartered in the Northeast. Its trim along the window line is light blue.

CHAPTER 40

Air One

In 1977, CAB head Alfred Kahn, with Senators Kennedy and Cannon—and at the considerable direction of Mark Morris—got a bill introduced that paved the way for deregulation that next year. After the Airline Deregulation Act was signed into law by Jimmy Carter in late 1978 the work was not over, so in subsequent years Mark Morris would serve as a cleanup man of sorts by continuing to represent all CACA members (see Chapter 32). Kahn was head of the CAB and that body was now a vestige that still provided the major airlines a few competitive advantages. Ironically, Kahn, with the help of Morris, would lobby Congress and the major airlines to *abolish* the CAB once and for all, which occurred on January 1, 1985. The free market was now "reasonably free" to determine routes, pricing, etc. Also, Mark's continuing role with the New Entrant's CEO club helped restructure the system, including the formulation of policy for ticketing, gating, and the general integration of the coming onslaught of new airline entrants.

With airline deregulation well underway, in early 1982 I see a local St. Louis TV news report that a new airline is coming to town called Air One. It is to be all-jet with Boeing 727-100s and would charge *standard coach fares* which are *fixed* for each flight, in exchange for premium service—meaning "first-class." Attractive flight attendants—one per every 27 passengers—were combined with real first-class meals and drinks, real china, wide leather seats with individual telephones, and four-abreast seating meaning no middle seat with a large pitch between rows for *excessive* leg room. This was a deliberate throwback to the piston/propliner *First Wind* era of the 1950s when only the elites could afford to fly and they were served first-class restaurant cuisine, prepared right there in the aircraft galley, and served on real china with real silverware. They had to be treated that way—the average en route flight time was *long*!

The person I see interviewed on the TV news report is Eugene A. "Gene" Cernan, the last man to walk on the Moon and an astronaut I was familiar with. He had been meeting with Mark Morris on his new airline idea and agreed to serve as its first Chairman of the Board. Without airline deregulation that Mark helped usher in, his Air One could *not have happened*.

Mark Morris is in the news—including every local and national medium—which is how I learn that he had also been the man who had been behind PAT Air and Mark Aero. I am glad to finally learn who the main personality was behind all my spying on those operations and find it interesting that he is now pulling together a jet airline. It turns out it was the stillborn Missouri Air Commuter with its proposed use of old Martin 404s that caused Mark to start developing the idea of this type of airline service.

Air One was part of a wave of Part 121 new entrant scheduled airline startups in these early years of deregulation of which there were approximately 21 at the final count. Most of the regulatory barriers that had repeatedly slammed the Morrises were gone and federal government protectionism of established airlines was unraveling. Government sentiment was shifting in favor of new competition, very much due to the earlier congressional testimony and committee work of Joe and Mark Morris on the decline of the supplemental airlines during the middle and late-1970s.

One of Mark Aero's de Havilland DH-125 corporate jets under maintenance at its Greenville, Illinois facility near St. Louis during the 1960s. These, a Hansa Jet, and Mitsubishi MU-2s were used for its corporate flight departments outsourced to them, including Peabody Coal (later Peabody Holding then Peabody Energy). Both Mark Morris and Jerry Riebold cut their "jet teeth" by getting type rated and their ATP's (<u>A</u>irline <u>T</u>ransport <u>P</u>ilot rating) with this aircraft. (Mark G. Morris)

Mark would serve as Air One's president and chief operating officer. Mark himself came up with the "Air One" name which truly stood out among the *first wave* of post-deregulation new entrants.

How did Air One get started? After leaving DHL and his subsequent unsuccessful attempt to re-acquire and salvage PAT Air, Mark went to work as a consultant for Interstate Airlines out of Detroit, which was Dave Clark's newly-formed airline within his mega air freight forwarding operation, AAC. Interstate now wanted to expand into scheduled passenger service. Mark resurrected a *variant* of the MAC business plan for a standard fare, but more upscale service airline, but Dave Clark/Interstate ultimately turned it down.

So, Mark Morris decided to run with his idea and start such an airline himself. He had jet experience by driving DHL's expansion from heavy-recip iron into long-haul jet transport aircraft. Plus he had earned his Airline Transport Pilot's rating (ATP) a decade earlier at only 23 years old (the youngest age you can get the ATP) in the de Havilland DH-125 corporate jets operated by Mark Aero that he had been type-rated in earlier. So, he rallied interest and pulled together an executive management team made up of long-time business associates from the airline industry and from St. Louis law firms. Jim Johnson had been EVP marketing at Continental Airlines and would now serve in that same capacity at Air One; Vic Pruitt had been SVP Tech services at Northwest Orient and serve in that position at Air One; John Dvorak was a guru in financial planning for Frank Lorenzo who was controlling shareholder and CEO of Continental

Last man on the moon. Astronaut Gene Cernan inside the Lunar Module as it sits on the lunar surface in December 1972 after he and Harrison Schmitt spent record hours on extravehicular activity (moon walking, that is). A decade later Mark Morris reached out to Cernan cold turkey and suddenly they became close friends and Cernan became Air One's first board chairman. (NASA)

Airlines/Texas International and later Eastern Airlines. He would be Air One's chief financial officer. And finally, Dennis Fitzgerald would serve as Air One's chief pilot and SVP-Flight Operations. He had previously been the chief pilot at Garuda Indonesia Airlines and assistant chief pilot at Midway Airlines. On top of this, he was—of all things—an attorney as well as a C-9 Nightingale (DC-9-30) pilot with the Air National Guard out of Scott Air Force Base (see photo page 96). Mark's General Counsel was Ken Wideman – an experienced corporate attorney and friend from earlier days while running PAT Air. The next-level staff members were filled with similarly well-qualified individuals. Mark and most of his team put up considerable equity and there were additional private debt placements – much of which was underwritten by a large Hong Cong bank which was then under British rule.

There were a lot of problems to be addressed that Mark had not previously had to deal with, but that was what his experienced brain trust was for: How to secure ticket counters, gate slots, and ground support services for a scheduled operation at St. Louis and various destinations; what reservation system would you be able to use; and would a host airline favor Air One over other airlines when it could not fill the reservation request internally.

There were endless marketing issues as to how to gain the favor of travel and booking agents, etc. The headquarters and hub would be in St. Louis with initial daily round trips to Kansas City, Newark, Reagan National Washington D.C., and Dallas, with 9 round trips flown daily to start. Air One secured seven older Boeing 727-100s—three from Pan American (at $1.9 million each) and the rest from Piedmont (at $2.5 million each). All of Air One's wide first-class seats came from the defunct Braniff International Airways, and with the later acquisitions of 727-200s he acquired the wide seats from KLM airways. Chinaware and other commissary supplies came from Braniff. Air One obtained CAB approval and its Part 121 certificate allowing scheduled services in 1982. Charter services began in February 1983 while Air One was still attempting to gain gate slots for scheduled services— with such services inaugurated that April once the slots were secured.

An Air One Boeing 727-100 is ready for departure after a successful launch of operations. The lower fuselage is white; the upper fuselage and #1 on the tail are dark grey and the overall tail is light grey. The St. Louis business community loved this airline and many in that community "bragged" about flying with them. (Wikimedia Commons, Jon Proctor GFDL 1.2)

Why Gene Cernan? From its inception, Mark decided he *first* needed a well-known and highly respected public figure to take the helm of the new Air One. In his own words:

When I decided to start Air One, I made a list of important industry leaders I thought I needed as chairman to get a scheduled airline started in the U.S. So my priority list for my board of directors was 1) astronaut, 2) energy leader, 3) well-known academician, 4) real estate guru or 5) well known retired airline executive. I originally called Neil Armstrong [first man on the moon] *and he was actually listed in the phone book in Denver and I called him and he actually answered the phone. I was quite shocked but happy to talk with him—I told him my plans—and he said it was an interesting proposal but he was currently on the board of United Airlines.*

So then I thought if I couldn't get the first guy on the moon, I would go for the last one on the moon. I actually had to look that up in the encyclopedia Britannica and found the last man was Gene Cernan but I couldn't find him in the phone book. Just by chance, I was talking to a friend in the travel business who happened to know Cernan, and he gave me his office phone number. When I called his secretary put me right through and he asked me to come to Houston and I spent about a week with him there—and he came on as chairman.

We brought on his close buddy Tom Short, the only flying General in the Vietnam era and he was flying C-118s which as you know is the military version of the DC-6. Tom and I had great discussions on flying those old aircraft. Tom had also been head of all Mercury and Gemini ground operations at North American Rockwell, and then later on Apollo when Rockwell got the contract to build Command Module. With a variety of management experience in other businesses (oil wildcat drilling in Canada and a large software company in California), Tom was one of the best business guys I ever worked with.

We also brought on Ed Phelps our longtime friend and partner from Peabody Holding, real estate mogul Lynn McCarthy who ran the big commercial real estate developer JC Nichols in Kansas City, and we even snapped up longtime Ozark marketing executive Paul Rogers which did not sit well with my friend Ed Crane of Ozark. Paul was the nicest guy you could ask for and I brought him on as President as he was highly recognized in the U.S. scheduled passenger industry—where I had charter passenger and cargo experience only but no scheduled passenger experience. When Air One went public in late 1983, there were some disagreements on management style. Gene thought it was best was for him to step down as chairman and go to vice-chairman role, Paul would become chairman and I became the president and later CEO when Air One went public.

During these startup months, Mark Morris was primed to continue the fight with the regulators on all kinds of issues including new carrier entrants—so that they could obtain the infrastructure to operate—from gates to ticket counters to computerized ticketing systems. Not only was he working with Kahn, Kennedy, and Cannon in Washington, he talks about how he began to establish clout with the airlines themselves:

*In late 1981 I became Chairman of the New Entrants CEO Club – formed to troubleshoot problems for new entrants from the post-1978 deregulated era. The club was started at the time of the 1981 PATCO air controller's strike where President Reagan fired them all. This greatly complicated the mission. I was voted in at 32 years of age by all the new entrants to chair that committee – why? Probably because none of the others wanted it – new entrants were considered at the time to be any existing **intrastate** carrier that was now able to expand into the interstate markets – those included large established airlines like PSA; Air California; Air Florida, Southwest Airlines, plus the "from scratch" startups, a new phenomenon at the beginning of the deregulated era. None of those [intrastate] carriers had previously been under the regulation of the old CAB [just their respective state authorities].*

*The ATA (Air Transport Association) – comprised of the CEOs of all the airlines – decided to split the New Entrants CEO club into two divisions – one for the established carriers like the intrastates, and one for the from scratch startups, which most existing airlines still did not consider legitimate. Herb Kelleher [founder and CEO of Southwest Airlines] was my mentor in the CEO club and he was the big 800-pound gorilla in the room and he championed me to be chairman – plus as he said we need at least one airline pilot heading up their airline – and he told them that not only am I an airline pilot – I am also the only **line qualified** pilot running an airline [with both PAT Air and the new Air One] – in fact, he said that he thinks I was the only line pilot qualified that ran any airline*

236

– ever. I don't know that to be true – but certainly, there were ATP pilots running airlines, but being "line qualified" is a whole different kettle of fish . . . so I was not only a "stick-and-rudder" pilot I was also a qualified line pilot – for all the airlines I ran from Petroleum Air Transport [PAT Air] and beyond.

The resultant problems of integration of new entrants were complicated by the FAA controller shortage—the "rusty supervisors" had to step in to do the "controlling" which resulted in an industrywide bottleneck in airline operations. As logic would have it, there were far fewer supervisors than practicing controllers. At the same time, a deregulated airline industry required many more gates, ticket counters, and other infrastructure than the regulated industry, and this existing infrastructure from the unregulated days had to be seriously rationed until more could be added. These sudden problems demanded the attention of President Reagan's Department of Transportation, led by Elizabeth Dole. With the help of New Entrants, Herb Kelleher and Mark Morris, a creative bidding system similar to today's NFL draft was devised and proven successful. As a result, Mark was made an official advisor to the Department of Transportation for evolving new entrant integration issues.

At this pivotal point, Air One was off to a great start, and Mark was also off to an interesting start in the political world. But trouble was just around the corner.

Mark Morris (center left) looks on as Air One's first president, former Ozark executive Paul Rogers (center) and chairman Gene Cernan jointly man the scissors for the Air One inaugural ribbon-cutting ceremony. (Mark G. Morris)

CHAPTER 41

It's Not Just Me

With the PAT Air dream job out the window, I leave the industrial sales world and am admitted to Washington University in St. Louis and over the next couple of years earn my MBA in finance. With my graduate degree in hand, Karen and I are engaged in December 1983, but not before I land the career mismatch of a lifetime by joining a small suburban bank called Mark Twain Banks which has multiple bank locations in St. Louis. That means they have a lot of bank presidents. My new boss is the president of Mark Twain Bank Fenton is a good guy who *makes* me want to work for him, and he offered me more money than I ever dreamed of. My title of "Assistant to the President" is impressive, but that is the title that our bank holding company gives to most of its MBA hires who are mostly freshly-minted Wharton or Harvard MBAs.

Also, my new boss is a well-known, high-profile St. Louis banker with influential people on his board, so, I take the job. Fenton, Missouri is just outside southwest St. Louis County but I view this town as a backwoods "Hooterville" kind of place (not so anymore), but what the hell? But after a week on the job, I find I'm having a hard time adjusting to the peddling of intangible financial products to "mom-and-pop" businesses and real estate developers. In my previous IBT life, I was comfortable selling tangible machinery components to big manufacturers. Now I'm hawking certificates of deposit and loans feeling as though I am "selling air." It's not my "PAT Air dream job," but I accept things and try to get used to it.

I continue my flying, but the demands of my new job curtail this, and most of my flying time consists of just keeping up with and exceeding my "six-and-six" IFR currency—shooting six approaches under the hood with a "safety pilot" or in actual IMC conditions, every six months. You will recall we met Doug Teel in Chapter 35 when his Cessna 172 was almost clobbered by that beat-up Super Constellation just before it flew over me. These days Doug owns a vintage 1957 twin-engine Cessna 310B. While he flies it occasionally, it's not cheap, so he looks for any excuse to fly in anything else just to be in the air. Sometimes we practice in actual IMC, and I don't need Doug for that, but I don't argue with the extra safety measure. More than once we get caught in unreported icing conditions in an aircraft not certificated for known icing. I always return to base OK, making necessary speed adjustments on final approach. Doug and I also do cross-country flights together in his 310, or using one of my rented planes if it was likely that IMC conditions would be encountered.

In January 1984 I see news reports of a fatal heavy-recip night takeoff crash out of Lambert, almost a repeat of the Fleming International L-188 Electra crash 6 ½ years earlier. This time it's a Canadian-registered DC-3 auto parts freighter flown by Skycraft Aviation, backhauling to Toronto. Two takeoff attempts are made on runway 30L, resulting in power losses and aborts. On the third attempt, the plane becomes airborne, only to lose both engines during gear retraction. The pilot attempts to "glide" the DC-3 onto I-70 which is parallel to their westerly direction of flight, but a wing first hits a sign pole resulting in a wheels-up crash landing along the north highway embankment, tearing the plane to pieces. The pilot is uninjured but the co-pilot dies in the emergency room.

The DC-3 had been *misfueled* with 200 gallons of Jet A aviation kerosene by a newbie 18-year-old ATS ground handler. It was dark when this young handler couldn't start the fuel truck that contained the proper 100LL avgas. He went to another truck that *did* start, but he *didn't notice or check* that it was a "Jet A" fuel truck. This mix-up results in expected bad publicity for ATS for a while. The sickening wreckage of the bright red DC-3 is stored for a few weeks on the former Mark Aero ramp, the second time I've seen this kind of thing since 1973. I also notice considerable scrapping of propliners occurring on this premises during this period— wing panels, chopped-off cockpits, and fuselage pieces littered all over—mostly DC-3 and DC-6 hulks. So, the DC-3 pieces and parts of the crashed one blend in well.

By April, I'm finding I'm not fitting in with most of my "Assistant to the President" Ivy League peers. On top of that, I still don't identify well with the majority of my client base—mostly retail and residential real estate developers and small construction companies. But my boss likes me and thinks things are just fine, and I do enjoy some aspects of the job. St. Louis Cardinal football great and NFL announcer Dan Dierdorf is on our Fenton board, and my boss and I, along with a few peers, often drink with him after work at his restaurant Dierdorf and Hart's and other places. It is fun hanging out with a big sports celebrity while everyone is looking at you.

The bank holding company founder and CEO is a fine art collector, and his crazy artwork, mostly weird and sexual in nature, adorns the halls and offices of all of his banks. My credit training is in the form of a brown-nosing "Policy Study Group" made up of all of us "assistants to the presidents," as closely monitored by our art-loving CEO. This group seems to spend more time on "art appreciation" and corporate culture indoctrination versus the credit training that I truly needed. Don't get me wrong, a company reflects its leader, and our CEO was brilliant. He hired the "best and the brightest" from the nation's top business schools, and many of his hires went on to be top banking leaders in St. Louis and beyond. But within these few months, I'm running off the rails. I don't mix very well with our CEO's Ivy League brown-nosers.

One cool and windy late afternoon I decide to forget about my situation and sneak out of the bank early. I had reserved a Cessna 172RG and decide to take off just before sunset to log some night flying time. As I drive by the east end of Spirit of St. Louis Airport, I am stopped in my tracks. A natural metal cargo DC-6B, N861TA, with all four propellers spinning in idle, is taxiing into position on Runway 8 for takeoff, *right next to me.* "Universal" is painted in large navy-blue letters over the window line (no trim line), with the letters "UA" on the tail. I pull over to the side *just* as four R-2800 CB engines thunder up to takeoff power, shaking the ground around me. At the initial climbout into the setting sun, the DC-6 silhouette banks to the left to a southeasterly heading, trailing four streams of exhaust behind the engines.

I had never heard of Universal before. I assume it had just unloaded auto parts for the GM Wentzville plant (I was correct). This DC-6 experience added to a pleasant sunset flight in the 172RG, including a touch-and-go across the river at Alton Civic. This clears my mind of my daily annoyances at the bank. It turns out this DC-6 is owned by Miami freight hauler Trans-Air-Link and on temporary lease to Universal, a new "bottom feeder" in the Detroit auto parts business, with only three aircraft. It would have blown me away on the spot had I known that in a few short years I would have a close relationship with—and fly with—this Miami corporate owner.

In May, my fellow "policy studiers" at Mark Twain sense my culturally divergent attitude. The founder/CEO gives these Ivy Leaguers a lot of say as to who "fits" and who "does not." For me, it's a big "does not." My bad karma finds its way to the CEO, who immediately tells my regional manager (my boss's boss) to fire me on the spot. So, on a late Friday afternoon—after

The telltale "UA" on the tailfin was my "identifying mark" when spotting this DC-6B (using my binoculars) operating around St. Louis in 1984. It made a lot of empty transfer flights between Spirit of St. Louis Airport and Lambert for backhauls to Detroit, after unloading auto parts at Spirit for the GM Wentzville assembly plant. This aircraft had previously been refurbished by Atlas Aircraft Brokers out of Miami and leased to Universal by its offspring-owner and DC-6 freight operator Trans-Air-Link, who I would get to know well and fly with—though 7 years later.

hours no less—and just after landing a promising new banking client, I am fired in cold blood with no empathy, no customary fake apologies, no goodbyes, no nothing, except for a merciful two-month severance (considering I worked there for only four months). This timing could not be more perfect. Karen and I have a wedding date set for two months from now and had just ordered an expensive new bedroom set. Still, I am somewhat relieved.

We cancel the bedroom set but not the wedding. So, I now have extra time on my hands during what would become a five-month job search. Despite our planned wedding, our paid-for honeymoon to Mexico, and my continued flying activities, I decide not to worry about finances until after our July honeymoon. I take my time with my new job search because I *have* to get it *right* this time. Karen still has a good job, and I'll damn well enjoy life in the meantime.

In the coming months, my apartment is regularly overflown by that UA DC-6. On other occasions, I sight it on the tarmac in front of where the historic Old Terminal stood. I find the overflights are transfer flights from Spirit to Lambert for backhauls to Detroit. After late 1984, I never see the UA DC-6 again. However, I do cross paths with a sister ship the following year.

A week after my firing I find that a Douglas C-124C Globemaster II heavy military transport will be flying to Scott Air Force Base for its May 1984 Saturday open house. What? A C-124? This is historic. The last one that *ever flew* in military service was 10 years earlier in 1974 and the last one I saw flying overhead was 1972. All had been long relegated to boneyards in Arizona and Maryland, due to fatigued wing spars that were cost-prohibitive to fix. One thing is for sure, I *will* be going to this open house. Just fired? Who cares!

The Travis Air Force Base Museum outside San Francisco had assembled a group of experienced volunteers who had pulled the aircraft from the Aberdeen, MD Proving Grounds and whipped it into shape for a ferry flight to Dobbins Air Force Base in Georgia for further restoration. This was in preparation for a multi-stop trip to the Travis Museum where it would be put on permanent static display. The Scott Open House would be the first of these stops.

Since the retirement of the ten-engine B-36 Peacemaker strategic bomber in 1959 (six R-4360 pushers and four J-47 turbojets) in favor of the growing B-52 Stratofortress strategic bomber fleet, the C-124 would remain the largest heavy-recip aircraft in operation over the next 15 years. It was powered by four 28-cylinder Pratt & Whitney R-4360 air-cooled radials developing a whopping 3,800 hp each at takeoff power. In the early 1970s when learning about propliners I noticed several C-124s over St. Louis at their maximum 9,000-foot cruise altitude (they were non-pressurized and non-turbocharged). Even though they were straight-stacked engines (strait exhausts from the cylinders—no turbochargers or exhaust collector rings in the way), they sounded muffled, though forceful, in flight.

Doug Teel and I head on over to Scott on open house day. The C-124 is enormous up close and is clean-looking—as though it was still in first-line service with the USAF Military Airlift Command. I think to bring my camera this time so I photograph it in detail. We are allowed inside the cavernous cargo bay and to peer into the flight deck.

There is also a U.S. Navy Reserve C-118 on display that I also photograph extensively. I find out that it had been based at Scott for several years, though I'm not sure why a Navy transport plane would base out of an Air Force base. Before 1990, this C-118 would be sold to Basler Air Services of Oshkosh Wisconsin, and would be outfitted to FAA requirements to see further service as a commercial freighter, but for whom?

In late June, Karen and I are shopping for wedding stuff at Northwest Plaza Shopping Center only a couple of miles southwest of Lambert. At shopping centers, I always go into B. Dalton Bookstores. My eye is caught by a pictorial book called *Sky Truck* by British aviation author

C-124C 0-21000 formerly of the Georgia Air Guard is landing at its final home at Travis Air Force Museum, California in May 1984. Doug Teel and I visited it on its stopover at the Scott AFB Illinois Open House a few days earlier. Three years later I visited it again while on one of my routine business trips to San Francisco. But later in 1984, one other C-124 would fly again, under a similar scenario from Detroit Michigan to McCord AFB in Washington State. That would be it for the C-124. As we've said before, there was no piston engine like its R-4360 ever manufactured for aeronautics, before or after. (Wikimedia Commons, SSgt Bob Simons, USAF)

Stephen Piercey who is a couple of years younger than me. I look inside the book and find captivating, close-up color photos of worn-out propliners living out their last days in Miami, the Caribbean, Mexico, and South America. Piercey travels the four corners of the earth seeking the few remaining propliners in revenue service. He does this with the assistance of his business partner who flies him around in an old Piper Aztec Twin for some of the trips.

This is the first time I have evidence that someone else besides me is interested in this stuff, but he commands an *actual audience*. I feel like there are now *two of us*, but he had taken it to the next level. Without hesitation, I buy *Sky Truck* and my obscure obsession is now validated. This puts me in high gear on the topic so I plan to contact Piercey to see if there is any way we can

This is the "C-5 Galaxy" of its day. Here we get an idea of the overwhelming size of the Douglas C-124 Globemaster II which became state-of-the-art for heavy military air transport in the late 1940s— that's three-quarters of a century ago.

collaborate. But, at the time of my purchase I didn't know that only six weeks before, Piercey and his pilot friend had been killed in a midair collision while doing an inflight photo shoot of a vintage aircraft. When I find this out, I feel as though I just lost a partner who I never knew. I'm now fired up even more—to do something like Steve Piercey—go all over the world and photograph the last of these planes. I'm unemployed so I think seriously about this.

On the flip side, I come to the sober realization that the *Tiger on a Leash* can maul a simple, innocent propliner *enthusiast*—just like me—to death!

A good view of the C-124s open stacks all of which dumped over the top of the wing, keeping things quiet on the ground. I am not sure if "keeping things quiet on the ground" was deliberate on the part of Douglas Aircraft designers or not. Probably not.

This is Navy C-118 BuNo 13167 that was on display at the May 24, 1984, Scott AFB Open House where Doug Teel and I visited the C-124C. For some reason, this *Navy Reserve* C-118 was based at Scott AFB for a time, and I may have seen it overhead many times on the St. Louis-Millington run during the 1970s. This is the same plane at EAA AirVenture Oshkosh, Wisconsin 6 years later in 1990 when it was owned by Basler Air Services. It was repainted and modified to FAA requirements went on for a few more years as a commercial cargo hauler, but I never found out who operated it.

CHAPTER 42

"Needle! Ball! Airspeed!"

May 30, 1984

Two weeks after being fired from Mark Twain, I'm working on my job search in my Maryland Heights apartment when I hear news about a disturbing inflight breakup of a Zantop L-188 Electra freighter over Chalkhill, Pennsylvania. To me, this is significant because I see Zantop Electras at St. Louis all the time, in the air, and on the ground. The breakup Electra had leveled off at flight level 220 (22,000 feet) on a return cargo flight from Baltimore to its home base of Ypsilanti, Michigan when it entered a tightening spiral and disintegrated in flight. It happened in the pitch darkness after 1:00 AM, in marginal VFR (Visual Flight Rules) conditions under a normal IFR (Instrument Flight Rules) flight plan whereby the horizon was obscured by an overcast layer at 10,000 feet. The first officer's electrical-driven *artificial horizon* instrument (called an "approach horizon" on the Electra) failed and the crew couldn't tell whether the captain's or the first officer's instrument was correct. They became spatially disoriented before they could sort that out and in seconds the plane entered the death spiral of increasing speed, leading to overstressing and breakup. The three crew and one non-revenue passenger—surprisingly the brother Jeff Whitesell (the restorer of Martin 404 N636X)—perished. Someone on board was recorded as saying *"we're dead"* as the wingless fuselage spiraled in.

This was almost a carbon copy of an earlier Electra inflight breakup I instantly recall that occurred just south of Salt Lake City on the afternoon of November 18, 1979. That one was a TransAmerica cargo Electra on a military LogAir flight from Hill AFB to Nellis AFB, Nevada near Las Vegas. This accident occurred at the *exact time* Les Neuroth was giving me my private pilot checkride over St. Charles County, Missouri (another big air disaster that happens at the exact time I am flying a plane). But this first Electra crash was caused by a more massive electrical failure than the current Pennsylvania mishap, also resulting in similar conflicting artificial horizon readings during climbout, this time in full IMC (Instrument Meteorological Conditions). In the first case the massive disorientation which started at around 12,000 feet, the flight recorder caught the pilot verbally reminding himself *"Needle! Ball! Airspeed!"* as he struggled for control in his last seconds of life. This refers to the turn-and-bank indicator or "turn coordinator" (which gives limited primary roll and yaw coordination information and is very sensitive) while checking the airspeed indicator for pitch information (speeding up = diving, slowing down = climbing, steady speed = level flight). Neither of those two primary instruments is electrically powered so they would be operable during massive electrical system failures. The NTSB *did not fault the crew* in this first accident.

Regarding the first crash, I am irked when I read a "safety article" in the leading general aviation magazine which is entitled "Needle! Ball! Airspeed!" This piece described the circumstances of this Hill AFB crash and was written by a well-known and highly respected general aviation pilot and editorial staffer. He quotes the disoriented Electra pilot trying to calm himself down by repeating *"Needle! Ball! Airspeed!"* to himself as he struggled to regain control of the plane. The main point the author made was, *"Had this pilot followed his own advice he and his crew would be alive today."* This is the most simple-minded and misleading conclusion I'd ever seen from a renowned aviation author. No, I never flew a plane in the class of an L-188 Electra, but I certainly know more about that big plane than this short-sighted light-plane, ink-slinging idiot, who I'm sure never flew one either.

The L-188 Electra has four massive propeller discs turning at a constant speed of just over 1,000 rpm and absorbing *tremendous* torque. The four associated 3,750 shp (shaft horsepower) GM Allison 501 turboprop packages are mounted on unusually short-spanned wings with a resultant high wing loading. This, by design, gives the aircraft the power response, handling, and performance qualities that rival a fighter plane—something pilots always *like*. It seems *all* airline pilots who flew it loved it and some even liked it more than pure jets. On the negative side, these large props produce very high gyroscopic forces that are amplified at slower airspeeds—and even during normal power adjustments. Such gyroscopic forces also exist on piston propliners and smaller aircraft but are less pronounced and easier to manage. The more-pronounced tendencies on the Electra make the transition to primary needle-ball-airspeed references in a disorientation event *virtually impossible* using the turn-and-bank indicator alone. A few years later my conclusions on this are vindicated when I get my hands on the NTSB accident report on the Pennsylvania Electra breakup (the second crash in 1984). It states:

> *Flying by "needle-ball-airspeed" is not feasible in the Electra, since small power changes result in large torque differentials and yaw excursions that can fully deflect the turn needle and the ball, even in level flight.*

A Zantop L-188 Electra freighter at rest on the ATS tarmac on the northwest corner of Lambert in September 1984. The hangar partially visible on the right is the old Navy hangar closest to Banshee Road to the west. The "A" part of "ATS" over the main hangar door is where the "Mark Aero" name was once displayed. As with all Zantop planes, the trim is bright red. Note the overwhelming size of the propellers.

In other words, it was not humanly possible for the TransAmerica pilots, the Zantop pilots, or *any other human being* for that matter, to react fast enough to arrest the rapid stop-to-stop turn-and-bank deviations that occur with an upset Electra. Reacting to the needle and ball would only aggravate the situation already in progress, which it did in both cases. It's this same gyroscopic phenomenon that makes it nearly impossible for a human to *manually* fly at slow airspeeds or hover a helicopter in zero visibility conditions, even with all the proper pilot scans and instrumentation. A helicopter pilot cannot humanly react fast enough to the moving instrument indications (reference the Kobe Bryant helicopter crash). Autopilot engaged—*no problem*—as long as the damn thing works, but the autopilot can become a crutch that causes overconfidence. The best suggestion is to never fly a helicopter in IMC if you can help it. The NTSB accident reports for both Electra inflight breakups point out that:

> *An independently powered standby attitude indicating system, designed to provide attitude indications on large turbojet aircraft in the event of major failures of electrical systems, is not required on large turboprop aircraft and was not installed on the accident aircraft.*

The NTSB accident report on the Pennsylvania crash as adopted on March 19, 1985, makes the following recommendation to the FAA:

> *Amend 14 CFR **121.305(j)** to extend its application to all large turboprop aircraft to require an additional attitude-indicating instrument, for bank and pitch, operating from a source of power independent of the normal electrical generating system as is now required on all large turbojet* [and turbofan] *aircraft.*

I don't know if this recommendation was ever adopted and/or enforced for the remaining in-service Electras, but it would seem to be good advice. By 1984 less than a third of the 168 Electras built (since 1957) were still flying, mostly as freighters, with their numbers dwindling every day. Of those no longer flying, more than *forty* had been destroyed in crashes since 1959, with even more in coming (post-1984) years. In the 1984-1985 timeframe, I see an unusual surge of Electra freighters humming over my Maryland Heights apartment to and from Lambert—and likewise see them cruising high overhead at our lake house.

In January 1985 when I am finally employed again I take note of another Electra crash, this time an exceedingly rare passenger one. This time, there are 71 souls (including six crew members) aboard Galaxy Airlines Flight 203 on a returning gambling junket departing Reno, Nevada for a return trip to Minneapolis. All except for a single passenger on board are killed. The first thing that comes to mind is that I can't believe they are still flying passengers in these things in 1985.

The passenger Electra had a simple access panel fly open on climbout, causing insidious and worsening vibrations that rattled the pilots. Thinking that it was an engine or propeller issue about to tear the plane apart, the captain throttled back too much at a critical time, causing a stall and ground impact. Hindsight showed that *had* the crew "tuned out" the vibration a normal emergency return to the airport could have been executed without the power reduction—easy to say. Only seven days later, another Galaxy L-188 Electra, this time a freighter, crash lands at Dobbins AFB Georgia due to a jammed landing gear after takeoff. The plane is written off, but fortunately, the entire crew walks away unscathed, but these bizarre crash circumstances are such that Galaxy ceases operations.

It now seems that the Lockheed Electra, which started its life in 1959 with a rash of disastrous fatal crashes, has been trying to end its useful life in much the same way that it started. In the beginning, the unstable gyroscopic characteristics of its propellers alone were the cause of two highly publicized, passenger-filled inflight breakups in 1959 (Braniff over Buffalo, Texas) and 1960 (Northwest over Tell City, Indiana), respectively. Both upsets started propeller-induced wing separation. This phenomenon, called "whirl-mode" is a force that exists in all prop-driven aircraft, but as we've learned, its effects are severely amplified with the Electra. The two whorl-mode failures forced Lockheed to strengthen the wing/nacelle areas of all in-service aircraft and modify ongoing production. That modification program was a success, but the production line was shut down prematurely due to market preferences for pure jets. Its military derivative, the P3 Orion antisubmarine patrol aircraft version of the Electra was a resounding success with the U.S. and international navies, but that's another story. There had been 757 P3 Orions built before production ceased in 1990.

Despite its choppy safety record, pilots liked flying this airplane and *swore* it was safe. However, like the big piston propliners, the turboprop L-188 Electra was a formidable *Tiger on a Leash* that could bite hard. In 2021 only one or two Electras, both freighters, remained in operation with Buffalo Airways in Northwest Territories Canada, in addition to a couple of converted Electra fire bombers that operated in Canada by a company called Air Spray. There is not an operating Electra to be found anywhere else in the world.

CHAPTER 43

A Honeymoon and a Flying Crock

July 8, 1984, Chicago O'Hare International Airport

Bright and early Karen and I board an American Trans Air (ATA) Boeing 727-100 charter flight at Chicago O'Hare, bound for Cancun Mexico. ATA is a big Part 121 supplemental charter airline with major travel company ties. We had tied the knot the day before in St. Louis and are ready for our honeymoon trip to Mexico. On the flight down our captain gets on the PA and outlines our southerly route and even the VORs we will be tracking. That is fun because many of those I regularly track myself when flying, including Troy, Illinois, Farmington Missouri, and Malden, Missouri. The aroma of freshly brewed airplane coffee this early morning is intoxicating.

Earlier, while researching the brochures we got on Cancun, I find you can go on side trips to the large island Cozumel, 50 miles to the southeast of Cancun. It's a scuba diving and cruise ship destination, but not much in the way of general vacation resorts (back then, that is). Airline transportation between Cancun and Cozumel is the mode of choice versus the ferry. My further research shows that two airlines provide this service: AeroCaribe and AeroCozumel. The former has three piston Convair 240's and some small Britten-Norman Trislanders in its fleet. I note that the latter has a single piston Convair 440 and a Fokker F-27 twin turboprop. Never having flown on a heavy-recip, I think about my impossible wish from two years earlier while hearing the piston Convair freighters taking off at Lambert from Karen's apartment. I realize I now have that *one-time shot* at fulfilling this wish, so we book a flight on AeroCaribe the airline that has the *most* Convairliners. But I don't realize you can book on either of these airlines, but you might still fly on the other airline or its equipment. Nevertheless, I have cornered two of the very last scheduled passenger heavy-recip operations in the world and I am hellbent on getting a flight on one.

I schedule our side trip for the fourth day of our stay in Cancun. We grab a cab to the airport where I see two orange-trimmed AeroCaribe 240s on the ramp. I am suspicious because a half hour before our boarding time they are still idly "parked" with no passenger steps, support equipment, or ground personnel around them. While standing in the small boarding line of only around six other people, we meet a pleasant couple from Los Angeles, JoAnne, and John, who will be on our flight. Right outside our gate is an AeroCozumel Trislander. Damn! it looks like my idea of a Convair ride is *out*.

Well, it's buzzkill to the max. We board the small Trislander—not an Aero Caribe Convair. The Trislander is a light tri-motor aircraft that packs in us 10 passengers like sardines. It's powered by three Lycoming O-540 flat-six engines, with the third engine unconventionally mounted in the middle of the reinforced vertical stabilizer. Being a passenger in one of these is about as claustrophobic as it gets—to get to the rear seats you have to fold down the ones in front of them. Emergency exit? Where? My first thought is that if one of these augers in you would have the perfect mass grave—forget about digging up and identifying the dead passengers.

As a consolation, we hit it off well with JoAnne and John, and we decide to explore Cozumel together. John says he is a musician who was the lead in a mid-1960s rock band called

This is a Britten-Norman Trislander like the one we flew in from Cancun to Cozumel. You can cram 16 passengers into this thing. This sardine can is certainly not a Convair 240 like I was expecting. The Trislander has one less O-540 engine than the 4-engine de Havilland Heron as described (and pictured) in Chapter 30. (Wikimedia Commons, NMOS332 CC BY-SA 2.0)

"Gamagucchi," but I never heard of him. He says he performed in 1965 on the popular TV rock show *Shindig!* Now that's cool, we're hanging out with a rock legend and his wife.

At Cozumel, the four of us catch a cab to head south for a strip of western coastline called San Francisco Beach. On the ride down, Cozumel doesn't look like a vacation spot, but a junk-ridden ghetto. During the ride, I spot a southbound DC-6 passing overhead along the coast cruising at around 5,000 feet. I wonder if it's a Corrosion Corner resident like F.A. Conner, on its way to Honduras, one of its regular destinations.

At San Francisco Beach we sit in the sun, swim, and snorkel—the usual—but a light overcast cloud layer is moving in to spoil this. There's a band playing on the beach, and our new friend "Rocker John" grabs the mic and does some great lead singing that mesmerizes the band and everyone else at the beach. But my mind isn't on this. I begin mental plans for my own damn trip to Marco Island, Florida, to ride on one of Marco Island Airway's last Martin 404s still in service. They're supposed to be retired in a matter of weeks so I better get serious about this *now*, unemployed or not. I don't mention this ludicrous idea to Karen—a trip to Marco Island just to ride on an airplane.

Late in the afternoon the four of us cab back through the squalor to Cozumel Airport. The "Me-no-English" driver is not taking the direct route, but zig-zagging through side routes. Through open cab windows, we see families dressed in rags, sitting down for dinner inside concrete block structures without roofs. The cab driver is signaling them, making Rocker John and me nervous. We both move closer to the driver and gruffly say *"aeropuerto NOW!"* He gets the picture and the signaling stops. When we get there my hopes are raised as I spot the white and blue-trimmed AeroCozumel Convair 440 at a gate, along with a crowded gate area. This is encouraging. The smiling ticket agent confirms to me in broken English that yes, we will be *"taking the Convair"* back to Cancun. Only minutes ago there was no God. Now suddenly there is.

Tickets to Ride—boarding passes for an AeroCozumel Convair 440 return trip to Cancun. Last name, departure time, and gate only. No date, first names, control numbers, etc. Welcome to 1984 in Mexico.

As clean as the aircraft appears, the first thing I notice are 55-gallon oil drums under each engine with black hoses protruding from the tops, sitting in shallow pools of oil. I presume they are replenishing the engine oil reservoirs. Several mechanics are also checking over the plane, yelling back and forth. We have a little time before boarding so we leave the gate area to get a snack, and when we get back the mechanics are doing runup checks on the number two engine. After the shutdown, the oily ramp under the plane receives a comprehensive hose down.

When called to board the Convair I reflexively rush to be first through the gate metal detector, leaving Karen and our famous friends behind. I want to be sure I grab a good seat adjacent to one of the engines—as though everyone else would have the "same idea." As I climb the stairs in front of the number one (left) engine, I turn around to photograph it. All we have is Karen's cheap, miniature plastic "cereal box" camera she packed it as a spare. As usual, I forgot to pack my good Pentax camera. I don't recall why I did not take a wider-angle photo of the entire plane with Karen's plastic camera. I was probably concerned that we might be low on cereal box film which had to be mail ordered and not available in stores.

I secure our third-row seats long before Karen, rocker John, and JoAnne board. The cabin interior seems to be in the original 1950s configuration. It's immaculate with brown-tinted, roundish rough-cloth seats, reminding me of the interior of a new Volkswagen. Small fans, spaced every four rows, are hanging from the overheads pointing down on the seats, with two additional fans over the flight deck above the windscreens. The semi-musty aroma inside the cabin, mixed with a tinge of oil scent does not smell like the interior of a Volkswagen or a modern jetliner, but it sure puts me in a pleasant frame of mind.

This Convair 440 is a near-carbon copy of the one we experienced with AeroCozumel on July 12, 1984 (except for the paint job). I, unfortunately, failed to take a wide-angle photo of our plane but I had a lousy camera anyway. (Wikimedia Commons, Finnair via Tom Edvardsson)

The young Latino flight attendant greets me at my seat. She is short and kind of dumpy, with buck teeth and black wavy hair, and is smiling constantly. She speaks no English but professionally assists the passengers as they settle in. The first officer enters next. He looks much younger than me and seems American. He looks like a tanned beach stud with loosely curled brown hair containing his propped-up sunglasses, a pressed white shirt, and epaulets. He looks like he could just as well be flying for Pan Am or Eastern. He has a conversation with an older couple in their seats who turn out to be his parents. Our neatly-mustached captain is an upper middle-aged Mexican (no surprise) who radiates seasoned professionalism. Our flight is 100%

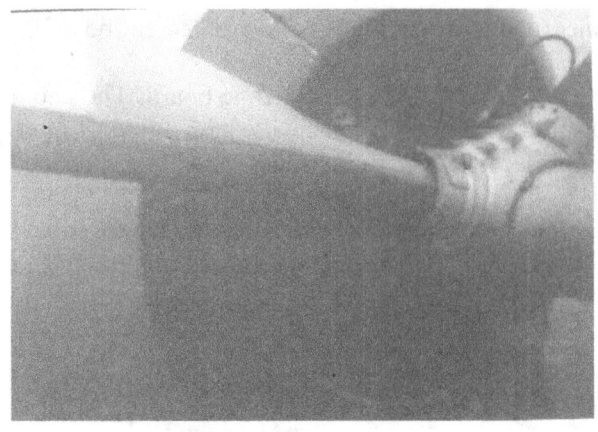

From the boarding steps I snap a photo of the number one engine, using the cheapest camera in the world, as I climb the steps to enter the AeroCozumel Convair 440.

The first passenger to board (me) waits in his window seat for his new wife and new friends (in front of the engine cowl) to board at the onset of darkness. Overblown enthusiasm on my part? Yes.

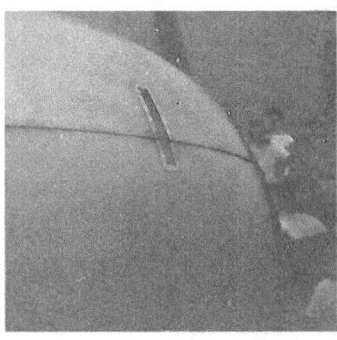

booked and while I am the first to board, the more sane and much calmer Karen, JoAnne, and Rocker John are the last.

I barely hear the whine of the number two starter motor as it turns the right engine, sounding like a quiet dentist drill. The magnetos are engaged after "twelve blades" (four propeller rotations) and the engine catches on a few cylinders, which are muffled due to the long exhaust augmentation system extending to the trailing edge of the wing. It then seems that all eighteen cylinders catch in rapid succession to burn off the prime. Then a pause and a whirring down of the planetary gearbox as the first officer moves the mixture control from auto-lean to auto-rich. Quickly, the eighteen cylinders cough back to life again in a muffled roar that shakes the plane, before settling down to a stable idle with propeller paddles beating smartly. It idles so quietly it doesn't seem this engine is part of the aircraft. The process is repeated for the right engine which effortlessly comes to life. The cabin cooling fans start turning, resulting in instant relief from the boiling cabin heat— at least for Karen. I never notice the hot cabin temperature.

Then, a startling BANG-BANG-BANG emanates from somewhere in front. Number one engine is shut down, then number two, with propeller blades gliding to a stop. The electric cabin fans go off too and now it's nothing but silence—not a peep out of the passengers except for the occasional *"Uh Oh"* and then some mumbling. The cabin air stops circulating and it's hot once again and an impatient Karen starts fanning herself with a magazine. My first thought is that this plane is "down for the count" and they'll be sending in a couple of Trislanders to take us back to Cancun. Great. Suddenly there is no God again—or he's just having fun messin' with me.

CHAPTER 44

Let's Try This Again

July 12, 1984, Cozumel Airport, Mexico

The petite flight attendant smiles at the passengers—what else can she do? My reckless thinking is that I want the pilots to get this thing off the ground no matter how bad the mechanical situation is. That goes against my advice as to how a pilot should think. I stare out my window at the number one engine and notice clear heat convection waves and diminishing smoke traces rising out of the Convair's small upper cowl flaps. Well, I guess *this* will be the extent of my heavy-recip "ride."

I observe around five grungy mechanics with toolboxes approach the plane and start to make a racket outside my window. Spanish words are flying in all directions. The mechanics are smiling and gesturing toward the front of the plane, seemingly joking around rather than trying to analyze the situation. The first officer then emerges from the flight deck and announces a fifteen-minute delay because *"we're having a little problem with our front passenger door."*

The young first officer then settles in the opposite first row of rear-facing seats and chats in Spanish with a group of scuba divers. The captain then works his way out of the flight deck and converses with the mechanics that are climbing the steps and surrounding the door. They are jovial and banter with each other. We then hear all kinds of hammers and other tools banging on the airframe and door, and socket wrenches going full blast while the incessant jabbering back and forth continues. Then, in about 10 minutes all the racket stops and we hear the electric passenger door slowly open and close several times. Success maybe. By now, darkness is setting in, making it harder for me to use our cheap camera.

Engines are started and then almost immediately shut down so Mexican ground personnel with hammers and socket wrenches work on a stuck passenger entrance door that also won't latch. It sounds like they are beating the hell out of the forward fuselage with their hammers, and I'm sure the flight will be canceled. So, I just snap this cereal box camera photo of the Cozumel Terminal with the top of the R-2800 power package in the foreground. The word "Cozumel" is barely visible on the terminal building.

In another 10 minutes, the crew returns to the flight deck and the R-2800s are restarted and the cabin fans go back on. Whew, God exists again—he's gone back and forth a lot today. Brakes are released and we slowly creep into a left turn to taxi to runway 29—propeller blades beating, pistons pounding and engine nose gearboxes whirring. As we taxi into takeoff position the small cowl flaps slowly close. As the engines run up to about 50% of takeoff power the propeller tips generate white spiraling moisture ribbons in the humid air. Throttles are advanced to max power as they generate their characteristic harmonic roar. They're *not* muffled now, the whole plane becomes a noise bomb that vibrates like hell. Compared to a jetliner, the takeoff roll is slow and labored, lasting *forever*. By the time we rotate it seems we use most of the runway. The rate of climb is nil, we're just skimming over the treetops before leaving the western coastline behind.

Looking south along the now-lighted Cozumel coastline, there are large docks and lit-up cruise ships tied to them. They fade behind us as we slowly build speed. After power reductions to METO and then climb power, I start to relax. A couple of the raggedy, door-banging mechanics remain on our flight. One of them opens the flight deck entrance and starts chatting with the pilots like they are all office workers at the water cooler.

The powerplants quiet down after the third power reduction to cruise power. After leveling off at only around 2,500 feet for the short 20-minute flight across the channel to Cancun, we pierce through sheets of a dark stratus scud layer far under the high overcast. Soon I see the Yucatan coastal lights easing toward us from the northwest and then we adjust course to roughly parallel it. Gradually we crisscross the coast over the jungle greenery. Engine power is reduced for descent and things get even quieter.

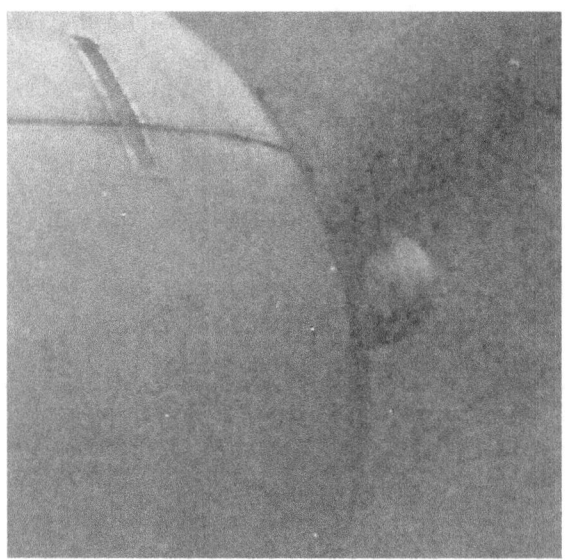

Finally. Enroute in the AeroCozumel Convair 440 over the strait back to Cancun as the darkness deepens. We're in and out of a stratus scud layer over the channel. Karen fully understands that for me this event is a close second to normal honeymoon activities.

We enter left downwind for runway 30 at Cancun. As we turn base and it becomes noisier as the props go into fine pitch and RPMs increase for approach and landing. On left base, I see what appears to be a long-ago ditched DC-6 sitting level but half submerged in the swamp below, with the wings and engines barely visible below the water surface. This confirms I am definitely in Mexico in the *Second Wind* era. Scenes like that are typical in all of the Caribbean and Latin America.

Then, the cabin is filled with a whirring sound as the gear doors open and the landing gear comes down, which I can see from my seat. We turn final and our pilot greases on one of the smoothest landings I would experience in both this life and the hereafter, with a short burst of prop reversal for initial braking. The small cowl flaps open on the rollout and light smoke starts pouring out of them. We taxi in front of the flood-lighted terminal and come to a slow stop with an immediate engine shutdown.

After deplaning, I talk Karen, JoAnne, and Rocker John into standing in front of the 440 for a cereal box photo. We had free reign to walk around the plane before heading across the apron to the gate. The pilots and the raggedy mechanics walk around with us with pride, as if they had just singlehandedly crossed the Atlantic. They did a post-flight inspection of the aircraft, almost giving each other high-fives.

While we have a great time with Rocker John and JoAnne in Cozumel, decades later I google "Shindig!" and get a comprehensive list of all performing artists who appeared on this show for its 16-month run time from 1964 into1966. Not one of them was a band or performer named "Gamagucchi" nor could I find *any* musician or band that ever existed by that name.

Karen with Rocker "Gamagucchi" John and his wife JoAnne posing in front of our AeroCozumel 440 after deplaning. After that, it took me 35 years to find out that there was no such thing as a popular rock band or performer named "Gamagucchi"—so just who were these people? He may have been a performer on the Shindig! TV show in the mid-1960s, but maybe I just missed something in the translation. However, the way he sang on the Cozumel San Francisco Beach was convincing.

CHAPTER 45

Apron Queen

I was born in January 1955. At that time, *all* commercial airliners were piston-powered. Though there was an earlier jetliner false-start, the British de Havilland Comet, that ended with disastrous crashes and prompt withdrawal of the plane from use for several years. Otherwise, state-of-the-art North Atlantic air traffic in 1955 consisted of big-piston Douglas DC-7Bs, Lockheed L-1049G "Super G" Super Constellations, and Boeing 377 Stratocruisers, mostly operated by U.S., Canadian, and European airlines. Transatlantic flights typically carried small passenger loads, something like 40 to 60 on each crossing (the lower density was for comfort and more fuel), compared to 200 – 400 on today's widebody 747s and twinjets. However, in the mid-1950s these piston planes had a problem. None of them could make consistent nonstop westbound North Atlantic flights against prevailing westerly winds, often requiring an inconvenient fuel stop at Gander, Newfoundland.

Douglas Aircraft was the first to solve this problem with the introduction of its DC-7C. It had a stretched fuselage for more elbow room but was not specifically outfitted for more passengers than the -7B carried. It had a larger tailfin to accommodate the fuselage stretch and the wingspan was increased by 10 feet to 127 feet through the insertion of 5-foot plugs at the wing root on each side. This allowed more fuel to be carried and moved the four engines farther from the passenger cabin for a quieter cruise. A small side-benefit was greater efficiency of the wing, decreasing fuel burn slightly. The 3,250 hp Wright R-3350 Turbo-Compound "D-Series" engines mounted on the -7B were replaced with 3,400-hp "E-Series" engines on the -7C. For the first time, we had consistent, nonstop transatlantic flight in *both directions*.

The DC-7C was introduced by Pan American Airways in June 1956 and other major first-tier operators included SAS, BOAC, KLM, and Northwest Orient, among several others. This aircraft became the most efficient piston transoceanic transport aircraft ever, even after its main competitor was introduced over a year later—the L-1649A Starliner Constellation (see photo page 89). The DC-7C remained the backbone of transoceanic traffic for just a few short years until the 707 and DC-8 jetliners were introduced in 1959 (and the introduction of the British turboprop Bristol Britannia and the return of the Comet jetliner). The -7C pioneered "over-the-pole" routes between the U.S. west coast and European destinations. First-tier operators understandably phased out the DC-7C during the early 1960s as they went all-jet. While many -7Cs were passed on to supplementals, smaller commercial operators, and travel clubs in their original passenger configurations, many were converted to freighters. Remember, back then the supplementals made more money hauling freight. We will see that less than a single handful of these DC-7C freighters (and converted fire tankers) survived into the early 1990s.

Starting in 1979, I had noticed a derelict DC-7C freighter sitting on the former Mark Aero (now ATS) ramp. While it had been moved around from time to time, its nose gear tire was always flat so I knew it was not being flown. On September 13, 1984, Doug Teel and I arrive mid-morning at the ATS-occupied Navy hangers—what was once Mark Aero. We find access into the west

Inactive Apron Queen DC-7CF N90251 as seen for many years at the ATS/former Mark Aero ramp. This view is seen from Banshee Road looking east across the ramp.

hangar and walk across the inside. There are several big R-2800 C engines and DC-6 QECs (quick engine change "power eggs") mounted on cradles and sitting on pallets. I assume these are on standby for transient cargo propliners that might arrive with a blown engine. It's otherwise empty. We approach a side office on the far side that says "ZANTOP" above the door. We walk inside and there are a few occupied desks and big fat computer monitors with those old green displays, teletypes hammering away, and a few dispatch workers. We had just stumbled upon a Zantop satellite office. The office people are welcoming and pleasant, asking how they can help us.

We ask our friendly Zantop guys as to how we might gain access to the ramp to photograph the old DC-7C sitting outside about 200 yards away. While they acknowledge the nostalgic significance of the plane, they tell us that they are not sure where to go for permission. After all,

Douglas DC-7C N90251 as I shot it from around 200 yards away outside the west ex-Navy hangar door at the Zantop satellite office. I figured this may be as close as we get to the plane. The unusual placement of the engines farther out from the fuselage is apparent. This allowed for more fuel and made for a quieter passenger ride on 12-hour trips across the ocean. On the right is the rear 1/3 of ex-Shamrock and ex-Trans Continental DC-6B N90777, sitting for years and now an engineless hulk (see photo and description next chapter).

their job is *not* to grant prying strangers access to their landlord's property. Their purpose is to get arriving cargo on its way and fill their DC-6s, Convair 640s, Electras, and DC-8s with backhaul loads to Detroit and other satellite cargo terminals. But we are on a mission. There is a fully intact, but seriously neglected Douglas DC-7CF sitting on the apron that *begs* to be photographed.

We thank our Zantop friends and head toward the main passenger terminal on the south side of Lambert. We find the office of airport administrator Colonel Leonard Griggs in the northwest part of the terminal. His administrative assistant grants us a short meeting with one of his bureaucratic sidekicks who's not a nice man like the Zantop guys. He doesn't converse, he barks, *"That airplane is private property, and neither can I grant you access to the property nor permission to photograph that plane."* Damn, he's a bozo for sure, cutting us right down to "size" so he can feel like a big shot—he's probably failed in everything else in life.

While Doug and I wait in the Lambert airport authority offices to seek permission to enter ATS's northwest ramp, I snap this photo through a panoramic airport office window. It's a Convair C-131B (Convair 340) serving as a "transport hack" for the 110th Fighter Squadron of the Missouri Air National Guard based there. The 110th had just transitioned from F-4s to F-15 fighters. This Convair spends more time parked than in the air and will be retired to the boneyard soon. Note that the "orange peel" cowling is open for mechanics to tweak the #1 (left) R-2800-99W engine.

He shows us the door, almost telling us not to let it hit us in our asses on the way out. As we leave I wonder why we need permission to photograph "private property" that has remained in the full view of thousands of people who over the past five years who had driven by it on Banshee Road and Lindbergh Boulevard—every single day. It was my understanding that permission is not required to photograph private property as long as you are not trespassing on it. We just go home.

DC-7C N90251 started life with French airline TAI in 1958 which was absorbed by a larger French airline, UTA, in 1963. UTA immediately sold it to the French Air Force which operated it until 1978 when they sold it to Engine Air, Ltd. who immediately turned it over to GCA, Inc. of New Orleans. GCA gave it its current registration, positioned it in St. Louis, and then just abandoned it. In June 1982 it was sold to Commercial Leasing, Inc. of New Orleans while the plane continued to deteriorate in St. Louis. I never knew the intended game plan for this aircraft after it arrived here way back in 1979.

That afternoon I get a phone call from Teel. He giddily announces that he made arrangements to get us both on the ATS ramp *now*, so get ready and don't forget the camera. His aircraft mechanic Ollie has a pass for the old Mark Aero ramp. Ollie and Doug swing by my Maryland Heights apartment in Ollie's beat-up white and green pickup, and we drive to the ramp at Lambert. Ollie opens the chain link gate with his key card and we drive straight up to the DC-7C among the tarmac crack weeds and rusty support equipment. The only other planes on this ramp are a Zantop cargo Electra, an old, faded Cessna 150, a Beech 18, and a bare-metal, engineless ex-Trans Continental DC-6 hulk. Tucked in a corner is another apron queen—a single ex-PAT Air DC-6 N44DG (see photo page 210). Ollie tells me to get my photos of the -7C as quickly as to avoid attracting security—our purpose for being here is "not official' and difficult to explain. In about ten minutes I secure everything I need and we jump back into the truck and exit the ramp onto Banshee Road. I instruct Ollie to drive us to Balducci's Pizza near my apartment. The pizza and beer for three of are on me.

Yours truly standing in front of the DC-7C wing root extension, with his "catch," holding on to the #3 prop. The trim is aqua blue. Now that I caught it, what do I do with it? Note the "tarmac crack weeds" everywhere.

To get ahead of ourselves for a minute, two years later in August 1986, I drive by the DC-7C as I had done so many times. The plane is still there, but things are changing. I see engine cowl panels removed and mechanics on scaffolding diligently working on the R-3350 Turbo-Compounds. What's going on here? Then a month later I'm sitting at the TWA gate before boarding an L-1011 for a business trip to Los Angeles. I glance out the window to the northwest toward the northwest ATS facilities. DC-7C N90251 is *gone*. It had been flown out at some point but to where?

Commercial Leasing had been years behind on parking and other fees for the plane and the airport authority was getting sick of this eyesore. At some point, its owner had died and his elderly widow now owned the company, ignoring it the plane whole time which is not surprising. Under court order, the local sheriff arranged to have the aircraft auction where it was sold to T&G aviation of Chandler, Arizona to secure at least a partial payment on these accumulated fees. The plane would start a new life as an insect sprayer. For the next several years the revived N90251

I take numerous close-in detail shots of the DC-7C Apron Queen. The neglected condition of the ATS/former Mark Aero ramp is obvious, including monster sprouting weeds, rusty scaffolding, expired ground equipment, and parts scattered all over.

Doug Teel, New Year's Eve 2016 at Karen's and my house.

sprayed for locusts in Morocco until 1990 when it was returned to Chandler and parked. In 1995 T&G sold the plane to Brooks Fuel in Alaska who converted it to a tanker for hauling diesel fuel to the arctic regions. It went through several iterations of flying activity and storage—mostly storage—and was ultimately scrapped in 2018 or 2019. Such is the typical *Second Wind* career path of a propliner. That said, Apron Queen N90251 would only represent the starting point for my close association with the Douglas DC-7C.

To this day, Doug Teel and I are glad to have preserved our Apron Queen's images for posterity.

CHAPTER 46

An Icarus Moment

In Greek mythology, Icarus tried to escape from the Minoans in Crete with the help of his father, Daedalus. Daedalus constructed wings made of eagle feathers bound together with wax and attached them to each of his son's arms and his own. Father Daedalus warned Icarus to stay at a moderate height—if he flew too close to the sun, the wax would melt and the feathers would fall off. But Icarus was so enthralled with being able to fly like a bird he ignored his dad's advice and flew too close to *Mr. Big Yellow Fireball* and all the wax melted and the feathers came off. Icarus fell to his death. This well-known myth parallels the fate of nearly *all* of the *first wave* of new airline entrants that emerged after the airlines were deregulated in 1978. As we mentioned, there were about 21 of these new entrants in the early 1980s—including Air One.

As Air One finally gets underway I see well-choreographed, if not provocative local TV commercials of sexy flight attendants giving gentile "hand-on-shoulder" attention to male passengers, almost like you'd see at a high-end spa (or, more crudely, "massage parlor"). There are all kinds of articles on Air One in every magazine and paper that counted—*Forbes, Fortune, Aviation Week, Business Week,* and *The Wall Street Journal.* Since Air One flies to Los Angeles, even Hollywood gets in on the action. Movie stars and industry giants fall in love with Air One's novel premium-class concept. Mark Morris and Air One are regularly written up in the Hollywood society and gossip pages. It seems at this time Mark is a "miniature Howard Hughes" out there on the west coast—except that he didn't make movies (but both were in segments of the oil business). St. Louis businessmen/businesswomen comprise Air One's core customer base. These customers like to brag about flying with Air One—the airline seems to have the name and the chutzpah that business folks admire. Its employee culture is something close to that seen with today's Southwest Airlines, except with those *big* luxury add-ons that business people like to boast about (which was not Southwest).

The experienced Air One crews were highly qualified, down-to-earth, and personable. After a flight, they would sometimes let interested passengers take photos of the cockpit and the crews just like during the *First Wind* propliner days (*not* allowed now). Air One tried to get FAA approval to allow passengers in the cockpit in the spirit of what Joe Morris did with his Pegasus Club DC-6 passengers. But Pegasus was a travel club and not a common carrier, and the FAA told Air One—a common carrier—to forget that idea.

In the 1950s and 1960s cockpit tours were normal public relations, so why not in the 1980s? Because aircraft were being hijacked almost daily during the 1960s and '70s, mostly to Havana, Cuba. In November 1971 the legendary air pirate D.B. Cooper jumped out of the back airstair door of a Northwest Orient 727-100 somewhere over the Pacific Northwest with a ransom of $200,000 cash—Cooper was never found, though some of the cash and remnants of some of his items were. The mystery was never solved so D.B. Cooper "cults" began to spring up and still thrive. The Cooper 727-100 jump plane, formerly N467US (and since re-registered N838N) ultimately became one of Air One's first fleet planes. Mark acquired it from Piedmont Airlines through a continuing leasing arrangement with United Technologies. When Mark found out about the significance of the plane he had a plaque mounted on the forward galley. After a few subsequent operators—the last one being Key Air—the plane was scrapped at Greenwood, Mississippi in 1996. Over the years much reference has since been made to the plaque, but nobody seems to know that Mark put it there—or who may have possession of it now.

Starting an airline in the early days of deregulation was far from easy. In hindsight, Air One's 1982 startup year was probably the worst year ever to do that. Maybe the *federal government* was finally coming around for newcomers, but not the established airlines, airport authorities, or local governments. In Mark Morris's words:

Lambert Airport Director Leonard Griggs preferred to be called "Colonel"—so that pretty much describes him. He did the bidding for TWA and his buddy Ed Crane, CEO of Ozark Airlines. With the help of John Tucker of Midcoast and St. Louis Mayor Vince Schoemel, they worked to keep Air One out of the passenger concourses. They forced me way out near the Charter Wing which was just remote tarmac located near the jet blast fences to the east of the main terminal concourses. The International Wing [note that the Old Terminal had since been demolished and at this time the International Terminal was not yet part of the Main Terminal] *was the same arrangement only closer to the concourses. Not only that, they pushed me to where I could not even get counter space for ticketing. Interestingly, Tucker would be handling all the fueling via ATS at the Charter Wing, where we would prove to be his biggest customer by far. As things got underway, we would do at least 100,000 gallons of jet fuel a day out of St. Louis.*

At that time Herb Kelleher, founder, and CEO of Southwest Airlines was planning to enter St. Louis' already overcrowded market. As you know I got to know him fairly well when I was Chairman of the New Entrant Airlines group in the CEO Club where Herb was a member. He thought TWA would start a fare war with any new entrants and despite Herb's aggressive billboard campaign advertising that Southwest was coming to St. Louis, he postponed his inaugural plans. Once I got the funding to start scheduled service with Air One, Herb called me and offered me his counter space, which I grabbed without hesitation.

Tucker, through his Midcoast subsidiary ATS, also operated the purpose-built "people mover" shuttles between the concourses and the remote International Wing and offered these services to me. I thought this was a crappy arrangement for our passengers, but it turned out that it worked super well. The blast fences where our planes were parked were probably a quarter mile away from the main concourses. We would load deplaning passengers on a shuttle and by the time they settled on board the shuttle, our baggage guys could unload the baggage and have it on the main international terminal carousels just as the shuttle arrived. These carousels were literally 20 feet away from the disembarking shuttle passengers. Upon exiting the shuttle, passengers would have their luggage ASAP and head right for the ground transportation a very short distance away.

Mark asked Jerry Riebold if he wanted to get type rated in the Boeing 727-100/200 and fly for Air One. What an opportunity—finally the chance to fly a *big jet airliner* with a *scheduled* airline. However, Jerry had his steady job with Peabody Holding flying smaller corporate jet hotrods. Preferring job security over flying with the big boys, Jerry declined the offer to remain Peabody's chief pilot until his retirement. However, Mark did bring on Patti Finot Riebold, now

Publicity shots of Air One business travelers enjoying wide leather seats providing "decadently excessive" elbow room, and "silver platter" champaign meals aboard an Air One 727—at "coach" prices. (Mark G. Morris)

married to Jerry, so the PAT Air "working family" relationships continued into the Air One era. On her first day, she was simply told to "buy fuel." She called Midcoast and figure out the rest.

As mentioned, between 1979 and 1986 there were 21 *first wave* new entrants in the U.S., including Air One. This group did not include preexisting intrastate airlines that converted to interstate operations post-deregulation such as Alaska, Air California, PSA, and Southwest, or preexisting charter operators that started scheduled services after deregulation such as American Trans Air, World Airways, and Tower Air. Other familiar names among the *first wave* of 21 included Jet America, PEOPLExpress, MGM Grand Air, Muse, New York Air, and Sunworld. Each new entrant had a boutique strategy such as "discount fares no frills," "discount fares normal service," and "regular fares, premium service," the latter being the Air One and MGM strategy. Two-thirds of the *first wave* folded after just three or fewer years of operation. The longer-term survivors eventually hit the wall of financial distress and some were lucky enough to be acquired. *None* of the *first wave* brands survive today.

Most of these corporate deaths were caused by external factors such as competition-driven predatory pricing, gate slot hoarding, or the inability of the new entrant to raise financing for the necessary infrastructure as the entire industry fought for limited space and otherwise struggled to adapt. Also, most airline startup managements were comprised of *experienced* airline executives that had previously worked within rigid corporate structures, so they did not possess entrepreneurial mindsets. That possibly contributed to some of the failures.

Another component of the strategy was the route system. Should it be a "hub-and-spoke" structure as pioneered a few years earlier by Federal Express, or the traditional point-to-point? New entrants choosing the early hub-and-spoke realm could grow *fast* if the hub was underserved. Unfortunately for airlines, most hubs quickly became adequately or over-served. Air One's hub was Lambert-St. Louis, shared by two competitors—Ozark and TWA. This made St. Louis seem "over-served." That could be perceived as a problem for Air One right out of the starting gate, but Wall Street disagreed with that premise and enthusiastically backed Air One's case.

With its first 727-100s and inaugural route system, Air One needed at least a 62% load factor to break even at the lowest anticipated fares. It was soon proven that Mark and Wall Street were correct—within months Air One achieved the highest load factors in the industry at 94%.

That, along with Air One's $34.5 million IPO in late 1983, covered all of the airline's sustained losses in the first 15 months of operations.

The not-so-apparent reality was that *any* new airline entrant starting during this early period of deregulation had about as much chance of long-term survival as a person diving head-first into a tree chipper. Fuel costs were skyrocketing and the fog of deregulation was hampering the decision-making of established airlines, causing them to be unpredictable, reactionary, and even *irrational*. This started a furball of endless fare wars in a high labor cost environment. The new non-union airline startups could charge at-or-below coach fares because they had no "legacy" union costs, first thinking they could win over passengers with low fares alone. The problem was the established carriers simply matched their prices, or worse.

In early 1982, Robert Crandall – the CEO of American Airlines—was asked while guest lecturing to a class at Stanford University (with the press in attendance), *"what are you going to do about all the new entrants starting up all over the U.S.?"* His answer was *"all we can do is match their fares, add more flights, and overschedule their flight times."* But that combination would cost them big time, so the majors had a real problem. Because of their high legacy fixed costs that accumulated over the decades (i.e. labor and pension debt costs) their managements could not just snap their fingers and quickly adapt.

Even though he was running an old-fashioned legacy airline, Crandall was a flexible and innovative manager. He was the "father" of today's frequent flyer loyalty programs that dominate the industry today. He also changed the face of post-deregulation route planning by being the first besides Federal Express to adopt the hub-and-spoke route system. Most major airlines eventually followed suit on both accounts. But in continuing his answer at Stanford, Crandall indicated that neither American nor any other legacy carrier could compete with the Air One concept of premium service at coach fares ("premium" meant the *way it actually was* during those luxurious piston days of the *First Wind* in the 1950s). I should note that when Crandall said all this, Air One was still a "paper" airline.

Crandall's lecture was captured by the trade journals and *The Wall Street Journal* picked it up too. That alone lit the fire under Mark to "push the paper aside" and accelerate Air One's certification process. Crandall inadvertently opened the eyes of the investment community to Mark's new airline concept and he was inundated with phone calls from investment banks. Eventually, this led to Air One's initial financing and later public offering. According to Mark, that is how American's Crandall "started" Air One. The next year, Mark himself would be the guest lecturer for graduate management students at Stanford discussing startup problems with new entrants and the plethora of issues surrounding the legacy airlines.

During this period the established majors were losing tons of money and fare wars were making it worse. Despite their inflexibility, the majors still had long-established resources to fight the new competition. On Air One's first day, TWA took its cheapest one-way flight from St. Louis to New York and dropped the price from $189 to $179; then Air One matched and TWA lowered the price by another $10. Ozark was the other competitor on this route but never initiated cuts, but always matched those of TWA. Fair enough, Air One could handle that for now.

In the meantime, Air One got almost all the press. During one of the New Entrant CEO meetings in Washington D.C., Herb Kelleher asked Mark how Air One got *"five times more press"* than Southwest Airlines. Mark answered that he had cut a deal to haul bundles of newspapers for the startup of a brand new nationally syndicated daily newspaper. That paper was *USA Today*. The newspaper had first come to St. Louis to propose giving away free papers for TWA and Ozark passengers as a barter for the haulage—remember, in those days, daily media

Mark Morris and his boys Jeff and Brad (above) are joined by wife Susan (left), to savor one of the freshly-painted Air One 727-100s during some of Mark's extremely rare downtime. (Mark G. Morris)

was *bulk and volume-centric* and needed lots of airplane capacity! Both airlines turned them down, as did every other one they approached. Mark then met with the *USA Today* editor to let him know that Air One was about to start scheduled service and that he would do the barter if *USA Today* would go "overboard" with favorable articles, photos, and follow-ups on Air One. They shook hands and that was it. *USA Today* took off and the editor lived up to the handshake—for a long time one could not get a *USA Today* newspaper where Air One wasn't at least mentioned—but it was usually "more than" mentioned.

As an example, Anchorage Alaska had a major snowstorm which was the front page headline on *USA Today* that included a piece on blizzard-induced flight delays. Even though Anchorage wasn't even close to Air One's route system, the associated *USA Today* photo was of one of Air One's busy ticket counters with its big logo. Mark says that alone caused a temporary spike in Air One load factors.

By September of 1983, two airlines had broken the glass ceiling for *average* load factors in the airline business – which was 80%. This was PEOPLExpress—started and run by Don Burr—and Air One. These two airline entrants represented the business model bookends of the newly deregulated industry. PEOPLExpress was "discount no-frills" and Air One was "coach (standard fare) all-frills." NBC's *The Today Show* wanted to do a special on the "All Frills versus No Frills" airline CEOs. So, Mark Morris and Don Burr were together in the hot seats for 30 minutes—which was unusually long for *The Today Show* business segment (that would *never* happen today). PEOPLExpress had just racked up a 92% quarterly load factor average and Air One was slightly higher.

A month later Air One went public with its $31 million public offering underwritten by the St. Louis investment banking firm of Burns Pauli & Co., Inc. and the New York firm of Sherwood Securities. With the IPO, two 727-200s from each of PSA and the now-defunct Braniff were also added, along with new services in the spring of 1984 from St. Louis to Houston and Los Angeles. Although fares were dropping industrywide, TWA began slitting its wrists trying to put Air One out of business. Even though Air One could be considered a gnat on the TWA elephant, it *still* got consistently superior press—and was voted as the best first-class service in the U.S. in a major annual survey for two years in a row, as conducted by the Airline Passenger Experience Association (APEX). Delta normally won that award hands down, so they were furious. They sent its employee spies on Air One flights to try and figure it out.

When Air One went public, TWA had all it needed to know about Air One's strategic plan, including route structure pricing and balance sheet, and funding sources under SEC full disclosure rules. With its more expansive resources, TWA began the implementation of a computerized "yield management" system that the majors were adopting. With this, an airline was allowed to match (but not undercut) new entrant fares in many of its threatened markets. They could sometimes, but not always, offset this decrease in revenue by increasing fares in some of their more inelastic markets as determined by the yield management formulas.

Another motivating factor for TWA was that they knew that Ozark wanted to buy Air One and TWA *did not want that*. It really needed to cut Air One off at the knees—*now*! Thus, TWA started cutting into its own muscle and bone by overscheduling combined with predatory pricing—essentially flushing its employees down the toilet in the name of getting rid of Air One. TWA put its *grossly oversized* widebody Lockheed L-1011 jumbos against Air One's single-aisle Boeing 727s and then cut some of those L-1011 fares by as much as 85%. As a result, Air One could not maintain its minimum 62% load factor on a one-way ticket to New York when TWA was charging only $19 for an L-1011 seat on that route.

As Mark Morris puts it:

We were carrying 92%-94% load factors and their load factor on these routes was less than 15%. The cash was gushing out of TWA, but as Air One found out later via Carl Icahn (after he purchased TWA in late 1985) TWA was deliberately losing over $400 million on an annualized basis [on Air One's routes alone] *for the sole purpose of crushing us. Ticket prices did begin to increase* [with continuing economic recovery in 1984] *but the cash was dwindling. Air One's load factors stayed high but the fares were not going back up to the pre-Air One days in the marketplace. By late '84 Air One was just a few hundred thousand dollars a month short of breaking even – but couldn't sustain operations of scheduled service and filed for Chapter 11 bankruptcy and was reorganized. Ironically, Air was just one of a few* [first wave] *startups that "survived" operationally* [though the brand did not]*, because when it was later purchased, its certificate and corporate entity were still alive* [as we shall see].

A sample of one of Air One's marketing pieces. (Mark G. Morris)

With its bleeding cash and a negative balance sheet, Air One could no longer fly scheduled services for now. As it entered Chapter 11 bankruptcy its jetliner fleet was temporarily parked, out of the way, in one big sad cluster at the old Mark Aero ramp right in front of where the Old Terminal once stood. In a Chapter 11 bankruptcy, the CEO usually retains decision-making power while the board of directors resign. As CEO, Mark and others formed the debtor-in-possession group to work out a reorganization plan. He remained CEO of Air One for the next two years while working on many different options and deal structures. One of his first actions was for Air One to fly charters to help offset bankruptcy costs during the proceedings. Though his board was gone, Mark maintained his relationships with Cernan, Phelps, McCarthy, and others. In all this, however, there was a glimmer of hope. It could be argued that Air One's demise as a scheduled passenger airline was caused primarily by the illegal actions of a juggernaut competitor—

predatory pricing. As everyone knows, *predatory* is a *bad word* at the federal level.

A well-known law firm in Washington DC wanted to take the Air One case for anti-trust violations by TWA. Alfred Kahn was to be the economist for the case. The only problem was that the law firm needed a $2 million advance to cover initial expenses to take the case, agreeing to take the rest on a contingent basis. This was unheard of for a federal bankruptcy case at the time. Mark got a commitment for the $2 million from a group of investment institutions which was supported by a revenue sharing agreement based on the final settlement that contained a necessary "upside" component.

About two weeks before funding, Congress passed a law that you could not sell "upside participation" in federal lawsuits—only the principal amount advanced could be recovered by investors—killing investor interest. Mark's institutional backers did not want to test a method on how to work around this new law, so they politely backed out.

During Mark's bankruptcy challenges with Air One, he remained in the eternal regulatory fight like a pit bull—some of his and Joe's early problems lingered even after deregulation. The redundant CAB remained a lagging deterrent to full open competition in the new world. Mark Morris and Alfred Kahn successfully reenlisted Senators Howard Cannon and Ted Kennedy to join them in convincing the airlines, particularly United, to go along with abolishing the CAB. United was the largest U.S. airline and the staunchest opponent of the proposed CAB dissolution. Kahn told United he would make every effort to use its "beloved" CAB to freeze its growth until the other airlines "caught up" with them under deregulation. That solved that problem. The clean-up team was successful and the CAB was formally dismantled on January 1, 1985. This nearly 10-year fight gave Mark a top reputation in Washington on airline regulatory matters. Revenge had finally been exacted on the monster that kept Mark Aero, Standard, Missouri Air Commuter, and all the successors "in their place" all those years. With the CAB finally brushed aside, most of Mark Morris's future airline struggles would just involve the competition, local constituencies, and financing. As Fred Smith at FedEx had always wanted, Mark Morris helped get the federal government "*out of the way.*"

During the bankruptcy period, Mark had begun managing an investment banking firm called Quest Capital, along with partner John Stanger, who had the controlling interest in the firm. Stanger was the former CEO of GE Capital. This was the beginning of a deal that evolved to sell Air One to Dave Clark's Interstate Airlines (formerly AAC which, as will be recalled funneled much of its automotive business to PA Air) which had since moved to Little Rock, Arkansas.

In 1986 Interstate acquired Air One for several million dollars plus several times that value in tax loss carryforwards. Interstate Airlines was mostly interested in piggybacking Air One's superior operating certificate to fly scheduled passenger and freight operations, but in the meantime, Air One would have to continue operating charters only. This added 727s to Interstate's current stretched DC-8 fleet that it was operating on behalf of UPS, Emory, and the U.S. Government—the latter almost solely related to wartime operations in Central America. UPS was Interstate's core *bread-and-butter* customer at this time as UPS had no in-house fleet.

After the sale of Air One to Interstate, Quest made its first major investment for its "Alternative Situation Fund" it shared with New York Life. They teamed up to acquire an 80% controlling interest in Interstate Airlines and Mark moved to Little Rock to run the combined airline. At around the same time, President Reagan's Secretary of Transportation, Elizabeth Dole, who was long familiar with Mark's work starting with the New Entrant CEOs and the 1981 controller's strike, tapped him to chair various advisory committees to further hammer out air transportation policy, which led to a sideline activity of his being appointed as National Finance

This is the remains of former DC-6B freighter N90777 seen on the former Mark Aero ramp in October 1984 at about the time Air One was "going under." Typical eyesore hulks like this were seen for more than a decade after Mark Aero was liquidated. The last owner of N90777 was freight hauler Trans Continental Airlines, and before that it was registered with Shamrock Airlines though I'm not sure if either actually operated it. My guess is that this was a PAT Air spares aircraft that was cannibalized for engines and other rotables before being left to rot in place. This plane started its career with American Airlines in 1953.

Co-Chair for Senator Bob Dole's 1988 bid for the Presidency. Mark also became the Chairman of Dole's Arkansas campaign, with co-chairs Jack Stephens (investment banking firm of Stephens, Inc.) and Sam Walton (founder and Chairman of Wal-Mart).

However, before the election, Morris and Stanger decided to dissolve Interstate after winning a major lawsuit in a complex dispute with UPS. In return, UPS got to piggyback the lucrative Air One certificate *which it operates under to this day*, and received most of the Interstate jet fleet to establish its first dedicated air operations. At this point, the Interstate balance sheet *looked* to be in great shape—but projections showed that continuing the "leftover" operations *without* UPS would *eat the balance sheet alive* in a matter of months. The dissolution alternative got them out of their $100 million of debt, leaving Morris and Stanger with some upside.

From here, Mark would leverage himself into many aviation and non-aviation entrepreneurial and consulting ventures involving private companies and both U.S. and foreign governments all over the world. He would not, however, be directly involved in running an airline *for now*. His investment banking and regulatory consulting activity would grow and consume most of his time.

In the second half of the 1980s, my activities are not nearly as intense or far-reaching. I realign and fix my post-Mark Twain finance career while simultaneously forging ahead into the diminishing breezes of the *Second Wind*, a space where Joe and Mark Morris had since exited. My reinvented career path *does* carry me well into the periphery of aviation and the jet age, but at the same time, the dwindling heavy-recips that are *operating on borrowed time* are consuming my spare thoughts. So, I decide to spend whatever spare time I have mulling around this technological hospice—to the bitter end.

CHAPTER 47

Climbing the Horizontal Ladder

In the late spring of 1984 after having been canned from Mark Twain Banks, I'm more careful about which potential employers I talk to and do a lot of informational networking that takes five months. I take my time because Karen has her job at Peabody Holding (later to be renamed Peabody Energy with a change in ownership from a six-company consortium that included Boeing Company to Hanson PLC out of the U.K.). I still want to "get into aviation" with my marketing and finance degrees, or at least interact with it. While a hard engineering degree in the mix would have been preferable, my five years of sales engineer experience with industrial distributor IBT might help some. Through my dad's church contacts, I'm introduced to Midcoast Aviation (and ATS) President and CEO John Tucker, who helps me with part of my job search. Tucker's father was Raymond Tucker, Mayor of the City of St. Louis from 1953 to 1965, so son John was obviously connected. So he connects me with aerospace heavy-hitters including Ed Crane of Ozark, Sandy McDonnell of McDonnell-Douglas, and astronaut Pete Conrad, the third man to walk on the moon and now Director of Marketing at Douglas Aircraft (McDonnell Douglas) in Long Beach, California.

While they are all helpful with information, I do not have the background necessary to push me over the top. I wind up in the Credit Division at Mercantile Bank, a large regional bank in St. Louis. This is *not* another career mistake. It's a serious bank and finance training ground, which is nothing like the useless Policy Study Group I endured at Mark Twain. Mercantile has a large portfolio of clients in the aviation, aerospace, and defense realms. In 6 months I am promoted to the National Division which handles these accounts, and secure my initial position as a corporate banking officer. At my request, I am assigned to handle most of their aviation and aerospace portfolio, so my territory includes the west coast.

As it has been said, in any business organization there are three types of workers—"minders," "finders," and "grinders." During my working career, I was mostly a combined "finder-grinder" and only sometimes a "minder." That is, I progressed well horizontally in business development and implementation, but not vertically into management. I enjoyed my finder-grinder roles anyway and was able to advance normally.

But back in 1985 through 1987 my National Division assignment is to cover our Fortune 1000 client base in St. Louis and on the west coast from Seattle to San Diego and cold-call prospects. In this role, I become involved with several legacy airline clients including Ozark Airlines, Flying Tiger Line, and Western Airlines, as well as manufacturers such as Boeing, Northrup, Rohr (during the *First Wind* Rohr designed and build most of the propliner engine installations for the Douglas and others), Singer, and Garrett AirResearch while I continued flying my rented Cessna 182 Turbo Skylane RG out of Spirit of St. Louis Airport and photographing the last heavy-recips whenever I can. Regularly going out west helps facilitate this.

I become Ozark's lead banker and facilitated their merger transition with Carl Icahn's TWA in 1986. In the end, this did not bode well for TWA, as it set the wheels in motion for Icahn to siphon off TWA's cash through various operational and financial maneuvers. This led to the airline's ultimate brand destruction in 2001 when they were acquired by American Airlines—just as Lambert was in the middle of a *major* expansion to further accommodate TWA's hub. This would send Lambert-St. Louis International Airport into a tailspin from which it has not yet fully recovered, but it is now slowly gaining.

Just before TWA acquired Ozark, both were bleeding cash out of the jugular. St. Louis had no room for two hub airlines during this airline recession, much less new entrants. The St. Louis mess was one of the early side-effects of deregulation and therefore Icahn had no intention of acquiring TWA without *taking out* Ozark, which is what he did. It turns out that Mark Morris advised Icahn to do this nearly about a year before it happened.

To keep Ozark afloat during this critical acquisition period, my boss Maury Matthews and I work with Ozark CEO Ed Crane, CFO Al Rose, and controller Bob Bohbrink to structure a $10 million bridge loan which is promptly approved by our credit committee. But this takes Mercantile and participant Chase Manhattan over their credit limits with Ozark. We had millions already out to them. I bring in Boatmen's National Bank in St. Louis as an additional participant, which verbally signs on without hesitation. Problem solved. Despite Ozark's cash bleed, none of us banks are seriously worried as long as the merger goes through which we know it "has to." We have around 4:1 collateral coverage with Ozark's pool of Pratt & Whitney JT8D turbofan engines, the

Modest trinkets given to me by Ozark executives during my 1-year tenure as their final lead banker (1985-1986). This now fading autographed baseball came to me out of nowhere by Ozark board member and Cardinal Baseball legend Stan Musial. For that moment, the towering Musial made me, at 36 years old, feel like a little kid again. The trim and lettering on the MD-80 model are "Ozark Green," as expected.

most commonly used jet engine by the airlines at that time.

After the bittersweet final shareholder meeting before closing with TWA, Al Rose, Bob Bohbrink, myself, along with the Chase and Boatmen's officers, go to the St. Louis Hilton Inn across from the airport for lunch. This hotel is majority-owned by Ozark board member and Cardinal baseball legend Stan Musial, who is now a successful hotel and restaurant entrepreneur with investments all over the U.S.

As the five of us sit down at our table for a sentimental toast to "the end" of Ozark Airlines, the tall and lanky Musial approaches us, sitting down next to me. He asks me, *"what's your name, young man?"* As I tell him and he pops a baseball out of his suit jacket pocket and autographs it for me. He does the same for the other two bankers who are likewise transformed into kids as though they were just invited into the dugout. The first thing I think is that Stan can sure hide a lot of baseballs in his jacket. The next thing I think is *what a true and total gentleman he is. There is nobody like him.*

Over most of my career my roles would span from commercial banking, equipment and project finance/leasing, and corporate trust—with national and international banks and trust companies—to business valuation, mergers, acquisitions, and legal expert witness with a CPA and consulting firm. In the trust role I was often a *minder* when it was required that I manage a client's entire business in a fiduciary capacity. I was the corporate trustee for closely held equity blocks held in trust, many of them controlling (over 50% of the issued and outstanding stock) or near-controlling interests, which as a fiduciary required me to assume CEO and board of director responsibilities of these private mid-sized and larger companies. I was bound to do this to keep things on an even keel and to guide them through difficult challenges in the interest of protecting shareholder value—that is, surviving family wealth. I sat on boards and executive committees of companies such as a midwestern regional railroad, a west Texas contract oil driller, a plastics manufacturer, and an industrial machine manufacturer. I still specialized in aviation and aerospace-related clients during this time. Also, as a loaned executive, I served several months as interim treasurer for the largest healthcare organization in the St. Louis area.

As a corporate trustee, one of my clients was Airport Terminal Services (ATS). Just before being acquired by TWA, Ozark was desperate for diversification (for both survival and as a deterrent) and had therefore acquired Midcoast Aviation and its subsidiary, ATS, which had long-since had taken over the ground service support previously provided by Mark Aero. But with the explosion of new airline entrants, ATS expanded to major airports all across the U.S. After acquiring Ozark, it took TWA nearly a decade to jettison "non-strategic" Midcoast and ATS. They spun each off separately, with ATS going to private investor Dick Hawes, who previously had a plastics empire called KSH.

Hawes needs a corporate trustee to hold much of the family stock, so Boatmen's Trust (that is, me) bid on the appointment and won. Fellow corporate trustee Skip Schumacher and myself are placed in advisory (non-voting) roles on their board. Skip happened to be the operations officer (number four in command) on the ill-fated USS Pueblo where he and his crew were tortured prisoners of the North Koreans for an entire year. I am still proud to have had the privilege of working with Skip for several years. ATS founder John Tucker was the sole outside *voting* board member.

ATS survived through the unforgiving business environment during Gudmundsson's *first* and *second waves* of airline entrants—and exits—in the post-deregulation period, making this an interesting assignment for me. Coordinating and transporting resources all over the map to respond to new entrants, failures and sometimes arbitrary management decisions of client airlines

TWA

ADMINISTRATIVE CENTER, P.O. BOX 20007, KANSAS CITY, MISSOURI, U.S.A. 64195

February 6, 1987

RECEIVED
NATIONAL DIVISION
FEB 12 1987
Secy:
Officer:

Mr. Maury Matthews
Vice President
Mercantile Bank
National Division
St. Louis, MO 63166

Dear Maury:

Many thanks for the putter which Al Rose delivered to me this morning. It will certainly be "in use" when the weather gives us a break.

Maury, I wish to express my appreciation to you and your associates for the many years of fine cooperation that existed between Mercantile and Ozark with which I was fortunate to have been involved. Give my regards to John Reed who spent many hours with me in ironing out the small problems that need attention.

Best regards,

Bob

J. R. Bohbrink

Mercantile National Division's final correspondence from its former client Ozark Airlines post-merger. This is a thank you note from former Ozark Controller Bob Bohbrink for an engraved golf putter we had presented to him. Both Rose and Bohbrink stayed with TWA for a while in finance capacities but relocated to Kansas City.

was an interesting jigsaw puzzle to witness.

In late 1997, Boatmen's is acquired by Nations Bank which almost immediately morphs into Bank of America. These bozos enthusiastically tell me they will *"have a job for me somewhere"* meaning it could—according to them—be a bank teller slot (they were serious!). What kind of BS is that? To their credit, they offer me a promotion as the division manager of their Dallas Special Assets Group, but they are too cheap to pay my moving expenses. That's a signal not to trust them at all. Once I get down there, I'll probably be arbitrarily demoted or let go, so I turned it down. That's exactly what happened to the guy from our department who relocated his whole family to take that slot.

With that I drop everything to get out of Dodge, jumping right over to a business valuation consultant position with CPA firm Grace Advisors, Inc. (later UHY Advisors), where I work to obtain my credential as an Accredited Senior Appraiser (ASA) in Business Valuation with the American Society of Appraisers. While I do much business valuation and expert testimony work in court, I do a boatload of general business consulting as well.

It's here I start consulting for Exec-Jet Air (name changed—any similarity a coincidence) at Spirit of St. Louis Airport. They have a charter operation with 10 or more corporate jets that are mostly sale-leasebacks with the St. Louis aristocracy (in a similar fashion as the PAT Air fleet). They have a complete technical services division that does jet overhauls, modifications, and refurbishments. They are the home base for several corporate jet fleets and also handle fueling and all other ground support services at Spirit. The Who's Who of St. Louis society could no longer fly with Mark Aero as it no longer existed, so now many of them flew with Exec-Jet Air.

I am asked to pull together an industrial revenue bond (IRB) issue for Exec-Jet Air's proposed big new hangar expansion by enlisting the investment banking firm of Stifel Nicholas and St. Louis law firm Armstrong Teasdale. We obtain Airport Director Dick Hrabko's verbal assurances that he would get St. Louis County approval for the expansion.

Exec-Jet Air's founder and CEO praises me to the sky for pulling all this together *quickly*. But then only days later, Exec-Jet Air presents a *very bad* financial quarter (after many quarters of only slight losses but slightly positive cash flow). This defies its original, rosier financial projections that I had been provided to pull together our IRB team. Exec-Jet Air's revised financial forecasts take it "further south" into negative cash flow land for the foreseeable future. The deal is *tanked* on the spot after all that work and Stifel has no choice but to pull out.

After previously praising me to the heavens, Exec-Jet Air's CEO turns on me and fires me as his consultant—blaming me personally for *"screwing up,"* saying that *"you don't understand the aviation business!"* I silently agreed with him—I don't understand any business that cannot *just once* earn an old-fashioned, organic profit and cash return. In retrospect, and as we will expound upon later, Exec-Jet Air's CEO was right about me. My reactive bean-counting attitude showed *I truly didn't understand the aviation business*. Remember Mark Aero's bean counter?

In the meantime, another UHY consultant who *truly doesn't know anything about aviation* takes over the relationship, but the hangar is never built. Exec-Jet Air has no alternative but to reorganize under a new investor group, which turned around (slightly) and sold out to a national FBO chain. While disappointing, I've always known that setbacks like this are a normal part of the financing and consulting world, and I continued my work with UHY for another 15 years.

During my banking years, it is no surprise that I make every effort to track the rapidly dwindling movements of propliners within the St. Louis region and the western hemisphere. I initiate a campaign of shoehorning-in visits to rare propliner operations, including firebombing stations and air museums. I photograph the equipment during my business trips out west and on the west coast. I continue maintaining my heavy-recip data gathering using all kinds of sources including vintage aviation publications such as *Air Classics* and *Propliner* and much later from internet sources. The snowballing impact of the Mark Aero on me is far from over. In truth, it is just beginning.

As busy as I am, I'm concerned that I am not able to fly enough to keep my proficiency edge and decide to take a pause, rationalizing that I can restart flying activities at any time. Due to a multitude of bad excuses, I remain in that long "pause" to this day.

CHAPTER 48

Heavy-Recip Revival—and Another Downer

Toward the end of the previous chapter, we had to get chronologically ahead of things, so we now rewind back to the mid-1980s where we left off. During the years 1985 through 1987 while still at Mercantile, I witness a significant uptick in vintage propliner freight activity in and around St. Louis, almost to the level of the early 1970s. Once again I'm sporadically witnessing one or more sightings per day, mostly piston Convair twins, but also heightened DC-6 and Electra activity. But the utilitarian C-46 freighters have been gone for at least ten years, and there was also not a Martinliner to be seen. Heavy-recip passenger service is fading away. By this time, all seven of the former Mark Aero 404s had since been scrapped or destroyed in crashes. A few surviving passenger 404s are now winding down in Florida and the Northeast—flying commuter service with Provincetown-Boston Airlines (PBA). PBA is providing *scheduled* passenger service that Mark Aero had been *twice denied* a decade earlier—but not for long. They would soon be shut down by the FAA for safety violations. And that would be it for the passenger Martinliners.

There is a rationale for the increased propliner freight activity. President Ronald Reagan's economic policies are kicking in full force, literally ripping the economy out of the grips of the double recession of 1980-1983. Pro-business policies are given loads of adrenalin by Fed Chairman Paul Volcker's monetary actions that break the back of hyperinflation and resultant high interest rates that prevailed over the previous decade. The automotive industry is firing back to life and the adolescent overnight courier industry is exploding and seeing further innovation, along with general air cargo. The military is being revived and rebuilt as well, lending support to the LogAir business. This is the perfect storm for the few surviving heavy-recips to be pulled out of storage, serviced, and cranked up—for just *one last time*.

On a clear June afternoon in 1985, Karen and I are getting ready for a dinner party at a friend's house in west St. Louis County. The deep sound of four R-2800s overhead brings me to the south-facing balcony of our Maryland Heights apartment. It's a descending DC-6B, heading southwest toward Spirit of St. Louis Airport when the landing gear drops. The wings gently bank side-to-side a couple of times as the pilot lines up on the back course approach to Runway 26 at Spirit, just over 10 miles away, which happens to be a slight detour on our way to our dinner party. I hurry Karen up and grab my camera and off we go to our first stop at Spirit. This becomes the first and only overflying aircraft that I actually chase to the ground.

There it is, an *Aerial Leviathan* I'd never sighted before, right on the ramp behind the chain-link fence at Spirit, right along Edison Avenue. It's *Universal Airlines* DC-6B auto parts hauler N400UA, but not the bare metal one that frequented Spirit and Lambert last year. The fuselage is solid white with festive-looking red and blue stripes along the sides, making it look like a Mardi Gras float. Years later I learn these are the markings of its previous Venezuelan operator. Universal had just acquired the plane from Atlas Aircraft Brokers out of Miami. They were a sister company of a new DC-6 and DC-7 cargo operator out of Corrosion Corner at Miami International, Trans-Air-Link, who in coming years I would work with. Atlas didn't alter the Venezuelan paint job

The DC-6B I chased for 10 miles to the ground. Universal Airlines N400UA shortly after arrival at Spirit of St. Louis Airport on the late afternoon of June 22, 1985. I was tipped off after it had just flown over my Maryland Heights apartment while lowering its landing gear. The upper trim stripes are shades of blue, the lower ones are red.

while the plane was in its possession.

I jump out of the car. As I move closer in to photograph the plane, I hear the muffled echoes of shouting ground handlers inside the freight hold, rolling pallets of auto parts and the clanking of pallet jacks. The plane is subtly shaking and creaking with the movements inside and a forklift is pulling the pallets out of the rear side cargo door, carefully staging them near an eighteen-wheeler flatbed rig that is about to be loaded for the short ground run north to the GM Wentzville plant. The pallets carry orange racks of unpainted auto door panels lined up sideways like a can of Pringles chips. I see a young, lean, and dark-haired sun-glassed pilot, smartly uniformed with shoulder epaulets as though he had just climbed out of a 747. He inspects the front of the plane and the nose gear before walking to the terminal. I hurriedly bust out onto the ramp to snap photos so we won't be late for our dinner. N400UA would subsequently fly on with several other operators well into the turn of the century when it operated in Alaska with Woods Air Fuel under Part 125 bulk fuel service. The last I heard it was reported to be hauling bags of gold concentrate out of northern Alaskan mines. But now N400UA is probably long out of service and converted to pots, pans, and Budweiser cans.

In July 1985, one month after my encounter with Universal, Doug Teel presents me with photographs he took of a Trans Continental DC-6 unloading auto components at Spirit. He had just shot the photos starting at 6:00 AM that day as he was coming home from work. The crew invited him up into the plane and permitted him to "have at it" with his camera (try that today). While he was inside, the crew left and the ground handlers shut the cargo doors, unknowingly locking him inside for almost two hours. So, before the age of cell phones what do you do when this happens? Just keep shooting photos.

Very late that summer I spot a curious Convair 340 parked in front of the west ex-Mark Aero ATS hangar. It has the normal white-topped fuselage but with a three-tone varied-green

Front view of the ex-Venezuelan N400UA at Spirit. Note the forklift barely visible behind the #2 engine and the just-unloaded auto parts racks under the #1 engine (far right) bound for GM Wentzville by flatbed truck.

Trans Continental DC-6B N616SE after an early morning arrival with auto parts for GM Wentzville at Spirit of St. Louis airport in July 1985, just 3 weeks after I photographed Universal N400UA here on the way to a dinner party. Note the rack of stamped car body panels at the lower right. (Douglas E. Teel)

Close-up of Trans Continental N616NE at Spirit of St. Louis, July 1985. A stubborn #3 engine cowl panel has seen some obvious abuse by heat, weather, and mechanics over the years—typical for heavy-recip iron still flying in 1985. (Douglas E. Teel)

"sunburst" pattern cheat line along the plated-over cabin window line, then shooting up the front of the vertical tail like a hockey stick blade. On the tail at the same 80-degree angle behind the "hockey stick blade" is the word "GENERAL" in large letters. I have no idea who the operator is. In a few months, I would know, but in the meantime, I sort of forget about these ramp sightings while Karen and I are preoccupied with moving into our first house that we had just purchased in Kirkwood. It was located due south and much further from Lambert than the Maryland Heights apartment we had just left and about 3 miles southeast of the house where I grew up.

On New Year's Eve 1985, Karen and I are back at our friends' house in west St. Louis County for a quiet dinner—the same people we visited the previous June when I was sidetracked by the Universal DC-6B freighter at Spirit. On a relaxed New Year's Eve like this, the 1980s-era tubed box television is usually just tuned to one of those network New Year's Eve specials, which it was. There were no flat-screen hi-def TVs then.

The flight deck of Trans Continental N616SE photographed just after sunrise at Spirit of St. Louis Airport in July 1985. The DC-6B crew permitted Doug Teel to take photos of the inside of the plane. The ground handlers forgot he was on board and locked him in the plane for nearly two hours until the crew returned for its empty return flight to Detroit. (Douglas E. Teel)

In those days "cable TV" was still rare. Only three national networks, NBC, CBS, and ABC dominated the TV airwaves, and any serious breaking news—and it had to be *serious*—resulted in a scary programming interruption. The screen on the TV would flash "Bulletin" or "Special Report," and the announcer would bark, *"We interrupt this program to bring you a special news bulletin."* Every time this happened you wondered if nuclear-tipped missiles were on the way (I took note of my first experiences with such bulletin interruptions during the Cuban Missile Crisis when I was only 7 years old—and at that young age I knew full well what was going on). So there we are, socializing with our friends watching gala New Year's Eve specials when suddenly, *"We interrupt this program . . ."* rudely barges in, snapping us to attention. The news bulletin is that actor, singer, and rock star Ricky Nelson had, only within the last couple of hours, died in a plane crash near DeKalb, Texas.

In 1985, American Jet Aviation is the primary FBO at Spirit and this is their headquarters operation. Exec-Jet Air Corporation, described in the previous chapter, replaced American Jet only a few years later. "Backup photographer" Doug Teel shot this photo while he was inadvertently locked inside Trans Continental DC-6. (Douglas E. Teel)

Rick Nelson was first known as a teenage idol on his parents' 1960s TV show *The Adventures of Ozzie and Harriet.* By 1985 Nelson had long-since morphed into a "country rock" trailblazer and rock star, influencing major artists such as Paul McCartney and Dan Fogarty. At 1714 local time (5:14 PM Central Standard Time) Rickey Hilliard Nelson, along with his fiancée and 5 band members, died in another damn propliner crash, this time a DC-3. It was a half-controlled crash landing along an open country road that unfortunately happened to have a large grove of trees in the way. The two pilots escaped with serious burns and survived. The Douglas DC-3—as an aircraft type—had just been celebrated on all three national TV networks, just two weeks earlier, on the 50th anniversary of the plane's maiden flight.

Nelson was en route to Fort Worth Texas from Guntersville, Alabama after completing a concert at a small venue there. Nelson's DC-3 was built in 1944 and was converted to a plush executive aircraft by our old St. Louis friends, Remmert-Werner, in 1959. The handsome gold and black-trimmed plane had uprated R-1830 engines of 1,350 hp (removed from scrapped four-engine Consolidated PB4Y-2 Privateers—a type that Joe Morris flew for Consolidated Vultee during World War II) and had several panoramic cabin window modifications, making the plane appear a step above the average DC-3.

Around 7 years earlier I had seen this plane, N711Y, featured in *Air Classics* magazine, in the very same paint job. Ricky Nelson had purchased it earlier in the year to replace, of all things, a Learjet he was using. Previous owners of this DC-3 had included singer/rocker legend Jerry Lee Lewis and a prominent member of the DuPont family at some point afterward. Nelson is said to have preferred this DC-3 over the Learjet due to its spacious and ultra-plush interior—in an era where propliners were considered retroactive junk. You can stand fully erect to walk down the DC-3 aisle but must bend at the waist almost 90 degrees forward to walk inside a Learjet. The other band members weren't so happy about this DC-3—they sensed there was something fishy about it and its crew—with some even having premonitions they would die in it—just like those members of the Lynyrd Skynyrd with the Convair 240 eight years earlier.

Rick Nelson, as the likable and respected guy that he was, was not knowledgeable or informed in aviation matters and would not be expected to be. He seems to have assumed that necessary currency, maintenance, and regulatory compliance issues would be properly handled by his "people"—if he thought about that at all.

The plane had not been re-registered after Nelson's purchase. After the crash, the pilot survivors couldn't produce maintenance or operating records including AD compliance records, even though the plane was supposed to be operating under Part 125 for private operators of large aircraft. It was being operated like a half-baked Part 91 flight—and the pilots didn't seem to have the required working knowledge regarding this DC-3 and its systems. In the previous six months that Nelson owned it, there was an emergency landing due to an engine failure and in a second instance, both engines quit during the first part of a takeoff roll. These incidences were both said to have been caused by inexcusable procedural errors.

During the fatal trip to Texas, the pilots got an "overheat" light on the cabin combustion heater located under the rear of the cabin. For the DC-3 the required procedure for the overheat indication is to shut the heater down—period. Instead, the crew went to the back of the cabin to fiddle with it, take things apart and troubleshoot the problem while cruising at 6,000 feet, causing a spark-induced fire and the cabin to quickly fill with dark, noxious smoke. This required an immediate emergency landing. They were not close enough to *any* alternate and were forced to crash land in the field along a country road, winding up in that tree grove that tore the plane up. One of the engines was reported to have remained idling in the rubble for some time before the fire consumed it. The NTSB stated the accident was both preventable and survivable from an impact standpoint, but the thick smoke asphyxiated the passengers and a post-crash fire immediately engulfed the plane, finishing them off. The primary cause of the crash was determined to be the crew's simple failure to follow proper procedure after getting the overheat light, and the other things we just mentioned are certainly factors.

In the world of aviation, it's all about following "by the book" protocol and good habits. You either adhere to good habits or you don't. There is rarely if ever, an in-between realm that works. By now we all know that the bad effects of habitual corner-cutting were highly magnified during the era of *Second Wind* and its vulnerable propliner equipment. The *Tiger* strikes again, this time only maiming its masters while killing the innocents. So, even though 1985 ended in a notable but preventable propliner disaster, we still had a good New Year's Eve gathering.

Starting in the first week of 1986, I notice an overhead phenomenon every Saturday morning around 10:30 AM. At that appointed time, one of the GENERAL Convairs would fly right over our new Kirkwood house on a southerly heading. Each time the engines are droning away at climb power. While this Saturday morning phenomenon continues for months, it abruptly stops around October.

"GENERAL" was short for an operation known as "General Aviation," which leased eight piston Convair freighters from Orion Air out of Raleigh Durham, North Carolina, ultimately purchasing them in 1988. Orion Air was a wholly-owned subsidiary of The Aviation Group. Of the eight freighters, four were ex-military T-29s (240s), two were 340s, and two were 440s. All were powered by the same old, over-reconditioned, and "now less than" 2,400 horsepower Pratt & Whitney R-2800 CB-16 or -99W engines. The Aviation Group provided the GENERAL aircraft to feed Purolator Courier, Emery Worldwide, and UPS (remember, at this time UPS did not yet have its in-house aircraft fleet and Interstate in Little Rock handled UPS's primary air transport requirements). GENERAL and others like it were at the time tying up the loose ends of the exploding overnight courier industry that started with DHL a decade-and-a-half earlier.

The tail fin of a "GENERAL" Convair 240, a scene similar to what I saw at the ATS (former Mark Aero) ramp starting in the fall of 1985. The headquarters building of my then client Ozark Airlines was just south of this location, which is why I sometimes sighted this parked Convair during this timeframe. On weekend mornings starting in early 1986 I regularly caught these prominently-marked Convairs flying over my Kirkwood house on what I think were backhaul operations. They always seemed headed for Memphis. The "sunburst" trim into the tail is different shades of green. (David L. Troupis collection)

During this year I would see and hear numerous other piston Convairs flying overhead in various colors (or no colors at all), flying in all directions to and from Lambert and Spirit, and would often catch them in all phases of ground operation at Lambert. I would also still see a few unidentified DC-6s and Electras overhead. All this 1985 and 1986 vintage propliner "supernova" activity seemed to flame out to nothing during the early part of 1987. I presume the creaky old propliners were being deliberately "run-out" before being cannibalized and scrapped—like driving your car past 300,000 miles until the transmission finally lets go. Their routes are being replaced by smaller second-hand commuter turboprops, first-generation DC-9, and 727-100 freighter conversions that blend with everything else in the air. A Deja Vue—just like the disappearance of the 375th Aeromedical Wing Convairs out of Scott AFB a decade earlier.

CHAPTER 49

"They're Fixing It Up to Fly Freight"

In February 1986 I see a photo in an issue of Challenge Publication's *Warbirds International* magazine, of a dilapidated L-1049H Super Constellation which had been sold at auction in Mesa, Arizona in October 1985. The caption reads, *"A sad sight. Dilapidated Lockheed Super Constellation freighter awaits its turn on the auction block. N6937C, sold for $4,000. It will be a minor miracle if this classic aircraft ever flies again."* I agree with this sentiment—that thing flying again would be wishful thinking.

The seed of my future propliner involvement. In early 1986 I see a magazine photograph of *this* Lockheed L-1049H Super Constellation, N6937C, rotting away at Mesa, Arizona in 1985. It was purchased for $4,840 by a conscientious buyer who threw in a low bid just to clear his conscious that he gave it his "best" to *prevent it from being scrapped.* Much to his dismay, nobody else bid on it so he became its proud owner. So, "the dog caught the car"—now what? Actually, for me, *everything.*

A year later while reading through an issue of *Air Classics* magazine by the same publisher, I find out about a Kansas City aircraft preservation group called "Save A Connie" (SAC). While I was never excited about the name, I must admit this became a "can do" organization for many years. To my amazement, I discover that they pulled *that very same* rotting Lockheed L-1049H Super Constellation out of the Arizona desert, restored it to bare-minimum flying condition, and ferried it to Kansas City for a comprehensive multi-year restoration to its former TWA passenger configuration. The goal was to fly this restored classic airliner to airshows for 10 years. I think this is insane—that will *never happen.* However, the core members of this group are from the TWA Kansas City operations base going decades back, representing the *largest* concentration of manpower with the *most* years of collective Super Constellation experience on the planet, from pilots and flight engineers to mechanics and maintenance inspectors.

Regarding the October 1985 Mesa auction, the winning bidder was Paul Pristo, of Scottsdale, Arizona, who acquired the Super Constellation for $4,840 (not $4,000 as the magazine said). He threw in a low bid to clear his conscious that he gave it his "best" to prevent it from being scrapped. Much to his dismay, nobody else bid on it so he was horrified to become its proud owner. A few months later after the SAC group contacted him, he donated it to the group, to become its first Charter Member. The SAC Constellation experts went to Mesa, restored the plane to ferriable condition, and flew it to Kansas City in July 1986.

In January 1987 I have a long phone conversation with SAC co-founder and President Larry Brown and join the group *immediately,* and soon become one of their other 45 "Charter Members" by contributing a specified over-and-above dollar amount. One of these Charter Members is TWA Chairman Carl Icahn—that "villain" corporate raider. What prompted *him* to join this group? Optics—just optics. Over the next three years, Karen and I spend a weekend per month at Kansas City Downtown Airport to help restore the aircraft, even though I am convinced this project is going nowhere. Touching and working on the plane, the smell of its machine oil and grease, assemblies, and parts is my ambrosia. These greasy lubricants penetrate my clothing, almost ruining the upholstery in my car, but I don't care.

As we begin and end each of our many trips west on Highway 40/I-64 from St. Louis to Kansas City, we pass by Spirit of St. Louis Airport. Light industrial buildings have since hidden most of the airport from the highway, but I notice two Convair 240 tails and even a DC-6 tail protruding above the building roofs. They seem to "live" there, but don't seem active. What gives?

For years I had flown out of Spirit, renting Cessna 172 and 182 aircraft from FBO Roederer Aviation, a Cessna dealer. Characteristic of the day, the proprietors were brothers Bob and Jay, who looked and acted like "long hair-hippies." They were personable with good senses of humor and they knew their business inside and out. As mentioned earlier their founding dad Herb Roederer was that former Northwest DC-7C captain, who was less active at this point.

Bob sometimes calls me to ferry brand new Cessna's from wholesalers located in places such as Palwaukee Airport near Chicago to their Spirit Airport headquarters. While Doug Teel can take advantage of this free flying time (no monetary compensation allowed for Part 91'ers), I am not able to do so due to my work hours. Doug worked nights so he was always ready at dawn. So instead, with my finance and leasing experience, Bob still calls me in after work and on weekends to steer customers into aircraft sale-leaseback arrangements with Roederer, in exchange for free flying time and free beer after hours—I think I get the better end of that deal.

One day we are grounded due to a blizzard, so Bob, Doug Teel, and I buy some bottles of red wine and drink them inside one of Bob's tied-down aircraft while talking airplanes. We keep the wine bottles cool in the growing snow banks just outside the airplane doors. After a couple of hours, Bob remembers an upcoming in-office appointment with a prospect to discuss an airplane sale-leaseback—and he wants me to be the deal closer. We are both drunk and I am slurring my words, with wine on my breath for sure, but I somehow get the prospect to sign on the dotted line (I have no idea how this happened). The happy new customer was not phased that we were drunk.

On another day I ask Bob about the Convairs and the DC-6 that so far seem to be inactive apron queens. *"Oh, that's Sundance, they fly cargo only but only do a flight about once every couple weeks or so."* I ask, *"But what about the DC-6 sitting there?"* *"Oh, that's Sundance too but it's not airworthy. They called in a bunch of Cubans from Miami to work on it. They're fixing it up to fly freight."*

Sundance Convair 240 N156PA "The Plantation Mistress" sits on the tarmac at Spirit in July 1987. It's modified with a Convair 440 radar nose cone. The plane's stenciled name is barely seen below the pilot's side window.

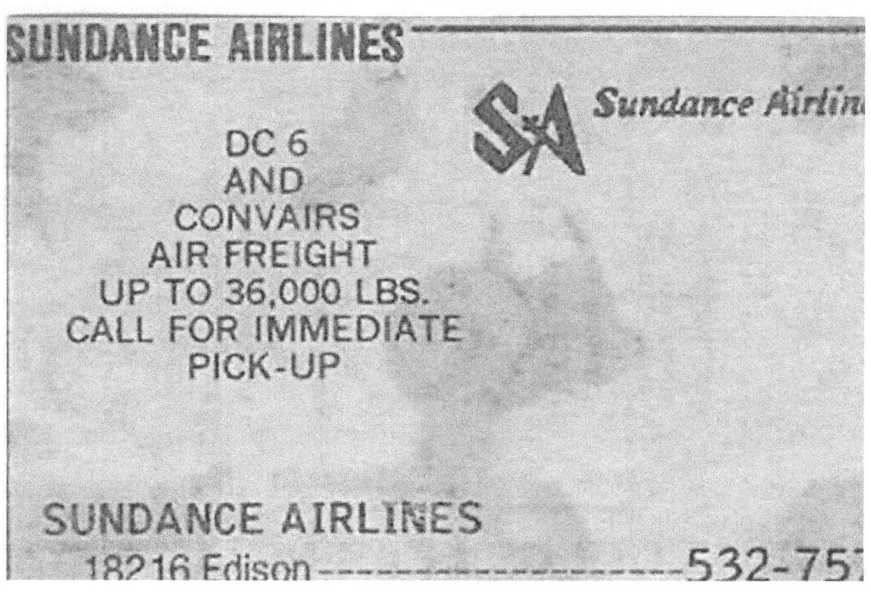

Taking advertising visual graphics to the limit (sort of). This is a simple 1987 ad in the Southwestern Bell Yellow Pages. This is reminiscent of the similar, but slightly better Interstate Airmotive ad I saw in the same publication 17 years previous (see photo page 117).

Sundance Convair 240 N150PA at Spirit, July 1987. It has a white "nipple radome" on the tip of its nose, more common with the 240 than the full nose modification that *The Plantation Mistress* had.

Rear view of the nameless Sundance 240 N150PA on the Spirit tarmac. This shows the two exhaust augmenter tubes exiting the trailing edge of the left engine nacelle—all exhaust exited out these two tubes and it was claimed that the venturi effect of the tubes added thrust to the exhaust, adding a knot or two to airspeed. This venturi effect also sucked most of the cooling air through the R-2800s cylinder cooling fins, requiring only the two small cowl flaps seen on top of the nacelle. The competing Martin 404 and other propliners did not use venturi augmentation. The 404 had five conventional cowl flaps and a simple exhaust collector ring dumping out of two stacks. Exhaust thrust augmented recips were slightly quieter than conventional ones, but otherwise sounded similar.

I further research Sundance Airlines by conversing with corporate pilots, mechanics, and other FBO personnel at the Blayney's airport pub. It will be recalled that is where years earlier I had learned of those alleged job opportunities at PAT Air. Doug and I have a habit of frequenting this place and we had gotten to know the two owner/bartender/waitresses well. They were nice-looking entrepreneurs named Betty and Elaine—who are also good information sources. It turns out Sundance is headquartered in San Juan, Puerto Rico, but the planes are being operated out of here by St. Louis-based Jet Service, Inc. Jet Service also operates lighter aircraft on a more frequent basis. The two Convairliners and the DC-6 seem to be a serious capacity overbuy. That's no way to make money.

Late one Saturday afternoon that July, I let myself out onto the tarmac and photograph the Sundance Convairs and the DC-6B. Convair 240 N156PA has the name "The Plantation Mistress" stenciled on its nose just below the flight deck. It had been modified at some point with the longer radar nose that came standard with the Convair 440 making me think at first that's what it was. The other 240, N150PA had no name on it and has a small "nipple" radome mounted at the tip of its roundish nose. Strangely enough, these two freighters "met" sometime way back and became inseparable. For some reason, they always stayed together in those endless second-hand markets. They formerly flew courier and general freight with Combs Freightair out of Denver, Colorado between 1978 and 1984, when Combs went bankrupt (but not before crash landing one of their 240s at Lambert during its last year of operations—nobody hurt). Coombs Freightair was absorbed by Providence Air Charter (PAC) out of Rhode Island and Seymour Indiana, before the two planes wound up at Sundance in 1986.

The two Sundance Convairs I photograph represent a closing chapter for me. They would be the very last "revenue ready" piston *Aerial Leviathans* I would see or photograph on a St. Louis area tarmac. In a strange irony, "non-revenue ready" Sundance DC-6B N72522 goes a step

Sundance DC-6 N72522 in the late afternoon sun at Spirit, July 1987. This is a former PAT Air and DHL plane—and one of DHL's *very first* in-house fleet aircraft. I am not sure of the purpose of the strange hodgepodge of scaffolding. This image represents the end of the line for me as far as spotting propliners on a St. Louis area tarmac. Ironically, it sits at about the same spot where I first sighted the Pegasus Club DC-6 N90710 that ignited everything for me in August 1969 at the National Air Races—almost two decades earlier. An even greater coincidence is that both of these DC-6 "book ends" had been operated by a Mark Aero affiliate or alumnus. This is the last photograph of a four-engine heavy-recip I would capture in the St. Louis area.

further, taking things full circle. It, like Pegasus Club DC-6 N90710 that I first spotted near this *very spot* in 1969, was a Mark Aero/PAT Air *alumnus*. It had spent several years with the PAT Air fleet and then was absorbed into the DHL Island Airways fleet as one of its initial freighters before winding up here.

Though Sundance acquired the DC-6 and the two Convairs in 1986, they ceased their "non-operations" by October 1987. Sometime that fall I notice all three planes had disappeared. A couple of weeks earlier I happen to catch that DC-6B on its way out as it flies over my Kirkwood home on its way back to Miami. My first assumption is that it is finally on a revenue flight and would wind up back at Spirit in a day or two. However, it never came back and was written off in Miami just 18 months later due to circumstances unknown to me.

After Sundance, these two Convair sisters went through a series of owners that included names such as Pandora Air, Rhodes International (based in Columbus, Indiana where that Fish Salmon Super Constellation bought the farm), and Cool Air, Inc. By 2020, and after a few more owners, they were still flying together out of Opa-locka near Miami on odd jobs to the Bahamas with Miami Air Lease. They represent one of the last, if not *the last*, piston Convair operations in the world.

So, for me, a significant era comes to a close here in St. Louis—at dusk on this sultry July evening in 1987. The *Second Wind* is calming down *fast*, but this is only the end of the beginning of my involvement. While July 1987 was the last time I saw a "revenue-ready" heavy-recip sitting on a St. Louis ramp, I still caught Zantop Convair 640 turboprop conversions delivering auto parts to both Lambert and Spirit as late as January 1999 when I was consulting for Exec-Jet Air. The DC-6s and Electras were long gone by then. The Convair 640 could carry only half the freight of those two earlier aircraft—reflecting St. Louis's curtailed demand for auto parts deliveries. During this period, St. Louis auto plants were being shuttered and/or relocated, resulting in only one

At the turn of the millennium, Zantop Convair 640s like this one closed out the great JIT auto parts propliner operations in St. Louis for good. (Wikimedia Commons, Torsten Malwald/JetPix GFDL 1.2)

remaining plant at Wentzville. Originally powered by piston R-2800 C engines, many 440s were converted to these 640s with Rolls-Royce Dart turboprop power at approximately 2,750 shp each, representing a 15% power increase. In the early 2000s, Zantop lost their LogAir military contract (like everybody else), causing them to shut down for good in 2005.

CHAPTER 50

Hands Getting Dirty—Finally

In January 1987, Larry Brown, founder, and president of SAC invites me to join their organization and help with the restoration of that 13,000 horsepower 1958 Lockheed L-1049H Super Constellation N6937C that had been ferried to Wheeler Kansas City Downtown Airport from Mesa, Arizona. I become a full member in about two seconds.

This "Super H" Super Constellation was one of the last three to come off the Lockheed assembly line, in 1958. These were -35C, -36C, and -37C, and they remained as "white tail" inventory into 1959. Soon, Slick Airways, a supplemental cargo operation out of San Francisco, acquired all three when it received a military contract for routes in the Pacific. A few years later they began flying LogAir missions into Tan Son Nhut airbase near Saigon, South Vietnam. Slick became insolvent in 1965, and in 1966 -37C was sold to Airlift International which continued Slick's former Southeast Asia missions until 1968. At that time commercial heavy-recips were banned by the military on all contracted international military routes due to increasing reliability issues with the old iron. If you had Canadair CL-44 turboprop or 707 or DC-8 jetliner capacity (like Flying Tiger Line), your contracts continued uninterrupted.

So, in 1968 -37C was sold to an outfit called Bal Trade, and flew freight and livestock out of Miami to Puerto Rico and most other Caribbean destinations. During one of its short-term lease periods to another operator, -37C was seized as evidence for smuggling arms and drugs. The feds later sold it at auction to a Canadian budworm spraying concern in Quebec, rigged it as a forest sprayer, and operated it there from 1973 to 1975. In 1975 it was acquired by Globe Air and flown to Mesa where it flew only a handful of spraying missions—but mostly sat rotting until months after the 1985 auction. Welcome to the career path of the typical heavy-recip transport. However, the rest of -37C's life was not-so-typical.

When Larry Brown and Richard McMahon came up with what then seemed a fruitcake idea of "saving a Constellation," the logical place to start was the Arizona desert and that's where they met winning auction bidder Paul Pristo, who kindly donated the plane. SAC then sent a crew of experienced volunteers and prepared and tested the plane for a ferry flight to Kansas City, which was completed in July 1986, but not without incident. On the first test flight attempt at Mesa, at least two of the engines lost significant power on climbout. Pilot Harry Ward barely nursed the sick plane back to the runway for a textbook landing. After rectifying the problem and running up all the engines again, the ferry flight to Kansas City took place a few days later—without as much as a hiccup.

SAC's ambitious goal was to fully restore the plane in TWA colors *"and fly it for 10 years to airshows."* Over the next 3 years it was to be fully rebuilt into passenger configuration as an iconic TWA "Super G" model, even though it was a lesser known "H" model (a convertible passenger/freight configuration known as a "combi") which is a model TWA did fly, but in much fewer numbers. This was at least a half-realistic goal for Brown and McMahon because there was a huge concentration of retired TWA personnel right there in Kansas City who had piloted and worked on Constellations in the 1950s and '60s. If anyone had any chance to succeed with this, they did. It was only the largest and most complex aircraft restoration ever attempted at that time.

As new members, Larry invited Karen and me to monthly membership meetings inside the dual hangars on the east side of the airport, after which the group would work on the airplane for the rest of the day. When we got to our first meeting, major restoration had not yet begun. It was still in its faded red colors of its last owner, Globe Air. We were welcomed with open arms. Most

The way Karen and I found N6937C on my first working trip to Kansas City in February 1987—pretty much a mess in need of a major rebuild which had not yet begun. The trim is red. The bulk of the restoration work and later operations were conducted by about 20 retired ex-TWA veteran volunteers, even though numerous inexperienced volunteers like Karen and me chipped in where they could.

meeting attendees are in their late '60s or well into their '70s and '80s. I'm only 32. They can't figure out *why*—at half their age—I'm so interested in this stuff—and *how* I know so much about all of it. I develop a particularly good rapport with the flight engineers who became real friends along with most of the other crew and many volunteers. I learn a ton from them and, as hard to believe as it is, they even learned a few things from me. Approximately 15 to 25 volunteers were working on the plane each weekend we were there. However, the bulk of the restoration was spearheaded by authentic Super Connie pilots, engineers, flight attendants, and maintainers from the *First Wind*. Those 10 or so people made up the brain trust to properly execute the bulk of the work and I was perhaps only 5 years old or younger when they were at the peaks of their careers on the Super Constellation.

That February day I'm sort of there in Heaven—Karen probably isn't. She is a good sport, however. The flight deck of this Super Constellation is so decrepit and decayed it appears non-functional—but that is the condition it was in during the ferry flight from Arizona only 7 months earlier.

With our St. Louis home being 250 miles away, Karen and I could only volunteer a weekend per month. Karen is a good sport and accompanies me on most of those weekends over the first 2 years—before she understandably finds other things to do. But not me, I keep going. All through this process I still give this group a 50-50 chance of actually finishing the restoration and flying the plane as planned—in many ways, it is more complex than a DC-6, but I don't care. I just want to experience this once-in-a-lifetime opportunity to crawl all over and work on a heavy-recip, even if the whole thing flops as I expect.

Since we are not even close to being A&P mechanics, Karen and I are instructed on how to take things apart, which is the first phase of a restoration anyway. We are put in charge of flap and fillet removal as our first job. Each flap hinge had something like twenty washers, snap rings, nuts, bolts, cotter pins, etc. where I can't possibly memorize how to reassemble them in exact order. When I bring up this concern, the mechanics tell me, *"Just toss all of them in this bucket—we'll worry about that later."*

We remove hydraulic hoses and pipes, help remove the outside vertical stabilizers and scrape layers of paint off of them with a nasty acid that turns the paint into "rubber" to make it easy to scrape off. However, it burns the hell out of our skin, despite the tight rubber gloves. We scrape down to the Slick Airways' original thick blue stripes across the vertical tails. During this time I sometimes think about Mark Aero employees who did this kind of thing for decades. I start

Pulling down run-out #4 engine late in the evening of November 7, 1987—one of three that had to be replaced with low-time Air Force surplus R-3350-93 Turbo-Compounds. This commercial "H" model Super Constellation used the commercial EA-3 version of this engine and neither that engine nor parts for it, were available anymore.

to feel like I'm "one of them"—but am I am not. My experience is *for fun*, theirs was a deadline-intensive, nerve-wracking, life-wrecking *job*. I do later get involved in some reassembly of the aircraft under A&P supervision.

At SAC's July 4th, 1987 party under the plane outside the hangar, I spend time with a special guest, Slick Airways former pilot William Willoughby, who flew -37C from the day it was delivered in 1959 until 1964. He tells me he flew exclusively on far east missions, mainly Vietnam, via Honolulu and Wake Island. He said that -37C was the "runt" of those three Super H Constellations purchased for the military contract for $1.2 million each because it was the only one delivered *without weather radar*—back then radar was an "option" and not a requirement. A common reaction to Slick pilots assigned to the plane on a mission was, *"Aww s**t! Not -37C!"* Understandably, they didn't like the extra guesswork required in navigating around those nasty thunderstorms in that part of the world, or anywhere else for that matter.

Willoughby also mentioned that Slick pilots were always nervous about flying into Ton San Nhut as they could not trust the Vietnamese cargo handlers. They were always worried about "pencil bombs" that might be planted inside the cargo boxes but lucky for him that never happened. Willoughby did show me small sheet metal patches on the rear fuselage underside of -37C covering small arms bullet holes. He even supervised some of that very patchwork he showed me. This was common with any aircraft that flew in and out of any air facility in South Vietnam.

One of the outer vertical tails undergoing acid paint stripping. The paint stripper volunteers (which included me) are on one of their frequent breaks as it's hard for anyone to take in too much of the acid fumes and burning skin—rubber gloves were a joke. The original Slick Airways dark blue horizontal tail stripes are visible. For some reason, the acid was not strong enough to remove that original blue paint.

Then Willoughby shares more somber stories. While -37C flew weapons, ammunition, personnel, and miscellaneous cargo in, they were assigned to fly the first trickle of fallen servicemen out of South Vietnam. The metal coffins were carried only in -37C's belly cargo bay which had to be loaded and unloaded through the nosewheel bay because the other lower cargo hatches were too small to shoehorn in the long metal coffins. Crews said you could always tell when you had a cargo of bodies when the telltale stench of embalming fluid permeated the aircraft on the return flights, and that gruesome stench often remained for weeks after stateside unloading.

A few more well-known personalities cross paths with SAC while I'm there. Joe Corr, then president of TWA and Carl Icahn's right-hand man, pops in one day to inspect things (I wasn't there that day). So does John Testrake who arrives in his vintage North American Navion private aircraft on a day I *was* there. Who was he? He was the TWA 727-231 pilot that was held captive in the internationally-publicized 1985 Beirut hijacking by terrorists. Passenger Robert Stethem, a U.S. Navy diver, was identified by the terrorists as "U.S. military" so they murdered him in cold blood inside the cabin and threw his floppy, lifeless body out the door to slam onto the tarmac. This infuriated me—and the rest of the civilized world for that matter.

After months of negotiation with the irrational "governing" factions, the badly abused 727, N64339, was recovered, repaired, and went back into service with TWA. In the year 2000, it was

Looking forward into the #2 engine accessory section from inside the gear well. This illustrates why early on I mentally give the SAC group of overzealous "70-somethings" a 50-50 chance of meeting their outrageous goals for the airplane. The highly motivated, knowledgeable, and experienced group ultimately put me and *uninformed opinions* in their places. This is the kind of mechanical, electrical, and hydraulic soup that Joe Morris, Mark Morris, Mark Aero, and PAT Air mechanics were faced with 24-7 x 30 airplanes. This picture easily illustrates that it never pays to cut corners with propliners (or any airplane), which so many operators did, often with disastrous consequences.

This mega heavy-recip enthusiast (me) may know something about big radial engines, but his blank look accurately suggests he doesn't have a clue regarding which screw to loosen first.

the very last 727 TWA retired before American Airlines acquired them. I had a fairly long conversation with Testrake about his flying career and his ordeal. At Larry Brown's request that day, Testrake agreed to be a keynote speaker at our planned July 1988 dedication of the plane.

On another day when I was not present, Darryl Greenamyer, a six-time winner of the Unlimited Class National Air Races in Reno, Nevada, stops by with a Super Constellation he is ferrying from the west coast to Washington D.C.—and he is seeking help and advice from us. That Super Constellation is now on display at the National Air and Space Museum Steven F. Udvar Hazy Center. In 1969 Greenamyer broke a 30-year-old FAI piston/propeller closed circuit

Inside one of the highly claustrophobic wing tip fuel tanks. I am tasked with checking for loose fittings and banging out dents in the aluminum skin with a rubber mallet. I'm 80% coated in preservative oil which gets through to my car upholstery on my drive back to St. Louis, even though I lined my seat with a plastic tarp.

The left Fowler flap had been re-installed by November 7, 1987, six months after Karen and I removed it.

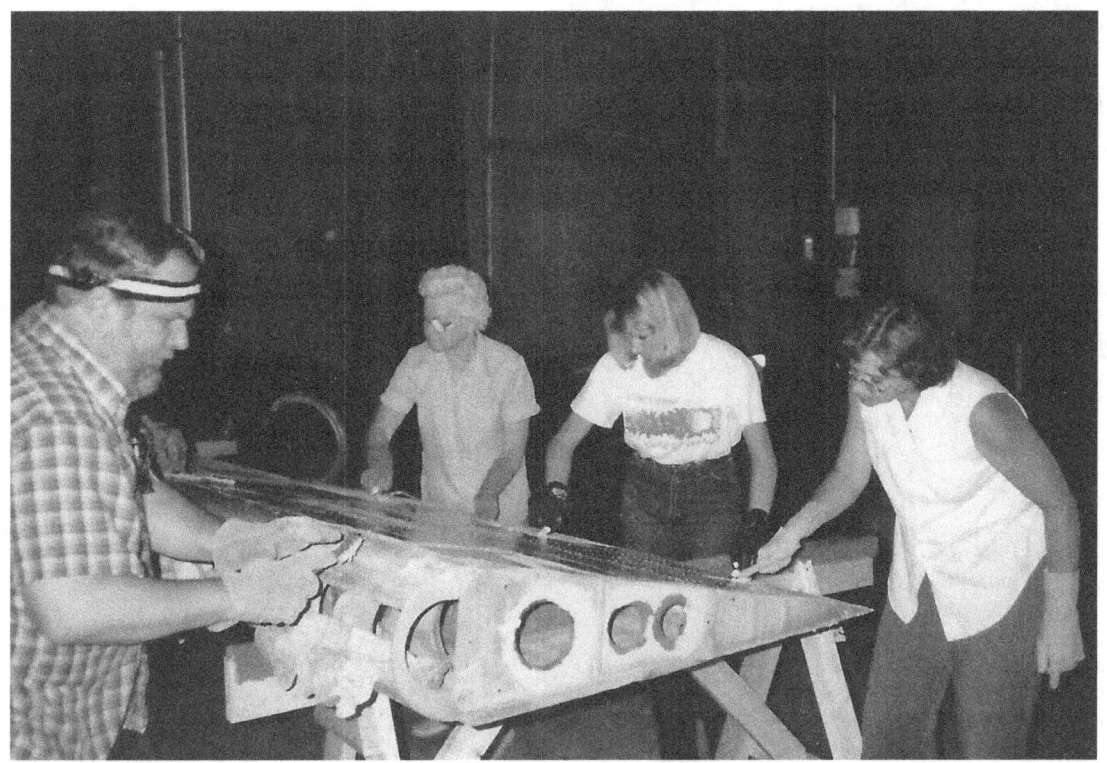

Stationed between two former TWA flight attendants (back then, "stewardesses"), Karen helps clean up an aileron. She is a good sport for two straight years, but can go along with this only so far—she has her own stuff to do.

SAC founder and president Larry Brown approaches retired TWA pilot-hero John Testrake in front of the paint-stripped -37C in April 1988. He is asking Testrake if he can be the keynote speaker at the planned dedication of the plane this coming July, only three months away. He accepts on the spot. Sterling Lacquers out of St. Louis would donate the paint and SAC members would at least get the paint job done in time. The people under the nose gear doors are part of a Dutch film crew who were doing a documentary on Testrake, which is why he was dressed in his full captain uniform. Testrake, who just flew himself in from St. Joseph, looked funny emerging from his vintage single-engine North American Navion light plane in fully-pressed captain formalwear.

Getting ready for paint. Burnishing along the rivet lines can be seen in the foreground in preparation for painting. All three of the low-time R-3350-93s had been installed at the time this May 1988 photo was taken. It's clear that everything is "not quite hooked up" just yet.

The July 1988 dedication of Save A Connie N6937C "Star of America," photographed from the upper deck of the historic old terminal at Kansas City Downtown Airport. That building has since been defaced beyond recognition with "leasehold improvements." Star of America looks great, but wouldn't be ready to fly for another year. In addition to John Testrake, "Original 7" astronaut M. Scott Carpenter addressed the crowd. Carpenter flew the second U.S. orbital Project Mercury mission in May 1962.

speed record in his highly modified Grumman Bearcat called Conquest 1. That record had been previously held by the Nazi Party in a specially designed Messerschmitt 209 and that pilot, Fritz Wendel, personally congratulated Greenamyer on breaking his 30-year record.

Our big dedication ceremony takes place in July 1988. Joining John Testrake on the podium is Mercury 7 astronaut M. Scott Carpenter, the second U.S. Mercury astronaut to orbit the earth However, at the time of this dedication and fanfare with the personalities, the plane would still be a year off from its first post-restoration test flight, but it was at least painted and presentable. Even my mom and dad come to Kansas City to attend this event.

Save A Connie wanted to paint the plane in authentic TWA livery, but the TWA legal department forbade it for fear that the general public would think the Super Constellation was still TWA's front-line equipment—*for God's sake, are people that dumb?* So, instead of painting "Trans World Airlines" above the window line, they had to use "Save A Connie" which I was not crazy about, but I kept my mouth shut. After a year or two of successful airshows, TWA management finally saw the incremental publicity advantages and changed its legal mind by allowing the "Trans World Airlines" title, which was promptly applied.

To my disbelief, the day arrives in July 1989 for the first post-restoration test flight of Super Constellation "Star of America." It looks like they're pulling all this off after all. For that purpose and considering the increasing possibility of my riding in the plane, I purchase a video camera (a novelty then) and am the only one witnessing this first flight with this "highly technical" capability. The short, one-way maiden flight to Kansas City International Airport (KCI) for avionics testing goes off without a hitch, almost as though it was never a big deal, and I film every aspect of the departure. Three months later in October *Star of America* flies to its very first airshow in Nashville, the only one it attends that year. That I can't go because of work obligations drives me insane!

Famed ex-TWA pilot John Testrake getting ready for his keynote address at the dedication. "Original 7" astronaut M. Scott Carpenter is in a tan suit with his back to the camera. Carpenter flew the second U.S. orbital Project Mercury mission after John Glenn did it first for the U.S., in May 1962.

In 1990 *Star of America* has a busy airshow season, making its debut at the world-class EAA AirVenture at Oshkosh. Karen and I drive up to Wisconsin and we work the SAC display area, giving tours of the plane, and selling trinkets from SAC's tent store. I have a conversation with James Woolsey, editor-in-chief of *Air Transport World* magazine. He's interested in doing a short article on *Star of America* which appears in the publication a few months later. I am filming the hell out of all the Super Connie operations at Oshkosh, including startup, taxi, takeoff, flybys, landing, and shutdowns. Why is nobody else in our organization is doing this baffles me.

Around 11:00 PM on September 27, 1990, just as I get back from a tiring business trip in eastern Tennessee, SAC pilot Frank Fitzgibbon phones me and in an apologetic tone asks if I can be at Kansas City Downtown airport by 8:00 AM *tomorrow*. Of course, I ask "why?" and he says that the Charter Member scheduled to go on tomorrow's (Friday's) Super Connie flight for a weekend airshow at Jefferson City Missouri just canceled and (unbeknownst to me) I was on standby to fly as "alternate crewmember" or ACM on the Super Constellation and to work the

Star of America performing one of its early flight demonstrations at EAA AirVenture Oshkosh in July 1990, as commanded by one of my friends, former TWA Captain Frank FitzGibbon. The Super Connie still has the short, "radarless" nose as it came out of the factory. Later in the year, the iconic "long" radar nose that characterized most of the TWAs Constellation fleet would be fabricated by SAC. I would unexpectedly fly in the plane two months after shooting this photo. Save A Connie leaders thought *Star of America* would be a "shoe-in" for the EAA Oshkosh "Best Transport" award. After her several trips to Oshkosh in subsequent years, that never materialized, probably because getting enough authentic Constellation passenger seats for the interior was an endless work-in-progress that was never completely fulfilled—so they never got the award. However, this plane found itself starring in several commercials, documentaries, and movies, including the 2004 blockbuster on Howard Hughes, *The Aviator.*

weekend airshow—and could I go ahead and "fill in." Duh!!

I immediately phone (and awaken) my boss at CIT, Steve Powell, who had always been interested in my involvement with SAC. I tell him the situation and *can I have tomorrow off?* In a laughing tone, he responds, "*Absolutely—you earned it, you can fill me in on Monday.*" This is the worst time for me to approach my boss with this kind of request. Just that afternoon on our drive back to St. Louis from a steel minimill in Harriman, Tennessee he admitted that our St. Louis office was on the brink of shutdown due to missing our volume targets over the last 18 months—and that it might be wise for me to start looking for another job. We had both expected this for months. Because of my low seniority at the St. Louis office, I am the first to go, but the rest of our coworkers would rotate out the door one by one in the following months. In the meantime, who cares—I am now a "crew member" on a Lockheed Super Constellation.

CHAPTER 51

Cease and Desist?

February 16, 1991

On an unseasonably springlike winter afternoon, I retrieve my second pile of videotape orders from my post office box in the St. Louis suburb of Brentwood. I pull a green ticket out of the pile that says I have "registered mail." My antenna goes up and I freeze. The registered piece is an official-looking envelope with the "Save A Connie" logo on it. Now the alarm bells go off—something's not right. I open it up and am shocked and paled. It's from SAC's new president—and obviously written by an attorney. It's a "Cease and Desist" order for a new business I just started. But I am out of work and *need the money* from my new business—*now*! I'm getting ahead of myself, so let me explain.

As it turns out, my friend Larry Brown thought there should be term limits on the organization's officers, so as a result of that board action he stepped down as president to make room for someone else. I thought I had a good relationship with the new president, Leslie Smith, who just now turned on me like a pit viper. Yes, over the past 24 months I'd gone wild with my video camera. This is mainly because no one else at SAC thought of it, and I thought the SAC restoration and events should be recorded for posterity. Three months earlier I'd filmed the Kansas City arrival of the museum's new addition, a former Eastern Airlines Martin 404. Nobody else has or utilizes video cameras. However, I like to record everything I have a personal stake in, and I had a personal stake in the Martin—I had previously helped fund its $80,000 purchase price, along with other donors while I still had my job at CIT. Just over 2 months earlier in late September, I had also filmed every aspect of my short-notice round-trip on Super Constellation N6937C *Star of America* to the Jefferson City Airshow.

Due to the recent loss of my job, I decide to form a one-man operation called Regulus Productions to produce and market aviation videos, focusing on heavy piston transports. My timing seems ideal. Active propliners are dwindling by the day—I don't see any in St. Louis anymore. No producers are covering the subject, even within the vintage aviation community which was almost exclusively focused on World War II warbirds. So, I become the pioneer of the "in-cockpit" propliner flight video that continues to be emulated by aviation video producers to this day, but now with modern jetliners and commuter planes—mostly on YouTube. But back then, there is no internet, social media—or YouTube—so I have a *temporary monopoly* on the inflight video experience and can command a retail price of $40 per tape almost anywhere in the developed world. For me, this is a living example of arbitrage or a "hole in the market." Two decades later with the explosion of iPhone video capabilities that *everyone has*—and social media—this kind of arbitrage is now impossible.

My first video is entitled *Flight of the Super Constellation*, which covers in detail my round trip in the Super Constellation between Kansas City and Jefferson City, as well as the technical and operational history of that aircraft type. I design large display ads and purchase space in aviation enthusiast magazines that have worldwide circulation and realize brisk sales

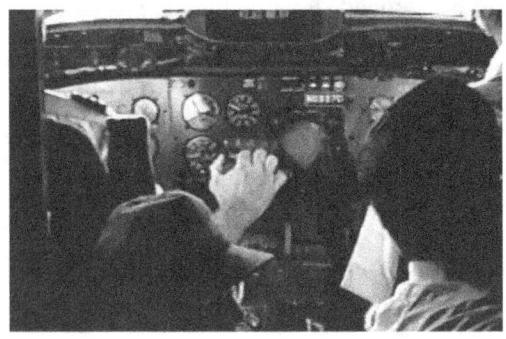

Above, Captain Harry Ward and First Officer Chris Clark go through final takeoff checklist items while in position on Runway 1, Kansas City Downtown Airport on September 28, 1990. Then Captain Ward pours on the coal (left). In the foreground are flight Engineers John Stark and Walter "Willie" Davis.

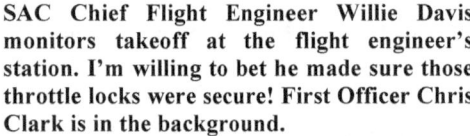

SAC Chief Flight Engineer Willie Davis monitors takeoff at the flight engineer's station. I'm willing to bet he made sure those throttle locks were secure! First Officer Chris Clark is in the background.

internationally among current and former pilots and the growing cult of propliner enthusiasts that was ignited by Stephen Piercey. I also obtain wholesale distribution through a company called World Transport Press (WTP) located at Miami, International Airport and they cannot stop ordering. I had also just published a feature article on the evolution of the postwar heavy piston radial engine in *Airliners* magazine in the first issue that contained my initial display ads. *Airliners* was an affiliate of WTP, resulting in my establishing relationships with well-known aviation writers and historians.

My goal in this endeavor is to establish a journalistic link between the *overserved* coverage of World War II combat warbirds and the *underserved* coverage of *postwar* military and commercial aviation that as a stopgap used this very same (yet further developed and more powerful) piston technology. As an example, the same basic R-2800 engine that powered the single-engine Vought F4U-4 Corsair fighter of World War II also powered the postwar four-engine postwar Douglas DC-6 airliner/transport that flew on for decades. So, I want to establish some level of awareness that would help expand the fledgling postwar "propliner cult." The big hurdle is that air combat is more glamorous and exciting than just flying passengers and freight, but I rationalize that if the *railroad enthusiast* crowd is *so much larger* than the air combat cult (it is and always has been), why not propliners? The last I checked there were not too many "combat railroads."

This all starts after my filming that Martin 404 arrival in December 1990, I tell our new president Leslie Smith that I'm going to produce and market a videotape on *Star of America* at my own expense. I make it clear that I would also donate to Save A Connie 10 percent of *top-line* revenues to them on all sales, which would leave little if any profit for me. Leslie's face lights up. *"That would be great—we'll take all the publicity we can get! That's just what we need—creative ideas like that!"* Maybe he didn't take me seriously that day, but a few months later he sees my

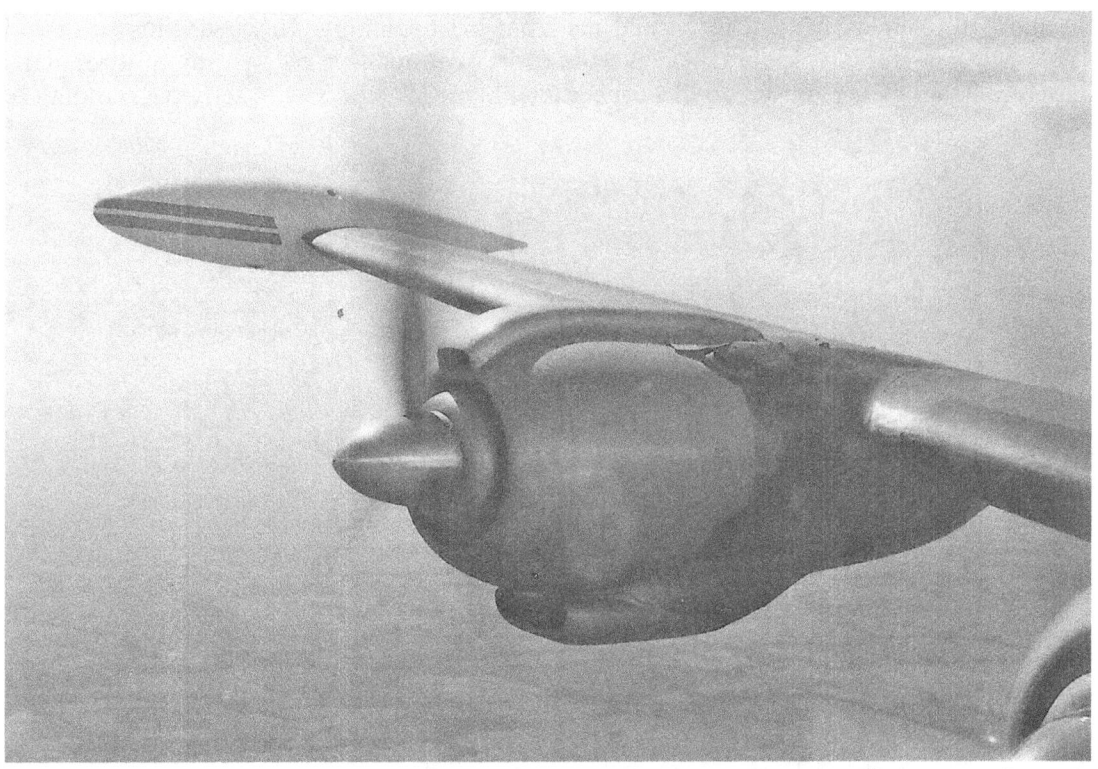

Winging east on a Super Constellation near Booneville, Missouri. This was the simple photo I used in my first magazine display ad. This photo was "attention getting" for enthusiasts because by then it was such a rare sight.

magazine ads, blows a gasket, and contacts Save A Connie's attorney. He had seen that I was now "for real." I am forced to take immediate action and hire one of the best trademark attorneys in the U.S. named "Jack" (I long forgot his last name), who is the lead practice partner for intellectual property at the St. Louis law firm of Armstrong Teasdale—the namesake of the "Teasdale" that owned Martinliner operator Interstate Airmotive years earlier. Jack's legal team views *Flight of the Super Constellation* and then he instructs that I do not need to halt sales or marketing. He then responds with a letter to Save A Connie's counsel.

It turns out that a few years earlier Jack and his team had defeated SAC's counsel in a high-profile Beechcraft case, and after reviewing our response to their allegations, Save A Connie was probably advised by their counsel to stand down, so they did. I presume their concern was that further legal action might bankrupt the group or risk its not-for-profit tax-exempt status. For all they know I could be a deep-pocketed millionaire with an unlimited expense budget—after all, I made oversized donations for both of their aircraft. But I am bluffing out of necessity—the reality is that I'm unemployed and cannot afford a big lawsuit.

I do not withdraw my 10 percent offer but SAC ignores it. All this ignites a chain reaction of sorts that starts a civil war among Save A Connie members, at first focusing on me, and then more broadly on aspects of Smith's twisted governance. His true colors are showing and he is turning into an absolute jerk. The members divide into two opposing factions. While I never asked for nor expected this counterproductive garbage for the entire group, Larry Brown and many of my member friends have empathy toward me. Others whom I thought *were* my friends are now "enemies." I am receiving and responding to all kinds of unsolicited support letters from the "friendlies" all over the U.S. who backed me from the beginning. However, this snowballing Hatfield-McCoy internal dispute takes on a life of its own, focused on an array of dysfunctional governance issues. The feud spread like cancer into many areas of SAC's activities, eroding both

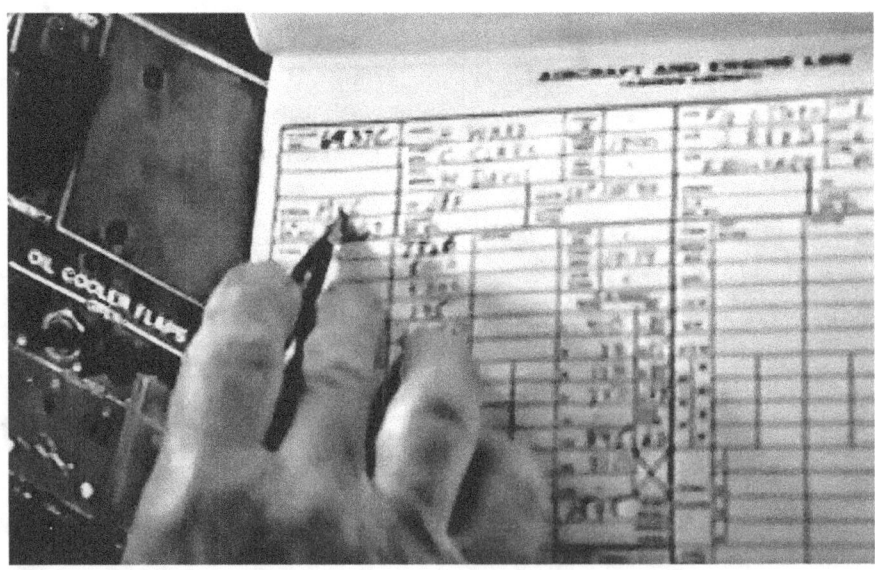

During a "free moment" in cruise flight, Willie Davis shows me the flight log. The crew names are listed in the second column from the left, and my name, as "alternate crew member" or ACM is the middle name in the second column from the right.

member and public relations. As my army friends tell me, *"a Company becomes its Commander."* Over time the conflict intensity lessens but never fully abates, and many aspects of Smith's totalitarian governance never go away. At least I get to keep the 10 percent—I sure need it.

Fortunately, none of this seemed to hamper Star of America's 15-year flight schedule to airshows. Yes, I thought the plan to fly it for 10 years was a pipe dream, but SAC actually flew it for that—plus 5 more years. But going back to 1992, I decide it best for me to sever my ties. I don't want to continue pouring gasoline on their fire by my mere presence. My *Flight of the Super Constellation* video does very well despite all this. I get rave reviews, letters and phone calls from numerous former Constellation crews, including some of the very recent crews still flying the very last Constellation freight runs in the Caribbean, as well as from renowned aviation journalists.

I can never resist taking inflight shots of heavy piston power packages hard at work in their element.

Forty miles out from destination Jefferson City Airport.

During the mid-1990s I spot the rumbling *Star of America* loitering over my Kirkwood house on several 4th of July weekends. Its annual visits are being sponsored by TWA as part of the annual Fair St. Louis "flyby airshow" along the Mississippi River with the Gateway Arch in the foreground. That would always culminate with a huge Fourth of July fireworks display each night. TWA is taking full advantage of Star of America as a relatively cheap promotional tool. If they can fill countless 747 tanks with Jet-A each day they can certainly spare the occasional cost of a few thousand gallons of 100 LL avgas for a TWA Super Constellation flying billboard.

Flight engineers John Stark (L) and Walter "Willie" Davis pose for a photo at the Jefferson City airshow. John holds a dipstick used to manually check fuel levels in the wing tanks—an absolute necessity. Rule number three in aviation: *"Never trust your fuel gauges."* Rule number two? *"Fly the plane."* Rule number one? *"Airspeed, airspeed, airspeed."* Note the Missouri capital building rotunda across the Missouri River above Willie.

Another shot, this time at Oshkosh 1996. It's no secret that for me it's all about the powerplants.

Star of America at Oshkosh 1996, four years after I left the organization. The iconic nose radome was added two months after my September 1990 flight. Here I run into SAC founder Larry Brown behind the sales tent and we get caught up—we are both glad to see each other—it had been five years. We reminisce about old times. However, he is more than anything else interested in "how Karen is doing" as she wasn't with me on this trip.

Karen and I tour the plane incognito at the 1997 Spirit of St. Louis Airport airshow. I do not recognize any of the current SAC volunteers there, and my friend Larry is not here this time. When I had flown on *Star of America* seven years earlier the passenger cabin was still an empty shell. But today I notice that the original Dreyfuss passenger interior is as complete as possible (actually, *well done*) but with only *a handful* of original Super Constellation passenger seats—the rest are buzzkill seats from a 747. Little do these 1997 SAC volunteers know that *this* airshow attendee once gave these crowds tours of this airplane just like they are doing now. I feel invisible and do not reveal myself to them. They probably don't care anyway.

The last time I spotted Star of America in the air was in St. Louis over my Maplewood office in July 2003. This was two years after the demise of TWA and two years before the plane was grounded forever due to a blown R-3350 on runup while training a new flight engineer. That's how thin their budget was in 2005, and, in a later chapter, it will become obvious as to why. One more *Second Wind* propliner is grounded for good.

CHAPTER 52

South to Corrosion Corner

By July 1991 my one-man Regulus Productions company needs more videos to grow, so I shift my focus to a most logical place—that place known as the infamous "Corrosion Corner." That was where some of Mark Aero's and PAT Air's heavy-recip fleet aircraft came from and in many cases where they returned, but now those two successive St. Louis companies are long gone. Practical consumer-grade videotape technology did not exist during the Mark Aero and PAT Air eras, so there was never a window for anyone like me to video that activity. But in 1991, Corrosion Corner, at the northwest corner of Miami International Airport still has some signs of life where video technology can be applied. It remains the largest surviving bastion of propliner operations in the world, but that is shrinking fast. Most of its propliner movements are pure freight, and some of the operators *still* have bad reputations and rough safety records.

Years of accumulated propliner crash sites involving dubious Corrosion Corner operators were littered throughout south Florida, the Caribbean, and Latin America. To add insult to injury, the few *legitimate* U.S. registered propliner operators who flew "by the book" with good safety records had to compete with Dominican and other foreign operators where the FAA gave them a "pass" on the strict (and costly) U.S. regulations that hog-tied these good domestic operators. Foreign operators could fly under a FAR Part 129 Foreign Air Carriers certificate that allowed them to operate in the U.S. under their country's otherwise lax rules. Part 129 even allowed such foreign carriers to operate aircraft with U.S. registrations. It's no surprise that the Dominican and other foreign operators easily underbid the legitimately run domestic ones—making life rough if you played by the rules.

To the relief of the good guys, the FAA eventually banned Dominican operations on US soil after a rash of fatal accidents and then the FAA finally tightened the rules for other non-U.S. operators. In 1991, Trans-Air-Link (TAL), Bellamy-Lawson d.b.a. Aerial Transit, F.A. Connor, and Agro Air were the largest heavy-recip operators at Corrosion Corner. While the latter two were headquartered in Miami, they still operated under foreign flags with U.S. registrations under the relaxed rules of Part 129. All except TAL had serious fatal crashes, not always due to those pervasive poor practices, but sometimes just due to bad luck.

Over the decades, Corrosion Corner was a curious mix. It was big a junkyard of cannibalized propliners, pieces, and parts, with fully intact operations sprinkled about, using worn out, often unmarked DC-6s, -7s, Constellations, Super Constellations, DC-3s, Convairs, Electras, and a few passenger Martinliners. Even civilianized R-4360-powered Boeing C-97 "mechanical nighmares" could be found, operated by Agro Air. Repair and maintenance of the R-4360 was difficult and expensive in the 1990s—something that got in the way. Naturally, these complex engines often broke down, but Agro Air had so many of these cheap engines in inventory that they would just replace a bad one with a low-time good one—buying a little time before it too failed. There was minimal maintenance and almost no repair to speak of.

As we had previously discussed, by 1991 most heavy piston radials of all sizes had been overhauled so many times over the decades that their structures were weakened to a point that none of them could generate the full power they were originally designed for. But many operators would not reduce payloads accordingly—they stuck to the original manuals in the name of bigger profit margins. This was aggravated by the discontinuance of the high P/N 115/145 avgas that these engines originally required, derating these engines further. By now, only 100LL was available, requiring reduced power settings, especially during takeoff.

Aircraft and parts brokers and dealers were everywhere at Corrosion Corner. Some of them were shysters. The economic fortunes of each airline in this volatile business unpredictably flipped back and forth. The fortune of an individual operator could flip to the opposite extreme on a dime. Shysters or not, the brokers and dealers shifted assets between those operators who were currently experiencing famine and those who were simultaneously feasting. Obsolete propliners were the *true currency* in this strange corner of the earth. The life of an operator was often measured in days, weeks, or months, but some lasted for years.

Typical. In 1990 a Dominican-flagged A.M.S.A Super Constellation freighter loses it just after takeoff. The crew initiated the fully-loaded flight on only *three* operable engines when another one quit just after takeoff, resulting in this ditching off of San Juan's Munoz International Airport. The engine that stopped after takeoff had known problems beforehand. This ditching resulted in the loss of the captain, but luckily the copilot and flight engineer got out after trying to rescue the captain who was irretrievably pinned down. A.M.S.A. and this Super Constellation, HI-515, visited Miami several times weekly under the dubious FAA Part 129 certificate for foreign carriers. This accident was said to be the straw that broke the camel's back for the FAA—setting the wheels in motion to accelerate the banning of Dominican and other foreign operations on or over U.S. soil. That edict came down within 2 years of this incident.

Corrosion Corner was also an epicenter for illicit arms and drug commerce in the western hemisphere. A few of the propliner operators were the actual traffickers. Just like the CIA, these organizations often put up a front as legitimate operators that haul normal cargoes such as livestock, fish, processed food, pharmaceuticals, clothing and fabric, auto parts, restaurant, hotel, and kitchen equipment.

Yes, a few of the operators at Corrosion Corner were *legitimate*. Legitimate or not, stowaways from distant places sometimes hid inside landing gear wells (some were crushed to death in the process and others were converted into pop sickles before reaching Miami). Drugs

A typically unmarked DC-6 (ex-C-118) pulls into its equally unmarked Corrosion Corner freight terminal in March 1992. Such terminals were usually simple concrete block shanties or butler buildings combined with linked portable trailers with moldy window air conditioners. I never knew who the operator of this DC-6 was and you probably don't want to know the exact number of likely safety violations this aircraft may have represented at the time this video frame was taken.

were sometimes hidden by third-party traffickers inside legitimate-looking cargoes such as fish carcasses that are in turn packed in dry ice boxes. Back then, if the legitimate propliner operator was unaware of hidden contraband in the cargo, they were not normally held responsible for the illicit shipments as long as they cooperated with authorities. This is no longer the case.

The intrigue of the dwindling propliner population and the seedy reputation of Corrosion Corner attracted propliner cultists like flies from Europe, Canada, Australia, and New Zealand. These were the countries where most of the world's growing propliner cult resided. Some were from the U.S. (like me), but *very few*. Many of the Corrosion Corner visitors were professional journalists obsessed with the *Second Wind*. Their media of choice was simple photography along with the written article or book. *None* of them used videography to record history and I am about to change that.

So, by the summer of 1991, I had been aware of the Corrosion Corner freight operator Trans-Air-Link, (TAL) for some time. They had been covered in historical aviation print media in recent years, and are considered a legitimate, safety-conscious operator with an impeccable reputation and no fatal crashes. Engine fires, failures, mechanical emergencies, and close calls, yes, but no crashes (yet). They are a FAR Part 121 Supplemental carrier (rare for a 1991 propliner operation) that flies both scheduled cargo routes and cargo charters and has been around for a decade. With this authority, they have to keep the same records and follow the same operating standards as the major U.S. airlines. TAL started operations a year or two after PAT Air shut theirs down, but the TAL family-owned predecessor company, Atlas Aircraft Corporation—who were brokers and refurbishers—had been around for much longer.

At this time TAL is flying three DC-6/C-118s and the very last DC-7C in Part 121 airline service and all are freighters. TAL is owned by Gary Balnicki, son of the founder of Atlas. In the early 1980s, they formed TAL to "get into the airline business" (sound familiar?). The new airline did so well that Atlas closed its doors in 1986. This represents a last-ditch opportunity for me and my video equipment.

Time is wasting so I need to get down there. I write Balnicki to ask him if I can come down and shoot videos of all aspects of his operations and perhaps catch a trip on one of his DC-6s. I receive his written reply in less than a week. He gives me all the answers I want to hear, welcoming me down and mentioning that aviation historians and enthusiasts have visited them in recent years and he always accommodates them as best he can. He says I can shoot video all I want as long as 1) I don't interfere with crew or ground operations, and 2) my end product does not insinuate "illegal operations." I assure him I will not get in the way and that I am a truth teller and not a sensationalist, so and we set up a week in late September for my visit. In the meantime, I find that several key TAL personnel are familiar with my video, *Flight of the Super Constellation*. Still, I have to be careful. Gary Balnicki *despises* the term "Corrosion Corner" and its stigma. So, I don't refer to that my resultant videos involving TAL. Also, my trip is timely in that the transition from prop to jet freighter transports is happening quickly at Corrosion Corner. Even TAL is working on acquiring jet or turboprop replacements.

I spend $2,000 that I don't have on a new video camera that shoots in the "semi-professional" SVHS format which is being adopted by lower-budget industrial producers like myself. The most advanced video format of this era is the professional "Beta Cam" format (not to be confused with the consumer "Beta Max" format) being used by TV news networks. Beta Cam equipment would have set me back around $60,000. By comparison, today's best off-the-shelf cameras are in high-definition digital ACHVD formats, and those, and now even iPhones are light-years better in quality than Beta Cam and can be purchased for just a few hundred dollars

One night a week before my trip I'm watching *CBS Evening News with Dan Rather* which has a story on the illegal arms trade into and out of Miami International Airport. While the field reporter is talking, I'm shocked to see helicopter footage of the TAL ramp with a few of their parked Douglas DC-6s flashing by on the TV screen. The blue "TAL" markings are clearly visible. I'm sure Gary Balnicki isn't happy about this. Otherwise, I think, *what am I getting myself into*?

As late September rolls around, *Flight of the Super Constellation* sales are booming and even putting real food on the table. I'm about to leave for Florida to a retrieve treasure chest of new material for contemplated and future productions. I pack up my Subaru wagon and head south early on a Saturday morning. On the trip down, I am always concerned about runaway expenses or screwing up once-in-a-lifetime shots, either by poor timing or otherwise. I know that rapidly-evolving scenes cannot be "re-shot" and I am *not* a seasoned videographer.

After two full days of driving, interrupted only by gas station stops and a Motel 6 overnight at Cartersville, Georgia, I arrive at Corrosion Corner in Miami Springs about an hour before sunset on Sunday evening. The sun is setting and everything is fresh from a recent rain shower. There is a hodgepodge of old concrete-block liquor stores, tattoo shops, and nail shops with barred windows all over the place and the buildings are painted in all kinds of bright pink, green, yellow

P.O. BOX 521298, MIAMI, FLORIDA 33152

July 29, 1991

EEGULUS PRODUCTIONS
621 N. Woodlawn
ST. Louis, MO 63122

                    Attn: Mr. John A. Reed

Dear Mr. Reed:

TAL and its employees would be happy to participage in
your film as long as it does not interfere with our
operations.

By your "adding flavor" to the story, I trust will not be
in any way insinuating ilegal operations.

TAL is a certificated Part 121 Supplemental Air Carrier
that has an impeccable reputation with the FAA and its
customers. We are always cooperative with orgniazations
doing educational or documentary work on our type of
equipment.

Please advise when and for how long your project will take.

Sincerely,

TRANS AIR LINK CORP.

Gary J. Balnicki
President

PHONE: (305) 871-3301   TELEX: 4941133   FAX: (305) 871-5785

A welcoming favorable response from president Gary Balnicki of TAL. You will see that executives of such aviation operations—reputable or not—were not always big on proofreading. I have always found this to be the case.

and blue colors with ugly graffiti here and there, and there are no people around.

Along the south side of Perimeter Drive is the heart of Corrosion Corner, featuring all kinds of unmarked DC-6s, and a couple of DC-7Cs that are dormant or being cannibalized with their "propellerless" R-3350s exposed. Propliner junk and half-hulks are everywhere. TAL is further east along the south side of this road on the eastern periphery of Corrosion Corner so I continue driving. There's no human activity on the ramps, just parked planes on this quiet Sunday evening. The white noise of idling jet airliners uninterruptedly fills the background, pierced only by an occasional thundering takeoff—or reverse thrust on landing.

I as drive further east looking for my Hampton Inn on NW 36th Street (just north of and parallel to Perimeter Drive), I spot three silver DC-6 tails behind the chain-link fence, towering above some mobile trailers and flat shanty-like buildings. On each tail is a large blue "TAL" logo. As is the case, Gary had told me when I arrive on Sunday there would be no activity since they usually did not work on Sundays, so just go straight to the hotel. The Hampton Inn is only a half block further down, so I check into my room. Then, as the evening darkness descends, I decide I'm hungry, but don't know where the feeding troughs are around here.

I figure my best bet is to go further east along NW 36th street. I stupidly don't take my car but decide to start walking on the north sidewalk in the pitch dark along the seedy neighborhood. In retrospect, this was probably a not-so-bright move, but I guess I'm still here. About half a mile down, I pass by two expansive, modern-looking hangars sitting on an expanse of empty tarmac. In outsized brightly-lit letters, it says "Pan Am" on one and "Eastern" on the other. Both *giant* structures are empty and ghostly silent amid the background airport noise. I pause and reflect for a moment. These are two of the "*most legacy*" of the legacy airlines that appeared in the late 1920s and '30s. Eastern had just ceased operations for good and Pan Am would follow in just a few months. I am reflective and otherwise fall in a state of overwhelming reverence.

One of the several DC-6 "TAL" tails that greet me on the other side of the chain-link fence as I drive by the TAL operating headquarters heading east on NW 36th Street for the first time on a sunny/showery Sunday evening. I feel a combination of high excitement with a tinge of apprehension. All TAL lettering is navy blue.

Eastern, which had marketed itself as *The Wings of Man,* fell victim to some of the most militant and out-of-control union activity ever to be seen in the airline industry, though management certainly shared the blame. Its CEO at the time, and its final one at that, was former Frank Borman, the first to command an orbital mission around the moon. Captain Eddie Rickenbacker, the famed World War I ace, ran Eastern through most of its high growth years during the heavy propliner era from the late 1930s into the "great jet transition", but he let quality and service go in his later years. Pan Am, once called *"The Chosen Instrument"* for the world's international routes by its founding CEO, Juan Trippe, is still operating a few skeleton routes mainly out of New York City as though in its final nerve twitches before death. Neither airline had been able to navigate through the first decade of deregulation—but neither was doing well beforehand either. I realize I'm witnessing the sickening end of an era *right before my eyes*. The real lesson is that a government, be it democratic or totalitarian, is always "good" as long as it favors "you." Good luck if it one day spits you out and you have to go it on your own.

After I shake out of this sobering reflection, I proceed to locate the dirtiest fast food place I'd ever seen which is the only eating place anywhere. It is a unit of an internationally-known chain and is staffed by unfriendly employees, who don't want to be here, nor do they want *me* here. I'm the sole patron at this late hour. But I'm hungry, so I consume the driest and most tasteless hamburger known to man. I don't want to think about what they might have put in that hamburger.

CHAPTER 53

Getting Acclimated

I arise at the crack of dawn and arrive at TAL headquarters promptly at 6:00 AM Monday. Gary had told me that Mondays normally involve a light schedule of planning and aircraft maintenance for that week's flights, so I would probably only get footage of limited ground operations. He told me that by the afternoon, planes on the ramp would be started, run up, and tweaked in preparation for flights starting on Tuesday. An exception was that the DC-7C was down in Curacao over the weekend and would return just after midnight tomorrow morning (Tuesday).

TAL's "shanty town" TAL headquarters, Building 1012. The main structure is mainly the freight staging and quick engine change (QEC) storage spaces. There is also a comfortable pilot's lounge with a coffee table, vending machines, and magazines in this section. Most of that main building is "open air" on both the east and west sides, protected only by a tall chain link wall. Partly visible on the far right are the dispatch and operations portable trailer offices featuring window air conditioner units.

The freight and staging building, Building 1012, has a minimal concrete block half-wall to the west, secured only by an open chain-link main entrance door. I peer inside and see a huge R-2800 CB-17 engine sitting on a stand next to an even larger R-3350 Turbo-Compound, mixed with pallets of cargo and a pilot lounge space with a coffee table and magazines. There is nobody inside. As a brief downpour starts pelting me I let myself in and walk across the small cargo staging area to the main offices on the north side of the building. I knock on a door with a sign that says "Guy Cottington" and he says "come in." He is cordial and says that initially there will be a lot of downtime for me as employees filter in, so I can just "start taking pictures." He gives me a laminated ramp pass card with ribbon that I must wear at all times both on and off the ramp.

Guy is a 60-something who is in charge of TAL personnel matters—hiring, firing, and crew scheduling. He has a reputation at the Corner for being a "horses' ass" to pilots and others inquiring about job availability. The most common word in his vocabulary is "no." TAL pilot jobs are highly sought by Corrosion Corner propliner jocks and TAL is the hardest place for them to land one. If you are lucky enough to "get on" at TAL, there is no room for missteps.

This scene greets me upon my first early morning arrival at TAL. In the foreground is a freshly overhauled R-2800 CB-17 that will eventually go on a DC-6. In the background is an overhauled Curtiss-Wright R-3350 Turbo-Compound QEC package destined for the DC-7C when required. That would probably be "sooner" rather than "later." Size differences between these two large propliner engines are apparent.

Company president Gary Balnicki arrives and invites me to his office and we have a nice chat. He is a short, feisty "Type A" kind of guy, perhaps in his late '40s with jet black hair. He says that once the dispatchers begin piecing together this week's flight schedules, we'll know more about available flights for me, and I can go on any flight I choose. He maintains that FAA Part 121 cargo operations allow for *"required crew only,"* and says that by issuing me a dry-cleaned pilot uniform, I magically become one of the "required" crew. He jokes that if anyone asks, I'm the "loadmaster." He shows me the closet with freshly laundered uniforms for me to try on later.

Then Bill Winn, head of quality control, shows up and Gary introduces us. Chain-smoking Bill is a former DC-6 pilot who is now somewhere in his late '60s with a full head of gray hair and a constant smile and pleasant personality. He will take me under his wing during my visit and becomes my advocate during my stay. His office is next to a few dispatchers housed in a group of musty smoke-filled trailers joined together on the south side of the staging room, cooled by moldy, nicotine-stained window air conditioners. It is comfortably cool inside but the humidity in there seems like it's 110 percent. In front of each dispatcher is a big, boxy computer monitor with that old-fashioned green display, each of which is plugged into freight forwarder and airline systems. Most of the dispatchers are middle-aged women. Bill says he will assist me in both securing and preparing for my flight, and tells me to keep an eye on the scheduling chalkboard located at the outside break patio area on the ramp. A parked DC-6B nose almost protrudes right into the patio. As the day goes on, tentative scheduled flights and messages are written in the blank spaces under seven columns, each representing a day of the week.

Bill has to start his day so he turns me loose on the ramp for much of the morning where I get my maintenance activity film segments. I freely crawl into the cockpits and cargo bays and walk out on the wings for different video angles. It smells worse than a barnyard inside several of the cargo bays. I hope I don't get a flight full of pigs or chickens, which is common, but *I must take what I can get.*

In the early afternoon, Bill and I go to lunch across the street at a popular pilot hangout called Bryson's. He invites a couple of visiting retired pilots to go along including a former TAL pilot now flying DC-6s in Africa. I am pleasantly conversant with this group and love every minute of it, and can tell I'm "accepted." Bill and I then return to his musty office with its window air conditioner working overtime, and continue our chat as an afternoon of scattered rain showers begins. I feel I'm taking up too much of his time, but he refuses to kick me out. Another operator's DC-6 suddenly powers up to takeoff power on runway 9L just outside Bill's window in the middle of a sun-filled shower, shaking the place up. His phone rings and he tells me that the weekly *scheduled* TAL DC-6 run to the West Indies is now on the chalkboard. They call that their "Duty Free Triangle" trip. He suggests I grab this two-day trip to get the most comprehensive coverage. I agree.

In-cabin and on-the-wing shots during the endless routine maintenance. The shanties and trailers that comprise TAL's facilities would be more typical of somewhere in Cambodia or India, not here in the U.S.

That flight will leave here for St. Maarten at 1:00 AM Wednesday with mixed cargo, and then on to St. Croix, St. Thomas, San Juan, and then Borinquen International at Aguadilla, Puerto Rico in the early evening for a night's rest while the plane is loaded with pharmaceuticals and textiles for the return leg to Miami. We will depart for Miami at 2:30 AM Thursday and arrive back at TAL headquarters at about 8:30 AM. The legal waiver guy comes into Bill's office and I sign away, causing me to think *it won't happen this time!* Well, guess what, I just don't care!

Bill then asks me for my passport. I turn as white as a ghost. Dammit, I didn't think of it and did not bring it. This a decade before 9/11 and back then a passport was not required for vacations to Mexico or the Caribbean. But Bill tells me that passports *are* required of cargo crews. He calls Larry Martineau, the guy who handles all the flight paperwork. When he hangs up he tells me not to sweat it. *"Stay with the crew, they will cover for you. If things get "hot," you can just stay inside the plane. Nobody will bother you."* Whew! That was a close one.

On my scheduled DC-6 trip our manifest includes a pallet labeled "Live Tropical Fish" destined for St. Croix. Bill Winn is perplexed as to why we are shipping live tropical fish *back* to the place where it seems they should have "come from"—and why a "whole pallet" of fish is needed for such a small island. Strange stories like this have always originated out of Corrosion Corner (like the Super Constellation load of Christmas trees bound for Venezuela just 10 days before Christmas).

We discuss the state of propliner operations in North America, and the close relationships that TAL has had with Zantop, Trans Continental, Universal, and now Northern Air Cargo in Alaska. Depending on the feast/famine cycle, planes and crew had been traded/leased between these collaborators to accommodate shifting demand. TAL and their crews had made regular flights into the continental US, but not so much anymore. He said they did fly into St. Louis only a month ago. Then I come to a realization. On an early evening exactly four weeks earlier (late August), I saw a now-very-rare natural-metal DC-6 passing overhead climbing out of Lambert, while on an evening walk with Karen in Kirkwood—my first such sighting in years. Coincidence?

Bill also discusses TAL's close relationship with Douglas in Long Beach. Douglas has a kind of "obsolete aircraft group" that serves as a clearinghouse of sorts, for information sharing between Douglas and the few remaining operators of its legacy aircraft. TAL plays a big part in updating the shrinking handful of DC-6 and DC-7 operators with the latest operating data and Airworthiness Directive (AD) compliance information.

Guy Cottington pops in as Bill and I are talking. He delivers some big news to Bill. Next door neighbor DC-6 operator F.A. Conner had just today been shut down for good by the FAA. While this is to TAL's advantage, it could happen to anybody. Conner had been investigated for years by the FAA and the intelligence agencies for illicit operations, particularly illegal arms, even though Conner allegedly flew missions under covert CIA directives. It seems Conner might have crossed some agency in *some manner* at *some point*. Conner's DC-6 fleet was one of those foreign-flagged operators that had U.S. "N" registrations under Part 129. A few weeks later owner Gus Conner was found dead from a gunshot wound in his parked car due to an "apparent suicide" under suspicious circumstances.

As Guy leaves the room, the whole place begins to shake violently. The deep thunder of an

R-2800 firing up engulfs everything. The sweet smoke of avgas exhaust soon enters the room. Just like clockwork, the DC-6s begin a series of preliminary runups for this week's flights which will start tomorrow. I tell Bill *"goodbye, nice knowin' yah,"* grab my camera and run out the door to film engine runups from every conceivable angle for the rest of the afternoon. My new friend Bill understands.

That evening, high winds and rainy weather move in. Heavy rain is splatting against my big window at the Hampton Inn. A quick tropical depression is moving through. According to the local Miami news, the ocean sea state is hazardous, with warnings everywhere. I wonder if this mess will clear up before my trip. In the news, the Haitian dictator Jean-Bertrand Aristide has just been ousted in a military coup. I hope all this military action there doesn't impact my trip, either (it won't). Overnight, while I sleep the DC-7C arrives at TAL headquarters on schedule from Curacao in the middle of this lousy weather at 1:00 AM Tuesday. This trip had been commanded by veteran pilot Joel Reeves, who was considered one of TAL's best.

The next morning it's cloudy but the weather is calmed down when I arrive at TAL it's cloudy but the weather had since calmed down. The first thing I notice is the big DC-7C secured on the ramp. Later that morning it clears up. A young, energetic, and super friendly operations coordinator Matt Engel, escorts me, my equipment, and a DC-6 crew into a van, where we travel about a quarter mile to the customs terminal just to the west of us. There I will interview the crew and film the loading, startup, and taxi-out of the first DC-6 operation for the week to Freeport, Bahamas, a short "milk run." Captain Roberto Amador is a Nicaraguan who a few years earlier was shot down his DC-3 during the conflicts there—and he then enjoyed a few years of communist hospitality in one of their gulags. Customs officials here in Miami are said to now call him the "Nicaraguan Refugee."

The TAL DC-7C N869TA is back from Curacao on my second-morning arrival at TAL headquarters on Tuesday. It had arrived much earlier at 1:00 AM during some extremely nasty IMC weather that would be unpleasant to fly in, especially at night.

First Officer Bill Gonzales was a Cuban Air Force pilot during the Batista regime in the 1950s. He escaped the clutches of Castro's communist revolution by stuffing his family into a commandeered Stearman biplane. He flew them to the U.S. Naval Base at Guantanamo Bay, carefully avoiding Castro's military installations scattered about. There he and his family were granted asylum. Miami customs officials unapologetically refer to Bill as the "Cuban Mobster."

I also talked to the young flight engineer, Edgar Badillo, whose English was so broken I could not get the background on him. Next, I film all the loading, startup, and taxi-out operations at customs, and then a TAL ground guy drives me along the taxiways to the east side of the airport just northeast of the passenger terminals, where I video the takeoff and departure of the DC-6B to Freeport.

Bill Winn tells me the story of when Roberto was flying out of Nassau in a TAL DC-6 when the number four engine burst into flames. This was a "fuel fire," the worst one can have in a heavy-recip. Roberto cut the fuel and electrical feed to the engine auxiliaries and hit the fire bottles, which didn't put the fire out—it only worsened. As luck would have it, he was able to do a one-

Captain Roberto Amador, a.k.a. the "Nicaraguan Refugee" (L) with First Officer Bill "Gonzo" Gonzales, a.k.a. the "Cuban Mobster." Each of these professionals had an interesting background in escaping the communist regimes that engulfed Cuba and Nicaragua.

Roberto, Bill, and Edgar on initial climbout with "flaps ten" from Miami International, just after gear retraction, on their milk run to Freeport, Bahamas.

eighty and execute a successful emergency landing back at Nassau before the wing had a chance to weaken. The fire inexplicably extinguished itself during the crew's hasty exit. Roberto was rattled, without a word, and disappeared without a trace for several months. Then one day he showed up cold turkey at TAL headquarters and informed Guy Cottington *"I'm ready"*, who hired him back on the spot.

When I get back to TAL headquarters, Bill Winn gives me a detailed ramp tour of the DC-6A in which I will be flying. It's N870TA, a former Belgian Air Forced C-118 with 26,000 hours on its airframe. I'm happy to find out that my assigned captain will be Joel Reeves, the guy who just brought the DC-7C back from Curacao through those horrible weather conditions. Bill and I climb onto the flight deck of "my" DC6A and he shows me how to operate the radios on the pedestal. Houston radio will be tracking our flight to the islands and back on airway Amber 555.

Bill then goes home and I head north to downtown Hialeah to pick up Bill's recommended list of distilled water (this was before the days of bottled water), snacks, a flashlight, and other "survival" supplies for the trip. I then go back to TAL headquarters and pick out my pressed crewman uniform, and then film the late afternoon fueling and ramp cargo staging and loading of

N870TA. After completing my ramp video work for the day, I decide to retire early to my hotel room for some shuteye. By the way, I have to set my alarm for midnight. That's intolerable—but too bad. The problem is my adrenalin levels are so high that the "shuteye" part of the night never happens.

My DC-6A trip is about to happen: N870TA undergoing fueling and loading for my five-leg trip around the West Indies. We will leave first thing the next morning at 1:00 AM.

Bill Winn shows me how to work the comm radios on DC-6A N870TA should I wish to monitor communications. I don't have the heart to tell him that I don't have the proper cables to record cockpit communications into my video camera.

Rear cargo door loading of N870TA eight hours before our morning departure into the pitch blackness of night.

CHAPTER 54

West Indies Odyssey

Damn! I guess I better get ready. The clock says 11:45 PM. I lie there, after tossing and turning for 4 useless hours. The minute and hour hands on the clock seem to be in overdrive without reprieve while I lie there with my brain going a thousand miles per hour. I reluctantly pull myself up, shower, and put on my crew uniform. I go to the lobby where uniformed pilots are standing around, *checking in* after *completing* their trips! I feel like one of them except I'm *checking out*. I pay for a full night just to sit there awake a few hours—it would seem a hotel in this seedy area would have hourly rates, but no such luck.

At 12:30 AM in the tranquil pitch black as pierced by the street and airport lights, I drive the short distance to TAL headquarters, let myself in, and go to the waiting room. Soon I hear some male voices in the small hallway, getting louder. Two uniformed guys walk in, and one of them says, *"Hey, you must be John."* They introduce themselves as flight engineer Geno Gentile, flight and First Officer Edgar Alvarado. Captain Joel Reeves then walks in behind them and introduces himself. Edgar is an Argentine in his forties, and heavy-set Geno, in his late fifties is retired Air Force where he was a flight engineer on the four-engine Boeing B-50 Superfortress bomber in the early 1960s. Captain Reeves, perhaps a little older than the other two (back then 60 years was pilot retirement age under Part 121), is winding down his airline flying career and tells me he's having the best time of his life with the Douglas recips. They go out of the way to make me comfortable and our conversations flow well. We all go to the ramp and I start doing some filming of their preflight activity on the floodlit ramp.

DC-6 N870TA is *stuffed* with full pallets and cargo. There is not a single cubic inch to spare and it feels like we'll never get this thing off the ground. Did they weigh this? Did they balance the load? Yes, but the packed hodgepodge of cargo bay begs these mental questions—I feel like we are going to be a giant flying a anvil if we are lucky enough to get airborne in the first place. It is chilly inside and it reeks of raw seafood. There must be a lot of dry ice in here. We even have a caged Rottweiler dog in our cargo manifest, bound for St. Maarten, as well as sailboat parts, those "live tropical fish," raw textiles, generators, and brand-new Mercury outboard motors. Thankfully it's not a barn load of hogs.

Between the flight deck and cargo spaces, there is a solid protective steel wall with a thin opening for crew entrance and egress, so if we have a sudden impact the cargo won't (hopefully) crush the crew. After preflight, I help load all crew luggage and other items in the tight area around my jumpseat, including all those supplies I bought at Miami Springs. My seat is next to the radio rack behind the flight engineer's folding seat, which is between and just behind the pilot and copilot. I'm packed in my seat and can hardly move. I have to dig out a spot to stand so I can film the flight deck action. For me to get useable video, the crew doesn't require me to be belted in my seat during any flight phase*, including takeoffs and landings.* Yes—against the Part 121 rules. I am usually standing up, unsecured, and prepared to fly through the windscreen in the unlikely event that the brakes are slammed on an aborted takeoff or if we crash land. Rules aside, the

Cargo at one of TAL's staging areas, ready for loading on N670TA for my trip. It looks like the bulk of it is baled raw fabric. The box with "SXM" on it is headed for St. Maarten.

chances of a sudden deceleration event are still extremely low, but this goes to show that minor "corner cutting" can happen anywhere, by anybody, at any time, for any reason.

I film the crew doing their checklists and then the fire-up procedures for the four engines, which go smoothly. With the tape still rolling, I record taxi-out and engine runup at the "runup ramp" near the takeoff end of the runway (these ramps don't exist anymore), after which we taxi into position as the crew barks off final items. We are cleared for takeoff and without hesitation, First Officer Alvarado pours on the coal. I am engulfed in a cauldron of vibrating R-2800 acoustics as I've never experienced, as sweet-smelling exhaust smoke briefly enters the flight deck.

After liftoff, I film through the pilot's windscreen as power is hauled back to "METO" and then "Climb" power. Our initial climb rate is "flat poor" at only 200 feet per minute with this fully loaded aircraft. It seems like we are going to fly "through" and not "over" the magically lit

Sunrise over the Virgin Islands, heading southeast for St. Maarten.

Looking south from the left seat over St. Thomas just after sunrise. We will make a stop there later on this round-robin trip.

Captain Joel Reeves is flying by hand—no autopilot. It is clear I did some filming from the DC-6A's right seat during cruise flight, something the FAA later caught (on my resultant video production) and scolded TAL on.

Captain Reeves uses an early hand-held GPS unit as a navigational cross-check. Yes, that thing is HUGE. Also, the FAA had not yet approved the use of GPS for primary or secondary aircraft navigation—another minor infraction recorded by my camera and brought to TAL's attention by the FAA.

Geno works the throttles during our early morning descent into St. Maarten.

Miami skyline which is approaching fast. I sure was right about the "flying anvil" part. This is all an illusion as we handily clear the skyline, pass over the Florida coast, and into the dark abyss.

We cruise around 11,000 feet. It's a little chilly up here and I am glad I have my jacket. I have a conversation with First Officer Alvarado, who lets me shoot video from his right cockpit seat which is, yes, that's illegal—but Captain Reeves does not object. It is here that Alvarado mentions that he was the captain on a trip of *this very plane*, N870TA, that did a round-robin auto parts trip late last August on behalf of Zantop from Miami to Detroit to St. Louis to Oklahoma City and back to Miami—the one I likely saw overhead two months earlier over Kirkwood. It is also here that Edgar tells me he was in St. Louis around 1987 to "ferry a DC-6 out of there." Here That DC-6 turned out to be the ex-PAT Air N44DG that I photographed at Lambert that April, as well as the first plane assigned to PAT Air's JIT auto parts segment—and the last to leave Lambert (see page210). That was the ferry trip that was being made on behalf of FA Connor involving the emergency stop at Memphis. And the dots just keep connecting—I realize that the DC-6 world is now a small one for sure.

Through the flight deck windscreen, I witness a dramatic sunrise, framed in majestic towering cumulus buildups. Engineer Gentile and I hit it off well, just as I did with flight engineers at SAC. The morning brightens. At our first stop in St. Maarten, we are delayed for two hours as a TAL dispatcher instruct us to wait for a KLM DC10 to arrive from the Netherlands. Our mostly empty freight hold is repacked to the gills with white rolls of raw fabric out of the DC-10's belly, destined for St. Croix, our next stop.

As is typical on TAL's scheduled Duty Free Triangle trips, cargo is heavy on the Miami to St. Maarten leg, then fairly light on the short legs to St. Croix (except this time), St. Thomas, San Juan, and Aguadilla/Borinquen. The trip back to Miami the next morning is normally filled with

As the Dutch fabric rolls are loaded at St. Maarten . . .

. . . as flight engineer Geno Gentile grabs a short rest under the fuselage.

Cargo doors have just opened at St. Croix, ready for the forklifts to unload. Most of the time the crew had to bribe the island ground personnel with cash and rum just to get them started—no exception this time. It usually took Caribbean ground handlers a *long time* to turn a big cargo plane around.

Topping off the wing tanks at St. Croix. The aircraft on the left is civilianized Lockheed P3 Orion (Navy derivative of the L-188 Electra) operated by General Offshore Corporation. They were a private contractor with the U.S. Navy that tested their antisubmarine sonobuoys.

Geno with his trusty dipstick getting ready to "stick" the tanks just after our late afternoon arrival at Borinquen. Now it's time for a few beers and a relaxing dinner at the Cielo Mar Hotel patio bar in Aguadilla, complete with airplane stories and a bright orange sunset.

Baxter Labs pharmaceuticals and finished bluejeans from Wrangler. We arrive at the Borinquen airport just before sunset and the courtesy car takes us to the Cielo Mar Hotel in Aguadilla situated in a large half-moon bay surrounded by lush tropical vegetation. There is an open-air bar/restaurant with a panoramic view of the tropical scenery. Geno and I are the only ones who partake in a few brews (we have nine hours until wheels up) as we all share airplane stories over dinner overlooking they bay. The soothing tropical tree frogs and the beer make me sleepy as I realize I've been up for 36 hours straight. Since we have to get up at 2:30 AM to meet our 4:00 AM departure in the morning, we all turn in early.

In the morning, the four of us seem groggy and sluggish. Our plane is loaded with 15,000 pounds of Vicks Nasal Decongestant from the Baxter Labs manufacturing facility, so we are just over half our load capacity. There are no bluejeans on the manifest this time. One of the engines idles roughly and intermittently backfires after startup due to "wet plugs" Geno clears the plugs, and we depart for Miami in the pitch darkness, arriving there an hour after sunrise. The plane runs like a watch for the entire trip, which the crew says is *rare*. I thank my crew and everyone else at TAL, we say our goodbyes, and I immediately head home with an overnight stop in Macon, Georgia. My treasure chest of billions of priceless magnetic impressions is in tow as I drive north through the southeast through Nashville and across the Ohio River at Paducah, and back to St. Louis.

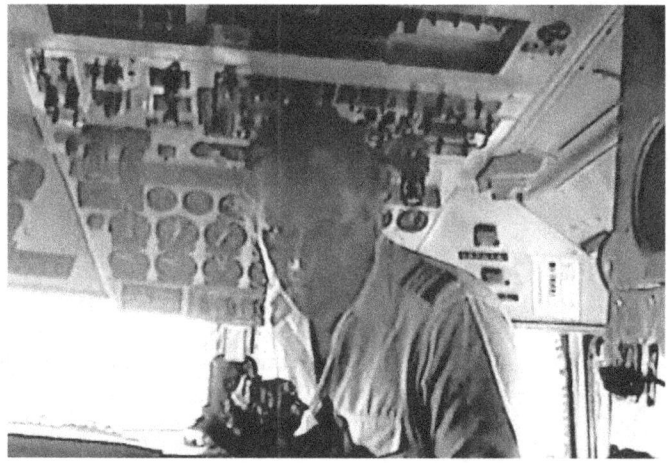

After our 7:30 AM arrival back at TAL headquarters in Miami and completing his shutdown checklist, First Officer Alvarado picks up the trash and is ready to *"take the rest of the day off"* in Captain Reeves' words. It would seem they should always deserve generous time off after a grueling Duty Free Triangle trip—often not the case. For me, I now have to drive over 1,200 miles back to St. Louis in my run-down Subaru wagon—roughly the same distance as our just-completed leg from Puerto Rico—which is easy by comparison.

N879TA rests after taking us on our 2,500-mile round-trip Duty Free Triangle journey. This photo served as the cover illustration on the video case cover for my resultant *DC-6 West Indies Odyssey* video release.

CHAPTER 55

Corrosion Corner Sequel

In late December 1991, I begin fulfilling my first orders for my new video release, *DC-6 West Indies Odyssey*. These are concurrent with when my half-page ad in the January 1991 issue of *Air Classics* magazine hits the stands. The spring issue of *Airliners* magazine with these ads would hit later. Aviation sales outlet *World Transport Press* at Miami International begins placing bulk orders that are refilled monthly. As in our Super Constellation video, we narrate in detail aircraft operations, power settings, speeds, altitudes, fueling, weights, cargo carried, etc. along with comprehensive details on TAL's overall operations and destinations. Video sales are brisk and I am happy.

Our audience is similar to that of *Flight of the Super Constellation*, consisting not only of current and former airline pilots, crews, and vintage airline enthusiasts but also current-day Caribbean cargo crews. I receive hundreds of "fan letters" that verify this audience mix. Because Karen was gainfully employed, I had long since postponed my job search to see where Regulus Productions leads. Over time she becomes increasingly irritated as I could be earning more money in the finance world, and this is understandably causing her to lose interest in joining me at airshows and other aviation activities.

I sell at cost many copies of the DC-6 video to TAL, which uses the video as promotional tools for their employees, customers, and remote station personnel. I write a letter of appreciation to Gary Balnicki commenting on my positive impressions of TAL and their enthusiastic employees who put their best foot forward for me. However, privately I know damn well that their employee morale is in the pits, but my letter is a reflection of my true experience. He frames and mounts my letter on the waiting lounge wall.

Because I borrowed some vintage Douglas Aircraft photos from Harry Gann, Historical Curator at McDonnell-Douglas Aircraft in Long Beach, he wants a copy of my video too. He passes it on to their obsolete aircraft support group which uses it for the orientation of new employees in that department. More air magazines do reviews on both our videos, including *Air Progress, Airliners,* and *Fine Scale Modeler*. Some of the reviews are unsolicited and almost all give them the equivalent of "five stars."

I figure I need to stay on the crest of this wave and do another TAL video ASAP. This time it will logically focus on their DC-7CF. After all, it is the last DC-7 in Part 121 scheduled and supplemental airline service and who knows for how long (about four others linger under Part 129 or as firebombers operating under Part 91). Gary Balnicki and Bill Winn are "all in" on doing a DC-7C project, and Bill keeps an eye on DC-7C scheduling for me. But now in January, it's down for a few weeks on a periodic "C" check.

Bill Winn tells me that their local FAA office got their hands on one of my video copies and saw something like 16 operational violations for which TAL should be cited (they weren't, however). These included things like not having a spotter with a fire extinguisher on startups (to put out "stack fires" that sometimes erupt); having a videographer illegally filming from the first

Trans-Air-Link (TAL) DC-7C freighter N869TA being readied for a 1:00 AM departure to the islands in March 1992, at the eastern edge of Corrosion Corner. Doug Teel came along with me for the ride to help me with the video work—this DC-7C had two jump seats. Recall that Doug is the guy who got us onto the ATS (former Mark Aero) apron to photograph "Apron Queen" DC-7C N9251. Now, 8 years later, we're hitching a ride on the very last one in airline service. (see Chapter 44).

officer's right seat during a Part 121 operation (a big "no-no"); classifying a videographer "required" crew; the captain's "unapproved use" of GPS as backup navigation; and of course, me standing up with no restraints during takeoffs and landings (there was just *no other way*). The FAA told Bill that I cannot do any more "operational videos" with TAL, especially since I'm not a "required" crewman. However, TAL and the FAA had such an otherwise good and positive rapport that Bill jokingly thumbs his nose at them. *"Yes he is going to do another video with us, so be sure to pop in for a ramp check when he gets here."* Bill knows full well that the FAA knows neither the time nor the place—well, maybe "the place," but certainly not "the time."

I knew from my first trip that DC-7CF N869TA had two adjoining jump seats and Bill said I could bring an assistant if both seats were open on the strip—so we'll just have a "required" crew of "two loadmasters." Doug Teel had just returned to St. Louis after working the previous 4 years in North Carolina so I asked if he wanted to go with me. You know his answer. Recall that was the one who helped me photograph the DC-7C apron queen on the ATS/former Mark Aero tarmac 8 years earlier, so he would not turn down a trip opportunity on the very last one in U.S. service. On a Monday afternoon in March 1992, Bill calls to tell me the DC-7CF is scheduled for a charter for Kingston Jamaica early this upcoming Thursday morning. Doug and I pack up, jump into my little Honda Civic, and head for Miami—we are both on "budgets" and have lapsed pilot certificates so we have to drive.

N869TA became the last DC-7C to see any airline service, be it passenger, freight, charter, or scheduled. Only several weeks after this photo was taken in March 1992, an active Part 129 Dominican DC-7C exploded on the Corrosion Corner ramp due to a lack of proper grounding during refueling. In the past, this Dominican operator had crashed a few other DC-7s. Nobody was killed this time but that again goes to show you that the *Tiger* can rip into you even when sitting on the ground. TAL's president Gary Balnicki called me on another matter after the explosion and commented that he now had the most valuable DC-7 in the world because of those guys! Five months after this photo was taken the open hangar in the background was destroyed by Hurricane Andrew. DC-8 operator Arrow Air operated from there (see DC-8 jetliner tails at the far left).

Our flight is being loaded to its full 35,000-pound cargo capacity at TAL headquarters.

We arrive at the TAL facilities on Wednesday afternoon. The first thing we see is the DC-7CF being moved with a tow. It looks like the plane is going to leave without us! It wasn't—it was just the normal juggling of equipment on the ramp. But we do find that the trip to Jamaica has been canceled. *Great!* We catch up with Bill who is his usual cheerful self and tells us not to worry. The three of us grab a late lunch at Bryson's across the street, and Bill tells us that -9TA has now been scheduled for the "Duty Free Triangle" trip—St. Maarten—St. Croix—St. Thomas—San Juan—Aguadilla/Borinquen, leaving 7 hours from now at 1:00 AM Thursday. Heck—a repeat of my grueling DC-6 trip last September! I'm not looking forward to no sleep again, but we grab the opportunity. As it turned out, this trip would prove to be anything but a "repeat."

Guy Cottington has us sign our waivers. It seems he is not in a good mood today and it appears were it his choice, he wouldn't let us go. As the sun sets, we head for a Holiday Inn near the northeast corner of the airport so we can find a place to "not sleep" again. Even though we could see this hotel in the dark from a distance, we had a hell of a time figuring out how to drive our way around all the tall chain link fences to get there. Finally, we stop the car on the side of the road and I scale several chain-link fences until there's nothing between me and the hotel, and then I backtrack around the chain-link maze back *out* to our car to memorize the way back *in*. That crazy idea works, and we uncomfortably lie awake in the hotel for three hours.

We get into our pressed flight uniforms and go back to the TAL pilot's lounge. Our captain is Jacques Magnin, and we have a woman first officer, Ky Adedeji. Jacques is a Swiss National and Ky grew up within an African mission family. The flight engineer is George Alvarez, a Cuban American. Our flight is packed to its full 35,000-pound capacity and this crew is as personable and welcoming as the DC-6 crew was last September.

Unlike the DC-6 trip, from start to finish this trip is plagued with mechanical issues.

Fueling the #2 saddle tank with 100LL avgas.

Remember, this is a DC-7, not a DC-6. The first problem is during our initial runup at Miami when one of the power recovery turbines (PRTs) begins making a funny popping sound. It is eerie, even scary in the dim cockpit lighting, and the crew is adamant they *never heard this noise before*, knowing that PRTs have a well-earned reputation for catching on fire. I see concerned looks on their dimly illuminated faces. Captain Magnin whispers to Flight Engineer Alvarez, *"What do you think?" "I don't know!"* is the reply. They all three mumble a bit longer, and I can almost see the question marks popping out of their heads. George runs that engine up a few more times and the noise lessens, so takeoff is initiated with all trigger fingers ready for an abort if the sound does not *stop* before the V1 takeoff commitment speed. The noise goes away in time and is not heard again—at least on this trip.

Funny noise or not, this takeoff is still unnerving because I know that with a fully-loaded plane, this DC-7's engines begin overheating after only *60 seconds* of max power, so we have to get to our cut to METO power ASAP. One problem—this loaded DC-7C has a funny quirk—after rotation, it *always* remains stuck just a few feet above the runway, held down by ground effect until it's "good and ready" to break loose on its own damn schedule. It does break loose, but long after the east end of our 10,000-foot runway comes into view.

The first leg cruise flight is uneventful and at the St. Maarten airport patio Ky tells me that PRTs are known for making strange, but harmless noises at times. As we all sip orange juice and coffee, Doug queries Captain Magnin about the reliability of the DC-7C on long trips like this. Jacques casually replies, *"Actually the reliability is good—except for hydraulics and fire."* That proves to be a premonition—we will "flirt" with both of those issues before this trip is over.

DC-7CF Captain Jacques Magnin is drenched in a blinding sunrise at about 200 miles inbound to St. Maarten.

First Officer Adedeji barks out the numbers as Flight Engineer Alvarez looks on.

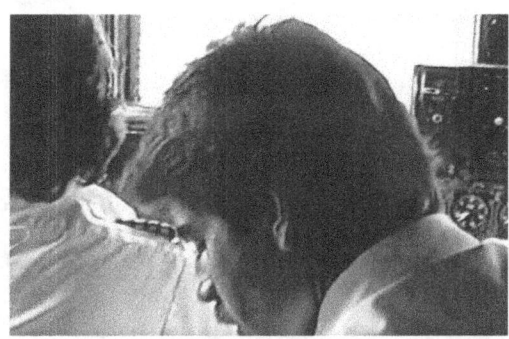

Flight Engineer George Alvarez.

After our cargo transfers at St. Maarten, St. Croix, and St. Thomas, we fly into San Juan in a low overcast. Just after the shutdown, Jacques gets a funny look on his face as he begins flipping switches back and forth on the pedestal. He barks, *"We're stuck. We ain't goin' anywhere."* I suddenly feel like we are sitting inside a 60-ton piece of junk. The master prop governor synchronizer on the number three engine had failed so the props will not automatically synchronize (match RPMs) in flight. It can be done manually, but that's complex, distracting, and somewhat dangerous in a big complicated heavy-recip, so you need an operable auto-synch as your primary. Another master synchronizer is kept in the aircraft belly "fly away kit." Located on top of the nose case of the number 3 engine, George changes out the master. After the loudest full-RPM runups I'd ever experienced, it's determined that everything works. During these runups, the engine spews the longest flame tongues I'd ever seen out of its three equally-spaced PRT exhaust ports. No wonder the original airline guys called the R-3350 Turbo-Compound a "Demon from Hades." George is an A&P so he can sign off on his own work when out in the field. We leave for Borinquen in the pitch dark, five hours late.

As we settle into cruise flight, there's another problem while we are mostly in the soup (that is, flying blind in the solid overcast). Hydraulics pressure falls to near zero. Jacques slows the plane down and uses most of the residual pressure to successfully lower the landing gear. We are speeding in and out of thick clouds at night which gives me mild bouts of disorientation as the gear *very slowly* extends. Whatever hydraulic pressure is left is needed for control boost, and some control inputs are getting harder. Jacques calls for us to prepare for a no-flap landing with "no reverse." The touchdown and rollout are normal. It is now late at night and I haven't slept in 40 hours, and am more fatigued than I can ever remember.

On the Borinquen ramp, George tears into the hydraulic manifold, accomplishing little other than spilling nasty Skydrol hydraulic fluid all over his hands, burning his skin. Originally, propliners didn't use this nasty stuff as it was designed for jets, but now it is often substituted. During all this, I become preoccupied with an extremely rare Tradewinds Canadair CL-44 four-engine turboprop freighter parked next to us, also experiencing problems. Its crew tells me they're having both hydraulic and electrical issues, so they will be here for a while too. Through its windscreen I see one of their crew inside the dimly lit flight deck, flipping overhead switches and shaking his head in frustration. At least we're not alone. They're trying to haul a load of Wrangler jeans to their headquarters in North Carolina. Like the DC-7C, this is the last "stock" CL-44 freighter in revenue airline service—though a single modified "guppy" version for outsized cargo

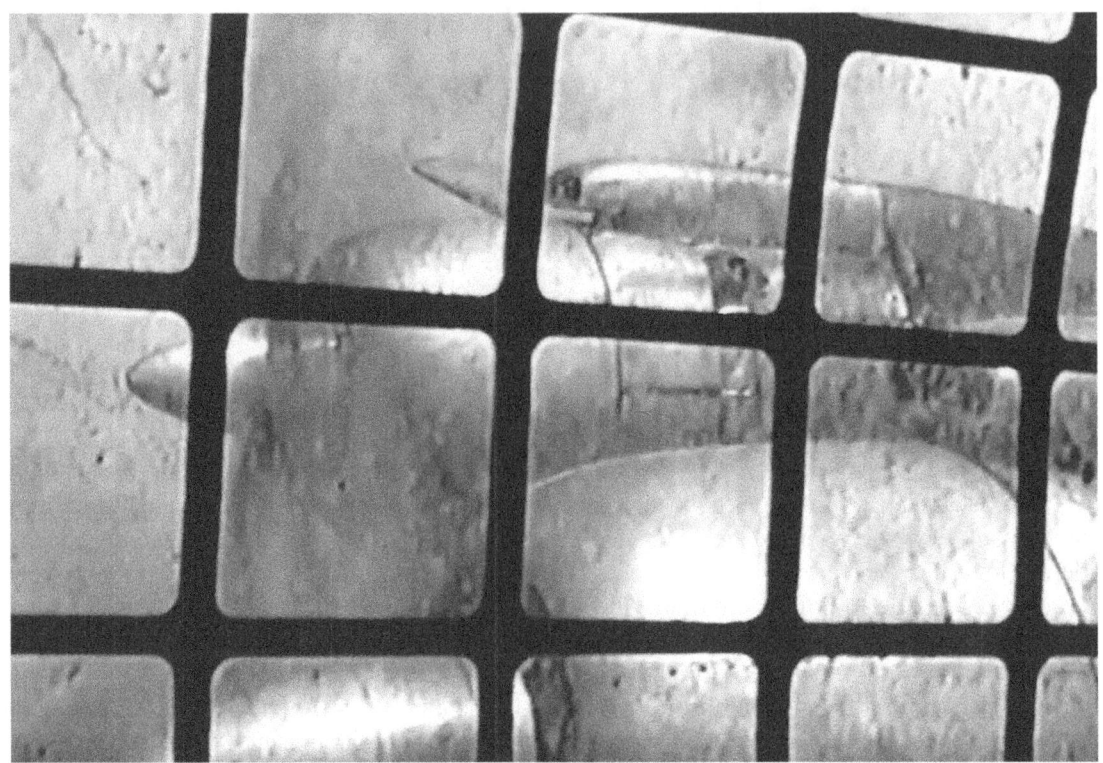

Numbers 3 and 4 doing their jobs somewhere over the ocean between St. Thomas and San Juan. R-3350 Turbo-Compounds could not even take the slightest abuse by crews. One such abuse event could turn one of these engines into a time bomb that could eventually result in total disaster. As discussed in Chapter 18, a DC-7C like this one is what baseball legend Roberto Clemente died in. Also, from this photo, it is obvious that there is no point in replacing crazed windows on these old freighters.

would continue to make isolated ad hoc cargo flights over the next decade. But for now, our exhausted crew pauses and decides to tackle our problem in the morning. We all pile in a courtesy car and head for the hotel.

Shortly after sunrise the next morning, we go back to the airport for a quick breakfast near the American Airlines gates. Then we head out onto the ramp. It is clear and a little cool, and the CL-44 is gone—they made it out. George isolates our problem. It's a decayed O-ring in the hydraulic manifold. While it is a common ring size, it is a "special" or nonstandard "square" profile, not the normal "round" one. We don't have one in our flyaway kit and can't find one anywhere else at the airport. My attention is drawn to an Arrow Air stretched DC-8-63 on landing rollout with engines in full, screaming reverse. It pulls up in front of us and shuts down. Jacques and George approach the DC-8 captain and ask if they can check their flyaway kit. He permits them to search and they find the right size, but with the standard "round" profile. George says we can improvise with this ring for *one flight leg* and he, with the help of Doug Teel, install it.

After several runups, the problem is deemed solved—George signs us off and without further incident, we depart Borinquen for Miami, full of cargo but *ten hours late*. It is a bright, sunny, satisfying trip back over the blue ocean until I spot a mist coming out of the number four engine. I call George back and he confirms number four is "pissing fuel." The R-3350 is one of

Engineer George Alvarez shows me the pitted O-ring that causes our hydraulics failure in the DC-7CF. It is a special "square' profile that we did not have in our "fly away" kit and we could not find one anywhere at the airport. George's hands had been scorched by the nasty "Skydrol" hydraulic fluid that is used by most airlines today.

the few big radials that are fuel-injected and this one seems to have a leaky injector. While unlikely, this could cause one of those dreaded fuel fires that are nearly impossible to extinguish. However, we are past the point of no return and an engine shutdown with our full load would put additional stress on the three good engines so we press on and make it back to Miami mid-afternoon without incident. Just after we shut down and exit the plane a TAL DC-6 pulls up and two of my old friends Edgar Alvarado and Geno Gentile come down the ladder. We have a great reunion right there on the ramp. They had just completed a round-trip to Honduras with a load of pigs. Geno tells me these were *"the best-behaved pigs he'd ever seen—they slept the whole way!"* So ended my DC-7C trip with Doug Teel. The *Tiger* growled at us this time—but at least our crew kept it in check.

The resultant video, *DC-7C: The Seven Seas Solution* is released in September 1991 and it does well. *World Transport Press* again gives me big orders. John Wegg, editor of *Airliners* magazine writes an unsolicited positive review in the magazine on this video. I get compliments and phone calls from historical aviation journalists such as Lockheed Constellation expert Peter Marson, and other known aviation journalists such as Len Morgan and Nick Veronico. Crews from other Corrosion Corner operators contact me to exchange information and share experiences. Former Pan Am transpacific crews from the 1950s and '60s call to "thank" me for capturing some of history that will soon be irretrievable.

George and Jacques haul our step ladder over to the Arrow Air DC-8-63 freighter. They get permission from its captain to search their "fly away" kit for the O-ring we need. They find the right size, but with the "standard" round profile, not the "special" square one we need. George says it will work--at least it can get us back to Miami.

Doug Teel, with his foot on the ladder, assists George Alvarez who is bracing himself on the right arm of the ladder in front of the right main gear wheels, as the number two engine is run up. This is to provide hydraulic pressure to the manifold they're working on. Success! We get pressure. The improvised O-ring substitution should hold for our last leg to Miami where a permanent fix is made back at TAL's facilities.

In this video production, I focus more on techno-historical aspects of the DC-7C rather than TAL operations as I did in the DC-6 production. Because of this different theme, Gary Balnicki was not as enthusiastic about this video as he was with *DC-6 West Indies Odyssey*, so he did not order copies for promotional purposes. I understood and sure had no problem with that.

Gary then leveled with me. *"This place has been for sale for a year and I've retained a broker, and if you or anyone you know is interested in a turn-key, going-concern operation, I'm ready to talk."* It is clear he is getting burned out—I think about the irony that the same TAL that puts me in "heaven" keeps Gary in "hell." I am surprised he considered me a potential buyer for a heavy-recip airline, but that idea scares the hell out of me. An otherwise qualified buyer remains elusive. For a couple of years, I stay in touch with Bill Winn and in one conversation I tell him that Karen and I are going on a vacation to Greece. He asks me if I can make a side trip to Cyprus to report on the external condition of an intact DC-6 that had been sitting at that airport for years. TAL will cover my expenses and then some. I say I will try, but ultimately our schedule with our traveling friends did not allow it, and Cyprus is still quite a distance from Athens anyway.

TAL sold its DC-6s and DC-7C during the second half of the 1990s, replacing them with turboprop Convair 580s and an L-188 Electra, both using the same 3,750 shp GM Allison turboprops. The DC-7C went to work with someone in Africa just to run out its hours. It was last reported as a stripped and faded engineless hulk, engulfed in tall weeds somewhere in West Africa.

By the late 1990s the residual propliner freight operations, including TAL, were exiled by Dade County to nearby Opa-locka just to the north. Here, the propliner population rapidly dwindled to almost nothing. All the intrigue, adventure, sweat, oil, grease, engine fires, daily mechanical delays, renegade cowboy pilots, and piles of propliner junk that go with it all are gone forever. They are replaced with the endgame of mundane *sameness*. In December 2001, TAL had its first and only major accident where a not-too-smart crew allowed one of its Convair 580s to suck its tanks dry forcing them to ditch in a shallow area just off of the Ft. Lauderdale beaches. Luckily, the crew walked away unscathed and the plane washed ashore with the tide and was scrapped on site. TAL was sold to an individual in 2003 but ceased operation shortly thereafter due to multiple, irreconcilable FAA violations.

With the bulldozing and redevelopment of the Corrosion Corner premises in the late 1990s, its cargoes moved into larger converted commuter turboprops and Convair 580s, and into the bellies of MD-80s, 737s, 757s, and 767s as well as into dedicated jet freighters. As an example, ABX Air out of Cincinnati, Ohio, which flies domestically for DHL, handles some of these Caribbean freight routes with a single, dedicated Boeing 767-200 freighter (see photo page 218). Today, it even flies TAL's old DC-7C cargo route to Jamaica on behalf of TAL's old customer, Air Jamaica. ABX indirectly traces right back to Mark Morris and DHL. In the early 2000s, DHL absorbed Airborne Express, spinning off that air operation which went public as ABX. DHL was later acquired by Deutsche Post of Germany. Foreign carriers are not allowed to operate domestic U.S. flights, so those domestic DHL flight operations have been contracted out to ABX ever since.

During the year after my DC-7C trip, I produce two other propliner videos using much of the unpublished raw footage that I had previously taken at EAA AirVenture Oshkosh, other airshows, and museums. These have a mediocre reception. By early 1994 I'm experiencing diminishing returns and I need more product. I don't want to spend time or the money to go to Alaska or the Yukon Territories to do more raw footage, and I feel as though my in-depth work with SAC, Corrosion Corner, and TAL was a lifetime windfall that would be hard to top. Mission accomplished—history preserved. Karen is getting tired of our eating out on the first day of the month only to hear me say *this blows our restaurant budget for the rest of the month*. It's clear I have to re-enter the "real job" market, so I'm able to secure one in April as an Assistant Vice President at Boatmen's Trust in its Special Assets unit—the beginning of a long fiduciary and business consulting phase of my career over the next quarter century—and where along the way I became an advisory board member to ATS. My resumed "normal" career path in consulting takes up most of my time and there are no vintage propliners left to distract me anyway. By default, I'm dormant on the topic over those decades, with a few abrupt, if not surprising interruptions.

In April 2008, Karen and I pass through Miami International Airport on our way home from vacationing in the Turks and Caicos Islands. We have a three-hour layover and we spend most of that in the bar before going to our boarding gate. At the gate, a panoramic window faces northwest, so I can see where Corrosion Corner used to be. It is now a few square miles of what looks like freshly-poured, off-white tarmac, with some modern hangars spaced far apart, and a big new distribution warehouse. Three or four spanking clean MD-11 and 747 wide-body freighters sit there in a neat row, including an MD-11 and two 747s, all freighters—and everything looks just as clean, modern, tidy, and sterile. I also spot three shiny 40-year-old Convair 580 freighters that look like they just came out of the conversion shops just recently—not 40 years ago when they actually did. I know this much, TAL isn't flying them now, but someone else is. . .

I recently looked up TAL's former address, 3501 NW 62nd Avenue on Google Earth. That real estate is now a *huge* FedEx freight and ship center and accompanying parking lot, all covering several hundred thousand square feet. On the west side of the street is an apron where those Convair 580s I saw back in 2008 are *still parked*, almost 15 years after first seeing them. And further west—where the old customs facilities were—is a similarly *huge* UPS facility. This is in stark contrast to what I once knew this area to be. A *political wind* had blown the eye of the *Second Wind* off the face of the earth. Yes, Dade County had *finally* won the war.

This March 1992 scene at St. Maarten represents one of my very last images in the heavy-recip realm—and the continuation of the wind down one of the longest chapters in my life. It's fitting that this last look involves the last DC-7C in airline service—an aircraft that was introduced as the state-of-the-art long-range ocean-spanning airliner only months after I showed up on this planet.

CHAPTER 56

"Porky Pete"

On a muggy, high overcast early evening in July 1995, I'm mulling around the Kirkwood Methodist Church parking lot, sweating through my suit and tie, waiting for Karen and her side of our extended family to empty the building after my sister-in-law's wedding rehearsal. I'm hungry and am only thinking about rehearsal dinner food and booze at Sunset 44 in downtown Kirkwood. Propliners had been in the background of my realm of existence for nearly 3 years—though spare change still trickles in from residual Regulus videotape sales. Suddenly I sense a deep thundering of a heavy-recip. It rumbles the *entire* sky like a low DC-4 and is coming toward me, *fast*. I had not experienced this in ages, and now I seem to be traveling back in time.

I look through the trees to the northeast and it registers that I am witnessing one of the most unusual overflights I would ever see. Through the trees is the silhouette of four-engine Aviation Traders ATL-98 Carvair, (a radical DC-4/C-54 conversion) climbing low overhead, heading southeast. I am now witnessing the *rarest* of propliners—even for the "back in time" days. I'd thought that the last few out of only 21 of these Carvairs built in the early 1960s had been long grounded or scrapped. Then it comes into clear view—yep, that's what it is—it looks like a 747 with propellers. What is one of these doing in St. Louis—in 1995? In due course, I learn it was N83FA, nicknamed *"Porky Pete"* by its original operator, and was the only airworthy Carvair in the world on this date. It was the 5th Carvair built and was now being operated by Custom Air Services out of Griffin, Georgia. The only other airworthy-capable Carvair is also operated by Custom Air. That is sistership N89FA called *"Fat Annie,"* which is not airworthy just now. It is parked at Griffin undergoing an extended airframe and powerplant overhaul.

All Carvairs were built in the U.K. A better word is "remanufactured." The brainchild of engineer and airline mogul Sir Freddie Laker, the Carvair was a major modification of the Douglas DC-4/C-54 and is powered by the same 14-cylinder, 1,450 horsepower Pratt & Whitney R-2000 engines that first appeared on the original planes by late World War II. As explained earlier, the R-2000 (see photo on page 42) was that scaled-up version of its ubiquitous R-1830 engine which powered the DC-3 and C-47, and the B-24 Liberator. The Carvair had a lengthened fuselage and an enlarged, squared-off tail that looked similar to that of the Douglas DC-7C. The forward fuselage bulged with an upper level that housed the flight deck, just like the Boeing 747. This allowed the full length of the fuselage as cargo capacity, and allowed for a large nose-entry cargo door that provided for direct frontal loading of oversized cargo. Standard DC-4s and other propliners could not do this because of their awkward side-loading doors.

One of the Carvairs is featured in the 1964 James Bond movie *Goldfinger* where bad guy Goldfinger uses one to transport his fancy yellow and black Rolls-Royce automobile along with his entourage. Laker designed the Carvair to ferry automobiles over the English Channel with greater ease, with their drivers and passengers seated in the rear fuselage behind the cars. British Air Ferries (BAF) was the largest initial operator of the Carvair, but the ferry operations always lost money and the Carvairs actually spent most of their decades with second-hand users in ad hoc

I built these two replicas that are in scale. They illustrate the differences between the ATL-98 Carvair (left) and the stock DC-4/C-54 on which the Carvair was based. Note that the Carvair's nose comprises its large main cargo door and the unobstructed cargo space under the raised flight deck. The C-54 like most other propliners has to load at an awkward angle through a side cargo door which is difficult to see here at the "Stars and Bars" marking on the aft fuselage. The maximum length of a piece of cargo that can enter the standard C-54 freight entrance is limited by the shape and width of the cargo, coupled with the awkward loading angle. This Carvair, British registered G-ADFW, is in original operator British Air Ferries markings who nicknamed it "Big John." It was the 12th Carvair built and it was scrapped in 1983.

cargo service all over the world because of their versatile cargo capabilities.

I find out that Carvair N83FA *Porky Pete* had been to St. Louis many times, mostly recently in the early- to mid-1990s. It first visited Lambert-St. Louis on September 21, 1979, for a fuel stop during an ownership-transfer ferry trip from the U.K. after being purchased by Falcon Airways of Addison, Texas. The young right seater on this transoceanic trip was the now well-known warbird demonstration and unlimited race pilot Stewart "Stu" Dawson. On that trip, *Porky Pete* sprung a bad oil leak in the number-three engine midway over the Atlantic and began losing altitude, requiring an unscheduled stop in Greenland. They barely made it. While there it was reported that the crew almost got beat up in a bar skirmish because they were simply talking to a local girl.

The next day an attempt was made to fix the leak and they continued the flight when the same problem arose again. The plane barely held altitude over the rough seas before successfully reaching Goose Bay Labrador where the oil leak was finally remedied. The flight stopped Lambert a day later while I was flying around that vicinity on a training flight, but I did not see it. Like Convair 240 operator Sundance in St. Louis, Falcon was a typical under-utilized and under-funded, *Second Wind* era heavy-recip operator that did not last long, making only a few revenue flights. *Porky Pete* sat in Texas and then had a sporadic stint in Alaska over the next few years before finding its way to Custom Air Services in October 1985.

Custom Air, a one-man show, was founded that same year. Their certificate was limited to a Part 125 ad hoc cargo carrier only, which was that "extension" of Part 91 for large aircraft. While they worked with freight forwarders like Emery while flying occasional emergency charters

ATL-98 Carvair N80FA, sistership with N83FA when they were both operated by Falcon Airways hauling cargo out of Texas. When I saw sistership N83FA overhead in July 1995 it had this same paint scheme, though faded, and without titles except for the word "Cargo" on the tail. N80FA is the 7th Carvair built. It passed through two previous nicknames while flying with earlier operator British Air Ferries: *"Big Louie"* and *"Plane Jane."* This *is the plane* that appeared in the 1963 James Bond movie *Goldfinger.* In 1997 it crash-landed in Alaska after suffering an engine fire. The plane was destroyed but fortunately, the crew walked away. (Wikimedia Commons, Richard Vandervord CC BY-SA 4.0)

hauling jet engines and other components for the airlines, their meat and potatoes was the "on-call" JIT automotive component business, just like PAT Air, Zantop, and Trans Continental—but nearly a decade later! Most of Custom Air's ad hoc jobs were "handshake only" with no written contract—a true "bottom-feeder" operation like Universal Airlines.

One of Custom Air's regular runs was the Americus Georgia to St. Louis for the big three automakers that lasted just past the mid-1990s. By 1995 when I caught Carvair N83FA overhead, the GM Goodfellow Corvette assembly plant had since been the first to leave St. Louis —for Bowling Green, Kentucky—leaving three plants remaining there. In just a few years, two of those would be shut down too—the Ford and Chrysler plants— leaving only the GM Wentzville plant. It is also clear that the logistical patterns of the automotive industry had since begun to disburse away from the traditional Detroit hub, with the opening of both assembly and subassembly plants in "right-to-work" states in the south, particularly by non-U.S. auto manufacturers such as Toyota, Nissan, BMW, Volkswagen, and others.

The overflight I witnessed that hot July evening in 1995 was confirmed to be *"Porky Pete"* as it was the only airworthy one in the world on that particular date as mentioned. It was probably being flown by lead Captain Larry Whittington and lead First Officer Ralph Josey back to their small, uncontrolled airport headquarters at Griffin after an Americus to St. Louis auto parts run. They were both high-time heavy- recip pilots, but for some reason, Josey always wanted to fly as the first officer and not as a captain. He was checked out as first officer on the DC-4, DC-6, and others, but possibly not type-rated in them to fly as captain. For nearly the next two years after my sighting, *Porky Pete* would continue to serve the St. Louis auto assembly market, though I never saw it again. So, this July day in 1995 would become my last 4- engine heavy-recip sighting in St. Louis that was tied to the JIT automotive realm.

At least one former employee of Custom Air has maintained that the company was lax in a few areas—particularly with procedures and checklists. By now it should be clear that it would be hard to pinpoint a single *Second Wind* heavy-recip operator that is, or was, 100% snow white. Just after midnight on April 3, 1997, Wittington and Josey entered the flight deck of *Porky Pete* at the quiet Griffin Airport. Just the day before the two had returned to Griffin in the plane from a St. Louis auto run. They were now departing empty on the 3,700-foot Runway 14 on a short hop to Americus, Georgia to pick up auto parts bound for Rockford, Illinois. Max takeoff power was applied, but more than halfway down the runway the pilots slammed on the brakes and the plane skidded from side to side, never coming off full throttle. There was a downhill embankment at the end of the runway and a retail strip center across a boulevard at the bottom. *Porky Pete* careened over the embankment and smashed into a grocery store in a strip center, instantly killing Wittington and Josey and destroying the aircraft in a ball of fire.

These two qualified professionals with thousands of flight hours had forgotten to remove the elevator control gust lock pin behind them when going through their pre-takeoff checklist—assuming they did their checklist in the first place. When they realized this during the takeoff roll, they kept on the power *while awkwardly twisting their bodies trying to remove the lock*, only to slam and hold the brakes when they realized it was way too late. The *Tiger* wins again, and from here Custom Air fades into history. We again ask the eternal question that repeatedly pops up in the heavy-recip world: *What else can go wrong?*

This is a bad ending tied to an otherwise memorable propliner sighting two years earlier. Now, the only remaining airworthy Carvair after the 1997 crash is N89FA *Fat Annie*, still sitting there in pieces at Griffon. It would not stay there in that condition forever. As chance would have it, I would have a "carbon-copy" experience in Kirkwood with *that* airplane too, the "new" only airworthy one, exactly *one decade later*.

CHAPTER 57

The Notables

Unlike me and my impulsive side adventures, the Morrises needed *good relationships* with prominent people for their basic economic survival. These included those already introduced earlier such as Edgar M. Queeny, Bob Werner, Howard Hughes, Ed Crane, Herb Kelleher, and John Tucker—not to mention the mover and shaker bureaucrats at the Lambert airport authority and the City of St. Louis mayor's office. That hardly scratched the surface.

John Tucker, St. Louis Mayor Tucker's son, was a U.S. Marine pilot in the same unit as astronaut Pete Conrad (the third man to walk on the moon) and Ed McMahon (you know, Johnny Carson's sidekick). Mark often partied with them as part of this ex-Marine airman "Good Ole Boys Club," even though he was an ex-Air America pilot and not a Marine. Also, Gene Cernan (Navy man and last man on the moon) was a "participating member." All were "hot" pilots. These impromptu long-weekend gatherings occurred in St. Louis, Los Angeles, and anywhere in between. Ex-Navy pilot Jim Holton, the banker, and insurance provider for the Morris's businesses (and in the early days one of the owners of Interstate Airmotive) often joined in.

Years back, John Tucker told me about these gatherings and said that Pete Conrad's favorite St. Louis restaurant was Dominic's on the Hill (the historic St. Louis Italian community), so these get-togethers often started with drinks and dinner there. The gatherings sometimes morphed into "mixed—then wild" affairs. Yes, this was a group of big-time ex-Marines and egotistical pilots no less—nothing ever changes from that perspective, even these days.

Pete Conrad (NASA)

Ed McMahon (Wikimedia Commons, Christa Chapman CC BY 3.0)

Joe and Mark had frequent dinners with James S. McDonnell and his son John, the aeronautical titans that ran McDonnell-Douglas as founded by James S., along with John's cousin Sandy. Mark was particularly close to John, the last CEO before the Boeing takeover in the 1990s. John—a very bright and philanthropic leader in the tradition of the McDonnell family—looked like a young, bearded college professor, not an aerospace titan. Mark relates the following regarding one of his dinners with John's dad, McDonnell Aircraft founder James S. McDonnell:

My dad was very close to James McDonnell. I was closer to John McDonnell after he took the helm from his cousin Sandy. I had a few dinners with both of them. I remember one dinner with James S. just after the 1979 fatal DC-10 crash at Chicago O'Hare that wiped out hundreds. There, he told me he should never have acquired Douglas Aircraft. He also told me that he and my dad were working on purchasing American Airlines [this was plausible after deregulation]*, and he was going to have my dad run it. I never knew that until James S. "Mr. Mac" told me that story at dinner.*

James S. McDonnell—Founder of McDonnell Aircraft and close friend and confidant of both Joe and Mark Morris. (Wikimedia Commons, Fair Use)

And before that, there was Howard Hughes, who liked Joe Morris from the beginning. Joe said that Howard repeatedly told him he hated the nickname "Spruce Goose" for his H-4 Hercules seaplane and that he would like to strangle the guy who came up with that silly name that stuck with the public. As previously discussed, in the mid-1960s Howard rescued the Morris family from the St. Louis mob. Mark relates his dad's premonitions about Howard Hughes:

My dad told me many times that it was after his [Hughes'] *big crash in the XF-11* [one of his twin-engine, twin-boom WWII reconnaissance plane prototypes, R-4360 powered] *that he started with big-time pain pills. He was always a bit eccentric, certainly like Larry Hillblom who at DHL was my boss via his ownership of DHL. Dad noticed that after 25 years* [of knowing] *Hughes was* [his] *getting completely paranoid with lots of psychotic breaks. Me - I spent a few minutes with him* [Hughes] *when he came to our house and I*

Howard Hughes on the cover of TIME Magazine, July 19, 1948 when he was the controlling shareholder of TWA. Behind him is an illustration of the eight-engine H-4 Hercules seaplane "Spruce Goose" that Joe Morris worked with him on. Hughes flew it only once which occurred in November 1947—only a few feet above the water for a short distance—then stored it forever. It is now on public display at the Evergreen Aviation & Space Museum in McMinnville, Oregon. I saw it from the highway through the museum's impressive panoramic window while there on a 2002 business trip. Hughes greatly respected Joe Morris, and in the mid-1960s rescued him from the St. Louis mob (see Chapter 6). (Wikimedia Commons, Time, Inc., Ernest Hamlin Baker)

was impressed with his smile and he looked right at me . . . decades later, except for the movie business, I sometimes thought of myself as doing a few of the same things as Hughes did with airlines, oil business, and test pilots, but yes, on a comparatively small scale.

Mark Morris tells a Vietnam-era story when in 1970 he was flying an unmarked C-47 for the CIA's Air America. He was doing around 90 knots on a long final approach with a full load to Clark Air Base in the Philippines after being vectored in front of a smokey U.S. Air Force F4 Phantom II which was much farther out on a much faster-moving final, perhaps at 150 knots. The F4 screamed right over the top of Mark's C-47 at a high throttle setting, emitting a ton of violent smoke and kerosene fumes that filled his flight deck, almost incapacitating him. After Mark landed he cornered the F4 pilot and verbally laid into him, telling the fighter pilot that he didn't appreciate being smoked by some f**k'n fighter jock. The F4 pilot in turn said, *"Yeah, been airborne for a long time trying to get over here – I'll buy you a drink."* Mark replied, *"You'll buy me more than one..."*

They went to the bar at the Officer's Club and got a table. Noting that Mark's copilot was an *ex*-Air Force major and not a *current* one, the F4 pilot told Mark, *"You don't act, look, or talk like an Army guy – who are you really with?"* Morris said, *"Well, I'm not into saluting..."* The pilot got the drift. We should mention that an Air America pilot was required to *not disclose*—and otherwise *deny completely*—for whom he was flying. It turns out that one of the F4 jock's sons was missing on patrol in Vietnam (later found to be OK), and so Mark's new beer buddy had to get there *now.*

The "smoking" of Mark's C-47 was an act of impatience more than anything else, as this F4 jock was *exhausted* after having just completed his second-to-last of a long series of extended legs from his base at Frankfurt, Germany to Tan Son Nhut airbase, Saigon to get there ASAP. Soon, Mark's new "friend" identified himself as Brigadier General Chuck Yeager. Yeager was best known as the first man to break the sound barrier, which happened in 1947. He was a central figure in the book by Tom Wolfe (and the related 1982 blockbuster movie) *The Right Stuff* at which time he became a household name. Because Mark Morris became friends with several moon-walking astronauts, Mark was invited to "astronaut parties" that sometimes included

Brigadier General Chuck Yeager in the year 2000. He was a well-known aerial combat ace and test pilot. He was best known as the first person to break the sound barrier, which happened in 1947. He was a central figure in the book by Tom Wolfe (and the related 1982 blockbuster movie) *The Right Stuff* **at which time he became a household name.** (Wikimedia Commons)

Yeager. At first, the astronauts were taken by surprise when Mark and Chuck greeted each other with back-slapping familiarity—"*You two know each other?*" They stayed in touch until Yeager's death in December 2020 at 97. Like Mark, it turns out that Chuck Yeager and many of his other jet jock and early astronaut peers had lots of C-47 heavy-recip time, mainly on "hack duty" during their military test pilot careers.

On a much later front in 1976 and 1977, Joe Morris provided congressional testimony on the decline of the supplemental airlines that helped spark the sentiment on airline deregulation. The government's favorable treatment of the major airlines was in the final stages of killing the historically leaner and more innovative supplementals who had no political clout causing them to dwindle to only six airlines (which included PAT Air)—from a high of around 140 supplementals in earlier decades. This was not serving the public good. Joe got a sympathetic ear from Congress and a few years later deregulation *reversed* the misfortune of the supplementals. As we mentioned that fostered new supplemental airline startups, but a few of the surviving legacy supplementals (originating before PAT Air) were so damaged by the previous bad policy (coupled with imperfect management and rotten luck) that they could not recover in the new environment.

Joe's work was simultaneous with Mark's involvement as chairman of CACA. As a result of his work there, Mark, as previously discussed, was recruited by Alfred Kahn to assist him in working with Senators Howard Cannon and Ted Kennedy. They were convinced and ultimately championed their cause to "break the back" of the airline-federal government oligopoly that was always doing its best to destroy small and startup airlines to protect turf. Kahn, though a political liberal who *would seem* to favor continued regulation, was not only the *head* of the CAB (as ironic as that is), but also a premier economist and professor of marginal-cost theory. So, he was a rare "liberal" who understood the ultimate public benefits of deregulating the airlines. Who knows what it took to twist the arms of fellow liberals Kennedy and Cannon to get on board. As we know now, the net result was the Airline Deregulation Act of 1978 (signed into law by another "liberal," President Jimmy Carter), which enabled Mark Morris to start Air One concurrently with the *first*

Professor Alfred Kahn, CAB head and "The Father of Airline Deregulation" (United States Congress)

wave of those other new entrants.

After enactment, the work of Morris, Kahn, Kennedy, and Cannon continued until the mid-1980s. The still-active CAB had become a vestige of the regulated era, and some of the major airlines still retained incremental benefits from it. United Airlines (the largest domestic airline) and Flying Tiger Line (the world's largest cargo carrier) were particularly adamant about keeping the CAB in place. Mark Morris, Kahn, and the two senators were not. So Kahn told United Airlines CEO Richard Ferris that United would not be awarded any more routes until the other majors grew to "equal" United's size. With that, United and Flying Tigers came around and the CAB was formally dissolved on January 1, 1985.

The resultant additional competition prolonged the major airlines' living hell until market equilibrium was re-established. The ones that could not adapt experienced slow, painful deaths. Braniff was the earliest dropout (even before the CAB dissolution), and within a decade Pan American and Eastern Airlines would also go. TWA was one of the sickest ones that would be absorbed by American Airlines in 2001 where all employee bargaining power was lost, including seniority. But many accepted the "reset." Others including Northwest and Continental were longer-term survivors. Like TWA now with American, these two now remain "invisibly intact" as part of Delta and United, respectively, resulting from mergers during the first two decades of the 2000s. It was just that their respective brands and autonomies had vanished.

Successful intrastate-interstate conversions, coupled with new entrants using precise business models—such as Southwest and Jet Blue—have been able to establish "permanent residence" for the foreseeable future. Commuter airlines that feed small communities were now partnering, branding, and code-sharing with major airlines, with appropriately-matched equipment. In more recent years, the majors themselves began developing or absorbing larger regional capabilities, and SATS was successfully implemented for the smallest communities and to reduce airport congestion. And again, Part 121 supplemental airlines staged a comeback. The natural laws of economics, including the "marginal-cost theory," seemed to be working.

After completing much of his deregulation work with CACA, the New Entrants, Congress, and the CAB, Mark would eventually do similar work with foreign governments in revamping their aviation regulatory frameworks. It was before the international work that he sold Air One's assets to Interstate Airlines of Little Rock, where he oversaw the now combined airline investment

Herb Kelleher, well-known founder and former CEO of today's Southwest Airlines. He was a mentor, friend, and confidante of Mark Morris. (Wikimedia Commons, Southwest Archive CC BY-SA 4.0)

that Quest Capital had made with the help of New York Life (see Chapter 46). That was the point in time in 1987 when he was approached by Secretary of Transportation Elizabeth Dole to continue his advisory work on loose-end deregulation issues as applied to new airline entrants. This led to another assignment. In Mark's words:

This entailed my meeting with her [Elizabeth Dole] *once a month to hammer out policy in the deregulated airline environment, at which time she talked me into becoming Finance Chairman for her husband Senator Bob Dole for his bid in a primary against George H.W. Bush. I had no idea how to even raise a dollar in political fundraising. However, I had two major hitters from Arkansas helping me – Jack Stephens of the investment banking firm Stephens, Inc. and Sam Walton of Wal-Mart. This enabled me to raise up to our fund limit* [$67 million] *before HW got his money raised. This was my only stint inside pure Washington politics.*

By 1991, after Interstate was dissolved and Mark's Department of Transportation work was complete, he found himself back in St. Louis. Because of his acquired investment banking acumen, he got a seller representation assignment representing Guarantee Electrical Co., a large established privately-held electrical contractor in St. Louis, for the sale of one of their "non-strategic" subsidiaries, GISMO, Inc. (Guarantee Industrial Systems of Missouri) Inc. which was a thin-margined, small manufacturer of custom electrical panels, control houses and metal containers for large corporations and the U.S. military. The investor group was led by prominent St. Louis banker and former Democratic National Committee Finance Chairman S. Lee Kling Sr. and Mark negotiated a deal for them to acquire GISMO. Once the terms were set, it turned out the new GISMO needed an interim CEO with "turnaround" experience (that would be Mark with his

Mark Morris with Elizabeth and Bob Dole circa 1988. (Mark G. Morris)

major-scale DHL experience) so they hired him to steer the company on a return path to profitability.

There was just one little problem—never mind that the economy had just entered a recession and the Gulf war was winding down. One customer comprised 90% of GISMO's revenues in the form of a single contract with one of the U.S. Army's prime contractors for portable storage units designed for desert operations. Just *one day* after the new investor group assumed control of GISMO with full intentions of immediate diversification—that big contract was canceled without warning, pending the resolution of an obscure design problem that was never communicated to GISMO. For starters, the U.S. Army is always concerned about *weight* in its logistical planning, and suddenly the Army said the containers *weighed too much*—requiring a major redesign that could not be accomplished overnight. Mark and the investors were fully aware of this single-customer risk exposure, but as most any of us would rationalize, *"it won't happen this time."*

But there was more. The union representing most of the 200 employees was demanding impossible increases in overtime pay among other workplace demands. The board just threw their hands up. So Kling's investor group just abandoned the assets which automatically reverted to seller Guarantee Electric. The investor group, the board, and of course Mark, just walked away but not before satisfying their various obligations. GISMO was promptly dissolved.

So, what do you do after your 43rd birthday when you've had successes and failures and you are available for anything around the world while in the meantime you've raked in a few million in change? You move to the new Russian Federation—and Moscow is where Mark Morris lived over the next 8 years until late 1999. This was during the years of Russian President Boris Yeltsin, which represented a massive thaw out of the Cold War between the U.S. and the former Soviet Union.

Why Russia? During the Yeltsin presidency, Mark was tapped to work for President Clinton's State Department in the peak era of "Perestroika" to help the U.S. navigate the sensitive economic and financial matters between the two countries, which undoubtedly included aviation and even more urgent policies between Russia, the U.S., and other former eastern bloc countries—the details of which still cannot be disclosed. During his time in that country Mark worked closely with various high-level Russians who would later run the country, including Sergei Ivanov, the First Prime Minister of Defense; Pavel Borodin head of the President's Fund (overseeing approximately 85% of all Russian assets) and later General Secretary of the Council of Ministers; and Vladimir Putin who was working up the ranks from Deputy Prime Minister to head of the FSB (the new name of the KGB) to Prime Minister.

By 1998, Boris Yeltsin was in seriously bad health with severe alcoholism not helping. Putin and his followers accused him of "selling Russia out" as a world power. Yeltsin resigned in 1999 and within a month Putin became President of the Russian Federation. Mark Morris had lived overseas over much of his adult life and felt it "wise" to return to the U.S., which he did. As time went on the Russian Federation under Putin gained strength, and the Cold War with the U.S. began "re-freezing" for lack of a better term. Today, we all know the outcome—the Post World War II world is not only back to "square one" but probably worse.

Well, in the meantime, *why not just start another airline*?

CHAPTER 58

Primaris

By the year 2001, Mark Morris figured the dust had settled on the mayhem that defined the immediate post-deregulation environment in the days of Air One. Thoughts of a new airline began popping into his head. The days of knee-jerk fare wars were over, TWA was gone and successor American Airlines was minimally committed to St. Louis and began disassembly of that hub after first promising to keep it in place. American Airlines would probably not replicate the 80% fare cuts that TWA did with Air One. St. Louis was *TWA's turf* back then. And Gudmundsson's so-called *second wave* of new airline entrants in the 1990s had gained more traction than the early 1980s *first wave* that Air One was part of. Most airlines, established and new, were finding their footing in the deregulated age. In effect, Mark decided "all systems GO." He would call his new airline Primaris. However, his route analysis suggested that St. Louis would not be a part of Primaris' initial plans—maybe as an endpoint sometime down the road.

Unlike Air One, Primaris would be a point-to-point operation (like Southwest) rather than a hub-and-spoke airline like Ozark, TWA, or Air One. That is, each route would have enough self-sufficiency that "through traffic" would not be necessary as with hub-and-spoke. The over-arching component of Primaris' business model was that it would mimic AirOne's model of premium first-class service at standard fares. Primaris would first seek the top five domestic routes and then expand internationally into Europe and Asia—more ambitious than AirOne's domestic-only strategy. Primaris' first scheduled routes would be slated to serve the New York, Los Angeles, and San Francisco markets.

Primaris was incorporated in Delaware in 2002 and headquartered in Scottsdale, Arizona with its operating base at McCarron International Airport in Las Vegas, Nevada. Mark Morris was heavily courted by airplane manufacturers Boeing and Airbus into 2003. This was before Primaris received—under the post-deregulation Part 121 structure—its comprehensive operating certificate. They could meet *operations specifications* to fly domestic, flag, or supplemental routes as long as the crews were properly qualified for a given flight, the properly-outfitted equipment and infrastructure were in place, and the specific procedures were followed. Boeing won the Primaris fleet order with an interesting strategy, as we will see.

Primaris could be considered part of Gudmunsson's *second wave* of post-deregulation new entrants. Starting in the late 1980s the *second wave* evolved for over a decade, compared to the "everybody at once" phenomenon during the uncertainties of the *first wave* of the early 1980s. This more conservative evolution contributed to the continued survival of several of these airlines today, the largest being Jet Blue which, after long delays, began operations several years before Primaris.

New York City-based Jet Blue remains a major success story that falls beyond our scope, but it should be mentioned that they followed the Southwest Airlines pattern business model of "low-cost-no-frills"—with their differentiation exception of "live TV" in front of every seat. They thrive today as the seventh largest U.S. airline operating in North America in terms of passenger volume. Other healthy survivors of the *second wave* category include Spirit Airlines as number eight, the "second" Frontier Airlines as number eleven, and Allegiant as number fourteen (these rankings may well change by the time you read this), and they all have one thing in common. Each of them follows some variation of the "low-cost-no-frills" model. On the other hand, Primaris would still follow the "normal-cost (coach)-high-frills" pattern of Air One that Mark Morris introduced two decades earlier, obviously requiring a different setup.

While Mark was negotiating with Airbus in France and Boeing in Seattle, both manufacturers were working with many new airlines, both proposed and established. For long-haul and international routes, Primaris was considering the Boeing 7E7, which is the developmental designation for its 787 Dreamliner, as well as the competing Airbus 350. In 2003, both of these aircraft were several years away from production and airline service. Mark was also looking at the Airbus 321 series of airliners then in production for shorter domestic flights, as well as the Boeing 737-800 then under development. However, the Primaris concept, along with its proposed managers and directors, were known quantities in Boeing's executive suite and board room. As well, the major Wall Street houses specializing in the airline industry reacted positively to the Primaris business plan.

So, what's going on here? Why was Boeing so concerned with "paper" airlines and "airline concepts"? Because Boeing had just been approved to make direct investments in airlines where previously the anti-trust division of the Department of Justice (DOJ) had forbidden them (or any aircraft manufacturer) from doing so—going back to President Franklin Roosevelt's "Airmail Scandal of 1934." Also, as a result of that scandal, mounting anticompetitive airline practices, and related stock market manipulations, the formation of "multiple airline" holding companies was also prohibited. Mark Morris was the first to breach the latter in his structuring of DHL. And now he was about to be the first to breach the "direct investment" side with an aircraft manufacturer.

That said, the president of Boeing Commercial and chief economist for the parent Boeing Company approached Mark to see if he was interested in being considered, among a group of other new entrants, as candidates for direct investment by Boeing. Primaris made the shortlist. Mark and Boeing worked together for six months to hammer out the definitive business model for Primaris and a potential partnership with Boeing when a deal was struck.

Jet Blue did not have this kind of heavyweight backing and took a long time to get its certification. On the other hand, after raising startup capital from a New York hedge fund, Primaris was able to quickly obtain its broad Part 121 certification and FAA operating permit in June 2004, months before acquiring the necessary assets and infrastructure. This would be unheard of in the hyper-regulated days of Standard Airways, Missouri Air Commuter, and PAT Air in the 1970s. In those days, to obtain an operating certificate it was *required* to have everything in place, including financing, aircraft fleets, gates, ticket counters, security plans, contracts, legal approval at every level, and so forth. In other words, you had to be ready to start operations *immediately* upon approval. Also, at that time any financing or ownership stake in a new airline (or any airline) by a major aerospace manufacturer was illegal. Accordingly, Mark's unusual partnership with Boeing made the front pages of most aviation journals and publications as well as the Wall Street Journal. So just what was the nature of this partnership?

After raising another $9 million from the hedge fund, and without infrastructure for scheduled service yet in place, Primaris was able to begin stopgap supplemental (charter) flight operations later in 2004 with a single Boeing 757-200 acquired from Air-Scotland (an Air France company). The plane was delivered with 222 seats—too many for his type of premium service. So, it was outfitted with 52 first-class seats plus 40 coach seats for Primaris' first big charter contract—with the reelection campaign for George W. Bush's second term. With the ICAO callsign "WHITECAP," Primaris would be the exclusive airline for the White House Press Corps during the Bush campaign, and this thrust the airline into solid profitability over its first nine months of operation. Before taking delivery of this first 757-200, Mark got his 757/767 type rating and then became "line qualified" as the stopgap charters commenced. This meant he not only was type rated in these two widebody aircraft types but was qualified to be pilot-in-command on revenue flights—continuing his line captain tradition as with his previous airlines—PAT Air (with DC-6s and Martin 404s) and Air One (with 727s). Since both the 757 and 767 fell into the FAA category of "Heavy" aircraft, it was here that Mark won a longstanding "competitive joke" with Jerry Riebold as to who would be the first to be able to use the term "Heavy" when communicating with ATC. At this point, Jerry probably didn't care that much, as he was in a "safer" position flying corporate jets for Peabody Holding.

Primaris' first 757-200 was acquired from Air Scotland (an Air France company) and is seen here on a customs stopover at Portland, Maine. On the left is John Pearsall, chief pilot at Primaris with Mark Morris. They spent ten days in France getting the airplane ready and then flew non-stop to this first point of entry. They had just completed ferrying the aircraft across the Atlantic from Nimes, France before their final leg to Evergreen's modification facility in Tucson, Arizona for interior, paint, and certification work. (Mark G. Morris)

Boeing committed to pre-deposit loans worth billions for the acquisition of Primaris' flagship aircraft fleet—as the domestic launch customer for its 7E7/787 Dreamliner. Primaris' slot was for 52 Dreamliners and 737-800s and an option for another 52 aircraft. Primaris would first have to raise another $100 million in infrastructure financing (needed for scheduled services) for deliveries to start. Then, Boeing would kick in another $30 million for working capital. Raising this kind of financing would not, and could not happen overnight.

At first, Mark hired a good friend Jim Douglas as Primaris' president and chief operating officer. He was the twin brother of Donald Douglas, Jr. and son of Douglas Aircraft founder Donald Douglas, Sr. Jim was previously the engineering chief on the McDonnell Douglas DC-10 and successor MD-11 widebody tri-jets. Douglas commuted weekly to Scottsdale and Las Vegas from his home in Newport Beach, California which wore on him, so Mark and Jim reluctantly agreed to part ways while maintaining their friendship. Mark's Senior V.P. of Operations, John Pearsall then became president. However, Pearsall proved to be a better chief pilot than a president, so Mark hired Bob Fleming who had run multiple charter airlines in the past, including Fleming International (remember the 1977 St. Louis Electra crash—see Chapter 30), and Trans International Airlines which operated stretched DC-8 aircraft. Bob Fleming was well known in the *Second Wind* propliner realm and later gained a reputation as a tough executive who knew the regulations and how to optimize international airline operations.

Mark ran the airline as its "line flying CEO" and when not flying spent most of his time on the road working on the $100 million private placement with Credit Agricole and Credit Suisse First Boston. In the meantime, three more aircraft were added—two more 757-200s outfitted with 126 low-density (2x2) first-class seating, and a wide-body 767. They leased and operated the 767 under contract with Blackwater Security Consulting. Blackwater was a paramilitary security firm that was the premiere "private highly qualified special force" operator that complemented special operations forces (Army Rangers, Navy Seals, Delta Force, etc.) during the Mideast wars that followed 9/11. They always seemed to get bad press because liberal politicians in Washington disliked them because some of their critical operations in Iraq involved "collateral damage."

The Primaris Boeing 767 was retained to fly covert Blackwater missions into dangerous areas in Iraq and Afghanistan. The plane was leased from Blackwater after a deal was struck

One of the three Boeing 757-200s operated by Primaris in its livery. Mark Morris got his 757/767 type rating and flew an average of about 30 hours a month. This was not as much as the standard 80 or so hours per month by a full-time line pilot but he enjoyed every minute of it. He flew mostly international charters. The lighter trim is bright red, darker trim is dark purple. (Wikipedia Commons, Pedro Aragao CC BY-SA 3.0)

between Mark Morris and Erik Prince (Blackwater's founder and owner) for contracts with the U.S. State Department.

To fly into declared war zones, a commercial airline had to be proficient at "tactical penetration letdowns" to air bases from high altitudes. This consisted of a high-speed, jinking (rolling side-to-side) down-spiral to the runway in an attempt to confuse anti-aircraft weaponry. Neither UPS, FedEx, nor any of the other U.S.-registered passenger airlines were authorized by the FAA to do this except as a *military operation* where they were specifically chartered and trained by the U.S. military to fly such missions. Big commercial supplemental passenger and cargo carriers like World, Kalitta, and Evergreen were broadly authorized and trained for these dangerous areas—even with their giant 747s—under these U.S. military contracts.

Prince needed Primaris to fly for the U.S. State Department, which was considered *non-military*. The State Department was having a real problem getting their people in and out of these dangerous places, and as mentioned the large supplementals with combat zone experience could *not* fly into these dangerous areas for the State Department. Mark worked with his contacts in Washington D.C. to become the first U.S. airline to be able to fly into war zones for the State Department using the approved high-altitude tactical penetration letdown. How? One of Mark's proponents was a four-star general whose staff took Primaris' proposal directly to the senior FAA people who approved it within days. Suddenly. Mark got calls from his fellow CEOs from Evergreen to Kalitta to World Airways to offer their congratulations followed by, *"How the hell did you pull that off? We've been trying to get that permission for years and still don't have it!"* Mark politely said he "didn't know" how he got it. Primaris' combat zone operations were highly classified and apparently uneventful.

While raising capital to start *scheduled* operations was a moving target, Primaris continued to build its stopgap charter network. They flew for TNT Vacations from Boston to Punta Cana and Cancun. They also became the first U.S. airline to resume Hajj flights to Mecca after 9/11, and corporate charters for companies such as Goodyear, First Data, TCS Expeditions, and Bertch Manufacturing, and also flew traditional charters and sub-service (flying under contract with other airlines) for professional sports teams. One of Primaris' big contracts was its Oakland to Kona, Hawaii shuttle for Silicon Valley executives and billionaires including Mondavi family members to/from their multi-million-dollar weekend homes in Hawaii. Another example includes a tour company's regular charter between New York to Trinidad. Primaris also did sub-service for Santa Barbara Airlines on the Miami to Caracus, Venezuela route for 18 months.

To do all this, Primaris got its 180-minute ETOPS certification in November 2006, enabling their 757s and 767 to operate over most (but not all) transoceanic international routes. ETOPS stands for "Extended Range Twin-engine Operational Performance Standards." This meant all such certified large twin-engine jetliners on an overwater flight must be routed within 3 hours of the nearest airport for an emergency landing in case one of the two engines is lost.

ETOPS addressed a holdover from when comparatively unreliable *four-engine* heavy piston airliners often arrived at their overwater international destinations on *three engines*. Accordingly, in those days four *working* engines were required for departure on a long transoceanic flight, which might involve an arrival on *three*. Through the decades, turbofan reliability improved exponentially compared to heavy-piston engines and *early* turbojet and turbofan engines. Jetliners became reliable enough for a lower, *three-engine* departure requirement on long transoceanic flights, permitting the use of jetliners such as the DC-10 and L-1011 widebody tri-jets. Single-aisle tri-jets such as the Boeing 727 did not have the range for long overwater flights. So, ETOPS allowed the design of large, more fuel-efficient *twin-engine* jetliners such as the Boeing 757, 767, and 777 for long-range transoceanic service where ETOPS rules could be maintained.

As time went on, Primaris garnered scheduled "wet lease" sub-service contracts with foreign airlines which grew to operations in over twelve countries in Europe, the Middle East, Africa, South America, Canada, China, and Russia. For instance, Primaris flew daily scheduled sub-services for Virgin Nigeria between Lagos and London and Johannesburg, South Africa. Most of these flights were 5 to 8 hours long. Strategic joint ventures were also entered into with certain foreign airlines that wanted to operate from their countries into the United States but were prohibited from doing so as they could not yet meet the U.S. regulatory certification requirements. This niche was pioneered by Primaris who would perform these transborder flights to U.S. destinations on behalf of the foreign carrier while assisting that carrier in obtaining U.S. certifications so they could eventually make the flights themselves. The kickoff foreign carrier for this venture was Air Peru at the request of President George W. Bush on a route between Lima and Miami. Also, at Bush's and Peru President Garcia's request, Mark Morris spearheaded the updating of Peru's air regulations as patterned after U.S. Part 121 regulations.

There was one problem in all this. Funding for Primaris' *scheduled service* infrastructure remained elusive.

CHAPTER 59

The Big Bite

Mark Morris's attitude had always been *"damn the torpedoes—full ahead."* In October 2004 only months after commencing charter operations, he announced that Primaris placed its initial *firm* order with Boeing for twenty 7E7 (787) Dreamliners and twenty-six 737-800s. This order was valued at $4.0 billion and Primaris had those other options for 52 more aircraft. Boeing was criticized for not reserving this domestic launch order of the game-changing Dreamliner to an *established* major airline. In a public statement, Boeing's then-head of the Dreamliner program said, *"The Primaris decision validates the plane as a catalyst for new business models."* The Primaris order more than complemented All Nippon's launch order for three aircraft earlier that year. The Dreamliner was scheduled to enter service with All Nippon in 2008 and Primaris was scheduled to launch its Dreamliner service a year later. These timelines proved slightly ambitious.

Up to the time Primaris ordered the Dreamliners, Boeing had spent an estimated $10 billion and more on R&D on the plane, with only the All Nippon order to show for it. Four months after the Primaris order, Continental Airlines ordered 60 or so and other major airlines (mostly foreign carriers) slowly got in line on the order books. A year later, Boeing had almost a thousand orders for the aircraft. Did Primaris have anything to do with the explosion in the Dreamliner orders? Probably not but Mark likes to think so and still ribs his Boeing friends about it.

At this point, anticipated initial scheduled routes under consideration would include New York to Los Angeles, San Francisco, Paris, Atlanta, Chicago, Denver, and Paris; Washington D.C to Los Angeles and San Francisco; Honolulu to San Francisco, Los Angeles, Beijing, Shanghai; and Las Vegas to New York and Honolulu. These city pairs remained moving targets throughout the scheduled service planning stage. Further expansion might include stations such as Boston, Pittsburgh, St. Louis, New Orleans, Miami, Seattle, Phoenix, Salt Lake City, Taipei, Mexico City, Seoul, London, and Singapore among others.

During the 2002-2004 organizational years, Mark Morris was introduced to—and became friends with—Jake Garn, the Republican Senator from Utah from 1974 to 1993, and the first congressman to fly on the space shuttle in April 1985. According to much of the ill-informed media coverage, Garn flew as a "token citizen" payload specialist and "congressional observer" on space shuttle mission STS-51-D. What the media didn't seem to mention was that Garn had more than 17,000 military pilot-in-command flight time with the Navy and later the Utah Air National Guard. This was multiple times more pilot time than most space shuttle commanders or pilots could even *think* of accumulating. That's got to be the most qualified "token passenger" I've ever heard of.

Garn started as an insurance executive before entering the Navy in 1956 and then the Utah Air National Guard in 1963. He was elected mayor of Salt Lake City from 1972 to 1974 before being elected to the U.S. Senate in 1974. He was re-elected to the Senate twice and served on banking, housing, and appropriations committees, and in 1982 was one of the co-authors of the Garn-St. Germain Act addressing the savings and loan crises. Eight years after his Shuttle

Boeing 787 Dreamliner on display at EAA AirVenture Oshkosh in July 2011, three months before service entry. All Nippon (ANA) would launch the first Dreamliner service on October 26, 2011, three years later than anticipated. A few years earlier, Primaris was Boeing's *domestic* launch airline for this plane, but the economy had other plans. However, Mark Morris's footprint is all over the 787. He and his VP-Inflight (head of flight attendants) Chris Iocca were part of a Boeing team that developed the flight deck and instrumentation layouts and ergonomics (Mark) and cabin ergonomics and procedures (Chris) that are in use today on the 787.

mission, Garn left the Air Force in 1993 with the rank of colonel.

Garn even had a load of time in heavy-recips going back to the mid-1950s. While in the Navy he flew twin-engine P5M Marlin patrol seaplanes on dangerous anti-submarine missions off the coast of China from 1956 to 1960. As we mentioned in Chapter 8, Marlins were powered by Curtiss-Wright R-3350 Turbo-Compounds like the DC-7 and Super Constellation. In 1963 he moved over to the Air Force to spend the next 16 years with the Utah Air National Guard. There he flew two other heavy-recip types, both using the 28-cylinder Pratt & Whitney R-4360 Wasp Major engine. These were the Douglas C-124 Globemaster II (see Chapter 41), then the largest capacity transport with the Military Airlift Command where he flew supply missions into and out of Vietnam, and later the Boeing KC-97 Stratotanker (see Chapter 7).

Garn was named Chairman of the Board of Primaris in 2004 while Mark was CEO. For Mark to carry out his ambitious plans, he surrounded himself with other highly experienced executives. These initially included the aforementioned John Pearsall, chief operating officer and later president. Pearsall was a former FAA executive and previous Vice President of Operations with Sun Air and National Airlines, and chief pilot for the Saudi Oil Minister and the Sultan of Brunei. Primaris' Board of Advisors included Rodney Slater, former U.S. Secretary of Transportation as its chairman; J. Randolph Babbitt, former president of the Airline Pilots' Association (ALPHA) and former Administrator of the FAA; and Neil Livingstone, CEO of Global Options, Inc. and world-renowned crisis management expert. Livingstone was a television commentator and the author of numerous books and articles on intelligence, national security, and terrorism and was considered a top authority, if not *the* top authority, on all these topics. He ran unsuccessfully for Governor of Montana in 2012, and despite that loss, *Esquire* and *Forbes* magazine dubbed him *"The Most Interesting Man in the World."* Livingstone was the real-life was

Primaris Board Chairman, and former Senator and Shuttle Astronaut Jake Garn. (NASA)

Jake Garn was a big "heavy-reciper" in his early days, starting with his pilot-in-command experience in the P5M Marlin Navy anti-shipping seaplane (U.S. Coast Guard P5M pictured). Recall in Chapter 8 that the Marlin was the last aircraft manufactured by Martin, with that production line closing down in 1960. Of course, Garn's heavy-recip time had little to do with his appointment as the Primaris board chairman,---except for its contribution to his impressive total flight time. Garn also had considerable pilot-in-command time in even larger piston planes, including the KC-97 (see Chapter 7) and the C-124 Globemaster II (see Chapter 41). (National Museum of Naval Aviation)

the subject of the main character in the TV series *The Equalizer* a spy thriller series that ran on CBS from 1985 to 1989.

In addition, Mark convinced Tony Fernandez, the founder of startup Air Asia that, when combined with his other airlines in that region, grew into the largest discount airline system in the world which compares size-wise to today's Southwest Airlines. These individuals, along with the

Mark G. Morris, shortly before his Primaris years, with some of his "heavy hitters." Left to right: Neil Livingstone (undisputed "Most Interesting Man in the World" and the real-life *Equalizer*), Mark Morris, Admiral William James Crowe (former Chairman of the Joint Chiefs of Staff under the Reagan and George H.W. Bush administrations), and Rodney Slater (former Secretary of Transportation under the Clinton Administration). Livingstone and Slater would later become part of Mark's Primaris "brain trust." (Mark G. Morris)

support of Boeing, provided the clout to grab the attention of a few of the world's largest investment banks.

In 2007 the private placement memorandum (PPM) was finally issued to raise the required $100 million in convertible preferred stock to provide the fixed investment and working capital for Primaris' formal entry into full-blown scheduled services. If successful, Boeing, as mentioned, would kick in that additional $30 million in working capital and proceed with the initial $4 billion in aircraft financing on pre-delivery payment requirements for that first set of 787 Dreamliners and 737-800s.

In the meantime, Mark and several on his management team were directly involved in Boeing's 7E7/787 flight deck ergonomics and interior cabin design. One of these design team members was Chris Iocca, Vice President-Inflight, who led the flight attendant group, Primaris' largest division. A veteran with TWA and later American Airlines, she first worked for Mark in the same capacity at Air One two decades earlier. For both of Mark's jet airlines, she developed "back of aircraft" services and procedures, including manuals, catering, flight attendant training, uniforms, emergency procedures, and so forth—resulting in Air One's two consecutive years of service awards that rattled Delta Airlines which, while certainly earned, seemed to be the "automatic recipient" of these awards for many years. Chris was FAA qualified in most Boeing and McDonnell-Douglas jetliner types.

Now that Boeing was the first airplane manufacturer to commit to a direct airline investment in 70 years, the contemplated partnership made the front page of *The Wall Street Journal*. Again, why was this so noteworthy? Back in 1927 aircraft manufacturer Boeing began underbidding on and winning airmail routes in the western U.S. Because the airplane manufacturing business was very profitable back then, they could undercut the pure airlines on virtually any route which

Chris Iocca. (Mark G. Morris)

consisted mostly of mail traffic—there was minimal acceptance of unprofitable passenger business at that time. They formed a holding company called United Aircraft Transport Co., or UAT, to make both horizontal and vertical acquisitions of aviation manufacturers including Pratt & Whitney, Sikorsky, Vought, Northrup, Stearman, and Hamilton Aero. This enabled UAT to acquire more airlines, notably Varney Airlines which began operations in 1926 and then underbid those routes. In the wake of the Air Mail Scandal of 1934 (a typical misguided federal government debacle beyond our scope), Boeing's predatory business practices came to light with the U.S. Government which broke Boeing's UAT apart under the antitrust rules, forbidding Boeing and all other aviation manufacturers from holding airline interests for at least the next 60 years. Boeing's forced spinoff of its airline interests became United Airlines, first run by legendary industry titan W.R. "Pat" Patterson. The year 2004 happened to be "year 70," so Boeing was free to invest in airlines again—and Primaris was their first contemplated partnership. So, for Boeing, the timing was perfect for the introduction of its revolutionary 787 Dreamliner as a "catalyst for change" in the rapidly changing airline industry.

Timing, timing, timing. Around 2006 during Primaris' extended rollout, investors became skittish about investing in airlines. The prices of petroleum products, including avgas and jet fuel, were unstable and rapidly rising. Credit Suisse First Boston, the lead investment banker for Primaris was completing the raise when a major investor backed out in favor of a "more fitting" deal with Virgin America. This started a negative snowballing effect with the rest of the Primaris investor group. As a result, in 2008 Primaris "temporarily" backed out of its big Boeing order while the rest of the world was in the midst of this thing called the "subprime" debacle. As the months wore on, numerous other instabilities were bubbling up in the financial markets, spurned by massive hedge fund implosions as precipitated by this subprime crisis in the secondary mortgage markets—ultimately resulting in the stock market crash to below 50% of peak value. In those days everybody was asking, *what the hell is subprime?*" That's beyond our scope too.

The "Great Recession" reared its ugliness in the second half of 2008 when Primaris was at its *peak* employee count. Several of Primaris' major sub-service contracts defaulted to the tune of $14 million, instantly slamming the airline into Chapter 11 bankruptcy in October 2008. Its cash position got so bad it couldn't continue to operate beyond December 2nd at which time

Primaris CEO and Line Captain Mark Morris and the proposed 787 Dreamliner. At this point, nowhere to go but UP! (Mark G. Morris)

operations had to be shut down. At that point, the bankruptcy judge had no choice but to convert Primaris' Chapter 11 filing into a Chapter 7 total liquidation.

Primaris was never revived, and its Dreamliner slots went elsewhere. As of late 2022, the total Boeing 787 Dreamliner orders stood at almost 1,500 aircraft, with total deliveries at just over 1,000 planes. It looks like that "1,000 plane" order backlog that Mark Morris took "credit" for earlier came to fruition—and then some.

CHAPTER 60

"Fat Annie" and Sunset on the Aerial Leviathans

In 2004, the year Primaris started operations, Karen had for 13 years been the executive assistant for Irl Engelhardt since he became CEO of Peabody Energy. She held that position through its 2002 initial public offering (IPO) until 2007 when Engelhardt left to run a spinoff, Patriot Coal. She later continued as his assistant there, and later with his agricultural ventures until she retired in 2022. While CEO of Peabody, Engelhardt propelled it to new heights, and its stock value quadrupled in just a few years after the 2002 IPO. Peabody became the best-performing U.S. coal company in history and remained the largest as it had been for decades. The coal industry will never see that again. During most of her time there, one of Karen's responsibilities was flight department scheduling.

On a clear, cool Sunday morning in early April 2004, Karen and I drive around the eastern perimeter of Lambert and then turn west on Banshee Road. Tomorrow—Monday—Air Force One with President George W. Bush will be arriving at the Lambert airport firehouse ramp on the north side just west of the Sabreliner FBO. Irl has been tapped to be one of the dignitaries to greet the President, so today he wants Karen to scope the place out so his driver will know the lay of the land for tomorrow—an "insurance policy" designed to ensure that her overcommitted boss isn't late. No, you can't "just use GPS"—widely available off-the-shelf and automobile units do not exist yet. In 2004, human "scouts" are still sent ahead to scope out a target area, just like 150 years earlier during the Civil War.

Karen asks that I do the driving because she has a poor sense of direction. After we get to the airport firehouse I draw a map and then decide to drive further west on Banshee Road to where it boomerangs south around the old Mark Aero facilities. I don't think I'd been by this place in nearly two decades. I am hit with some serious sentiments for what I see on this sunny April morning. At the boomerang bend in the road still stands the very same F-15 billboard I first noticed 34 years ago—except now it says "Boeing" not "McDonnell Douglas." I turn my head to the left— no Navy hangars, no tarmac, no nothing except a bright, greening *grass meadow*. When the hell did this happen? At some point, they bulldozed the sacred Mark Aero structures and ramp to oblivion, just like Corrosion Corner. This time, it's not redeveloped, but just vacant—no new tarmac or big new jets parked there. I just *stare*. There is nothing but *green*.

During this timeframe I do regularly fly with Karen on Peabody's Hawker 1000 and their slightly smaller 800 as a freeloading spouse on several Peabody trips to Naples Florida, Scottsdale, Arizona, and even on a boondoggle to the Grand Canyon. During these flights I spend time on the flight deck talking shop with Jerry and Dick who brief me on their navigation systems and flight progress as we cruise along.

Nobody else at Peabody except "sometimes" Karen seems interested in the flight deck (understandable). Irl Engelhardt seems to respect the pilots and converses with them on any topic. If Dick or Jerry decide to cancel a trip due to marginal weather—no matter how important the meeting or event—Irl concurs with their decision without question, *every time*. This is quite

Hawker 1000 which is similar to that flown by the Peabody Energy's flight department for several years. Jerry Riebold and Dick Horowitz spent quite a few thousand hours flying it and all other corporate jets in the Peabody fleet. (Wikimedia Commons, HaydenSoloviev CC By-SA 4.0)

opposite of some CEOs who would proclaim, *"If you can't do it, I'll find someone else who can."*

In June 2005 Karen and I throw a "pilots' barbeque" on our patio. I think one reason among others is that she wants to show off the house we built a few years back. Guests include Jerry and Patti (Finot) Riebold, Dick and Patsy Horowitz, and a few other Peabody couples. Doug Teel and his wife Judy, and my other good friend Al Bacon and his wife Pat are there. Al is a retired Army Lieutenant Colonel who flew UH-60 Blackhawk helicopters for the U.S. Army after having been involved with its engineering development and accident investigations. Everybody seems to have a good time and *then* I inadvertently make an unlikely connection.

I had known that Jerry had flown DC-6s in his past, but never knew "for whom." Then Jerry drops the big one. He tells me he started as a "lowly" Mark Aero primary flight instructor at Lambert. He goes on to say that Mark Morris saw his potential and pulled him off the line to begin getting him type rated on the big iron, along with his ATP rating. The rest is history. He and Patti tell me that PAT Air was where they met, and it is here where I find out that Patti was Mark Morris's right-hand person all those years. Jerry and Patti had gotten married during the Air One days. They tell me they are still in touch with Mark and remain good friends. I had earlier connected Mark Morris as the key figure with Mark Aero, PAT Air, *and* Air One during all of Air One's publicity in the early 1980s—but knew nothing else about him.

I am speechless but all questions (however you do that). This closes that big loop I *never knew existed* until this backyard party. I show them photos I had taken of Mark Aero and PAT Air aircraft since I was a teenager. Both Patti and Jerry recognize the "N" numbers, including DC-6 N44DG. Like a proud kid showing off his new bike, I haul onto the patio my R-2800 and R-3350 cylinders and other engine parts I collected over the years. Jerry says, *"Wow, we had all these same loose cylinder jugs and parts lying around everywhere, all the time! I just loved it!"*

Then it hits me. I realize it was by chance or providence that I met Karen at the Rodeo Bar in December 1980. Then she likes me enough to go out with me. She works at Peabody and soon thereafter she introduced me to Jerry Riebold, who *25 years later* connects the rest of the Mark Aero/PAT Air dots for me at our backyard barbeque. Then, *fifteen years after that*—due to a chance reunion of me and the former Peabody pilots over lunch—Jerry gives me Mark Morris's contact information. From there, Mark and I become friends.

Were it not for those events—separated by decades—the Mark Aero phenomenon I was glued to for years while growing up would have faded into an unsolved string of forgotten memories. Because of Joe and Mark Morris (people I did not know) and Mark Aero, I would befriend down the road heavy-recip entrepreneurs Larry Brown and Gary Balnicki, and now *Mark*

Morris—the *actual Mark Aero guy,* the *Pegasus guy*, and the *PAT Air guy* that sparked it all for me 50 years ago.

In early August, two months after our pilots' barbeque, Karen and I take a long weekend. It is typically warm today with a high light overcast. We decide to have lunch on the patio of one of our favorite places, Two Nice Guys, near our house. The wailing sound of a heavy-recip at medium altitude interrupts our lunch. What? Now in 2005? It sounds like R-2000s again, just like ten years earlier over the Kirkwood Methodist Church. Only this time the sound is weaker because it emanates from a higher altitude.

I look up. Damn, I cannot believe it. It's the dark silhouette of *another Carvair* heading east-northeast tracking airway Victor 88 from Vichy, Missouri (south-central) and Troy Illinois (just northeast of St. Louis) at around five thousand feet. I know the sound of a DC-4, but the fuselage is *way too long and the nose is too rounded*—again! Case closed. The Carvair and its four churning props fade to the east as I contemplate my *second* rare encounter with an ATL-98 Carvair—another *last airworthy one* in existence—again! I should have seen these two Carvairs

The extremely rare Carvair N89FA *"Fat Annie"* was my very last heavy-recip sighting over St. Louis in early August 2005. It is seen here in 1972 at Gatwick U.K. when flying for BAF. This is hard to figure—the two rarest propliners in the world are the last two I ever see on random St. Louis overflights, exactly one decade apart. Both are ATL-98 Carvairs, and each was the "only flyable" Carvair when I saw it. (Wikimedia Commons, 21c123 CC BY 3.0)

in 1967 when there were almost 20 of them in existence (only 21 built). Instead, I see the last two ever in 1995 and 2005—each over St. Louis.

In November of that year, I stumble upon the explanation for this second Carvair flyover. I find that this was *truly* the last airworthy Carvair in existence, N89FA *Fat Annie*, once the sister ship of the ill-fated N83FA *Porky Pete* that I saw over the church a decade earlier. But at that time in 1995, *Fat Annie* was not flyable, but in pieces at Griffon, Georgia. Now, in 2005 it's together again and winging over my head on the very *last trip* of *any* Carvair, *EVER*. It will also be my *very last* spotting of a heavy piston transport on an operational revenue mission, *EVER*. What are the chances of that? This is an impossible final ending to a 35-year era for me.

What I had witnessed was a glimpse of a repositioning flight from Texas to the former Chanute Air Force Base in Rantoul, Illinois for revenue work there. Hours earlier it had departed from its home base at Sherman-Grayson County Airport in Texas How did I figure this out? From the December 2005 issue of *Air Classics* magazine that I received in November. This issue outlined *this* final trip of *this* Carvair. The aircraft was being operated by Gator Global Flying Services headquartered at Sherman-Grayson. At the Chanute destination, the Carvair had served as a mass jump aircraft for the annual skydive event held there as part of the World Freefall Convention (WWFC). This was the very last of the few and varied odd jobs that Gator Global's *Fat Annie* performed.

The *Air Classics* article states:

> *Confirmation that the Carvair was going to appear at the WWFC arrived in the form of a call from propliner/skydiving enthusiast Mark Meltzer, who saw her unmistakable profile flying over St. Louis at noon on Saturday, 6 August* [2005] *heading in the general direction of Rantoul.*

This is another confirmation that I'm not the only *out-of-phase* person who looks up into the sky at the sound of *any* aircraft, vintage or otherwise. Mark Meltzer is a respected corporate attorney and sky diver. Oh yes, and a *propliner* enthusiast. The article also reported that on one Rantoul jump flight, *Fat Annie* was dangerously overloaded with 80 skydivers plus equipment. The takeoff acceleration was sickeningly slow, and it was apparent that *Fat Annie* might not get off the ground. She barely did, but at a dangerously high angle of attack, almost dragging herself into a tree line at the end of the runway. That would have been a mess. Sounds just like the beginning of a couple of Super Constellation disasters we are now familiar with. The *Tiger* struck both Carvairs I saw overhead ten years apart, this time lunging out almost to the point of disaster. *Porky Pete* was not so lucky.

The last I heard, non-airworthy *Fat Annie* was sitting somewhat intact but decaying at some other sleepy Texas airport. She had since been acquired by one or two "fix-er-up" enthusiasts looking for "crowdfunding" donations. These enthusiasts don't seem to have the background or manpower for that kind of project (nor DC-4/Carvair type ratings for that matter), so I don't expect *Fat Annie* to return to the skies any time soon—if ever.

CHAPTER 61

The Real Legacies

Legacy: of, relating to, associated with, or carried over from an earlier time, technology, business, etc. --Merriam Webster

What follows is not a "puff piece" or an advertisement. Mark Aero, which has been out of business for nearly a half-century, has nothing to gain from this chapter's "promotional" tone. Nor do the Morrises have anything to gain, and nor do I. Joe has sadly *passed on* and Mark has *moved on*. What we present here are just some facts. Until now these facts have never been formally articulated, but they *should have* long ago become prominent in the aviation historical record. This is not Joe's or Mark Morris's fault—these forward-looking entrepreneurs had *no time* to record their own history. That said, here we present the factual case that Joe Morris, Mark Aero, and Mark Morris, left sustaining, far-reaching, and untold aviation legacies that had a major impact on what transportation is today. Some are major and others are minor, some survive and thrive, and some do not, some are obvious, and some are not. The amazing thing is that most of these legacies started with a collection of forgotten, obsolete junk airplanes swept into the corner of a major airport. Out of that sprang the big legacies, in particular, DHL, the UPS operating certificate and fleet, and the post-1978 deregulated airline industry. No other pile of aeronautical junk in the corner can be associated with such a major worldwide impact. These are those legacies in no particular order:

- Joe Morris developed the standards for rough ocean seaplane landings and aircraft ditching that remain worldwide standard-practice procedures today.

- Joe Morris was one of Howard Hughes' key test engineers and advisors on his enormous H-4 Hercules "Spruce Goose" seaplane project. This *Leviathan of Leviathans* is a national treasure on full public display at the Evergreen Aviation and Space Museum, McMinnville, Oregon.

- Joe Morris was the architect of Pacific Northern Airlines' expansion into the big leagues, putting it into direct competition with Alaska Airlines, Pan American World Airways, and Western Airlines. This would result in a merger with Western in 1967 which in turn was absorbed by Delta Airlines in 1987.

- Mark Aero was the final steward for the many acres of real estate that represented Lambert's earliest history, as well as Charles A. Lindbergh's staging point from where he forged the rest of aviation history. Today, nothing remains on these sacred grounds.

- Mark Aero was the instructional starting point for hundreds of pilot careers, both civilian and military, spanning many decades, and it was the largest FBO at Lambert in its day. Mark Aero also served as the outsourced corporate flight department for several major St. Louis corporations, providing the framework and resources for these companies to eventually take their flight operations in-house.

- Mark Morris, at only 27 years old, started, owned, successfully ran, and flew as a line captain for the largest Douglas DC-6 airline in the world, Petroleum Air Transport (PAT Air) during the *Second Wind* era in the late 1970s, using 25 of these planes (in addition to the three twin-engine Martin 404s). The DC-6 was the flagship workhorse for most major airlines during the *First Wind* of the 1950s. In the *Second Wind*, PAT Air represented the last *major* DC-6 fleet in the world, and made the very last all-passenger DC-6 flight. Mark wore all hats—from CEO to line captain to human resources to insurance administrator. Before that—at age 25—he started Spiegel Oil Company in St. Louis by selling his British Leyland MGB sports car to finance its startup. Spiegel grew quickly and became a cash cow, generating a few million in net profits each year which he used to start Petroleum Air Transport. In my view, few 27-year-olds (especially today) have that sixth sense needed to capture, harness, coordinate, and operate complex heavy resources like that. By default, it was Mark Aero and PAT Air where Mark began to build his business, regulatory, and investment banking acumen, which he would utilize for a lifetime.

- Mark Morris was the last bastion of an earlier era when airline top managements and CEOs were also seasoned pilots (not to be confused as active "line pilots" with their respective airlines—they were not). These days most airline CEOs are not pilots or even "aviation people." With a few exceptions, they are bureaucrats, MBAs, and bean counters—almost as though their entry into the industry was an afterthought. Be certain that I am not implying that this disqualifies them—it obviously doesn't.

- Mark Morris was the first CEO of DHL Airlines when it was the *largest* domestic and international door-to-door overnight courier *well before* Federal Express or anyone else. Now the third-largest overnight courier, it is now under German ownership and generates revenues in excess of $65 billion (USD). That is more than Delta Airlines generates, now the largest U.S. passenger airline. Through the sale of PAT Air to DHL, Mark provided the original fleet hardware (DC-6s and Martin 404s) that formed the basis for DHL's "catch-up" international jet fleet that he initiated. During his four-year tenure there, he increased domestic revenues fourfold, and international revenues sixfold, providing the solid foundation for what DHL is today. Today's DHL aircraft color scheme of mustard yellow and red are taken directly from PAT Air, as originally designed by Mark's wife Susan. Years ago, as DHL was about to incorporated that paint scheme, they asked Mark Morris for legal permission to use those colors. To this day he wonders why DHL sought his permission. When PAT Air was sold to DHL it presumably included the transfer of any trademark, trade name, and other intangible rights. Still, Mark had to hire lawyers to formally document his permission.

- Mark Morris provided the initial infrastructure for what became UPS's air operations, now the core supporting UPS as the second-largest overnight courier. UPS's Part 121 operating certificate *originated* as the *Air One's* certificate as first secured by Mark in 1982. He, along with John Stanger also owned, operated, and controlled the UPS air fleet before 1988, when it was completely turned over to UPS as their initial dedicated fleet.

- Mark Morris was the first to take advantage of the expired federal airline anti-trust rules first enacted under the Air Mail Act of 1934. When running DHL, Mark was the first to form a holding company to own and control multiple airlines after 70 years, and that served as the precedent for other multiple airline holding companies. In the Primaris days, Mark was also the first since 1934 to form an investment partnership between an airline (Primaris) and an aircraft manufacturer (Boeing).

- Mark Morris, Chris Iocca, and other Primaris officials had a significant impact on the ergonomic design of the Boeing 787 Dreamliner.

- In 1976 and 1977 Joe Morris testified before Congress to lay the groundwork for the rescue of the supplemental airlines in the years before airline deregulation. The Morris impact on the proliferation and successes of current-day supplemental airlines cannot be overemphasized.

- Mark Morris was vice-chairman of the Commercial Air Carriers Association (CACA) and president of the New Entrant CEO's Club (representing about 26 established and startup *interstate* airlines) where he commanded the attention of airline titans such as Herb Kelleher of Southwest Airlines and Robert Crandall of American Airlines and built consensus among most airlines and airports regarding gate and ticket counter availability and sharing—a necessary step in ripping this industry out of its regulatory straightjacket.

- Mark Morris's work with CACA was noted by free-market economist and CAB head Alfred Kahn, who later asked him to steer a committee that included Kahn, and Senators Kennedy, and Cannon. With this, airline deregulation became a reality with the Airline Deregulation Act of 1978. That still did not put an end to lingering regulatory vestiges such as the Civil Aeronautics Board. Several established major airlines wanted the CAB to remain intact as they still retained residual benefits from it. Morris, Kahn, Kennedy and Cannon finally got the majors to consent, putting the final nail in the coffin of the CAB, and accelerating a revival of new airline entrants in all categories. The CAB was dissolved on January 1, 1985. Mark continued this work as a key advisor to President Reagan's Secretary of Transportation Elizabeth Dole.

- With Air One, Mark Morris was *the post-deregulation pioneer* in full-service jet travel at standard (coach} prices, later to be adopted by Primaris. Through Primaris, he also pioneered airline route sub-service and joint venture relationships with foreign airlines, paving the way for today's more relaxed "open skies" between international boundaries.

Maybe Mark Morris wasn't *the* primary driver of deregulation like Alfred Kahn, but he was both Kahn's and Elizabeth Dole's voice of practical experience. By default, Mark was forced into action after he and his dad Joe were repeatedly burned under the grip of the unfair government/major airline oligopoly. Add that main achievement to the other legacies described above—legacies that sprung from a collection of old junk airliners and hulks swept into the back corner of a major airport that was trying to radiate "civic progress." That scenario played a hundred times over at major airports during the *Second Wind* era, including Miami's "freight dog heaven," Corrosion Corner, but few of the operations associated with that junk had a far-reaching and everlasting impact on transportation as a whole. It was all that junk that attracted and inspired *me*, but as I dug more deeply, I became *more inspired* by its hidden broader impacts. Mark Aero and PAT Air, with that large fleet of long-obsolete DC-6 "prop jobs," *changed the course* of *the jet age forever*.

Despite Mark Morris's major successes with PAT Air/DHL, he still feels that a "standard-fare, all-frills" concept would work, even though none have since become fully established. You need the management, money, and timing to carry out this fragile concept, but the money will do an about-face and follow bad timing right out the back door before the managers do. Admittedly, the opposing "low-cost, no-frills" concept is more resilient when it comes to money and timing, explaining why most surviving *second wave* new entrants are based on that formula.

Timing aside, why didn't at least *one* of the Morris airlines achieve a long-term presence like Pan American, TWA, or Eastern—or even morph into current long-term survivors like American, Delta, United, or Southwest? Was their regulatory and economic timing off? Were the markets too saturated? Was the federal government too heavy-handed on the little guy? Were local governments and airport interests protecting gate availability for the established? Were the competitive furballs and mindless fare wars of the immediate post-deregulation environment impossible to react to? Yes, on all counts.

Successful airline management amounts to two things: Skill and luck. In the airline industry, skill is abundant and luck is fleeting. Go ahead and summon those ghosts that ran Eastern Airlines, Pan American Airways, Trans World Airlines, Braniff Airlines, and the dozens of other airlines that couldn't make it post-deregulation. The management expertise was there (the unions would argue with that one), but timing, high legacy costs, and capital constraints coupled with economic downturns couldn't put these Humpty Dumpties back together again.

Oh, one more thing. Did the Morrises place too much of their faith for too long in a *comfortably familiar* but *grossly obsolete* technology? Should PAT Air have started with second-hand, first-generation DC-9 or 727 jetliners instead of tired old DC-6s? According to Mark Morris, *"No."* A DC-9 was a *lousy* freighter conversion. Back then converted Boeing 727 freighters would be a better choice but *expensive* to operate. The old and cheap 1950s DC-6s *were* the *right* planes at the *right time* for PAT Air, and why PAT Air was *always profitable*—even in the jet age.

And then there was Air One and Primaris. Yes, it is true in aviation that *Fate is the Hunter*—as the prolific aviation writer Earnest Gann would say. *Fate is the Hunter?* That is the dark phenomenon that can arbitrarily override the collective brain trust of an airline—or a single, by-the-book, and careful pilot on a simple airplane flight. Again, welcome to the airline business.

CHAPTER 62

One Last Look

September 25, 2020

It's a pleasantly warm, sunny fall day. A light orange-brown haze covers the entire upper atmosphere, blown in from the major California wildfires that have been in progress for weeks. The unusual haze creates a surreal backdrop for my 250-mile afternoon drive from St. Louis to Kansas City, Missouri. After the dense-traffic negotiation of the complex maze of surprise exits, construction barrels, and lane changes on I-70 inside city limits, I exit immediately north, across the old Missouri River bridge leading right to Kansas City Downtown Airport, a familiar scene from decades past. I arrive at the Airline History Museum (AHM) now housed inside the former Slick Airways hangar on the southwest corner of the airport. AHM is the former Save A Connie (SAC) that houses Super Constellation *Star of America* and the Martin *Skyliner Kansas City*.

The AHM hangar and the museum signs are faded and the premises are otherwise unkempt with nasty weeds all around, featuring burrs the size of marbles. They stick to my socks and sting like a bee as I approach a beat-up side entrance door with a rusty bent lock latch with "No Entry" stenciled on the door. I walk all around the unfenced west side and can find no other entrance *anywhere*. On the north side behind the chain link fence, the wide main hangar door is open, and filling my field of vision is something I am familiar with—the three imposing, red-striped vertical tails of the TWA Lockheed L-1049H Super Constellation, N6937C *Star of America*. She has been sitting motionless in this run-down place over the last 15 years. She had been occasionally rolled out for an engine runup and taxi around the apron—but that's about it. During her post-restoration flying career, she lived in relative glamour, flying all over North America, and starring in various TV commercials and box office movies such as *Survivor (1992)* with Sam Shepard, *Ace Ventura: When Nature Calls (1995)* with Jim Carrey, and *The Aviator* with Leonardo DeCaprio *(2004)*. Astronaut Neil Armstrong, the first man to walk on the moon, hosted an A&E documentary called *First Flights*. In several segments, he narrated from inside the restored cabin of *Star of America*.

So, what do you do when you can find only *one door*, but it says "No Entry"? You just go through that door. It is musty and poorly lit inside, but I am promptly greeted by a few museum members who are waiting for me with sodas and refreshments. Some of these board members are a few generations removed from the people I knew in the early days of the organization. The museum seems in a state of slow deterioration, which could have probably been avoided had it not been for those years of cultural dysfunction and the ill-advised appointment of a slick-talking fraudster of a president during the first decade of the 2000s. This con artist promoter gradually replaced the board with his professional crook buddies—crooked lawyers, crooked bankers, and crooked entrepreneurs—who for several years bled the museum dry of something like two-thirds of total annual member donations. The crooked board awarded the fraudster president an annual salary of $120,000. AHM was finally able to excise the shysters and take the promoter to court, but this was too little too late. The damage was done and AHM recovered only $10,000 after being

N6937C Super Constellation "Star of America" in happier days. I took this shot in December 1990 when it was sitting where Missouri Air Commuter would have gated at the historic downtown terminal beginning 15 years previous. This old terminal has since been "renovated" and is unrecognizable today.

bilked out of *hundreds of thousands* of dollars.

Earlier this month, the museum contacted me after finding my AeroDinosaur YouTube channel which features a four-part video series on my early involvement with SAC. They are somehow impressed with my videos. None of these officers were there during the early days of the museum when Karen and I were there, and several weren't even born yet, so it seems I had something to share with them.

The next largest aircraft in the hangar is their Martin 404 that I am also old friends with. Thirty years earlier I videotaped its arrival at this airport from Florida in December 1990. After a "touchup" restoration and a single decade as a flying airshow exhibit, it had been tucked away in a corner of this hanger as another motionless exhibit, nose-to-nose with the Super Constellation.

There is also a shiny, though engineless TWA DC-3 on display. It's one of the rarer early DC-3 models that is powered by the 9-cylinder Wright R-1820s rather than the equally powerful 14-cylinder Pratt & Whitney R-1830s. Upon inspecting the polished engine firewall, it appears it is receiving brand-new plumbing for engine re-mounting. I am told this plane will be flying again in only a few months, but I am silently skeptical. Then there is also a rare old Northrup Gamma, and parts and pieces of several older small aircraft being stored among all kinds of dusty aviation "junk," including the wreckage of the World War II Ryan trainer that actor Harrison Ford crash-landed on a California golf course in March 2015.

My impression throughout is that this stalled museum is in dire need of money and manpower. This place is just out of gas. The problem is that the largest segments of the populace, meaning the bulk of millennials and even younger Gen Z'ers, have zero interest in anything aeronautical, much less mechanical, so why would they contribute to air museums? They don't even like cars so why in God's name should they be interested in airplanes? They all seem to major in liberal arts, humanities, and drama in college. This has dire consequences for our broader society—but few seem concerned about this. According to *Aviation Week & Space Technology*, in 1980 when I was actively flying, there were something like 360,000 private pilots in the U.S. Forty years later in 2020, there are only around 156,000 private pilots—a 55% decrease. The trend is the same in military aviation. Does anybody see a problem here? Maybe I should blame myself—I stopped piloting airplanes in 1985.

Now we are paying the piper. In 2022 we have a chronic airline pilot shortage that has been simmering for years and now worsening, with no end in sight. It is now becoming "normal" for travelers to spend holidays stranded at a distant airport—*should we care?*

The go-go days of AHM's high-powered fundraising and high-dollar embezzlement are gone. It peaked in 2007 when an aviation geek and vintage airliner enthusiast named John Travolta danced with the starstruck wife of a rich lawyer in exchange for $20 thousand (are you kidding me?)—on the very part hangar floor that I'm now standing on. It's not certain whether the dancing dollars went to Travolta or AHM—hopefully to the latter so we'll leave it at that.

AHM's Martin 404 stuffed away in a corner of their musty hangar on September 25, 2020. Just right of center is one of the R-2800 CB-16 engines that once helped power the plane. This engine was probably at work on the wing when I videoed its arrival at Kansas City Downtown Airport on December 11, 1990. The engine partially visible on the far left is an R-3350-93 Turbo-Compound (a military variant) which was used on Super Constellation *Star of America*. This is the engine whose internals blew up in the summer of 2005 while training a green flight engineer, crushing the budget and ending Star of America's flying career after a failed test flight one year later.

Three years *before* the Travolta fundraiser—and before it blew an engine for the last time in 2005—the museum's Super Constellation *Star of America* chauffeured Travolta and his beautiful movie star wife Kelly Preston to Cabo San Lucas, Mexico for his 50th birthday bash This was so this movie and aviation superstar could arrive in "Howard Hughes" style in front of his hundreds of celebrity friends in something *different* and *impressive.*

There was a problem with that. AHM was not certificated for what was in effect an international Part 121 charter flight, so they disguised the Cabo flight as a normal "airshow operation" under Part 91. That didn't go over with the FAA, but it appears they looked the other way, probably because the escapade involved Travolta. The celebrity could have used his own restored Qantas 707 jetliner that he normally flew, but that would not be *nearly as impressive* as the rare sight of a pounding four-engine heavy-recip Super Connie pulling up on the apron.

The current president of AHM is a personable guy named John Roper. He has an extremely impressive aerospace and engineering rap sheet and is an ATP who has commanded everything from single-engine Cessnas to large corporate jets, racking up thousands of hours. His appearance is uncharacteristic of his checkered career and his current role as AHM president. He's got long graying hair with a full beard, like Buffalo Bill or ZZ Top, and while his casual dress and appearance are clean, he does look like a well-seasoned hippie.

Surprisingly, one of the most enthusiastic people there is a tee-shirted, 12-year-old son of one of the AHM officers. The kid has long black hair and a baseball cap he wears "catcher style." He looks like a juvenile California skateboarder with a permanent smile. He knows everything about the museum and the airplanes it houses, and is extra excited to talk about them—atypical of his generation for sure. I am highly impressed with this kid. I know of no other kid his age that cares about machines that fly, but I am most impressed with his personality, maturity, and enthusiastic disposition. A friendly young woman is in charge of media or promotion, and the few other attendees are elderly retirees with not much to say. But one of them is the museum's talkative tour guide who has been in that role for years and is excited about showing me around.

My seasoned tour guide takes me around with all the others joining in. Scattered throughout the hangar and several storage rooms are more TWA airline memorabilia than I've ever seen in one place—models, uniforms, old schedules, airplane parts, avionics, instrument panels, seats, posters, banners, etc. Some of it is arranged in neatly organized displays, the rest of it scattered haphazardly along with the smaller museum airplane hulks. There is a big open space in the main hangar with a large, brightly-painted AHM logo that was the historic "John Travolta" dance floor.

We come to a side area consisting of a large cubicle where a bust statue of Charlie Taylor is displayed in the middle. He is the man who designed, machined, and built the 12-horsepower engine that powered the Wright Flyer in 1903. The walls of the cubicle are covered in framed black-and-white photos of people, arranged like a high school yearbook. As I scan these portraits, I realize that most of these people are the ones I worked with at SAC all those years ago. I am told that if there is a black ribbon under a photo, that person is now deceased. I get a sinking feeling when I notice that almost all my friends from three decades back have black ribbons. It seems like only yesterday I was working with, flying with, and joking around with them, but now I feel that I am attending *each* of their funeral visitations.

My guide takes me inside the Super Constellation cabin I'm long familiar with. I peer into the dark, Plexiglas-protected cockpit area from behind the flight engineers' station. It is bathed in an eerie, dim bluish light. I flashback to the times I spent in there with my friends, both on the ground and in the air. There is my good friend, chief flight engineer Walter "Willie" Davis (black ribbon), and good-humored engineer John Stark (black ribbon). Then I see pilots Frank FitzGibbon (black ribbon), Chris Clark (black ribbon), and Harry Ward (black ribbon). Just "yesterday" I worked closely with all these now *black-ribboned* guys in this very sacred space. Now it's just a ghostly silence, inactivity, darkness, and emptiness in there. My eyes water for just a second.

AHM has a serious problem that overshadows all others. Since its inception in 1986, it has bargain subleased or been granted rent-free space at several airport locations from Executive Beechcraft, the longtime FBO there. This was pursuant to the master hangar leases Executive Beech had with the City of Kansas City. AHM was written into the 2005 master lease to remain there rent-free until 2050, as long as AHM remains not-for-profit. But in 2019, Executive Beech

AHM's L-1949H Super Constellation *Star of America's* inert flight deck on September 25, 2020, from behind the Plexiglas. A strangely sentimental if not ghostly encounter for me, with the space bathed in an eerie blue light. This same week *exactly* 30 years ago, I was an alternate crew member on this very flight deck on brilliant sunny days, flying with my TWA-veteran friends Harry Ward, Chris Clark, Walter "Willie" Davis, and John Stark—all legacy TWA veterans of the *First Wind* piston era. All are now gone with black ribbons under their museum portraits. Davis' and Stark's flight engineer station is barely visible with American Flag on the right.

sold its Kansas City Downtown Airport operations (with *a lot* of empty hangar space) to another well-known corporate FBO chain that has quite the uppity jet-set image. Before closing, the new FBO renegotiated a new master lease with the City of Kansas City, whereby the city did not include AHM's rent-free clause. Ever since the new FBO has been attempting to evict AHM as an "eyesore" even though it has been said they have no intention of using that old hangar space or many of the other empty hangars.

AHM and the new FBO are now in the middle of a protracted court battle. If that fails, the hangar will likely be razed and the iconic Super Constellation *Star of America* and Martin 404 *Skyliner Kansas City* classics will be *scrapped in place* which is the intention of this classy FBO. This is Howard Hughes-level stuff they are seeking to trash in the name of their pristine image and nothing else. *If you succeed in destroying AHM, good luck getting rid of the ugly brownfield industry, pipeline terminals, extensive railyards, and old rusty bridges that surround the Kansas City Downtown Airport perimeter. All that alone tarnishes your flattering image.*

This reminds me of a startup airline called Missouri Air Commuter that ran into similar problems with a big-shot air carrier and Kansas City politics. That big-shot airline was TWA—ironically a legacy AHM has been trying to preserve. Why is it that there always seems to be a Martin 404 in the middle of these stupid Kansas City political airport battles?

The AHM website now says the museum is *"Temporarily Closed."* Not looking good.

Now and forevermore, once upon a time.

CHAPTER 63

Silent Skies

I still live approximately 20 miles south of St. Louis Lambert International Airport. If I had nothing else to do, I could sit on my pool deck for the rest of eternity and would never again see another heavy piston *Aerial Leviathan* growling overhead. And it's already been 15 years since my last such sighting (the ATL-98 Carvair)while eating lunch on that Two Nice Guys restaurant patio. Fifty years ago, I would count one or two DC-6s or piston Convairs overhead every couple of hours, and sometimes a Super Constellation. Over 60 years ago when I was 7 years old, I remember it was more like 10 or more such overflights per hour—mostly blue-nacelled Delta DC-6s singing slowly overhead on their way to Memphis, Nashville, or Atlanta—*and not a single jetliner*. Over my life, I witnessed hundreds of heavy-recips in operation. Today, that is all but a memory.

I'm fine with innovation, but I have never been an early adopter. This possibly explains my lifetime romance with the propliners. I have been a longtime subscriber to *Aviation Week & Space Technology* which is very much a crystal ball into the future regarding all aspects of aviation. Weird-looking hydrogen- and electric-powered experimental planes, and strange aeronautical concepts with funny airfoils adorn their pages. I've *never* been inspired by all that, but I do want to know what is going on.

Despite that, today I cannot imagine how I lived over 70% of my life in the age of landlines, pay phones, phone booths, letters on stationery with 4-cent postage stamps, and brick-and-mortar libraries. I know that compared to today's airline experience, flying 14 hours across the Atlantic on a DC-7, Constellation or Stratocruiser was probably an endurance test of sheer boredom, even with that "standard" luxurious five-star dinner service. The good old days were not *that* great, it's just that nobody knew any better. Jets now streak high overhead as they have over the last 60 years, where over the decades of my life Delmonico's-style dinner service has slowly eroded down to a package of crackers and a plastic glass filled with Sprite (Kelleher's Southwest started all that, providing the blueprint of consistency and profitability in the airline industry). But to me, there is an eternal void in the sky—the absence of thunder. You just *cannot feel* the void if you did not *live* it when it existed. The souls of the real aviation pioneers such as Lindbergh, Doolittle, Hughes, Rickenbacker, Trippe, Frye, Patterson, Douglas, Martin, and their collective thunder, will live with me and a dwindling few others for the rest of my time on this planet. The rest of the world has other fish to fry.

Long ago, the Morrises left the St. Louis aviation scene for good, leaving 52 acres of *faceless green meadow* at the northwest corner of Lambert. This is an anomaly in the now vast airport concrete desert of over-expanded runways and taxiways that *never saw* their intended traffic volume because of the demise of the TWA brand. This concrete vastness does have a handful of widely-spaced, white canvas "hoop house" portable hangars scattered among the few permanent ones on the north side, where a few FedEx, UPS, DHL (ABX), and Amazon jet freighters sneak in at night. It reeks of *sameness*.

The monster roaring piston engines, beating propellers, and giant screaming turboprops of the auto parts-hauling titans were long ago silenced. It seems over half of the majestic McDonnell Douglas manufacturing buildings that were once adjacent to Mark Aero and PAT Air have also been razed after McDonnell-Douglas, and later Boeing failed to win two big fighter contracts. Yes, what remains is that *sameness* with no soul—and this *green meadow*.

Green Acres. **I'm along for the ride on short final for 12L Lambert with Southwest Airlines just before sunset in June 2020. We're skimming directly over Banshee Road and the *green meadow* that was once Mark Aero, PAT Air, Interstate Airmotive, Pegasus Club, and the intense hub for propliner auto parts activity serving the St. Louis auto assembly industry. Barely noticeable at the "boomerang curve" is the F-15 billboard that remains in place after more than a half-century. Lindbergh Boulevard roughly parallels the left side of the photo. The concrete pad on the upper right is where one of the many McDonnell-Douglas assembly and finishing buildings once stood, formerly serving as a backdrop for the Mark Aero ramp. Compare this Banshee Road "boomerang shot" to the top photo on page 111. This green meadow was a focal point of my teenage life and for quite a few years beyond.**

As far as the majors go, Southwest Airlines now predominates at Lambert, replacing the incessant jet whine and kerosene exhaust smell that totally engulfed the entire airport when TWA and Ozark filled the main terminal gates—and reigned here—on a *much larger* scale. Overall, Southwest is now the third-largest U.S. registered airline—and resides on the far southeast corner at its East Terminal. This is where Midcoast once was, and now the ten-year plan is to raze the east terminal and move Southwest operations to the grossly underutilized main terminal. It's hard to believe that Herb Kelleher once gave away *all* his hard-fought Southwest ticket counter space at Lambert to Mark Morris so that he could start Air One. And now look at Herb's legacy—number *one* at Lambert, and number *three* nationally.

An "inconvenient truth" is that the combined airline industry has *racked up a baseline of sustained average losses* and *negative net worth* going all the way back to the Wright Brothers on Kill Devil Hill in 1903. That means that much of the time, both industry net worth and profits are in the negative. You might be reading these pages at a time when the airline industry is reaping "record" profits. Just wait—that happy spike will be erased and go negative in due course, keeping that long-term average below zero as it always does. From the beginning, perhaps more than 95% of all airlines that were started have eventually failed—putting the Morris's tumultuous track record into perspective. So why would be anyone crazy enough to risk his time and fortune in the airline industry, even after obvious and repeated failures?

It's a thing that some in the industry call the *Aviation Disease,* an incurable condition that a certain group is born with, mostly within the male species. A substantially smaller proportion of women are born with it. However, as hard as the industry tries, it cannot seem to break through that 5%-7% threshold of women pilots and mechanics as a percent of total participation in that part of the industry. Is it an XX-XY problem or the environment? Who knows, but probably some combination of both. We have made it obvious that Mark Morris's airlines unapologetically hired women pilots, flight engineers, flight attendants, and managers decades ago before the words "diversity" or "inclusion" were commonplace. Some or most of these women undoubtedly had the *Aviation Disease.* These days we seem to discount the most important term in this discussion, which is "qualifications." We should also make it clear that there are scores of woman pilots and aviation heroes going back to the very beginning—black, white, and in between—even before Amelia Earhart. Many of these women have far exceeded the aeronautical accomplishments of many men with *Aviation Disease*—and they've certainly left me in the dust. They had all attained the *qualifications* that this white male never came close to.

I developed the *Aviation Disease* before I was three years old, as my late parents would attest, and I will never be cured. It manifests itself in different ways. For me, it hardly developed beyond an all-consuming avocation whereby I was lucky to break through to, participate in, and contribute to, the real thing—but only along the periphery. It was a far easier path for me to earn a good living in other ways, mostly as an industry generalist in banking and consulting.

For the great airline titans that built the airline industry from scratch, it was very different. They had the most severe cases of *Aviation Disease* that put them to much more direct and productive use than me. A hundred years of industry losses and obstacles around every corner *do not stop them* to this day, even though more of today's airline executives do not exhibit evidence of the *Aviation Disease* or an aviation background. Because of the *Aviation Disease*, there will probably be another hundred years of average industry losses that will continue to accrue for the benefit of *public convenience and necessity.*

So, when my Exec-Jet Air CEO client told me *"You don't know anything about the aviation business,"* he was right. That business usually *doesn't* make money, even though I thought all businesses are *supposed* to make money. But in aviation, the general populace—and even the entirety of mankind—disproportionately benefit from and now *thrive* (or at least *survive*) due to this economic and social loss leader borne by the *Aviation Disease.* In 1986 at a Boeing banker's dinner in Seattle, I asked its CFO to explain to me just how Boeing Commercial Airplanes can stay in business when its customers cannot. He replied, "*Maybe they cannot, but at any given time they are all in business, and if they are not, somebody else is.*" There was no way to counter that one.

Mark Morris says he would not trade his tumultuous aviation life for anything in the world. He maintains he was "*born at the right time.*" He got to fly dozens of aircraft types—representing the full spectrum of technical evolution—from the Beech Super 18 to the Lockheed Lodestar, to the C-47/DC-3, to the Martin 404 and DC-6, and finally the 727 jetliner and the widebody 757s and 767s. In the process he accumulated over 25,000 hours of flight time in between, He hammered DHL into what it is today, gave life to UPS's dedicated air operations, and forged regulatory change. He, founded, built, groomed, and managed airlines for most of his working life and serve as a line pilot for each one he started—and he feels quite fortunate to have been blessed with those opportunities. In Mark's words:

> *I was privileged to personally interact with airline founders such as Juan Trippe of Pan Am, Bob Six of Continental, Del Smith of Evergreen International, and Ed Daly of World Airways. All these well-celebrated titans were great aviation guys but none of their great companies are around today except Continental in the form of United. All their airlines ultimately failed, but not before many on-and-off bouts of success and failure.*
>
> *It is no different than the risk profile of a B-17 heavy bombardment crew in World War II flying missions over heavily defended Europe. I don't recall the exact statistics— I'm just trying to do an illustration— but it works something like this: If you fly 20 missions you have perhaps a 70% chance of surviving the war, but you'll still get shot to hell in the meantime. If you do 25 missions it goes to something like a 50% survival rate. If you felt really confident and go for 50 missions you had a 10% chance of surviving the war. With these horrible statistics, the United States Army Air Force still prevailed and our democracy survived. So, it goes without saying that an airline titan that is infected with the aviation bug always goes for 50 missions, nothing less. It's in their DNA.*

And mankind benefits. Joe and Mark Morris had serious cases of *Aviation Disease*, and their channeling of that helped them overhaul and innovate the air transportation world, not unlike Juan Trippe, Howard Hughes, Ed Daly, Bob Six, Del Smith, and Herb Kelleher. As that old Southwest Airlines advertisement once proclaimed, "*You are now free to move about the country.*"

But then there is still that little 52-acre green space where Lambert *started*, and where *all* of Lambert's activity *was* in the 1920s and 1930s. I cannot say it enough and will say it again that this *green meadow* is where Charles Lindbergh once worked, hung out, ate lunch, and stopped by to thank his supporters on his way to Paris, and where celebrities, rock stars, professional sports teams, and dignitaries of foreign and domestic governments and militaries passed through. The days of Mark Aero, Edgar Monsanto Queeny, Pegasus Club, Interstate Airmotive, PAT Air, and scores of transient auto-parts-hauling heavy-recips and huge churning propellers that once dominated here—are all gone. But it is this *green meadow*—pictured in this chapter—that in many ways changed the transportation world forever.

Again, there is one thing that isn't gone. That F-15 billboard at the boomerang turn on Banshee Road remains *defiant and in place*—now watching over the now empty 52 acres after more than a half-century. That makes sense, as limited production of advanced versions of the legacy Boeing/McDonnell Douglas F-15 and F-18 continues a few blocks east of there for now, and the planned production of the Air Force's new Boeing T-7A Red Hawk advanced fighter trainer promises to keep St. Louis aircraft production lines open for the foreseeable future.

There have, however, been major changes in the *business aviation* world where Mark Aero had a major impact so many years ago. Over the past few decades, many Fortune 1000 companies, (including most of the 20 or so originally based in St. Louis) have been swallowed by large international concerns that voluntarily bow to the "green" agenda. Ralston Purina is now part of Nestle, Monsanto is now Bayer, and the Anheuser-Busch brands are now part of InBev. Concurrent with this, environmental activists—rightly or wrongly—have infiltrated board rooms all over the U.S. In the name of reducing "carbon footprints," and also in the more practical name of tightening budgets, most of the in-house corporate flight departments that originated at Mark Aero have since been shut down, and are *no more*.

Gone are the aviation departments of Peabody Energy, Ralston Purina and Anheuser-Busch, and others—not necessarily in that order. While airlines have been forced to adapt since deregulation, business aviation is now doing the same because of the "climate change" religion. It is moving away from big corporations toward celebrities and billionaires who seem to cherish "climate change," as well as fractional ownership companies such as NetJets and Flexjet. Fractional ownership in such private jet fleets is now the exclusive domain of the "descendants" of that same wealthy group that once dominated piston airliner travel during the *First Wind* in the 1940s and 1950s—when the rest of us took the train or the bus. Today, the rest of us just take Southwest.

Joe E. Morris left this world in 2005 at the respectable age of 93 years. Mark G. Morris lives in Scottsdale, Arizona, and now runs several software companies including a promising cancer treatment technology company that is seeing wide international acceptance. He also can't help himself—he tells me that he is looking at acquiring jet aircraft for corporate use, proving once again that the *Aviation Disease* is incurable.

Today, fewer than five DC-6s remain in service out of the hundreds built during the 1940s and 1950s. These holdouts fly freight *exclusively* in Alaska with Everts Air, where that state's arctic inhabitants have no road or water access. The DC-6 is the perfect vehicle in that environment where no other aircraft with its load capacity can match its performance on remote, frozen loose-gravel runways (gravel ruins jet engines). A replacement for these arctic DC-6s needs to be found soon. They are elderly, fully "cycled out," and have been "over-overhauled" throughout the last 70 years. Also, this handful of DC-6s still requires 100LL avgas. For both market demand and environmental reasons, this now-transitional aviation fuel is scarce and is being phased out by the refiners. The oil companies have long ago phased out the high-performance number (P/N) blends of avgas—the heavily-leaded 100/130 and 115/145 "hot fuels"— that provided for the *originally advertised* performance of factory-fresh propliners. While a few DC-6s survive, the last Martin 404 forever left the skies nearly 15 years ago as a demonstration and display airplane and not a revenue generator. There have always been practical jet-fueled alternatives to the Martinliner for short- and medium-haul passenger routes.

So, this is the story of the *Second Wind of the Aerial Leviathans*—and that of Joe and Mark Morris who inadvertently and unknowingly threw me into the middle of it for an interesting lifetime of experiences and memories. There were thousands of other great—and not so great—people and organizations who were part of the *Second Wind* era, but there were only a very few like the Morrises who were catalysts that reformed everyday air transportation for the better. So, this is where the two journeys, as described in these writings, meet. Yes, time *does* wash away all the evidence, but nobody seems to notice.

Selected Bibliography and Other Sources

BOOKS
M. Harris Yaeger, *Above the Labyrinth*, 2nd Edition (Michael H. Yeager, 2019).
Alan B. Hoffman, *Up There with the Biggest: The Story of Ozark Airlines* (Alan B. Hoffman, 2019)
R.E.G. Davies, *TWA: An Airline and Its Aircraft* (Paladwr Press, 2000)
David H. Stringer, *America's Local Service Airlines* (American Aviation Historical Society, First Edition 2016)
Brett Lane, *A Cargo Pilot's Life: Tales from Corrosion Corner*, (Brett Lane)
Sveinn Vidar Gudmundsson, *Flying too Close to the Sun: The Successes and Failures of the New Entrant Airlines* (Ashgate Publishing Company, 1998).
James C. Wetherbe, *The World On Time: The 11 Management Principles That made FedEx an Overnight Sensation* (Knowledge Exchange, LLC, 1996)
Daniel L. Rust, *The Aerial Crossroads of America: St. Louis's Lambert Airport* (Missouri History Museum Press, 2016)
Gary L. Killion, *The Martinliners* (Airways International, Inc., 1997)
J.M. Gradidge, *The CONVAIRLINERS Story* (Air Britain (Historians), Ltd., 1997)
Harry Gann, *Douglas DC-6 and DC-7* (AirlinerTech Series, Specialty Press, 1999)
Arthur Pearcy, *Douglas Propliners: DC-1—DC-7* (Airlife Publishing Ltd., 1995)
William Patrick Dean, *The ATL-98 Carvair* (McFarland & Company, Inc., 2008)
Scott E. Germain, *Lockheed Constellation & Super Constellation Vol 1* (AirlinerTech Series, Specialty Press, 1998)
M.J. Hardy, *The Lockheed Constellation,* (Arco Publishing Company, Inc., 1973)
Kenneth E. Wixley, *Lockheed Constellation, Classic Civil Aircraft: I* (Ian Allen Ltd., 1987)
Bill Yenne, *The 377 Stratocruiser & KC-97 Stratofreighter* (Crecy Publishing Limited, 2014)
Herschel Smith, *Aircraft Piston Engines from the Manly Baltzer to the Continental Tiara* (McGraw Hill, 1981)
Bill Gunston, *The Development of Piston Aero Engines* (Patrick Stephens Limited, 1993)
Graham White, *Allied Aircraft Piston Engines of World War II* (SAE International, 1995)
Graham White, *R-2800: Pratt & Whitney's Dependable Masterpiece* (SAE International, 2001)
Graham White, *R-4360: Pratt & Whitney's Major Miracle* (Specialty Press, 2006)

ARTICLES
Don Sims, *Trans Continental Airlines—Willow Run and Its Unusual Airlines Have Put Airpower Back into Airfreight* (Airline Quarterly, Challenge Publications, Inc., Spring 1980)
John A. Reed, *About That Heavy Pistonliner's Pistons* (Airliners, Spring 1991)
Dave Nichols, Reaching Back, *Box Canyon* (Airliners, Fall 1999)
Dave Nichols, Reaching Back, *Buying the Farm* (Airliners, Winter 1999)
Cristopher J. Buckley, *Miami's Fabulous Sky Trucks: Trans-Air-Link Celebrates its First Decade* (Propliner No. 47, Fall 1991).
Ralph M. Pettersen, *Classics Over Rantoul* (Air Classics, December 2005

ARTICLES (Continued)

Luann Grosseup, *The Wild Frontiers Supplemental Carriers Boldly Went Where No Scheduled Airliner Would Go* (Chicago Tribune, November 18, 2001)

William Garvey, *Inside Business Aviation* (Aviation Week & Space Technology, June 27-July 10, 2022)

Numerous articles on Mark Aero, PAT Air, Air One and Primaris from the following: The St. Louis Globe Democrat, The St. Louis Post-Dispatch, Management Saint Louis, St. Louis Business Journal, West County Journal, Aviation Week, Flight Magazine, Newsweek, Business Week, Forbes, The Wall Street Journal, The New York Times, The Hollywood Reporter, VanDusen Flyer, Primaris Airlines Executive Summary

GOVERNMENT AND LEGAL DOCUMENTS

Congressional Record, *Decline of the Supplemental Air Carriers in the United States* (HEARINGS before the SUBCOMMITTEE ON MONOPOLY AND ANTICOMPETITIVE ACTIVITIES OF THE SELECT COMMITTEE ON SMALL BUSINESS, United States Senate, 95th Congress, U. S. Government Printing Office, February 24 and 28, 1977)

Civil Aeronautics Board Reports, *ECONOMIC CASES of the CIVIL AERONAUTICS BOARD, Volume 92* (October to November 1981)

LOW-COST AIR TRANSPORTATION ACT, HEARINGS before the SUBCOMMITTEE ON COMMERCE, UNITED STATES SENATE, NINETY_FOURTH CONGRESS, First Session S.421, February 13 and 14, 1975

INDIANA LAW REVIEW, RECENT DEVELOPMENTS, ADMIINISTRATIVE LAW— Federal Aviation ACT—Civil Aeronautics Board ruling that Indiana-based travel club has become a "common carrier" in violation of 49 U.S.C. 1371(a) affirmed. –*Voyager 1000* v. CAB, 489 F.2d 792 (7th Cir. 1973), *cert denied*, 42 U.S.L.W. 3626 (U.S. May 13, 1974) ((No. 103).

NTSB-AAR-71-4 AIRCRAFT ACCIDENT REPORT, Martin 404 N464M 8 Statute Miles West of Silver Plume, Colorado October 2, 1970, report date December 24, 1970.

NTSB-AAR-74-2 AIRCRAFT ACCIDENT REPORT, Skyways International, Inc., Douglas DC-7C, N296 Near the Miami International Airport, Dade County, Florida, June 21, 1973, report date February 27, 1974.

NTSB-AAR-74-5 AIRCRAFT ACCIDENT REPORT, Ozark Air Lines, Inc., Fairchild Hiller FH-227B, N4215, Near the Lambert – St. Louis International Airport, St. Louis, Missouri, July 23, 1973, report date April 24, 1974.

NTSB-AAR-74-11 AIRCRAFT ACCIDENT REPORT, Aircraft Pool Leasing Corporation, Lockheed Super Constellation, L-1049H N6917C Miami, Florida, December 15, 1973, report date September 11, 1974.

NTSB-AAR-78-6 AIRCRAFT ACCIDENT REPORT, L&J Company, Convair 240 N55VM, Gillsburg, Mississippi, October 20, 1977, report date June 19, 1978.

NTSB-AAR-80-11 AIRCRAFT ACCIDENT REPORT, Transamerica Airlines, Inc., Lockheed L-188, N859U, Salt Lake City, Utah, November 18, 1979, report date August 26, 1980.

NTSB-AAR-80-14 AIRCRAFT ACCIDENT REPORT, Airtraders International, Lockheed 1049H N74CA, Columbus, Indiana, June 22, 1980, report date December 23, 1980.

NTSB-AAR-85-04 AIRCRAFT ACCIDENT REPORT, Zantop International Airlines, Inc., Lockheed L-188 Electra, Chalkhill, Pennsylvania, May 30, 1984, report date March 19, 1985.

NTSB-AAR-86-01 AIRCRAFT ACCIDENT REPORT, Galaxy Airlines, Inc., Lockheed Electra L-188C, N5532, Reno, Nevada, January 21, 1985, report date February 4, 1986.

VIDEO DOCUMENTARIES
John A. Reed, *AeroDinosaur* (YouTube channel)
John A. Reed, *Flight of the Super Constellation* (Regulus Productions 1990)
John A. Reed, *DC-6 West Indies Odyssey* (Regulus Productions 1992)
John A. Reed, *Fly DC-7C: The Seven Seas Solution* (Regulus Productions 1992)
John A. Reed, *HEAVY PROP DINOSAURS Vol. 1: SHORT-HAULERS* (Regulus Productions 1993)
John A. Reed, *HEAVY PROP DINOSAURS Vol. 2: FOUR-ENGINE GIANTS* (Regulus Productions 1993)

WEBSITES
planelogger.com
upi.com Bureau of Aircraft Accident Archives (Skycraft DC-3 and Fleming L-188 crashes)
flightsafety.org (Aviation Safety Network, Flight Safety Foundation)
baa-acro.com (Bureau of Aircraft Accident Archives)
Wikimedia Commons
wikipedia.org

OTHER
TECHNICAL MANUAL MAINTENANCE INSTRUCTIONS, R-2800 POWERPLANT, USAF SERIES C-118A and VC-118A AIRCRAFT (Douglas/USAF T.O. IC-118A-2-5, 15 November 1960 Change 17—15 June 1974)
Preliminary Prospectus Dated September 27, 1983, Air One, Inc.
Confidential Private Placement Memorandum, Primaris Airlines, October, 2007

ABOUT THE AUTHOR

John Andrew Reed is a retired business advisor and former commercial banker and industrial marketer who has had a lifetime involvement in several aspects of aviation as an instrument-rated private pilot, consultant, and board member, as well as a compiler, author, and videographer of legacy aviation history. He has written and published articles on the technical evolution of heavy piston aircraft engines and their twilight operations in the Caribbean. Mr. Reed has an MBA degree with a finance emphasis from Washington University in St. Louis, and a BSBA degree in marketing from the University of Missouri—Columbia. His YouTube channel *AeroDinosaur* features informative live-action documentaries on historical heavy piston aircraft, many of which are featured in this book. He lives with his wife Karen in Des Peres, Missouri, a suburb of St. Louis.

www.ingramcontent.com/pod-product-compliance
Lightning Source LLC
Chambersburg PA
CBHW082139120626
46553CB00010B/2708